Eliza Robbins, Mrs. Markham

History of England

From the Invasion of Julius Caesar to the Reign of Victoria

Eliza Robbins, Mrs. Markham

History of England

From the Invasion of Julius Caesar to the Reign of Victoria

ISBN/EAN: 9783337063047

Printed in Europe, USA, Canada, Australia, Japan

Cover: Foto ©ninafisch / pixelio.de

More available books at **www.hansebooks.com**

HISTORY
OF
ENGLAND,

FROM THE

INVASION OF JULIUS CÆSAR TO THE REIGN
OF VICTORIA.

BY MR ~~ANS BLAKE~~

A NEW EDITION, REVISED AND ENLARGED

WITH QUESTIONS,

ADAPTED TO SCHOOLS IN THE UNITED STATES

BY ELIZA ROBBINS,

AUTHOR OF "AMERICAN POPULAR LESSONS," ETC., ETC.

NEW YORK:
D. APPLETON AND COMPANY,
549 & 551 BROADWAY.
1879.

PREFACE

The History of England, entitled Mrs. Markham's, was written by a mother for the instruction of her own children, and it has been, and still is, extensively used in England. In its original form the construction is essentially domestic, and to the narrative portions are appended conversations between a mother and children on that most important part of history, the successive changes that have taken place in Britain, and other civilized countries, in manners, arts, and humanity.

Agreeable as this form of instruction may be in a family, it is altogether inconvenient in a school. There is nothing more needed in our schools than good histories; not the dry compends in present use, but elementary works that shall suggest the moral uses of history, and the Providence of God manifest in the affairs of men.

Mrs. Markham's History was used by that model for all teachers, the late Dr. Arnold, master of the great English school at Rugby, and agrees in its character with his enlightened and pious views of teaching history.

It is now several years since I adapted this History to the form and the price acceptable in the schools in the United States. I have recently revised it, and trust that it may be extensively serviceable in education. The principal alterations from the original are a new and more convenient division of paragraphs, and entire omission of the conversations annexed to the chapters. In place of these I have affixed questions to every page, that may at once facilitate the work of the teacher and the pupil. The rational and moral features of this book first commended it to me, and I have used it successfully with my own scholars.

The real author was Elizabeth, wife of the Rev. John Penrose, a native of England. Mrs. Penrose was a woman of rare gifts and accomplishments. She died at Lincoln, January 24th, 1837.

ELIZA ROBBINS

NEW YORK, March 8, 1848.

CONTENTS

THE BRITISH EMPIRE.

CHAPTER I. 9
Ancient Britons—Roman Invasion—The Druids—Antiquities—Prince Authur.

CHAPTER II. 19
Scots and Picts—Departure of the Romans—Saxon Invasion—Introduction of Christianity into Britain.

CHAPTER III. 23
Alfred—His education—His virtues—The Danes—Their ravages—Defeated by Alfred—Alfred's death—State of England in this reign.

CHAPTER IV. 35
Saxon Successors of Alfred—Clergy—St. Dunstan—Edwy and Elgiva—The Northmen—Danish Kings of England.

CHAPTER V. 43
From Canute to the Norman conquest—Saxon princes restored—Battle of Hastings—Condition of the people of England under the Saxons.

CHAPTER VI. 50
William of Normandy—Edgar Atheling—Robert and William, the conqueror's sons—Death of William—State of society under the Normans in England.

CHAPTER VII. 57
William II.—Injures his brother Robert—Robert goes to the Holy Land—William killed in the New Forest—Crusades.

CHAPTER VIII. 62
Character of Henry I.—Robert returns to England—Succession of prince William disputed—Prince William drowned—The Empress Matilda—Henry II. dies in Normandy—Arts, armor, and domestic manners of the English—Chivalry.

CHAPTER IX. 78
Usurpation of Stephen—Civil war in England—Stephen taken prisoner—Matilda abuses her own power—withdraws into Normandy—The succession settled on Henry Matilda's son—Stephen dies.

CHAPTER X. 84
Henry II.—his education—his abilities—grants a charter to the people—Invades and conquers Ireland—Thomas à Becket—his exaltation—his death—Henry does penance for the death of Becket—Henry's domestic affairs—his death—Learning and customs in England.

CHAPTER XI. 94
Richard I.—His foreign enterprises—Richard at Acre—Returns to Europe—made a prisoner in Germany—Ransomed—returns to England—Killed at Chalus—Disorders in England.

CHAPTER XII. 102
John, a despicable prince—Authur of Breiagne—John loses Normandy—quarrels with the Pope—persecutes the Jews—John makes submission to the Pope—opposed by the barons—grants Magna Charta—Depressed condition of the English people in this reign—John's death.

CHAPTER XIII. 109
Henry III. succeeds his father—attempts to recover Normandy—Civil war between the king and the barons—Prince Edward defends his father's cause—joins the last Crusade—Henry III. dies—Progress of society and of science in England.

CHAPTER XIV. 118
Edward I.—His policy—makes war with the Welsh—Affairs of Scotland—Edward loses Guienne—Sir William Wallace—Edward I. dies—his character—Trade in England—the Tournament.

CHAPTER XV. 125
Edward II.—a weak prince—Robert Bruce—Battle of Bannockburn—Queen Isabella rebels against her husband—Edward II. deposed and murdered—Manners of the Scots and English in this reign.

CHAPTER XVI. 132
Edward III.—an inexperienced youth, but soon manifests ability—a warlike prince—punishes his mother—makes war with the king of Scotland—with the French—the Black Prince—Battle of Cressy—Siege of Calais—War with France prolonged—King David Bruce—The Black Prince engages in the affairs of Spain—dies—Edward the III. dies—Amusements of the English.

CHAPTER XVII. 147
Richard II.—son of the Black Prince—the people rebel against Richard—Wat Tyler—Richard's presence of mind—his deterioration—loses his popularity—Battle of Otterburne between the English and Scots—Henry Bolingbroke banished—returns to England—assumes the Crown—Richard II. dies at Pontefract castle—Reformation commences—Wickliffe—Manners of the age—Language and literature—Liberty of thought.

CHAPTER XVIII. 160
Henry IV. succeeds Richard II.—Owen Glendower—Battle of Homildon Hill—The Percies rebel against the king—James I. of Scotland—a prisoner in England—his history and character interesting—Prince Henry—his good and bad qualities—The king dies—state of religion in England during this reign.

CHAPTER XIX. 169
Henry V.—abandons the follies of his youth—his generosity—Lord Cobham—one of the earliest Reformers in England—Henry V. makes war with France—Battle of Azincourt—Duke of Burgundy assassinated—Henry V. marries the princess Catharine of France—he dies—Comforts of life comparatively few in England in this age.

CHAPTER XX. 79
Henry VI.—Affairs in France—Joan of Arc—Henry marries Margaret of Anjou—The duke of York claims the crown—England thrown into a state of insurrection and tumult—The Yorkists prevail over the king's party—The Duke of York killed—his son proclaimed king—Parliamentary power—state of the English navy, and of trade in this reign

CHAPTER XXI. 193
Edward IV.—a warlike prince—Margaret endeavors to obtain the throne for her son—The battle of Hexham—Lancastrians suffer great distress—Henry VI. restored—Lancastrians finally defeated—Edward IV. reinstated—dies—Printing introduced into England.

CHAPTER XXII. 202
Edward V.—Richard, duke of Gloucester—his dissimulation—Lord Hastings beheaded—young princes murdered—Gloucester crowned king—Popular amusements in England in this reign.

CHAPTER XXIII. 207
Richard III.—conspiracy formed against him—Earl of Richmond—collects an army—Richard encounters the earl of Richmond—killed at Bosworth Field—The Plantagenet kings.

CHAPTER XXIV. 212
Henry VII.—His character—Simnel, an impostor, pretends to the crown of England—Perkin Warbeck does the same—Formidable insurrection—Henry at last reigns in peace—He dies—Extraordinary changes in tenure of property, and the military service in England—Discovery undertaken by the English.

CHAPTER XXV. 221
Henry VIII. succeeds his father—Cardinal Wolsey—Henry goes to France—his contemporaries Francis I. and Charles V.—Festivities in France—Catharine—Anne Boleyn—Cranmer—Henry quarrels with the Pope—Suppresses monasteries—makes war with Scotland—Henry dies—Bible translated in this reign—the Reformation advanced.

CHAPTER XXVI. 239
Edward VI.—Somerset the protector—Religious disturbances—Edward a Protestant—his health declines—He dies—Church of England—progress of Reformation.

CHAPTER XXVII. 245
Mary—Lady Jane Grey—Mary persecutes the Protestants—marries Philip of Spain—Gardiner and Bonner—persecutors of Protestants—Martyrs—Philip quits England—Mary dies—Manners in England during this reign.

CHAPTER XXVIII. 255
Queen Elizabeth—popular with the English nation—a Protestant—chooses wise ministers—refuses to marry—Mary, queen of Scots—her follies and misfortunes—a prisoner in England—Mary beheaded—Spanish invasion—Elizabeth conducts herself admirable in this juncture—Armada dispersed—Earl of Essex—Elizabeth dies—Condition of England.

CHAPTER XXIX 276
James I.—Lady Arabella Stuart—Sir Walter Raleigh—James a peaceable prince—Prince Charles marries Henrietta Maria of France—Prince Henry—death of the king.

CHAPTER XXX. 289
Charles I.—a well disposed, not a wise man—The duke of Buckingham—Sir Thomas Wentworth—Archbishop Laud—Charles unpopular in Scotland—Lord Stafford executed—Rebellion in Ireland—Civil war in England—Cromwell—war continued—religious Sects—Charles made prisoner by the parliament—Executed.

CONTENTS.

CHAPTER XXXI. 313
The Commonwealth—Prince Charles—Cromwell maintains his power—Charles withdraws to the continent—Cromwell abolishes the parliament—His sons—Cromwell dies

CHAPTER XXXII. 226
Charles II.—The Restoration—The regicides—Church affairs—Naval battles with the Dutch—Plague in England—great fire of London—Civil troubles—Charles dies—Profligacy of manners in England at this time.

CHAPTER XXXIII. 331
James II.—Monmouth's conspiracy—James a Catholic—William of Nassau invited to England—James abdicates the throne—takes refuge in France—Mr. Boyle.

CHAPTER XXXIV. 337
William III.—not well suited to the English—Battle of Killikrankie—James lands in Ireland—Battle of the Boyne—Massacre of Glencoe—Queen Mary dies—William dies—National debt.

CHAPTER XXXV. 345
Queen Anne—Whigs and Tories—Sir George Rooke—Marlborough—Lord Peterborough—The pretender—the Union with Scotland—death of Anne—Sir Isaac Newton

CHAPTER XXXVI. 351
George I.—Lewis XIV. aids the pretender—He lands in Scotland—his adherents punished—The South Sea Scheme—George I. visits Hanover—dies at Osnaburgh.

CHAPTER XXXVII. 354
George II.—engages in a continental war—Prince Charles, the young pretender kindles war in Scotland—advances into England—is forced back—defeated at Culloden—War in America with the French—Treaty of Aix-la-Chapelle—George II. dies—The last of the Stuarts.

CHAPTER XXXVIII. 361
George III.—European warfare—American war of Independence—Lord Chatham—pretences for war—French Revolution—Bonaparte—Peninsular war—Sir John Moore—Lord Wellington—Bonaparte sent to Elba—Battle of Waterloo—General peace in Europe—George III dies.

CHAPTER XXXIX. 381
Conclusion—George IV.—William IV.—British India—Queen Victoria—Chinese war—War in Affghanistan—Sir Robert Peel—Prospects of Britain.

ENGLISH HISTORY.

THE BRITISH EMPIRE.

Of all countries upon the globe there is none of which the history is more interesting to the American than Great Britain. To most of us it is the country of our ancestors, and is that from which our language and many of our institutions are derived. At the present time there is no nation upon earth of greater resources in learning and science, in wise men and useful arts; no nation, in despite of some traits of character which are neither to be admired or imitated, in which religion and literature, virtue and happiness, liberty of thought and freedom of speech, security of property and authority of law, are so generally enjoyed as in England.

We have only to go back in past time, a little more than eighteen centuries, and we shall find the present highly cultivated, civilized, and wealthy country of Great Britain, the abode of savage and hostile tribes, sunk in heathenism and ignorance, without comfortable habitations or decent garments.

> ' Time was, when clothing sumptuous or for use
> Save their own painted skins, our sires had none."
> COWPER'S TASK.

At the present time, (1848,) the country which was once so rude and poor, is not only a powerful and rich kingdom within itself, but its dominions extends to every sea, and every quarter of the globe. The following account of the British Empire is taken from Hale's Geography.

THE KINGDOM OF GREAT BRITAIN AND IRELAND

The kingdom of Great Britian consists of the ancient kingdoms of England, Scotland, Wales, and Ireland Besides these, the British empire includes a great number of foreign possessions, viz :—

In Europe, Gibraltar, the Island of Malta, in the Mediterranean sea, and Heligoland, in the German Ocean.

In America, Upper and Lower Canada, Nova Scotia, and New-Brunswick, Prince Edward's Island, and Newfoundland. Besides these Colonies, British America embraces extensive tracts of unsettled country north of Canada. Jamaica and other islands in the West Indies, also belong to the British.

Extensive possessions in India, New Holland, Van Diemen's Land, the Cape of Good Hope, and other parts of Africa, are subject to Britain.

ENGLAND AND WALES.

This country is bounded north by Scotland, east by the German Ocean, south by the English channel, which separates it from France, and west by St. George's channal, which separates it from Ireland. England consists of the *southern* part of the island of Great Britain, and Wales occupies the western part. England is divided into 40, and Wales into 12 counties.

The principal rivers in England, are the Thames, Severn, Medway, Trent, Ouse, Mersey, and Avon. The present population of England and Wales, is 16,000,000 About one-third of the inhabitants are employed in agriculture, and nearly half in trade, manufactures, and the mechanic arts. The nobility and great proprietors of land, being about one-sixth of the whole population, derive their subsistence from their estates.

England is the most commercial country in the world,

Of what does the kingdom of Great Britain and Ireland consist?
What are the British possessions in Europe?—In America?—Asia?—and Africa?
What are England and Wales, and how divided?
What is the population of England and Wales, 1833?
How do the people subsist?
What is the commerce of England?

and by its commerce has become the richest. Her merchants trade with all parts of the world, and particularly with her colonies in the East and West Indies and in America, with China, with South America, and with the United States.

The people of Great Britain have acquired great skill in the manufacture of every description of goods, particularly cotton, woolen, and silk goods of all sorts, as well as earthen and glass ware, and all articles made of iron, and other metals.

England is immensely rich in its mines of coal and iron, and its manufacturing operations are greatly aided by these treasures.

The government is a limited monarchy. The title of the sovereign is, King of the United Kingdom of Great Britain and Ireland. On the death of the King he is succeeded by his eldest son, if he have any, or by his eldest daughter in defect of sons, and, if he has no children, by the children of his father in the same order. The present sovereign of Great Britain is Queen Victoria, though Kings usually reign over this kingdom.

The King is personally responsible for little else than the appointment of his ministers. He often appoints only the prime minister, who with his approbation, selects all the rest. All the executive acts of the government are performed in the name of the King, but the ministers are responsible for them.

The King makes war and peace, negotiates treaties, raises armies, makes appointments to offices, civil and military,—in his name justice is administered—to him belong the forts, arsenals, and ships of war—he convenes, prorogues, and dissolves the Parliament at pleasure, and his assent is necessary to the validity of a law. But the revenues are raised, and laws are passed only by act of Parliament.

The Parliament is a legislative body, consisting of two branches; the House of Lords and the House of Commons. The House of Lords consists of peers of the realm

---

What are the manufactures?
What the mineral productions?
What is the present government of Great Britain?
What is the King's function?
What is the British Parliament?

and the archbishops and bishops. The peers are a part of the hereditary nobility, who among other privileges which descend from the father to the eldest son, have the right of a seat in the House of Lords. The King has the power of raising any individual to the peerage. This promotion is generally granted as a reward for distinguished services to the state.

The House of Commons consists of 658 members, who are elected, part by the electors of the counties, part by certain cities and boroughs, and two members by each of the ancient universities. They may hold their seats for seven years, unless the Parliament is sooner dissolved by the King, in which case a new election of all the members is necessary.

But a small part of the people of Great Britain possess the right of voting. Votes are frequently purchased. The members of Parliament receive no pay for their attendance.

There is an Established Church, of which the King is the nominal head, and in which there are two archbishops, twenty-four bishops, and a great number of inferior clergy. The number of the clergy of the Established Church is 11,600.

The present effective force of the British army is 88,000 men, exclusive of the forces employed by the East India Company. This force includes the troops which are stationed in Great Britain and Ireland, and those in the foreign possessions, except India. The East India Company maintains in addition a force of 20,000 men.

The British navy is much the largest in the world. The whole number of ships of war is 600. The number now in commission is 147, of which 14 are ships of the line.

There are two ancient universities, one at the town of Cambridge, and the other at the city of Oxford. Cambridge University has thirteen colleges, several of which are superb buildings, and four halls. It has many rich endowments, and has eighteen professors, and many other

---

What is the House of Commons?
How are members of Parliament elected?
What is the Established Church of Great Britain?
What is the British Army?
What is the Navy?
What are the Universities?

officers. Oxford University has twenty colleges and five halls. Many of these are large and splendid buildings. The revenues of the University are very great. The number of members of the University is about 3,000.

London is the capital of England, and of the British empire. It is the richest and most populous city in the world. It is situated on the River Thames, and embraces, besides what is strictly called the City of London, the City and Liberties of Westminster, and several out parishes in the counties of Middlesex and Surrey. It is seven miles in length, and from two to four miles in breadth, and contains nearly two millions of inhabitants.

SCOTLAND

Scotland consists of all that part of the Island of Great Britain which lies north of the river Tweed, and is bounded north, east and west, by the sea, and south by England. Scotland is divided into 33 counties or shires.

Scotland is divided into the Highlands and Lowlands. The Highlands, consisting of the northern and central parts, are mountainous and sterile, and but a small proportion of the lands are fit for cultivation. The Lowlands, consisting of the southern and eastern parts, have a resemblance to England, and abound in fertile plains.

The population of Scotland is a little over two millions. Their general character is that of a frugal, industrious, and well-instructed people. A portion of the Highlanders have not adopted all the arts of civilized life. They retain their peculiar dress, manners, and language. Education is much attended to.

Scotland, forming a part of the United Kingdom of Great Britain and Ireland, is under the same government, but its laws are in many respects different, and its courts and forms of judicial proceeding are entirely different. Scotland chooses 45 members of the House of Commons, in each Parliament, and the Scotch Peers, who are not Peers

---

What is the capital of Britain, and how described?
What is Scotland, and how divided?
What is the population of Scotland, and its general character?
What is the government of Scotland?

of Great Britain, choose from their number 16 to sit in the House of Lords.

The prevailing religion of Scotland is Calvinism, and the established form of church government is Presbyterian.

Edinburgh, the metropolis of Scotland, is a very handsome city, and has a population of 140,000. It is situated on the Firth of Forth.

IRELAND.

Ireland is an Island in the Atlantic Ocean, situated west of England. It is divided into four provinces, viz. Leinster, Ulster, Connaught, and Munster, and into 32 counties.

The population is estimated to be about 7,000,000. In consequence of the denseness of the population, and the difficulty of finding productive employments, a large proportion of the people are in abject poverty.

About four-fifths of the people are Roman Catholics, and it has been a subject of perpetual complaint, that they were excluded by their religion from a seat in parliament, and from other offices. These disabilities were removed (1729) removed by an act of the British parliament.

Dublin is the capital. It is a large and handsome city, of 240,000 inhabitants, situated on a beautiful bay, at the mouth of the river Liffey.

BRITISH INDIA.

The population of Hindostan is supposed to amount to 128,000,000. Of this immense population, 115,000,000 are subject directly or indirectly to the government of the English East India Company.

There are in Hindostan a number of native princes

What is the prevailing religion of Scotland?
What is the capital of Scotland?
What is Ireland, and how divided?
What is the population of Ireland, and its general condition
What is the prevailing religion of Ireland?
What is the government of Ireland?
What is its capital?
What portion of the population of India, is subject to Britain?
What Princes of Hindostan have become tributary to Britain?

called Rajahs, or Nabobs, who have become tributary to the government of the East India Company, and placed themselves under their protection. These tributary states have a population estimated at 33,000,000.

The rest of the country, containing a population of 82,000,000, is under the immediate government of the officers of the Company. For the purposes of administration the country is divided into three presidencies, in each of which there is a distinct government. These are the presidency of Bengal, which embraces the north-eastern provinces of India; that of Madras, which embraces the southern provinces; and that of Bombay, embracing the western provinces.

The East India Company, who are in fact the sovereigns of this country, is established in London, and the supreme government exists there, and consists of a Board of Commissioners, and a Court of Directors of twenty-four members. The government in India consists of a governor and council in each presidency. The governor of the presidency of Bengal has the title of Governor-General, and he is, in the name of the East India Company, the Supreme Chief of Political and Military Affairs, the other governors being subordinate to him.

The army of the company consists of 20,000 European and 180,000 native troops.

What territories in India are subject to Britain?
What is the East India Company?
What is the army of the East India Company?

ENGLISH HISTORY.

CHAPTER I.

Fifty five years before the birth of Christ, Julius Cæsar, the Roman general, was in Gaul. That country, now called France, is separated from the island of Great Britain by a channel so narrow in one place, between Dover and Calais, that the white cliffs of Dover are discernible from the opposite coast.

Cornwall, at the western extremity of the island, is still famous for its tin mines, and this metal was as useful to the ancients as it is to us. The merchants of the Mediterranean, from a period not exactly ascertained, had trafficked in tin with the Britons, and the features of the country were become familiar to the mariners who went thither in the age of Cæsar.

By their means Britain was made known to the Romans, and when Cæsar was in Gaul, he thought it desirable to get possession of that country. With the Romans, without regard to the rights and feelings of those they dispossessed, to desire and to seize was almost the same impulse, and without caring for the sufferings of the inoffensive inhabitants of the long-neglected island, the Roman general invaded their shores.

B. C. 55. With a force which he deemed sufficient to conquer the island, Cæsar sailed from Gaul to the British coast, but it is said that, on approaching Dover, the number and ferocious appearance of the natives rather daunted the Romans, so that they landed at Deal where the shore is flat, and they could more easily cope

---

What separates Gaul from Britain?
By what circumstances were the people of Europe made acquainted with Britain?
Had the Romans just notions of the rights of men?
When and where did Cæsar land in Britain?

with the natives, who attempted to prevent their landing which, however, the Romans effected.

The Britons, though slightly clothed, appear to have had at that time some knowledge of the art of defence and the use of metal, for they had war-chariots drawn by horses, and sharp scythes fixed to the axletrees of their wheels, which were very destructive in battle, nor did they fly from the invincible Romans without a struggle against their encroachments. Cæsar obtained little by the invasion of Britain, but from his time it is probable that a Roman garrison was stationed there, and that the Latin language was introduced. Perhaps some of the customs and arts of civilized people were also introduced and tribute may have been paid to the conquerors.

It is related by the older historians of Britain that the Romans were at first opposed by a British general named Cassibelan, (sometimes written Cassivelaunus,) and that a nephew of this general, at enmity with Cassibelan, became such a favorite of the Romans that he was sent to Rome to be educated. This youth, named Cymbeline, says the story, was caressed by Augustus, and called the *friend* of the Roman people.

In the early age of Roman conquests, the Romans were exceedingly cruel to their captives, but in later times they altered their policy. They liked to have hereditary princes of partially conquered countries come to their capital, and dwell there, that they might learn their language and laws, and respect their power; and, when they should return to their own land, they might dispose their subjects to submit to their wiser conquerors. The invasion of the Romans was the first introduction of civilization among the Britons.

The southern part of the island, since called Britain, was then Albion; and its northern portion, the present Scotland, was Caledonia. The southern country was divided among independent tribes of whom the chief were the Iceni, the Trinobantes, and the Silures.

What were the means of defence used by the Britons?
What were the first results of Cæsar's invasion?
Did the Romans show any favor to the Britons?
Was the Roman policy humanized as its power was extended ?
What were the ancient divisions of Britain?

A. D. 43. The Roman emperors for nearly a century paid little attention to Britain, but ninety-seven years after the invasion of Cæsar, an army of fifty thousand men was sent thither under the command of Aulus Plautius. The Britons defended themselves and their country with great bravery; but their imperfect skill in the art of war could not withstand the Roman power and discipline.

The last of the British princes who resisted the Romans was Caractacus. After several battles he was defeated, taken prisoner, and carried to Rome. In Rome, Caractacus, with his captive wife and children, were compelled to walk in chains through the streets; and the emperor and empress, and the inhabitants of that great city generally, being accustomed to such spectacles, were not probably much affected with this, which would so deeply grieve and offend us of the present more humane age of the world.

Caractacus did not submit tamely to this indignity, and made such a moving speech to the emperor, that he ordered his fetters to be taken off, and ever afterwards treated him with kindness. The Romans, notwithstanding their victories in Britain, advanced slowly in gaining possession of the island. They had only built a few castles, or forts, and established one military colony, when Suetonius Paulinus, a great general, resolved to finish the conquest

To convey a proper notion of the enterprise of Suetonius, it is necessary here to describe briefly the religion of the ancient Britons, for it was connected with their government, and aided resistance to their foreign enemies. According to Goldsmith, "The religion of the Britons was one of the most considerable parts of their government; and the Druids, who were the guardians of it, possessed great authority among them. No species of superstition was ever more terrible than theirs; besides the severe penalties which they were permitted to inflict in this world, they inculcated

---

What happened in Britain, A. D. 43?
Who was the British prince carried captive to Rome?
How was Caractacus finally treated by the Roman emperor?
Who were the Druids, and what were their doctrines?

the doctrine of transmigration of souls, and thus extended their authority as far as the fears of their votaries.

"They sacrificed human victims, which they burned in large wicker idols, made so capacious as to contain a multitude of persons at once, who were thus consumed together To these rites, tending to impress ignorance with awe, they added the austerity of their manners, and the simplicity of their lives. They lived in woods, caves, and hollow trees; acorns and berries constituted their general food, and their usual beverage was water. By these arts they were not only respected, but almost adored by the people."

The sacrifices of human victims implies a horrible religious faith, but it does not appear to be wholly inconsistent with fine qualities of mind and heart. The sacrifice of Jephtha's daughter, mentioned in the Hebrew scriptures, and that of Iphigenia by the Greeks, were induced by false notions of God. To give him the dearest of our possessions, may seem to ignorant men the most acceptable service, and those who were capable of such acts, often entertained sentiments of true devotion and humanity.

The Druids worshipped in the open air; and there still remain in England, circles of stones laid upon the surface of the ground, which, it is supposed, enclosed their sanctuaries. The oak was their favourite tree, and the mistletoe a parasitic plant, or one which grows upon trees, was used in their rites, and respected as a symbol of their faith. Some of the English poets regard the character of the Druids as that of simple-hearted and uncorrupted men, fond of contemplating the works of God.

Seutonius thought the most effectual way to establish the Roman power in Britain, was to extirpate the Druids, and therefore attacked their chief seat, the island of Anglesea, and got possession of it, and scattered the Druids and their attendants, and the *bards* or sacred poets, who assisted in their worship, and were highly reverenced by the native

---

What were some of the practices of the Druids?
What could induce men to offer human sacrifices?
What was the druidical worship?
What was the end of the Druids in Britain?

Britons. Probably many of the Druids and Bards were killed by the Roman soldiers.

The Romans boasted that their law "gave license to all faiths," that is they permitted to all conquered people the exercise of their former worship, whatever it was; and they may be vindicated in extirpating the religion of the Druids, contrary as the measure was to their accustomed policy, because it consisted partly of human sacrifices which humanity abhors, and which no power on earth should tolerate.

A. D. 60. One bold spirit yet remained to be subdued, and then the last of the Britons yielded to the Roman power. Boadicea, queen of the Iceni, held out against the enemy with a British army of 80,000 men under her command, and was opposed by the inferior force of 10,000 under Suetonius. But in this encounter the military skill of the foreign foe prevailed over the desperate but undisciplined valor of the natives.

Boadicea was overcome with anguish and despair when she saw her countrymen scattered, and murdered, and made prisoners. The Romans showed no respect to the unfortunate princess when she fell into their hands, but cruelly insulted her, and beat her with rods. Overwhelmed with her own misery, and the subjugation of her country, she put an end to her existence.

Boadicea's heroism has often been admired, and her misfortunes pitied in succeeding times. That she had not firmness to live, and bear whatever calamity awaited her, was owing to her ignorance of Christianity, which enjoins perfect submission to every evil however great or undeserved.

The Romans now easily established themselves all over Britain, and built towns and castles, and were entire masters of the country. Agricola, one of their generals, was a good, as well as a brave man, and prevailed with the natives to learn useful arts, and encouraged them to live in towns.

Did the Romans respect the religion of conquered nations generally and what in some sort justifies their severity to the Druids?
In what battle did Suetonius finally overcome the Britons?
What was the death of Boadicea?
What religion enjoins submission to misfortunes?
What was the character of Agricola?

and to build comfortable houses, and did all he could to civilize them.

Agricola also marched into Scotland. The inhabitants fled into the mountains, thinking that when winter should come he would depart. Instead, however, of going away, he built a line of forts quite across Scotland from the Frith of Forth to the mouth of the Clyde. The Caledonians, when they found themselves thus shut in, came down from the mountains, and ventured a battle, but were defeated, and then, overwhelmed with despair, many set fire to their dwellings, and killed their wives and children, for fear of their being made slaves to the victors. During this expedition, the Roman ships sailed quite round Britain, and so ascertained it to be an island.

For many years afterwards the country was in peace. During this period the Romans occupied themselves in making roads, of which some are still remaining, and in building castles, of which many vestiges are still left, and of which the ruins are so strong and massy, that they promise to outlast most of our modern buildings.

In the year 207, the Emperor Severus, though an old and infirm man, came to Britain with the determination to conquer Caledonia. He could not, however, succeed, owing to the nature of the country, and the bravery of the people; so he contented himself with employing his army to build an immense stone wall quite across from the Tyne to the Solway Frith, many parts of which are still to be seen. He soon after died at York.

For seventy years after the death of Severus we are ignorant of the affairs of Britain. At length the emperor Constantius came from Rome to take up his residence in the island. He did not live long, but died at York, in the year 309. His son, Constantine the Great, succeeded him; and being in Britain at the time of his father's death, there assumed the rank of emperor. While he lived, the country was at peace. Constantine died in 337.

The governors who came from Rome, by appointment

Did Agricola subdue Caledonia?
What were the public works of the Romans in Britain?
What was the principal work of Severus in Britain?
What happened from the death of Severus to A. D. 337?

of the emperors to govern Britain, were called *legates*, and sometimes *vicars* of Britain.

It does not appear that any considerable number of Romans domesticated and settled themselves in Britain. The imposition of taxes, and traffic in some of the productions of the country, were the advantages obtained by the conquerors, and they became, in fact, the benefactors of the Britons, by improving their arts, and teaching them their language, and introducing Christianity among them.

The Romans preserved their conquests by the establishment of colonies in the conquered countries. The Roman colonies differed from colonies in later times; because, though the Roman soldiers had lands given them to live on, yet, when they died, they could not leave them to their children; for the lands were then given to be held by other soldiers. The Roman settlers, therefore, could never feel as if what they had really belonged to them; which was the reason that, when they finally quitted Britain, the whole body of them went away together, and left none of their people settled in the island.

A. D. 414. Wars in Italy made it impossible to maintain the Roman Colony in Britain, and the legions which had kept the islanders in subjection were recalled 475 years after the first landing of Cæsar. The departure of the Romans was an occasion rather of grief than rejoicing to the Britons, for it exposed them to the incursions of their northern neighbors the Scots and Picts.

Those Caledonian nations were never subdued by the Romans, and retained the ferocity of their primitive barbarism. The improved condition of the southern country, its flocks, and harvests, and the articles of use and comfort which the houses contained, tempted the savage tribes, whose clothing was the skin, and whose precarious food was mostly the flesh of the slain beast, and who thought rapine no robbery.

In despite of the wall of Severus, which had been built

What was the Roman policy in Britain?
What were Roman colonies?
Why were the Romans recalled from Britain?
How long were they in the Island?
What was the condition of the Caledonians at that time?

to confine them within their own limits, the Scots and Picts after the departure of the Romans, made frequent and destructive inroads upon their neighbors, the Britons.

Stonehenge.

Before we proceed to the ensuing period of English history, it may be interesting to describe some of the *monuments* of the Romans, in England. By a *monument*, we do not mean merely some object which shows that persons have lived, have been remarkable for something, and are dead; but we also mean some work which they performed while living, which afterwards serves to show what they were capable of, and what were some of their customs.

The *monuments* of the ancient Britons, which may be found at the present time in England, are *Barrows, Cairns* or *Tumuli, Druidical Temples,* or circles of stones, *monumental* stones, *Cromlechs,* and remains of *Intrenchments.*

A Barrow, Cairn, or Tumulus, is a mound of earth, or a hillock of stones raised over the dead. Some of these are of great magnitude, and to raise them must have required immense labor. Perfect skeletons of British warriors have been found by digging deeply into these tumuli, or barrows. Spears, lances, bows and arrows, are generally found with these skeletons, and sometimes *pots* and *pans.*

The pots and pans probably at first contained food. Pa-

What is understood by the phrase "monument of antiquity?"
What monuments of the ancient Britons exist now in England?
What monuments of the ancient dead are found still in England?

gan and uncivilized nations seem to have believed that the articles necessary to the living, were acceptable to the dead, and this custom of supplying such articles to the tenants of the tomb may be discovered among the savages of America, as well as those of ancient Europe.

The skeletons in the British Tumuli have been found very entire.

> "Secure beneath his ancient hill
> The British warrior slumbers still;
> There lie in order, still the same,
> The bones which reared his stately frame,
> Still at his side, his spear, his bow,
> As placed two thousand years ago."

The *Cromlech* is nothing but a large flat stone placed horizontally upon other stones set upright in the ground. The whole forming a rude table which served, as is supposed, for the altar of Druidical worship.

As all savages live in a state of warfare, many contrive the defences called *fortifications*. The defence of a modern house is its locked and barred gates and doors. The defence of an ancient city, before the invention of fire-arms, was its walls and towers—the defence of savages against a hostile neighbor, is sometimes an *Intrenchment*, or high bank of earth, behind which the endangered people conceal themselves, and avoid the arrows of an enemy without. An Intrenchment, called *Wansdike* in Wiltshire, is eighty miles in length.

The remains of the works above mentioned form what are called British *antiquities*. Roman antiquities also exist in England. The Roman mode of interment resembled that of the Britons. *Antiquaries*, persons acquainted with the customs of ancient times, and the remains of ancient art, can distinguish between the Roman and British—the articles of Roman being of more elegant workmanship than those of British origin.

What custom prevails among savages in all countries?
Are the ancient dead well preserved in the Tumuli?
What is a Cromlech?
What is an Intrenchment?
Are there Roman antiquities in Britain?

The principal Roman antiquities, besides *tumuli, roads*, and *intrenchments*, are remains of *walls, houses, pavements, baths, hypocausts* or *stoves, urns, altars, statues, stones with inscriptions, coins, medals*, and various small articles of use or ornament.

The Roman *roads* in Britain were constructed by the soldiers with great art and labor, and so durable that they yet remain. Roman *Intrenchments* may still be seen. They show the spot where once was a *Pretorium* or *Roman Camp*. When these camps were permanently fixed to a certain place, they were carefully surrounded by Intrenchments, and were called Roman Stations.

When the Romans took possession of a town, or planted a colony in it, they generally took still greater care of themselves, and surrounded it with walls. These are so extremely hard and thick, that it is even now almost impossible to destroy them. Their first *colony* in Britain was Camulodunum, now Colchester, and there is their wall now standing, though not so high as it once was. When it was wished to make a gap in it some years ago, it was necessary to blow it up with gunpowder. The most astonishing wall, built by the Romans in Britain, was that of Severus, which was continued from one side of Scotland to the other.

Of their *houses*, or *villas*, there are few remains to be seen; but in digging, and in ploughing, their beautiful floors, called *tessellated pavements*, are often discovered. They are made of a vast number of very small bricks, of different colours, which are placed in ornamental figures, somewhat like the arrangement of cloth which we call patch-work, or the more elegant ornamental work of Mosaic. So fond were the Romans of this kind of ornament, that large sacks of these *tesseræ* often formed part of the baggage of their armies.

The sepulchres of the Romans were vaults, built for their dead, distinct from their *tumuli*. In these are found, sometimes, skeletons; in others, ashes, contained in urns

---

What are the principal Roman antiquities?
What are the military antiquities?
Are there any Roman houses in Britain?
Are there any Roman remains of the dead besides tumuli?

The urns are, most of them, beautifully made of very fine clay, and covered with a lid.

Altars, statues, and stones with inscriptions, are very scarce in England; but enough have been found to show that the Romans had leisure, and considered themselves settled. Of their *coins* great numbers have been found of brass, copper, lead, silver, and gold. Wherever history tells us there was a Roman station, there are often discovered quantities of their money and medals, which were usually stamped with heads, or figures, in remembrance of important public events.

Respecting these, it has been said by Mr. Addison, that, " As soon as an emperor had done any thing remarkable, it was immediately stamped upon a coin, and became current through his dominions. It was a pretty contrivance to spead abroad the virtues of an emperor, and make his actions circulate. A fresh coin was a kind of *gazette*, that published the latest news of the empire."

The ancient Britons, as has been mentioned, were divided into tribes, and were governed by their own chiefs. These petty sovereigns, it appears, thought it expedient in any great emergency, such as invasion, like that of the Romans, or in the Pictish ravages of the northern border, to choose one of their number to lead their united armies, and to preside in their councils. This supreme chief was the Pendragon, and his function resembled that of the Roman Dictator.

Arthur, prince of the Silures, the son of Uther, was made Pendragon when the Saxons usurped the sovereignty of Britain. Arthur's history, as it has come down to us, is partly true and partly false. In fact, he resisted the Saxons, and often prevailed against them, but Mordred, a powerful Pictish chief, went over to the Saxons, and by his treacherous assistance, they defeated Arthur in the battle of Camlan. In another engagement, Mordred killed Prince Arthur.

The more doubtful part of Arthur's history, are certain

What small and curious Roman antiquities still exist in England?
What in some sort served for a gazette in the Roman empire?
What was a British Pendragon?
What is the probable history of Prince Arthur?

wonderful achievements which are related in legends and ballads; among these are many stories of the Knights of the Round Table, who were friends of Arthur, and were represented to assemble sometimes at festivals held at a Round Table. from which their appellation was taken.

After the death of Arthur, the bards sung that Merlin, an enchanter, preserved and re-animated his dead body, and conveyed him to Fairyland. It became the common belief of the Welsh, that King Arthur would re-appear, would expel the Saxon conquerors of Britain, and reign again in the land. This fiction is often alluded to in English poetry.

CHAPTER II

During the occupation of Britain by the Romans, the natives lost much of their original hardihood. Their country was improved by cultivation, and their fruitful fields, and more numerous cattle, tempted their predatory neighbors, but as they had long found defenders in their Roman masters, they were become incapable of defending their property without the assistance of the Romans.

The ravages of the Scots and Picts not only impoverished but discouraged the Britons; and, in fear that they should not reap the harvest, they neglected their fields. In consequence of this neglect they suffered famine and disease. In their distress they called upon the Romans to return and protect them.

A letter which was addressed by them at this time to the governor of Gaul is still exant. It is the following:

"*To Ætius, thrice Consul. The groans of the Britons* The Barbarians drive us to the sea. The sea throws us back on the swords of the Barbarians: so we have nothing left but the wretched choice of being either drowned or butchered."

What is the poetic history of Arthur?
What was the popular belief of the Welsh in respect to Prince Arthur?
What effect had the protection afforded to the Britons by the Romans upon their character?
What was the condition of the Britons after the departure of the Romans?

The Romans were not in a condition to relieve the Britons, and they next had recourse to a nation at that period becoming powerful in Europe. The Saxons were a people dwelling in the northern part of Germany, and may be called a tribe of the Northmen. These were *properly* the people of Scandinavia—the inhabitants of Sweden, Norway, and Denmark. The dwellers on the *south* side of the Baltic resembled the Northmen in many particulars

The Northmen were never subject to Rome. From time immemorial they had been free and independent tribes, roaming over their own fields or deserts, without fear of, or subjection to, foreign enemies. They were the first natives of Europe who began to explore the open sea for subsistence, and when their vessels had penetrated to the inlets of Gaul, of Spain, and of Britain, the mild climate and cultivated soil of those countries allured their rapacity.

A. D. 448. Vortigern, a British prince, advised his countrymen to entreat aid of the Saxons, who, on their part, gladly promised to assist them against their enemies. In compliance with the request of the Britons, there presently arrived three ships, under the conduct of Hengist and Horsa, two brothers, who landed their troops, and being joined by the Britons, marched against the Scots, who had reached Stamford, where they were met by the Saxons, and were defeated, and driven back.

A. D. 460. The Saxons soon saw the value and agreeableness of the country they had been invited to defend, and began to covet the possession of it for themselves. They were, in fact, a nation of pirates, and, without regarding the wickedness and cruelty of such conduct, they sent for more of their countrymen, and fell upon the unfortunate Britons, and defeated them in many battles. In one of these Horsa was killed, and Hengist then took possession of Kent, and made. himself king of it.

After this success of the Saxons under Hengist, swarms

Who were the Northmen?
What is the History of the Northmen?
Under what circumstances did the Saxons first appear in Britain?
When did the Saxons first attempt hostilities against the Britons?
Who took possession of Britain, and how did they divide their conquest?

of them kept pouring in from time to time, and by degrees got possession of almost all South Britain; and as each of their chiefs took possession of what he conquered, there thus at last arose seven different kingdoms, which are commonly called the Saxon Heptarchy—Kent, contained Kent and part of Sussex.—Sussex, Surrey and part of Sussex.—Wessex, included the coast from Sussex to the Land's End.—East Saxony, or Essex.—East Anglia, Norfolk, Suffolk, and Cambridgeshire.—Mercia, the midland part of the island.—Northumberland, from Mercia to the borders of Scotland.

It was now that Britain began to be called, from one of the Saxon tribes, Angle-land, and from thence England. Of the native Britons but few were left. Numbers had been slaughtered by the perfidious Saxons. Some fled to Gaul, where they settled in the north-western corner of that country, which has since, from them, being called Bretagne, or Brittany. The rest took refuge in the western side of the island, from the Land's End to the Frith of Clyde, which is, for the most part, hilly and mountainous. The present inhabitants of Wales, and of a part of Cornwall, are descended from these ancient Britons. Scotland was then inhabited by the Scots and Picts. So that Britain must, at that time, have contained at least ten different nations or tribes.

After the battle of Stamford, there is no account to be met with of the Scots or Picts, till the year 503 when there is some record of a king Fergus, who united the whole of the nothern part of the island into one kingdom, and is the first king of Scotland we hear of. From the year 600 after Christ, to the year 800, there was little but fighting and disputing amongst the seven Saxon kings.

During this time one of the kings of Wessex conquered Cornwall; and then the Britons had nothing remaining to them but Cambria, now called Wales, which they kept possession of till the year 1300, when it was conquered by Edward I. king of England.

What became of the native Britons?
What was the condition of Scotland A. D. 503?
Who retreated to Wales, and who afterwards conquered Wales?

The Saxons, being pagans, persecuted the Christians, and seem at length to have nearly extirpated their religion. The people then became worshippers of the false gods of the Saxons.

When the Romans possessed Britain they doubtless brought the intelligence of Christianity with them, and Christian converts must have been made in Britain, but how much this Christianity prevailed is not now known. The Saxon masters of Britain brought with them the tyranny of ignorance and of physical power; and Christianity was so little regarded after the time of the Saxon domination, that the popes of Rome considered Britain among the waste places of heathenism, and sent thither one of the first Christian missions upon record.

About the year 596 Pope Gregory I. sent St. Augustine, or Austin, with forty monks, to instruct the people of Britain in the Christian religion. England and Wales were divided into different principalities at that time. Ethelred, king of Kent, was among the first proselytes of Augustine, and became an important aid to his purposes. Augustine was a spiritual governor as well as teacher, and he baptized converts, and established churches and ministers from Kent to Northumberland ; he also penetrated into Wales, where he found a form of Christianity more simple than the Romish faith. It had been learned in the second century after Christ from the Romans, and was still cherished.

Augustine expected to be acknowledged by all the inhabitants of Britain, as head of the English church under the pope. The Welsh, not comprehending the authority of the pope and Saint Austin, thought fit to reject it, and the saint denounced vengeance upon them. A king of Northumberland took upon himself the accomplishment of this prophecy, and without affording them time for defence, slaughtered about twelve hundred of the Welsh Christians Fear, as well as confidence, served to establish the Catholic

---

What was the state of Christianity under the Saxons in Britain, and who revived it ?
Who was St. Augustine ?
Did the Britons universally receive the Catholic doctrines ?

religion, and after the sixth century it was acknowledged in Britain, by the kings and the people.

The heptarchy was at last put an end to by Egbert, who is commonly considered the first king of all England; but, in fact, some of the kingdoms still remained, though he made them tributary. Towards the end of his reign, the Danes began to make irruptions into England; and during the reigns of Ethelwolf, the son, and Ethelred, the grandson, of Egbert, they came so frequently, and in such formidable numbers, that they nearly overran the whole kingdom. Ethelred was killed in a battle with them, and left his kingdom, in 871, to his brother Alfred, one of the best and greatest kings mentioned in history.

CHAPTER III

Among the best examples of virtue recorded in history is the character of Alfred, one of the Saxon kings of England. This prince was born in 849, at a place called Wannating, which is supposed to have been that which at present bears the name of Wantage in Berkshire, England.

Alfred had two brothers older than himself, the elder of whom, according to the law and custom of that time in England, was entitled to become king on the death of his father; but king Ethelwolf, for that was their father's name, disregarded the right of the eldest son, and determined, when he was no more than four years old, that Alfred should be his successor. As he was not the heir to the crown according to the law, King Ethelwolf did an act of injustice to the brothers of young Alfred when he allotted the crown to that prince.

Ethelwolf could not have declared this arbitrary intention, if there had not been another prince in Europe who

How did the heptarchy terminate?
What sort of man was the Saxon king Alfred?
Did Alfred come to the crown of England by regular succession?
By whose authority was Alfred made king?

was above the laws of every country, gave kingdoms to whom he pleased, and the people of all civilized Europe submitted to his will. This was the Pope. Ethelwolf obtained the consent of the Pope to his project of setting aside the claim of his eldest son, and in order to engage the Pope's favor more particularly in Alfred's behalf, in 853, sent that prince to Rome, where his Holiness, as the Pope is called, resided.

Alfred was *anointed* king of England by the Pope, and afterwards returned to his kingdom. *Anointing* is a ceremony performed upon kings, at the season of introducing them to their great office.

Two years after Alfred's first visit to Rome, he accompanied his father, and went thither a second time. A sensible person, who has written the history of Alfred, supposes that the public buildings, and other splendid and curious objects which he saw at Rome in this second visit, were ever after remembered by him, and that the remembrance of them inspired the designs which he afterwards in some measure effected, of improving his native country.

When the Saxons conquered Britain, after the Romans had left it, they were too ignorant, ferocious and cruel, to regard the useful and comfortable arts of the Romans. They treated the Britons so ill, and kept them so constantly at war with one another, that, except roads and fortifications, they destroyed all which their predecessors had done; so that when Alfred was young the country was in a ruined state.

Alfred's mother died when he was a very little child. On the return of Ethelwolf from Italy, he married Judith, daughter of Charles the Bald, then king of France. The Franks were originally a tribe of Germans, more improved and civilized than the other tribes; they established themselves in the ancient Gaul, and it received from them the modern name of France. Franks signifies freemen.

Some of Ethelwolf's subjects were offended by his injustice in preferring the infant Alfred to the proper heir of the

---

What is anointing?
Where did Alfred form notions of improving England?
What was the condition of England in Alfred's youth?
Who was Alfred's step-mother, and who were the Franks?
Did the English people readily accept of Alfred for their king?

throne. While Ethelwolf was absent in Italy, these disaffected subjects proposed to make the prince Ethelbald king in his father's place; but others formed a plan to divide the kingdom between the father and son. Ethelbald did not discourage these projects, and when the king became acquainted with the undutiful conduct of his son, it is said to have afflicted him so much that he died soon after Ethelbald survived his father but three years.

Alfred was twelve years of age at the death of his brother Ethelbald: his education had been so neglected that he did not know how to read; but though unable to read, he loved Saxon poetry, to which he always listened with eager attention when others read or recited it. One day, when queen Judith was sitting in the midst of her family reading a Saxon poem, she observed that the young princes seemed greatly to enjoy it, and she offered to give the book to him who should soonest learn to read it.

The older princes did not think the reward equal to the trouble, but Alfred, after examining the book, resolved to make an attempt to possess it. He found a competent instructor, and applied himself to his work with such diligence, that he was soon able to read and recite the poem to the queen. She kept her promise, and Alfred no doubt valued her gift as it deserved.

Alfred had no sooner acquired the inestimable ability to read, than he found it—what every rational and cultivated person finds it—a source of unfailing occupation and delight, and he never again felt the fatigue of indolence. Alfred always continued to delight in the Saxon poetry, and made a collection of pslams and hymns for his own use He kept this book in his bosom. Soon after Queen Judith had disposed Alfred to improve himself she returned to France, and left him to advance in learning as well as he was able.

Alfred's brothers did not act with more justice towards him than their father had done to themselves; for they allowed the young prince but a small maintenance out of

---

Was Alfred's education neglected?
From what beginning did Alfred learn to read?
Did Alfred profit by the art of reading?
What made Alfred regardless of the neglect of his brothers?

the ample property left by Ethelwolf; however, Alfred was too deeply engaged in study to think with much pain of any thing, even the unkindness of his brothers. In the course of his studies, Alfred learned that there was other and far more desirable knowledge than any to be found in the scanty Saxon literature : he discovered that the finest books then in the world were those written in the Greek and Latin languages.

Before Alfred could read those beautiful and precious books, it was necessary for him to learn Greek and Latin. He earnestly desired to become acquainted with poets, philosophers, and historians, whose thoughts were to him locked up in unknown tongues—but his wishes were in vain. To the royal Alfred aids to learning that are now in every school-boy's hands were utterly denied. He not only wanted grammars and dictionaries, but a master capable of teaching him, for not one could be found in the kingdom. He afterwards lamented, as his greatest misfortune, that when he had youth and leisure, and permission to learn, he could not find a teacher.

From the time of his learning the art of reading to his nineteenth year, Alfred spent almost all his time at his studies. During this period, two of Alfred's elder brothers died, and Ethelred, the third brother, came to the throne Ethelred was not happy in his government, for large numbers of Danes crossed the North Sea, landed in England and destroyed much of the property, and many of the lives of the English.

All the soldiers that Ethelred could command were not powerful enough to defeat these cruel enemies. In his distress Ethelred called upon his brother Alfred to assist him Alfred was mild and peaceable like his father, but he was grieved for the sufferings of the poor English. He resolved if he could, to punish the Danes, and he fought many battles with his brother. About this period he married Elswitha, the daughter of a British nobleman. Ethelred was wounded in battle, and died soon after, in the year 871

Was learning easily obtained in England in the age of Alfred ?
When did the Danes invade England ?
When was Alfred called to defend England ?

At the age of twenty-two Alfred became king. In the first seven years of his reign he does not appear so great a man as he afterwards became. In a month after he succeeded to the throne, the Danes attacked and defeated Alfred's troops, and he did not attempt to punish them; and twice afterwards he gave them money to quit the country, which they promised to do.

The Danes afterwards called over great numbers of their countrymen. They destroyed so much property, killed so many people, and so terrified others, that some of the English fled to France, and concealed themselves in secret places. The king, who had lost the confidence of his subjects, because he had not endeavored to prevent these misfortunes, was then forced to wander about alone in disguise; so that at one time neither his friends or enemies could find him.

Wise and good as Alfred really was, his habits of study had not instructed him in the character of the Danes, nor in the duty he owed his subjects, who, before the Danes had committed their most violent acts, entreated him to protect them; but he did not believe the danger to be so great as it was in fact.

Alfred was twenty-eight years of age at the time when he was obliged to conceal himself, and to give up his kingdom to the Danes. An excellent trait in his character now appears—a resolution to reform his faults, to endeavor to conquer the enemies of his country, and to do all in his power for the benefit of his subjects.

Alfred escaped from court in the disguise of a soldier, and he was at first attended by a number of faithful followers, but the company was too small to defend themselves, and large enough to excite the suspicions of the enemy. Alfred thought it prudent to seek his own safety alone; and he wandered about in the woods and lonely places till he reached a solitary spot in Somersetshire, where he found a secure retreat.

When did Alfred begin to reign, and how did he govern?
Did the Danes persevere in invading England?
Did Alfred repel the Danes vigorously?
Did Alfred reform his own errors?
Where did Alfred conceal himself from his enemies?

In this journey Alfred once entered the cottage of a swine-herd, who, perceiving that he wished to hide himself, inquired who he was. Alfred dared not tell the man who he really was, lest he should inform the Danes; therefore he was obliged to deceive him by saying, that he was an attendant on king Alfred, who had fled from battle, and who wanted to be concealed. Alfred was doubtless unwilling to do this, for among his virtues a constant regard for truth distinguished him—so much was he celebrated for this excellent habit, that an historian who lived two centuries after him, called him " Alfred the truth teller."

The good peasant feeling compassion for him, and little suspecting who it was he was protecting, gave him shelter, and made him welcome to his own comforts, and Alfred in his turn endeavored to make himself useful to his benefactor. One day, when the swine-herd was abroad with his charge, his wife put her cakes on the hearth to bake, and desired Alfred, who sat by the fire, trimming his bow and arrows, to take care of the cakes while she attended to her other business.

But Alfred was just then thinking too much of his own affairs to watch the bread, and when his hostess returned, she found it so burnt that it could not be eaten. She was very angry with the soldier, and scolded him heartily, telling him, that though he was very willing to eat her bread, he would not even turn it from the fire to prevent its being spoiled. This was very provoking to Alfred, but he had the good sense to make no reply, and immediately offered to do better, if the angry woman would give him some more cakes, which she accordingly did, and he baked them to please her.

Soon after his residence at the swine-herd's, Alfred discovered another asylum from his enemies. It was a few acres of firm ground near the *confluence* of two small rivers, the Thone and the Parret. This little island contained a wood, and abounded in stags and goats, and there was no approach to it but in small vessels. In the month of March,

---

Who received Alfred in his disguise?
How did Alfred employ himself in the swine-herd's cottage?
What exercised the king's patience?
Where was Alfred's next asylum?

Alfred heard of the death of Hubba, one of the most powerful and dreaded of the Danish chiefs. At the same time he found means to collect about him some of his faithful subjects, to whom he proposed to accompany him to the island, which he intended to fortify, and afterwards to reside in with his family. This place is now called Athelney.

By the aid of his followers, Alfred completed this plan, and was soon joined by many of his dispersed friends When the number of this little band was sufficient, they began to make excursions against the Danes, and although they were not always successful, they were enough so to alarm the enemy. Alfred and his followers were furnished with provisions during their stay at the island, by the spoils taken from the Danes, and by hunting and fishing; but the stock thus obtained was not always abundant.

After Alfred had meditated for some time an attempt to attack the Danes, he ventured in the disguise of a harper, to approach the tent of Guthrum, a Danish chief; he contrived to enter and to divert the Danes for several days with music and poetry. There he had an opportunity of learning that the Danes were not acquainted with the power of the English, and that they were unprepared for battle with them.

The carelessness of his enemies enabled Alfred to give information of his place of concealment, and of his plans, to many of his brave and afflicted subjects, who had for a long time been ignorant of their master's safety. They heard the news with gladness, readily flocked to Alfred, and joined him in his march against the Danes.

This enterprise was conducted with so much discretion and expedition, that Alfred surprised the Danes, who, in their surprise and terror, made some opposition, but afterwards fled before the king. Alfred, however, pursued, and surrounded his enemies; they were thus deprived of provisions, and after fourteen days of fatigue and hunger, they implored the mercy of the conqueror.

Some lives were lost in Alfred's attack upon the Danes

Did Alfred's friends come to his aid?
Did Alfred visit the Danish camp?
Did Alfred take advantage of the carelessness of the Danes?
Did the Danes finally submit to Alfred?
How did Alfred treat the Danes?

but when the army acknowledged themselves conquered Alfred formed a benevolent design to make them good and happy. He offered to become their protector and friend if they would become Christians, and would promise to assist him against any other Danes who should attack his subjects, and he promised them a portion of land to cultivate and live upon.

Guthrum accepted Alfred's proposal, and he and his followers were baptized. Guthrum remained with Alfred twelve days as a guest, and then, after receiving presents from the king, departed for the place allotted to him. Here he and his soldiers became peaceable and useful citizens: exchanging their swords for plough-shares, and leaving the business of destruction, they learned to promote their own and other's prosperity and happiness.

Alfred did not claim all England as his kingdom. Some parts of the country were governed by other princes, and the generous Alfred conferred a portion of the island which fell into his hands by the conquest of the Danes, on a prince named Ethelred, who married his daughter Ethelfleda. Athelstan, the grandson of Alfred, was the first Saxon monarch of all England.

After Alfred had obtained peace, he employed himself in all the useful works in his power. He rebuilt towns and castles which had been destroyed, erected forts, and stationed a number of armed ships along the coast of England, to prevent the landing of enemies from the neighboring continent of Europe. These ships were the beginning of the British navy.

Alfred had great need of armed ships, for the Danes, after the defeat of Guthrum, still persevered in their attempts upon England. Hastings, a daring and experienced Danish chief, presumed that his countrymen in England would take part with him, if he should attack that country after the death of Guthrum, who always continued faithful to his engagement with Alfred.

Hastings sent 250 ships to one place, and 80 to another.

Did the Danes become quiet subjects of Alfred?
Did Alfred govern all England?
Did Alfred improve his kingdom?
Who was Hastings?
What became of Hastings?

twenty miles distant from the former, and he landed troops in both without difficulty; and thus commenced a new war which tried the skill and patience of Alfred for three years. Hastings, at length, worn out by unfortunate attempts, retreated with all his army from England, and left the nation at peace.

Alfred reigned prosperously fifteen years, from the first defeat to the last invasion of the Danes, and after their last expulsion he lived four years. On the 28th of October, this excellent prince died, in the fifty-third year of his age, and the thirtieth of his reign.

Alfred was so much pleased with his own acquirements that he wished all his people, who could, to possess the same knowledge. On this account he was anxious that the books written in Latin, which contained what it is desirable that all men should know, should be translated into English, "that all the youth in England, who are *free*, and those that have wealth, may be committed to learning, that they may apply to no other duty till they first learn to read English writing. Let them further learn the Latin language who will advance to a higher state."

To promote this benevolent design he established schools in all parts of his kingdom, to which all freemen, possessing two acres of land, were enjoined by law to send their children. He gave places in the church, or under the government, to those only who had made some progress in learning. Engaged as he was in frequent wars, and in affairs of government, he gained more knowledge, and composed more books, than most men who have devoted their lives to study.

Alfred was happy in being surrounded by intelligent and amiable children. Two sons and three daughters survived him. His son Edward succeeded him as king, and his daughter Ethelfleda was accounted the wisest woman in England. Alfred's last instructions to his son and successor, deserve to be remembered, and with them will be concluded this brief history of one of the best and wisest men that ever lived.

When did Alfred die?
Did Alfred honor learning?
How did Alfred promote learning?
Was Alfred happy in his domestic relations?

"My dear son, sit thou now beside me, and I will deliver thee true instruction. My son, I feel that my hour is coming. My days are almost done. We must now part. I shall go to another world, and thou wilt be left in all my wealth. I pray thee, (for thou art my dear child,) strive to be a father and a lord to thy people. Be thou the children's father and the widow's friend. Comfort thou the poor, and shelter the weak; and with all thy might, right that which is wrong. And, son, govern thyself, by law, then shall the Lord love thee, and God, above all things, be thy reward. Call thou upon him to counsel thee in thy need, and so shall he help thee the better to compass what thou wouldst have."

The state of society under the Saxons appears to have been extremely rude till the age of Alfred, who enlarged his views of the true happiness and glory of mankind by observation of the better condition of men at that time in France and Italy. The inhabitants of monasteries were the only persons who thought much of cultivating their minds, and many of them were unable to read and write, others, however, were better informed.

The more intelligent of the monks recorded the history of the times, and from their histories, we obtain the facts which are related in modern history. Among the older British historians, was one called the *venerable* Bede, who is honored for his fidelity of description.

Coined money was not in use among the English at that time. Things were bought and sold in the way of barter or exchange; and rents, till long afterwards, were paid in corn and cattle, instead of money. The Romans made use of money as we do; and though it is so long since they left the island, people to this day find their coins, and the more frequently because they had a custom of burying money with the dead.

What advice did Alfred give his son?
What was the state of society in England under the Saxons?
Who wrote history in England?
What money was used by the Saxons and Romans?

The houses of Alfred's time were very different from those of our age; his palace was probably inferior to our common habitations. Most houses were in his time made of wood. There is an account of the chief palace of the king of Wales called the *White Palace*, which was made of peeled rods woven together. Houses were then never built of stone, which was only used in constructing castles and strong places for defence. Even the churches were commonly of wood. William of Malmesbury, an historian of the twelfth century, says, that the first Christian church in Britain, was made with wattles, which are stakes interlaced, or interwoven with osiers. We are told that the first stone church was built at Lincoln, and that it was thought a great curiosity.

The first glass that was ever seen in England was at Hexham Abbey, in Northumberland, and was made by some workmen who came from France, and taught the English how to make it: but it was a long time before it became general. At first it was only used for the windows of churches. The windows of their houses were covered with cloth to keep out the wind, or else with lattice-work.

Clocks were unknown, as is proved by a contrivance of the wise Alfred. One-third of his time he devoted to religious exercises and to study; another third to sleep and necessary refreshment, and the other to the affairs of his kingdom. Thus every thing was attended to; and he was so much afraid of losing a moment, that as there were no clocks or watches, he contrived a sort of candle, by the burning of which he could measure time. These candles were painted in rings or belts of different breadths and colors, so many colors as he had things to attend to; and thus he knew by the burning of these candles, when he had been employed long enough upon any one occupation.

The Saxon nobles were not much better informed than the inferior orders,—they could neither write nor read Much of their time hung heavily upon their hands, namely

---

What was the early architecture of England?
When was glass first used in England?
Were clocks known in Alfred's time?
How did the Saxon nobles sometimes divert themselves?

the time when they were neither hunting nor fighting; and they were not fighting every day in the year, nor hunting every hour of the day. And in rainy weather and winter evenings when they had played with their dogs, and sharpened their arrows, and brightened their spears, (for to have bright arms was an essential part of a Saxon gentleman's appearance,) they often did not know what to do with themselves. A man who could sing a song, or play on the harp, or tell an entertaining story, was consequently much courted and valued; and this occasioned some persons to make it their business to learn all these accomplishments.

These persons, whom the Saxons called glee-men, but usually known now under the name of *minstrels*, used to rove about the country from house to house, and from castle to castle, singing their songs, and telling their stories, which were commonly in verse : and every body made them welcome, and was glad to see them. And even when the country was in a state of warfare, and other people could not travel without danger, they went every where without molestation, for nobody would hurt or molest the poor minstrel, who was always so acceptable and amusing a guest.

The Danes were acquainted with the game of chess. Backgammon was also played in England, having been invented, it is said, by the Welsh, and called by them, from two words in their language, *back cammon*, or little battle.

What was the condition of the Saxon minstrels?
What were favorite games of the Danes, English, and Welsh, in the time of the Saxons,—and when was that time? (Latter answer from the pupils' judgment.)

CHAPTER IV

SAXON KINGS AFTER ALFRED

[Years after Christ, 901—959]

ST. DUNSTAN.

Alfred was succeeded by his son Edward, who had a turbulent reign of twenty-four years, the early part of which was disturbed by the attempts of his cousin Ethelwald to wrest the kingdom from him. This cousin Ethelwald was the son of Alfred's elder brother; but, being an infant at the time of his father's death, the nobles passed him by, and made Alfred king. The nephew, now that his uncle was dead, naturally put in his claim to the crown. After much fighting, and the loss of many of his adherents, he was killed, and then Edward's right remained undisputed.

A. D. 925. Edward was a man of great abilities, but more warlike than peaceable in his disposition. He had also a sister named Ethelfleda, who assisted him in many of his enterprises.

Athelstan, his eldest son, succeeded Edward. His reign, like that of his father, was a continual conflict with the Danes. One of their generals, a prince called Anlaff, disguised himself like a minstrel, and went into Athelstan's

---

Who was Alfred's successor?
What was the history of Edward the Elder?
Who succeeded Edward the Elder?
What Danish prince entered Athelstan's camp?

camp. The king was much pleased with his music, and, thinking he was a poor boy, gave him a piece of money. Anlaff was too proud to keep it, and when he got out of the king's tent, and thought nobody was in sight, he buried it in the ground. It happened that a soldier saw him, and thinking this very strange, examined the pretended minstrel's face, and knew him to be prince Anlaff, but did not prevent his departure.

When the Danish prince had got some distance from the camp, the soldier informed Athelstan of the discovery he had made. The king reproved him for letting such a dangerous enemy escape. "I once served Anlaff," replied the man, "and gave him the same faith that I have now given to you; and if I had betrayed him, what trust could you have reposed in my truth? Let him die, if such be his fate; but not through my treachery. Yet now he has escaped, secure yourself from danger, and remove your tent, lest he should assail you unawares."

Athelstan was pleased with the honest soldier's answer, and took his advice, and it was well he did; for an English bishop, who came the next day, and pitched his tent in the same spot where the king's had stood, was in the night attacked by the Danes; and both he and all his servants were killed.

The noise of this attack waked the Saxons, and the battle became general between them and the Danes. It lasted all that night and all the following day, and is distinguished in Saxon history by the name of the *long battle*. It ended in Athelstan's gaining a complete victory, which secured to him the entire possession of the kingdom. But he did not enjoy it long; for he died three years afterwards, in 941.

Athelstan was succeeded by his brother Edmund, who was at first molested by the persevering Danes. They however, were soon subdued, and Edmund displayed so much bravery and wisdom, that there was every hope his reign would be a happy one; when a sudden end was put

---

What trait of honor was exhibited by one of Athelstan's soldiers?
Was Athelstan's life saved by the faithful soldier?
What battle is called the *long battle*, and when did Athelstan die?
Was the reign of Edmund the Saxon long?

to it. He was sitting at a feast with all his nobles about him, when a daring robber, named Leolf, came into the hall. The attendants tried in vain to turn him out; and the king, getting very angry, rose from his seat, and seizing him by the hair, threw him down. The robber upon this drew his dagger, and stabbed the king to the heart; and thus this hopeful young prince died, when he was only twenty-four years old, in the year 948.

Edmund left two little sons, named Edwy and Edgar but they were so young, that Edred, his brother, was chosen king. The Northumberland Danes revolted in the beginning of the new reign; but Edred soon subdued them; and, no longer allowing them to have a prince of their own, he appointed one of his own nobles to be their governor; by which means he prevented them from any more disturbing the peace of the kingdom.

This king would have led on the whole a quiet life, if he had not suffered himself to be governed by an ambitious priest, called St. Dunstan. It is now necessary to give some account of the state of the church at this period. There were then at the head of the English bishops, as there now are, two *arch-bishops*, those of York and Canterbury. Of the body of the clergy, a large portion were monks, who took on themselves some particular vow of living by a certain system or rule. Their ordinary practice was to live in *monasteries*, under the government of some superior: and they are often called the *regular* clergy.

Another portion of the clergy were *seculars*, who did not take on themselves any monkish vows, but professed to be priests, and prayed with the people, and performed other priestly offices. The way of life of the secular clergy has, in later periods, been altogether different from that of the monks or regulars. At first, however, both these classes lived chiefly in *monasteries*, in which they preached regularly, and established schools.

The monasteries, having no soldiers in them, and being

Who succeeded Edmund, and how did he manage the Danes?
What was the state of the church in the tenth century in England?
What were secular clergy?
Were the clergy particularly exposed to the ravages of any foreign barbarians who might enter their country?

quite defenceless, were in general the first objects attacked by the Danes, who, after killing or driving out the inhabitants, carried off all the plunder they could find, and commonly destroyed the monastery. Of those who escaped, many took refuge in the neighbouring villages; and this occasioned a great increase of parish churches, almost all the churches till now having been either *cathedrals*, or annexed to religious houses.

After a time many of the new parish priests became attached to the homes which they thus acquired, and married, and, in short, lived among their parishioners as clergymen do now. When Alfred rebuilt the monasteries, and wanted their former inhabitants to go back to them, many refused to return, and he was, therefore, obliged to invite monks from other countries to come and live in his monasteries. Perpetual quarrels and jealousies ensued, and the two parties did all they could to injure one another. Perhaps the unmarried clergy reproved the others because they were married. Celibacy of the clergy, or a single life is required by Catholics.

St. Dunstan was an English monk, of good interest and connections. He had been at first abbot of Glastonbury; and at last came to be Archbishop of Canterbury. He was a proud, meddling man, and very violent against the secular clergy, and persuaded king Edred, over whom he had great influence, to treat them in a very harsh manner. Edred, in the latter part of his life, which ended in 955, became indolent and helpless from bad health, and let St. Dunstan do whatever he pleased.

Edwy, the eldest son of king Edmund, and nephew to Edred, then succeeded to the throne. He was only eighteen years old, and was naturally well-disposed; but the cruelty and hard-heartedness of this St. Dunstan destroyed not only the happiness of his life, but also his life, as shall be related.

Edwy had a beautiful cousin, Elgiva, whom he loved very

What is meant by celibacy of the clergy?
Who was St. Dunstan?
Whose son was Edwy?
What example of ecclesiastical abuse of power is afforded by the history of Edwy?

dearly, and whom he married. St. Dunstan, and Odo, at that time archbishop of Canterbury, declared it to be sinful for a man to marry his cousin, and did all they could to disturb their mutual happiness. On this the king sent St. Dunstan out of the kingdom; but Odo contrived to seize on the poor queen, cruelly burned her face with hot irons, in order to destroy her beauty, and then had her carried away into Ireland, where she was kept a prisoner.

Odo then instigated Edgar, who was still a boy, to raise a rebellion against his brother. St. Dunstan also returned from his banishment, and joined in Edgar's rebellion. To complete Edwy's afflictions, Elgiva, having made her escape from Ireland, got as far as Gloucester in her way back to him; but she was there discovered by her savage persecutors, who put her to death. Edwy, not able to support such an accumulation of misfortunes, died, of a broken heart, in 959.

Edgar, the next king, was only sixteen years old when he succeeded his unfortunate brother Edwy. We are told that justice was so well and wisely administered in his time, that travelers had no longer any fear of robbers. It appears that he attended diligently to the maritime affairs of his kingdom; and he had so large a fleet, that the Danes never ventured to molest him.

A. D. 975. After having reigned seventeen years, Edgar died in 975. His reign was so free from wars and tumults, that he obtained the title of Edgar the Peaceable. He left two sons, Edward, the son of his first wife; and Ethelred, whose mother, Elfrida, was still living. Elfrida was ambitious that her son should be king instead of his half-brother; but the influence of St. Dunstan placed the crown on the head of Edward.

This young man behaved kindly and gently to every body, and respectfully to his ambitious step-mother; but this did not prevent her from contriving his death. One day, when he was hunting near Corfe Castle, in Dorsetshire, where Elfrida lived, he rode to the Castle, unattended by any of his servants, and unsuspicious of any ill,

---

What was one consequence of the cruelties of Odo and St Dunstan?
Who succeeded Edwy?
When did Edgar die, and who succeeded him?
Who killed king Edward?

to make the queen a visit. Elfrida received him with much pretended kindness; and as he declined dismounting from his horse, she presented him with a cup of wine. While he was drinking it, she caused him to be stabbed in the back.—Edward, finding himself wounded, put spurs to his horse, and galloped off; but becoming weak from loss of blood, he fell from his horse, and was dragged in the stirrup till he died.

Ethelred then succeeded to the throne; but though his wicked mother had now obtained her utmost wish, she found it impossible to be happy. She founded monasteries, and performed penances, according to the superstitious notions of those times: but could never regain her peace of mind. Edward, whom she had murdered, was, on account of his tragical death, called Edward the Martyr.

In those superstitious times, when any one had committed a crime, instead of making amends for it in a proper way, by sincere repentance, and by repairing to the utmost the harm he had done, the monks used to persuade him to do penance, or inflict voluntary punishment upon himself.

To do penance, was often to go barefoot, or to sleep on a hard board instead of a bed, or to do something else which should vex the body; but which would not make the heart, or temper, from which the fault arose, at all the better.

It was then common for priests to exhort rich sinners to leave their money at their deaths to build churches and monasteries. *Indulgencies* were privileges that were to be bought, allowing people to do things which were forbidden; but which still they had a mind to do. For instance, it was against the rules of the church to eat butter during Lent; but by paying a priest for liberty to eat butter, any person was permitted to eat it in Lent.

Ethelred had the name of *Ethelred the Unready:* for when the Danes made an attack upon his kingdom, instead of being prepared to drive them off, he bribed them with a large sum of money to go away. This, at that time, they

---

How did the murdress of Edward console herself for her crime?
What amends for crimes did the Catholic Church sometimes enjoin?
What is Penance?
What are Indulgences in the Catholic Church?
By what foolish policy did Ethelred keep off the Danes from England?

did, but it was only to return again the next year, in hopes of being again bribed. Ethelred, however, was now ready for them, and would have blocked up and destroyed their fleet, had not Ealfric, one of his own commanders, deserted to them, after having first given them notice of the intended attack. By this means they escaped with only the loss of one ship.

A. D. 993. The country was again invaded. Sweyn, king of Denmark, and Olave, king of Norway, commanded this expedition. They sailed up the Humber, landed in Lincolnshire, and remained nearly two years, overrunning and pillaging different parts of the country. At last Ethelred, by giving them a very large sum of money, prevailed on them to depart. But the kingdom had only one year's rest from these insatiable marauders. They again returned, and were again bribed to leave the country.

Some years before, a body of Northmen, under the command of a leader named Rollo, had made an incursion into France, and obtained possession of a fertile district, which has since been called Normandy. Richard II., duke of Normandy, a descendant of Rollo, was a very powerful prince; and the improvident Ethelred, who had entirely exhausted the resources of his own kingdom by repeated bribes to the Danes, thought that the making a friend of this duke, would be his best protection against them in case they should return again. To cement this friendship, he prevailed on the duke to give him in marriage his daughter Emma, who was accounted the most beautiful princess in Europe.

This marriage might, through the duke of Normandy's influence with the Danes, have been some security to the English, but for an act of barbarity, not less unwise than wicked, of which they were guilty. In revenge for the repeated sufferings which the foreign Danes had brought upon them, they made, in the year 1002, a general massa-

---

What occurred A. D. 993?
What northern adventurer first established himself in France, and why did the king of England seek his friendship?
What bloody act of the English brought upon them the vengeance of Sweyn?

cre of the Danes settled in England. Amongst others was killed a sister of the king of Norway, with her husband and children. When the news of this cruel murder reached Sweyn, he vowed to make a bloody retaliation; and, accordingly, in the year 1003, he brought a large army to England, where he established himself successfully.

In the course of ten years, Sweyn got entire possession of the kingdom; and Ethelred and his queen Emma, with their two young sons, fled into Normandy. But Sweyn, before he could be crowned, died at Gainsborough. As soon as Ethelred heard of his death, he came back into England, and conducted himself with such unexpected activity and courage, that he compelled the Danes, with their young king Canute, to return home.

If Ethelred had been wise and prudent, he might now have reinstated himself in his kingdom: but he suffered himself to be governed and misguided by one of his traitorous nobles, and caused some of his more faithful adherents to be put to death unjustly. Canute now returned; and Edmund, the eldest son of Ethelred, a brave and active young prince, struggled hard to preserve his father's kingdom, amidst the many and great difficulties occasioned by the cruelties of the Danes, the weakness of his father, and the wickedness of the nobles.

A. D. 1016. This prince, on the death of his father, became king; and, from his hardihood and invincible valor, was called Edmund Ironsides. He fought no less than five pitched battles with the Danes. Canute and he then came to an agreement to divide the kingdom between them, and to live in peace. It was settled that Canute should have Mercia and Northumberland, and that Edmund should keep all the rest of the kingdom. But, a few days after this agreement had been made between them, Edmund was murdered at Oxford by one of his own nobles, and thus Canute became sole king of England in the year 1017.

Why was not Sweyn crowned king of England?
What was the conduct of Ethelred, and his son Edmund?
How did Canute become king of England?

CHAPTER V.

FROM CANUTE TO THE NORMAN CONQUEST.

[Years after Christ, 1017—1066.]

The English showed, at first, some repugnance to accept for their king a foreigner and an enemy, in exclusion of the sons of Edmund Ironsides. But Canute, who was a wise and powerful prince, reconciled all their differences, and peaceably ascended the throne. His first care was to endeavor to bring about a reconciliation between his English and Danish subjects; in which difficult undertaking, it is said, he succeeded: and although he had profited by the wicked arts of those Saxons who had betrayed their country to him, he nevertheless inflicted on them the just punishment of their treachery, putting some of them to death, and banishing others.

Canute's conduct towards the family of his predecessor,

What was the general character of Canute's government?

is the great stain on his character. He not only caused the brother of Edmund to be murdered, but also sent away Edmund's two little sons to the king of Sweden, meaning it is supposed, that he should put them to death. But the king of Sweden took compassion on them, and sent them to Solomon, king of Hungary, desiring him to take good care of them. Edwin, the elder, died young; but the younger, who was called Edward, lived to grow up, and married Agatha, sister to the queen of Hungary.

Canute, when he was thoroughly settled in England, being desirous to show his new subjects what confidence he had in them, sent almost all his Danish fleet and army back again to Denmark, keeping only forty ships. He next offered himself in marriage to Emma, the widowed queen of Ethelred, and she married him, although he had been her children's greatest enemy. It was, however, a very fortunate marriage for Canute, as it prevented the duke of Normandy from attempting to place on the throne of England his nephews, Alfred and Edward, the two sons of Emma and Ethelred.

The conduct of Canute was so wise and prudent, that he has been called by historians Canute the Great. In a voyage to Denmark, to repel the Swedes, who were making an attack upon that country, he took with him some English under the command of earl Godwin; and they attacked the Swedish army with so much bravery, that Canute was greatly pleased with their conduct; and Godwin became one of his greatest favorites.

Canute staid in Denmark about a year; and when he returned to England he found the country in tranquility in which it continued for some years. During this time Canute employed himself in making new laws and regulations, and in building churches and monasteries.

A. D. 1035. Excepting a dispute with the king of Scotland about the tribute called Danegelt, which he demanded for a part of Cumberland that had at some former time been given up to the Scots, Canute preserved England in peace during the whole of his reign

---

How did Canute treat the sons of Edmund Ironsides?
Did Canute reign securely in England, and whom did he marry?
Did Canute govern wisely?
Was England tranquil during Canute's life?

a term of eighteen years. He died at Shaftsbury, and left three sons, Sweyn, Harold, and Hardicanute.

The succession had been settled on Hardicanute, who was queen Emma's son; but, he being in Denmark when his father died, Harold seized on the crown, and took possession of the late king's treasures. Earl Godwin and the greater part of the English, declared for Hardicanute; and the country seemed on the verge of a civil war, when it was prevented by an arrangement entered into for dividing the kingdom between the two brothers.

Harold was to keep London, and the counties north of the Thames. All to the south of that river was to be Hardicanute's; and his mother, queen Emma, was to live at Winchester, and govern the country for him, till his return from Denmark. Emma then sent for her two sons, Alfred and Edward, whom she had had by Ethelred, to come to England from Normandy, where they were living under their uncle's care.

A. D. 1039. Alfred, on his arrival, fell into the hands of earl Godwin, who had been secretly gained to Harold's interest, and was carried to Ely, where he was either actually murdered, or died in consequence of the cruel treatment he suffered. As soon as Emma heard of his fate, she fled into Flanders, and Harold took possession of the whole kingdom. He did not, however, long enjoy the fruits of his cruelty and ambition, for he died in 1039. He was remarkable for his swiftness in walking and running, which obtained for him the name of Harold Harefoot.

A. D. 1041. As soon as Hardicanute, who had joined his mother in Flanders, heard of the death of Harold, he came to England, and was received by the people with the greatest joy. But their joy was of short duration, for the young king soon showed himself to be of a very ferocious and vindictive temper. Hardicanute levied heavy taxes on his English subjects, to pay his Danish fleet and army. His reign, however, did not last long; for he died in 1041, having shortened his life by his excessive intemperance in eating and drinking.

When did Canute die?
What prevented a civil war in England at that time?
When did Harold Harefoot die?
When did Hardicanute die?

The violences of Harold and Hardicanute had so much disgusted the English with their Danish sovereigns, that they now resolved to restore the line of their own Saxon princes, and they looked about amongst the descendants of Ethelred for a successor to the vacant throne. They invited Edward, afterwards called the Confessor, the son of Ethelred and Emma, to ascend the throne. Edward, being of a timorous and unambitious temper, did not desire to be king, and would have declined the offer, had not earl Godwin, who was now become the most powerful person in the kingdom, prevailed on him to suffer himself to be crowned. This restoration of the Saxon line caused great joy throughout the kingdom, and was long celebrated by an annual festival called Hokeday.

Edward married Edgitha, daughter of earl Godwin, and began his reign by seizing on the treasures of queen Emma, who, he pretended, had treated him very unkindly during his adversity. He also revoked many grants the late king had made to the Danes; and took off the tax called Danegelt, a tax which was particularly odious to the English, and which had been first levied by Ethelred, to obtain money to bribe the Danes to leave the country. This arbitrary seizure of property shows how little kings then understood the rights of subjects, and how imperfectly subjects understood their own rights when they submitted to it.

Edward having been brought up amongst the Normans, had many friends and favorites of that nation, who came flocking over to him, and were loaded by him with favors and benefits. This gave great offence to the English nobles, particularly to earl Godwin, who considered himself as having a right to govern and direct the king, and who was indignant at the influence the Normans had over him. These jealouses became at length so violent, that the king banished earl Godwin, and gave his possessions to Norman favorites. Even the queen because she was the earl's daughter, was very harshly treated, and was obliged to go into a nunnery.

After a time, Godwin and his sons returned with a great

What induced the British nation to restore the Saxon line of kings?
What were the principal measures of Edward's reign?
What first brought the Normans to England?

fleet, and boldly sailed up the Thames, towards London. The king was then persuaded by the rest of the English nobles to restore Godwin to his possessions, and to banish the Normans, who all left the country as secretly as they could, for fear of being torn to pieces by the populace.

Soon after this, earl Godwin died suddenly, as he was sitting at table with the king. Godwin had married a daughter of Canute the Great; and Harold, his eldest son, who was quite as ambitious as his father, had set his heart on succeeding Edward, who had no children, in the throne of England. But the king, who was aware of his ambitious designs, and desirous of deafeating them, sent into Hungary, for the long-forgotten prince, Edward the Exile, son of Edmund Ironsides. The prince readily obeyed the summons; but died a few months after his arrival, leaving a son named Edgar Atheling.

The death of Edward the Exile strengthened Harold yet more in his hopes; and on the death of Edward the Confessor, which took place in 1066, he was crowned king. He did not, however, find the throne a peaceable possession; for William, duke of Normandy, immediately asserted his own claim to it, under pretence that Edward the Confessor had left him the kingdom in his will. William, in aid of his own preparations, excited Halfager, king of Norway, and Tosti, the brother of Harold, to make a descent in the north of England.

Harold gained near York a great victory over these invaders; but was then obliged to make a speedy march to the south coast, to oppose the duke of Normandy, who had landed, with a great army, in Pevensey Bay, in Sussex, on the 28th of September, 1066. On the 14th of October was fought the great battle of Hastings, a battle that completely changed the fate of England. Harold was killed by a wound in the eye from an arrow, and William gained a signal victory.

Why were the Normans expelled from England?
What successor did Edward provide?
Who succeeded Edward the Confessor, and who claimed the crown
When was the battle of Hastings?

LIST OF SAXON KINGS.

THE SAXON LINE.

Began to reign.	Reigned.	
827	9	Egbert.
836	21	Ethelwolf, son of Egbert.
857	14	Ethelred, } sons of Ethelwolf.
871	30	Alfred,
901	24	Edward the Elder, son of Alfred.
925	16	Athelstan, }
941	7	Edmund, } sons of Edward.
948	7	Edred,
955	4	Edwy, } sons of Edmund.
959	16	Edgar,
975	4	Edward the Martyr, } sons of Edgar
979	37	Ethelred the Unready,
916	1	Edmund Ironsides.

THE DANISH LINE.

'017	18	Canute the Great.
1035	4	Harold Harefoot, } sons of Canute.
1039	2	Hardicanute,

SAXON LINE RESTORED

1041	27	Edward the Confessor, son of Ethelred the Unready.
1066		Harold, son of earl Godwin, usurped the crown though Edgar Atheling, grandson of Edmund Ironsides, was the natural heir.

The Saxons continued in the country after the conquest, and were much more numerous than the Norman settlers: the present inhabitants of England, therefore, are chiefly of Saxon descent: and their language, and many of their habits and customs, sufficiently declare their origin.

It does not appear that the social and moral character of England was much changed during the period of one hundred and sixty-five years, which elapsed from the death of Alfred to the battle of Hastings. During the greater part of that time the English were in such a continual state of warfare with the Danes, that they did not make much progress in any peaceful arts. Books were so very scarce and dear, that they were only to be found in royal libraries.— Paper was not then invented, and it was not possible to pro-

---

Are the present inhabitants of England chiefly of Saxon origin?
During 165 years what was the improvement of the English people?

cure parchment enough for a great supply of books. Besides this, there were only manuscripts, (printing not being invented at that time,) and but few people could write. Some, however, of the few manuscripts remaining in the Saxon character, are very beautifully and carefully written.

The Saxons had also another difficulty in the way of their acquiring knowledge. They had not any signs, or *characters*, to express numbers, except the Roman letters M. D. C. V. I., which are at this time occasionally in use ; and till the figures 1, 2, 3, 4, 5, &c., were brought into Europe by the Saracens, by whom, it is said, they were invented, there was great difficulty in learning and practising arithmetic.

The Danish kings were not more friendly to learning than their Saxon predecessors. Some of both respected learned men. Edward the Confessor liked to have them about him. Canute was a pagan when he came to England, but he became a Christian. The Danes and Saxons resembled each other very much in dress and language : but the Saxons, though equally brave and warlike, appear to have been a less savage and more social people than the Danes.

The style of dress among the Saxons was quite different from that in present fashion. The loose dress, called a carter's frock, very much resembles the tunic which was worn by the Saxons. These tunics were bound in round the waist with a belt, and usually came no lower than the knee ; only kings and nobles wore them down to the feet. People of rank wore, over the other, a short tunic, or *surcoa*, made of silk, and richly embroidered and ornamented. a linen shirt, also, shaped much like a modern shirt, was now an indispensable part of dress amongst the higher orders of people.

The poor people wore no shirt, and had only a tunic made of coarse materials. The slaves wore an iron collar round the neck, and were clad in tunics open at the sides. According to the pictures we have of the Saxons, they

---

What prevented the Saxons from readily acquiring arithmetic ?
Did the Danes and Saxons regard learning, and did they resemble each other ?
What was the Saxon style of dress generally ?
What was the dress of the poor people ?

appear generally to have gone bareheaded; though they occasionally wore fur caps. The hair was worn long, and parted on the forehead, and hung in straight locks on each side of the face. The beard was shaven on the upper lip and top of the chin: the rest grew long, and was kept very smooth and neat, and was usually divided in the middle and hung down in two points. Their shoes came up high, and were more properly a sort of buskin.

The Saxon women wore a linen under dress, with long tight sleeves; and over that a wide robe, or gown, fastened round the waist by a belt, and long enough to conceal the feet. Their head-dress was a square piece of linen, or silk, so put on as to conceal the hair and neck, showing only the face. It ought to be remembered, to the honor of the Saxon ladies, that, while the men were continually adopting new fashions in their dress, there was, in 300 years, little or no change in that of the women. Both sexes wore mantles, more or less splendid, according to their rank, and a profusion of gold ornaments, fringes, and bracelets.

Loose trowsers were worn by the men: but this, perhaps, was more a Norman fashion, being introduced, with many other changes, by Edward the Confessor, whose early education had made him much attached to the Norman dress and customs. Amongst other changes, he caused his nobles to be called *barons*, instead of by the old Saxon name of *theyn*, or thane.

The title of Confessor has nearly the same meaning with that of Saint, and was conferred on Edward by pope Alexander III. about a century after his death.

CHAPTER VI.

WILLIAM I.

[Years after Christ, 1066—1087.]

By the fatal termination of the battle of Hastings, in which Harold was killed, and William of Normandy com-

---

How did the Saxon women dress?
What changes of fashion were brought into England by Edward the Confessor, and why was he called so?
Did the English bestow the crown without hesitation upon William of Normandy?

pletely victorious, the English were thrown into the utmost consternation. Some of the nobles assembled in London to deliberate on placing Edgar Atheling on the throne; but before they could come to any settled determination, the Conqueror was already at their gates. Some of the nobles fled into the north; but the rest, and amongst them Edgar Atheling, came out to meet the duke of Normandy, and offered him the vacant throne; which he, with a little pretended hesitation, accepted.

A. D. 1066. William the Conqueror was crowned at Westminster, on Christmas-day. During the ceremony, the English, to show their satisfaction in their new king, set up loud shouts of applause. The Norman guards, who were stationed on the outside of the abbey, hearing a great noise, and not understanding what it meant, thought the English were insulting their prince. In the sudden passion into which this notion betrayed them, they set fire to some neighboring houses, which, being of wood, burnt furiously. A violent tumult ensued which, though it arose only from a mistake, caused much ill-will between the two nations, and there was some difficulty in pacifying it.

William, however, began his reign with so much prudence and moderation, that his new subjects thought they had great reason to be satisfied: but afterwards, when he built castles at Norwich, Winchester, Hereford, and London, and garrisoned them with Normans, they began to feel themselves oppressed.

On an occasion offered by his going into Normandy, they broke out into open rebellion, but without success: and William, on his return, did what was right in his own eyes, without much regard for the feelings of his subjects, and compelled them to absolute submission. Many years passed in unavailing struggles on the part of the English to throw off the Norman yoke, and in reiterated acts of oppression on the part of the Conqueror, who deprived the Saxon nobles of their estates to bestow them on his Norman followers.

William deposed the English bishops, and filled their

Did the English proceed to open rebellion against William?
When did the English become dissatisfied with William?
Did William act justly toward the Saxons?
How did William govern the church affairs?

places with Normans or other foreigners, one of these, however, Lanfranc, an Italian, who was made archbishop of Canterbury, proved himself, by his wisdom and prudence, and by the influence he had with the king, which he used in trying to moderate the violence of his temper, one of the best friends the English had.

During this time, Edgar Atheling had taken refuge with Malcolm, king of Scotland, who had given a kind reception to him, and to several nobles who had fled out of England with him. Malcolm married one of Edgar's sisters; and, assisted by the king of Denmark, made an attempt to drive out the Normans, and place Edgar on the throne of his ancestors.

William soon obliged the Scots and Danes to retreat; and with a view, as is said, to place an impenetrable barrier between England and Scotland, he depopulated a tract of sixty miles north of the Humber, and made it quite a desert. The inhabitants, those who could, fled into Scotland, where they were humanely received. The rest perished miserably from cold and hunger; and the land, after this dreadful devastation, remained uncultivated for nine years.

A. D. 1071. Malcolm intending to make a fresh attempt in favor of Edgar, William marched against him with a large army. The two armies met on the borders of Scotland, and a battle was about to ensue; but the two kings made peace with each other: one of the conditions of which was, that Edgar Atheling should be given up to William, who promised, if he would renounce his pretensions to the throne of England, to give him a mark a day, which was considered a very handsome allowance in those days. Edgar assented to these terms, and both he and William ever after continued true to their agreement.

It seemed, however, as if William had been destined never to enjoy repose; for now that he had no more disturbances to fear from either the English or Scots, his throne and life were endangered by a conspiracy amongst his own Norman nobles, those very persons, to enrich whom he

---
What became of Edgar Atheling?
By what cruel measure did William repel the Scots and Danes?
How did William finally accommodate matters with Edgar Atheling?
Did the Norman subjects of William rebel against him?

had been so often guilty of injustice and cruelty. This conspiracy was, however, discovered to him by the conscientiousness of Waltheoff, the only Saxon whom he had retained in his favor, and the only one of the conspirators who was punished, though his voluntary confession had preserved the king.

Fresh vexations next awaited William in his own family, from the turbulent and ungoverned tempers of his sons; particularly of the eldest two, Robert and William. These princes had been in a state of enmity with each other; and it is said that a boyish frolic, in which one of them threw some water on his brother's head, was the beginning of the quarrel between them.

At last, Robert, who was less malignant than William, but more passionate and headstrong, proceeded, from this quarrel with his brother, to an open rebellion against his father, whom, in an encounter, not knowing who it was, he wounded, and struck off his horse. When he saw that it was the king with whom he had been engaged, his remorse and horror, at the thought of having been so nearly guilty of killing his own father, subdued in a moment all his rebellious and proud feelings: and he sprung from his horse in an agony of grief, and threw himself on his knees at the king's feet.

William was too much offended to forgive his son; and, saying many bitter words to him, remounted and returned to his own army: and it was some time before he would listen to Robert's contrite entreaties. At last, queen Matilda, who was a very good and pious woman, and who was made very unhappy by the dissentions in her family, prevailed with the king to pardon his son.

One would have thought that, after all these turmoils, William would have been glad of some repose; but, on the contrary, on some trifling quarrel with Philip the First, king of France, he marched an army into that country, destroying and laying waste every thing: and as it was in the month of July, when the harvest was ripe, the devastation

---

What was the character of Robert and William, the Conquerers sons?

To what occurrence did the rebellion of Robert against his father ead?

By whose intercession was William reconciled to his son?

With what king had William a quarrel?

he made was very dreadful, particularly as he burnt every town and village he passed through.

William's cruelty, at length brought on him its own punishment; for after burning the town of Mantes, his horse, flinching from the smoking ashes, made a violent plunge; and the king, being very corpulent, got a bruise, which in a few days caused his death. He died in 1087, at the abbey of St. Gervaise, near Rouen, and was buried at Caen. He was in the sixty-third year of his age, and had reigned twenty-one years in England.

He married Matilda, daughter of the earl of Flanders, and had four sons and five daughters: Robert, to whom he left the dukedom of Normandy; William, king of England; Henry, to whom he left his mother Matilda's fortune; Richard, who died young; Adela married Stephen count de Blois, and five sons and daughters that died young.

It is above 700 years since the death of William the Conqueror, and there are yet remaining two remarkable memorials of his reign and character. The one is the *New Forest*, in Hampshire; to make which, for the sake of enjoying the pleasure of the chase, he depopulated a large district, destroyed thirty villages, and drove out the inhabitants.

The other memorial is a less painful one. It is a book which he caused to be made, called *Doomsday Book*, being a survey of the whole kingdom, giving an account of the extent of every parish, with all particulars respecting it.—This book is still preserved in the Tower; and all possessors of estates, who are curious to know to whom their lands belonged at the Conquest, whether it was arable or pasture, what was then its value, and, in some cases, what cattle it was stocked with, may there make themselves acquainted with these circumstances.

The national appellation of Britons, that of the primitive Islanders, in time gave place to that of Anglo-Saxons—the

---

How and where did William die?
Who were William's wife and children?
What is the most memorable act of William?
What other memorial of William exists?
Who were the Anglo-Saxons?

latter signifying Saxons born in England, so that a history of the Anglo-Saxons relates to the people who inhabited England from the Saxon to the Norman invasion.

The Anglo-Saxons were divided into nobility and vassals; that is, into great landholders and the cultivators of their estates. The conquest changed the owners of property in England, but it did not much change the order of rank in the king's subjects. There were several degrees, and more distinct than classes of people in the present age.

The highest in rank, after the king, were the *barons*, who were made rich and powerful by the lands of the Anglo-Saxon nobles. Another class was composed of Norman and foreign soldiers, who had helped to achieve the conquest of the island, and who settled on the lands that had been given to their leaders, and became their *vassals* and tenants.

With this class became blended gradually the Anglo-Saxon *thanes*, or nobles, who were all degraded from their former rank, and stripped of the greater part of their possessions; and also the Anglo-Saxon *ceorls*, or farmers, who if they had never taken up arms against the Conqueror, were allowed, on putting themselves under the protection of some Norman baron, to live without molestation. We may suppose, in general, that from this extensive class are chiefly derived the English gentlemen and farmers.

Saxon and Norman are now melted together. But it was not till long after William and his followers were no more, that the descendants of the two nations could endure each other; the Normans holding in contempt the stupid ignorant Saxons; and the Saxons detesting their tyrannical oppressors.

The clergy also formed a distinct numerous body. At the time of the Norman invasion, nearly a third part of the land is said to have belonged to monasteries, nunneries, and the clergy; and this is supposed to have been one great cause of the duke of Normandy's easy victory. William

---

Who were the lords and tenants after the Conquest?
* What became of the Anglo-Saxon lords?
 Did the Saxons and Normans like each other?
 Were the clergy a numerous and wealthy class among the Anglo-Saxons?

suffered the laboring classes to remain very much in the condition in which he found them. The lowest rank of the people had few, if any, rights of their own. These were usually, like the Russian peasants of our own times, considered as annexed to the estate on which they lived, and were bought and sold together with it. *Domestic slaves* were numerous; and these were the most miserable and degraded class of any. The children of these poor people were slaves equally with their parents: and thus the number of persons in the condition of slavery was very great; though there were many ways by which emancipation might be obtained. Free laborers, then worked for hire, as the laborers of our own times do, though few, compared with the number of slaves.

In towns there was another class of people called *Burghers*. These were tradesmen, or merchants, who joined together in little societies, called Gilds: but in this reign they had not become a numerous, or at least not a powerful body.

William used every means in his power to introduce the Norman or French into England, and to eradicate the Anglo-Saxon language. He altered many of the old Saxon laws, and established Norman instead; which were all written in Norman-French; and he ordered that law-business should be carried on in that language.

William also required that French, instead of Saxon should be taught to the children in the schools: but it is easier to conquer a kingdom than to change a language: and after an ineffectual struggle, which lasted three centuries, the Saxon got the better at last; and, with some intermixture of the Norman, forms the basis of the language we now speak.

The Saxons were masters of England from A.D. 460 to A.D. 1066. Six hundred years were time sufficient to establish their language in the country.

Were slaves numerous in England under the Norman Conquest
Who were the burghers?
Did William succeed in introducing the French into England?
How did he modify the Saxon tongue in England?
How long did the Saxons rule in England?

CHAPTER VII

WILLIAM II.

[Years after Christ, 1087—1100.]

St. Michel.

William, second son of William the Conqueror, was twenty-seven years old when he became king. Like his father, he had great bodily strength and activity, and he resembled him also in the sternness of his countenance. His complexion was ruddy, and his hair red, on which account he obtained the surname of Rufus. He was brave and active in war, like his father, and like him was ambitious and rapacious; but had not any of his great or good qualities: for he was irreligious, a lover of low company, and of excessive drinking. He was very passionate, and had not high principles of honor or honesty.

His father was scarcely dead when he set off for England to secure the inheritance which was left him, and to seize upon the royal treasures. It is but justice to say, that with part of them he paid his father's legacy to his brother Henry. His fierce and imperious temper being well known

---

What was the character of William II.?
Was William an acceptable king to the Anglo-Saxons?

to the Anglo-Norman barons, they were sorry to have him for their king, and made a rebellion to place his elder brother Robert, who was a much greater favorite with them, on the throne.

William Rufus now found it convenient to make friends with the Anglo-Saxons, who composed the great mass of the people; and he promised to restore many of their rights and privileges. By their help, he speedily subdued the rebellion of the barons. The fair promises which he had made to the Anglo-Saxons he very soon forgot; but he never forgot his resentment against Robert, on whom he retaliated by attacking his possessions in Normandy; and this kept the two brothers in a continual state of emnity.

The only occasion on which they ever agreed was when they joined to oppress their brother Henry. Henry's inheritance had been left him in money. Robert, who was always extravagant and thriftless, had been glad to sell to him a part of Normandy, called Cotentin, and now, in concert with William, sought to deprive him of it. Henry, being both brave and determined, would not tamely give it up, and with a small number of men fortified himself in Mont St. Michel; but, after enduring a very rigorous siege, he was at last obliged to surrender for want of provisions Having thus lost every thing, he, with a few faithful followers, who would not forsake him in his distress, wandered about, often in want of necessaries, and always in want of a home.

Some time after this, Robert went on the crusade to the Holy Land; and to procure money for this expedition, he lent or mortgaged his duchy for five years to his brother William, for ten thousand marks. William extorted the money from his English subjects; and then took possession of Normandy. He did not find it a very peaceable possession, for it involved him in continual quarrels and wars, with the king of France, in which sometimes the French, and sometimes the Normans had the advantage In one of these encounters, Heli de la Fleche, a very brave baron, was taken prisoner by William. After some

---

What was William's treatment to his subjects, and of his brother Robert?
Did Robert and William love their brother Henry?
How did William II. obtain possession of Normandy

time he regained his liberty, and then, coming to William made him an offer of his services. The king rejected hem; on which Heli went out, saying he would be revenged for the indignity. William called after him, in a very rude and haughty manner, " to be gone and do his worst." As soon as Heli arrived in France, he attacked William's territories there, and obtained possession of the town of Mans

The news of this event was brought to William while he was hunting in the New Forest. He instantly left the chase and galloped off to the sea coast, and embarked for Normandy. It blew so furious a storm, that the sailors at first refused to put to sea. The king's impatience, however, was so great, that he would not listen to them. He insisted on their setting sail, and contrary to all expectation, landed safely at Barfleur the next morning.

Heli de la Fleche was soon driven out of Mans, and William returned to England to complete the preparations in which he had been engaged for taking possession of Guienne, which the duke of Guienne, had mortgaged to him, as Robert had mortgaged Normandy. But a sudden end was put to all his ambitious projects: for going to hunt in the New Forest, during the time in which he was awaiting a fair wind to take his army over to France, he was shot by an arrow from the bow of sir Walter, Tyrrel, who was hunting with him.

A. D. 1100. William was killed in the fortieth year of his age, and the thirteenth of his reign. He was never married. William built Westminster Hall and the Tower of London.

The remarkable circumstance of this reign was, that Magnus, king of Norway, made a descent on Anglesea in 1098. This was the last attempt on England by any of the northern nations. Those restless people learned about this time the art of tillage, which provided them

---

What baron rebelled against William?
Did William attack de la Fleche?
What prevented William from taking possession of Guienne?
When was William killed?
When did the Northmen make their last descent upon England?

with food, and gave them occupation at home, and thus freed the rest of Europe from their predatory invasions

To explain Robert of Normandy's expedition, it is necessary the reader should know what is meant by Crusades. The crusades were religious wars. After his death, the Romans were masters of Jerusalem, and of the whole country which had been the scene of the life and labors of Jesus. Near the middle of the fourth century, the Roman Empire became partially Christian, and Helena, the mother of Constantine, took upon herself to identify the very spot at Jerusalem "where the Lord lay," and also to erect churches and other monuments on the places consecrated by his living actions.

After the erection of these edifices, and the establishment of convents in the Holy Land, as Palestine began to be called, religious persons from different and distant countries of Europe thought it a duty to make journeys thither, in order to visit the shrines or sacred buildings, which had been raised in honor of Christ. These pious travelers were called *pilgrims*, and their journey was a *pilgrimage*.

The pilgrims chiefly begged their way through the countries over which they traveled, and were regarded with universal respect by all Christians. They usually dressed in a plain garb, carried a *scrip*, or bag for their food, and sustained themselves upon a staff surmounted by a cross and had fastened to the front of their hats a scollop-shell When they returned from the Holy Land they frequently brought with them a branch of *palm*, a tree of that country, whence they were called *palmers*.

One of these pilgrims, named Peter the Hermit, though only a poor priest, has made himself more distinguished in history than the most potent monarch of his time. On his return from the Holy Land, inflamed by zeal for religion

---

What were Crusades?
What were pilgrimages?
What were the habits of the pilgrims?
Who was Peter the Hermit?

and by resentment against the Mohammedans, he went about from country to country, exhorting the princes and nobles of Europe to go and fight against the pagans, and drive them from Jerusalem. The pope entered warmly into this cause.

Vast armies were fitted out by different princes, and from A. D. 1097 to A. D. 1248, about one hundred and fifty years, four different Crusades were undertaken. More than two millions of men from England and southern Europe, are supposed to have marched into Asia upon these expeditions, and the greater number lost their lives. These wars were called Crusades, from the circumstance that a figure of the cross was a badge of the warriors—it was painted upon their banners, engraved on their shields, and embroidered in their garments.

Having endured hardships of every kind, and contended against numerous hosts of enemies, the crusaders, under the command of Godfrey of Bouillon, possessed themselves of Jerusalem after a bloody siege. They elected Godfrey king; and the city remained for about one hundred years in the possession of the Christians, when it was re-conquered by Saladin, the sultan of Egypt.

It was considered a religious duty to go to the Crusades, and it was thought that those who died in the Holy Land were sure to be received into heaven, let their lives have been ever so bad. Those who returned gained the advantage of being much honored in their lives; and at their deaths had the privilege of having their figures represented on their tombs, to show to all succeeding generations that they had served in the holy wars.

Out of so much that was bad in these enterprises, God permitted some good to arise. The people of Constantinople, and some of the countries in the east through which the Crusaders traveled were much better informed than those in Western Europe. The Saracens also were very superior to the Europeans in their knowledge of the sciences, and in many of the arts and elegancies of life. Much of this knowledge was brought home by the crusaders

---

How many Crusades were undertaken?
Did the Crusaders make any conquests?
What induced men to go to the Crusades?
Did any good arise from the Crusades?

The private misery which those wars occasioned is now over, but the knowledge remains, and seems transferred to us. Whilst Europeans, and their American descendants have been improving and gaining knowledge ever since, all the people of the East have been standing absolutely still.

CHAPTER VIII.

HENRY I.

[Years after Christ, 1100—1135.]

Henry, the Conqueror's youngest son, who was hunting with William, in the New Forest, at the time when he was slain by Tyrrel, instead of showing any concern at his brother's death, or even waiting to see his body borne away from the spot where he fell, put spurs to his horse, and rode directly to Winchester, where he seized on the royal treasure. He then hastened to London; and by gifts and promises, disposed the people so much in his favor, that they crowned him King, by the name of Henry I., in violation of the right of his brother, Robert, who was still in Palestine.

Henry's character was made up of an extraordinary mixture of good and engaging qualities, with many bad ones. Courage, intrepidity, political wisdom, impartial administration of justice to his people, love for his children, a fine understanding, and facetious humor are described of him by the historians of his time, and incline us to admire him. On the other hand, his ambition and avarice, his unjust usurpation, and his wicked conduct to his brother Robert, and to his nephew William, (Robert's son,) oblige us to acknowledge that, notwithstanding his dazzling qualities, he must have been a bad man. He had

---

How did Henry, the brother of William II. act on the king's death?
What sort of a man was Henry I.?

received, what was considered in those days, a learned education; and from that circumstance, he acquired the surname of Beauclerc, or fine scholar.

Henry began his reign by promising to redress all the evils his father and brother had inflicted on the Anglo-Saxons, and granted them a charter of privileges; or, more properly speaking, restored Edward the Confessor's code of laws, to which the people were much attached. He banished from his court all William's profligate associates, and recalled from exile Anselm, archbishop of Canterbury, who had been banished by Rufus for refusing to receive *investiture* from his hands. The more to endear himself to his English subjects, Henry married Matilda, daughter of Malcolm, king of Scotland. He also remitted many debts that were owing to the crown, and omitted nothing that could endear him to the people.

In the mean time, duke Robert had returned from the Holy Land, and resumed the possession of Normandy. He lost no time in making preparations for invading England, and asserting his right to the crown. He was joined by some discontented barons, and landed with his army at Portsmouth, on the 19th of July, 1101. Henry now found the benefit of the conciliatory conduct which he had pursued towards the English, who remained firm to him, while the Normans chiefly adhered to Robert. Henry marched to Portsmouth, with a numerous army, to oppose his brother.

The two armies stood facing each other several days, as if awe-struck, without coming to an engagement; which gave Anselm, and some of the barons, who were desirous of peace, an opportunity of concluding a treaty between the two princes, in which it was stipulated that Robert should give up his pretentions to the crown of England, in consideration of Henry's granting him a pension of 3000 marks, and promising to restore to their honors and estates in England, those Anglo-Normans, who had joined with him.

By what measures did Henry commend himself to his subjects?
Did Robert acquiesce in the usurpation of Henry?
On what conditions did the rival brothers make peace?

It was further agreed, that, if either of the brothers should die without children, the other should succeed to his dominions. The two armies were then disbanded, and Robert spent two months with his brother in feasts and amusements, and then returned to Normandy. But as soon as Robert was gone, Henry took the first opportunity of degrading those barons who had taken his side.

When Robert heard this, he returned to England, and remonstrated with Henry on this breach of the treaty; but he soon found, that, instead of benefiting his friends by staying in his brother's dominions, he was endangering himself; and he only escaped in safety by consenting to give up his pension.

The Norman barons were now made discontented by Robert's imprudence, and mismanagement of his affairs. In 1104 they invited Henry to come over and settle their disagreements with their duke; an invitation which Henry gladly accepted: and he acted so craftily, that he weakened and humbled his brother's party, and prepared the way for obtaining Normandy for himself. During the two following years, Robert entangled himself more and more in difficulties, and Henry gained every possible advantage over his inconsiderate brother.

A. D. 1106. Henry made a direct invasion of Normandy, and in a battle fought on the 28th of September, he took Robert and many of his nobles prisoners, amongst the latter was Edgar Atheling. Edgar, however, was considered no formidable enemy, and was soon set at liberty and spent the rest of his life in harmless and enviable obscurity. His Saxon blood, and his mild and amiable disposition, made him the idol of the English; while his imbecility and want of enterprise, rendered him too insignificant to be feared by the Normans. The only spirited thing we hear of Edgar is, that he had accompanied Robert to the Holy Land.

Robert was brought prisoner to England; and his cruel and unrelenting brother kept him in perpetual confinement till his death, twenty-eight years afterwards

---

Was Henry faithful to the treaty which he made with Robert?
Did Henry ever avail himself of Robert's mismanagement?
What became of Robert, and of Edgar Atheling?
When did Robert die, and what became of his son?

The whole of Normandy now submitted to Henry. Robert's son William, a child of six years old, was found in the castle of Falaise, and was committed by Henry to the care of Helie de St. Saen, who had married a daughter of Robert.

Every thing had prospered with Henry, according to his ambitious wishes; but while his brother's son lived, he stood in the way of his secure possession of the crown. Henry therefore sent Robert Beauchamp to surprise the castle of St. Saen, during the absence of its lord, and to seize on the young prince: but, by the vigilance, and fidelity of the people who were left in charge of him, the child was carried to a place of safety.

Henry, enraged at his disappointment, confiscated all the property of Helie de St. Saen, who having no longer a home of his own, wandered about from court to court, claiming protection for his royal charge, who was every where pitied for his misfortunes, and admired for the beauty of his person. The earl of Anjou engaged to assist him, and promised him his daughter, Sibylla, in marriage.

Henry no sooner heard that his nephew had acquired so powerful a friend, than he determined to prevent the intended match, and offered his own, and only son, William, in marriage to Matilda, another of the earl's daughters. The earl found this temptation so strong, that he broke off the contract with William the son of Robert, and concluded one with William the son of Henry. The faithful Helie, and the unfortunate prince, then retired from the court of Anjou to that of Baldwin, earl of Flanders, where they were recieved with great kindness.

For the next five years, whatever conflicts the king might suffer in his own mind, the country, at least enjoyed tranquillity. Henry was, however, still so suspicious of his son's right to the crown being disputed, that he required all his earls and barons to swear fealty to him; and he

---

Did King Henry get possession of prince William?
Who befriended prince William?
By what selfish motive was the earl of Anjou alienated from the interest of Prince William?
If the earl of Anjou had been a just man would he have acted thus? Ans. *whatever the pupil thinks right.*)

4

endeavored, by great promises, to entice his nephew to his court. But William could not forget his unhappy father, still languishing in prison, and would not put himself in his uncle's power. In 1118, Louis le Gros, king of France, with the earls of Flanders and Anjou, formed an alliance against Henry, in favor of William, and were joined by several disaffected Norman barons.

Henry was now surrounded by enemies, both secret and declared, and knew not whom to trust, nor whom to fear He slept in armor, and with a guard watching in his apartment. Nevertheless, his vigilance and prudence did not forsake him. He contrived to win over the Norman barons; and detached the earl of Anjou from the alliance with France, by solemnizing the marriage that had before been contracted for between his son and the earl's daughter.

The king of France and the barons confederated with him met Henry in the plain of Brenneville, not very far from Rouen, and a fierce battle ensued, in which the English army was victorious, and the king of France and prince William escaped with some difficulty.

Henry spent the geater part of the year 1120 in Normandy, endeavoring to strengthen the certainty of his son's succession, who was now eighteen years old. But how useless was all this anxiety! This beloved son, for whose aggrandisement he had done and sacrificed so much, was suddenly snatched from him. He was returning to England with a numerous train, and many ships; one of which, called the *White Ship*, was allotted to the prince and his retinue. The prince had ordered some wine to be given to the ship's crew, of which they drank so freely that many of them were intoxicated. The rest of the fleet had meanwhile sailed, and Fitzstephen, the commander of the White Ship, crowding all his sails, and plying all his oars, to overtake them, the vessel suddenly struck upon a rock. A boat was immediately let down, into which the prince and some of the young nobles were hurried; and they might have reached the shore in safety, had not the prince

---

Did prince William come to his uncle's court,—and why not?
Did Henry enjoy life without fear of enemies?
Where did Henry defeat the French king?
What happened to the king's eldest son?

insisted on going back to rescue his sister, the countess of Perche, whose shrieks he heard from the ship, where all was terror and confusion. As soon as the boat approached the vessel, so many persons jumped into it, that it instantly sank, and every creature perished.

Thus died the prince, with many of the young nobles, and several ladies of rank. Of three hundred persons who were on board, a butcher of Rouen, of the name of Bertould, who by clinging to the mast contrived to keep his head above water till the next morning, when he was picked up by some fisherman, was the only one who escaped. The captain had also clung to the same mast, but when told by the butcher that the prince had perished, he would not survive so great a disaster, and thew himself headlong into the sea.

The news of this misfortune reached England the next day; but it was three days before any one had courage to tell the king of it. At last a boy was instructed to fall at his feet, and tell him that the prince and all on board the White Ship were lost. Henry immediately fainted, and it was a long time before the violence of his grief abated. He had now only one legitimate child left, his daughter Matilda, who was married to Henry V., emperor of Germany, but had no children.

The death of the prince of England encouraged the friends of his cousin William to make fresh attempts in his favor; but they were unattended with any permament success; and William returned to the court of Louis, and married a sister of the queen of France, with whom he received a small domain as her dower, and thus at last became possessed of a spot of ground that he might call his own.

A few years afterwards, the king of France put him in possession of a part of Flanders, to which he had a claim in right of his grandmother Matilda, wife of the Conqueror, who was the daughter of an earl of Flanders. But no

---

By what generous action did the prince expose his own life?
Who perished and who was saved in this shipwreck?
Who communicated to Henry the death of his son, and who was his only remaining child?
What happened to prince William, Robert's son?

sooner did fortune seem to smile on this young prince then he died of wounds received in a skirmish with the landgrave of Alsace. Before his death he wrote a letter to king Henry, entreating his favor for Helie de St. Saen, and the other barons who had followed his fortunes. It is pleasing to be able to add that this last request of the gallant and ill-fated son of Robert was kindly attended to.

A. D. 1126. Henry's daughter Matilda had become a widow. She then returned to live with her father, who made all his nobles swear fealty to her, as they had formerly done to her brother. The following year she was married to Geoffry, eldest son of the earl of Anjou; and Henry who was devotedly fond of her, spent the latter part of his life in Normandy, that he might be near her.

After living to see Matilda the mother of three sons, Henry died on the first of December, 1135, at St. Denis, a little village in Normandy, in the 67th year of his age, and the 36th year of his reign, A. D. 1135. His body was brought to England, and was buried in the abbey he had founded at Reading.

His first wife was daughter of Malcolm, king of Scotland. Their children were William, who married a daughter of the earl of Flanders, and was drowned, and Matilda, married first to Henry V., emperor of Germany, and secondly, to Geoffry, son of the earl of Anjou. Henry, by his will, left all his dominions to his daughter, to the exclusion of her husband Geoffry.

It is proper here to notice the state of society and manners in England in the 12th century, and subsequently for a considerable time. Anselm, archbishop of Canterbury, (as was stated page 63) refused to receive *investi-*

What affectionate and grateful act was the last of prince William's life?
Is gratitude due to benefactors? (Ans. *the pupil's own judgment*.
Where did Henry spend his last days, and when did he die?
Who were Henry's family?
Who refused *investiture* from William Rufus?

ture from William Rufus, and was banished. It has been related in what manner the Pope's power was established in England, but the Norman kings were only Catholics in their religious worship; they bestowed lands and other property upon churches and convents to support bishops and priests; they paid nothing to the Pope, and did not admit that he could choose ministers for English churches, or lay taxes upon English property.

Anselm maintained, when the archbishopric of Canterbury was bestowed upon him, that the place, with the power the Archbishop exercised and the riches he enjoyed, must be given by the Pope. Authority to bestow these dignities, he called the *right of investiture*, and maintained that it belonged to the Pope; and the Pope, Pascal II., claimed such authority. Henry I. disputed the Pope's right of investiture, and claimed it himself, but after a long struggle he acknowledged it. This authority of popes and priests is called *ecclesiastical power*, and from this time, for several centuries it increased in England.

Anselm made another encroachment upon the liberties of the English. By his influence a regulation was made that the clergy should not marry, and that those who had wives should put them away forever, under pain of severe punishment; and in his preaching he inveighed against the gay dress of females, who afterwards conformed to his regulations.

As gunpowder was unknown, the warfare of that age was different from that of later times. When the Romans landed in England, the Britons had no kind of armor, except a rude sort of shield; nor does it appear that the Saxons or the Danes had any other defence except the shield and helmet, till a little before the time of the Conquest, when the nobles and leaders of their armies

---

What power had the first Norman kings in the English church, and what the Pope?
What was the *right of investiture*, and was it established in the Pope or the king of England?
What circumstance has changed the art of war and what was the coat of mail?

adopted armor, something like that of the Normans. The whole dress was made of little rings of iron, much smaller and slighter than the chain of a horse's bridle; and these were all linked together so ingeniously, like network, that it fitted close to the limbs and body, and was at the same time as flexible as a stocking. Under this they wore a dress called a *gambeson*, which was like a shirt without sleeves or collar, and quilted or stuffed with wool; sometimes this was worn over the *hawberk* which was the name of the coat of *mail*, or chain armor.

This kind of armor was not found a sufficient defence against the point of a spear or arrow; in the fourteenth century *plate armor* was introduced, so called from being made of plates of iron, which were often so heavy, that when a knight arrayed in it was overthrown, he lay on the ground immovable till he was helped up: and there were many instances, in hot weather, and in the press of an engagement, of persons being suffocated with the heat and weight of their armor. There was also an intermediate kind, called *scale armor*, formed of little pieces of iron laid one over another, in the manner of the scales of a fish.

The knights fought with lances, spears, and swords, and the common soldiers with slings and bows, in the use of which the English excelled almost all other nations. The French were more active, but the English possessed more bodily strength. Besides these arms, which they carried about them, they used various machines for throwing darts and stones to a great distance.

The violence to which men were exposed in these rude ages from one another, obliged them to live in castles,— large stone houses, surrounded with walls, to keep off their enemies who were their neighbors. The Conqueror and his two sons built a great many castles. The barons lived like so many little kings, each in his own castle with his train of followers; and they even affected the ceremonial of kings; for their servants and attendants

---

Why was plate armor introduced, and what was scale armor?
What were the weapons used by the knights?
What were *castles*, and who dwelt in them?

instead of being called stewards, grooms, and footmen, were called treasurers, privy counsellors, heralds, and pages, and by other honorable titles.

The mode of living in these castles was exceedingly disagreeable to the Saxons. Such haughty seclusion was entirely contrary to their own habits, which were remarkably convivial and social. They did not care for the shabbiness of their dwellings, which were only built of wood, and thatched, if they could but eat and drink, and have merry-makings; while the Normans, on the contrary, were frugal in their manner of living, but very costly in their buildings.

The space within the wall was the court of the castle, and in all castles there was an enclosure called the *inner bailey;* which contained the square tower, or *keep,* in which the baron, or governor, and his family dwelt, and in which all the stores, and arms, and valuable things were kept. Under the keep was the dungeon for prisoners The chapel also stood in the *inner bailey.*

The servants lived between the walls of the outer and inner enclosures, which space was called the *outer bailey*, there was always room enough for the soldiers' lodgings, the stables, and workshops for the blacksmiths, carpenters, and other artificers—all the articles which were used by the great family within being manufactured by the *retainers—* that is by persons who belonged to the lord of the castle.

The *postern gate* was a small private entrance in th' outer wall, through which the lord and his confidential servants might pass and re-pass privately. The best apartments were always in the upper stories of the castle, because the windows at the bottom part were only little slits in the walls, while those above were made the larger, the further they were from the ground. The upper parts of the castles were, of course, in less danger from the enemy. In those rooms, therefore, the inhabitants indulged themselves with air and daylight.

Did the Saxons like the manners of the Norman lords?
What was the construction of an ancient castle?
Where did the soldiers, &c. live?
What was the postern gate and what were the accommodations of a family in an ancient castle?

The soldiers then were hardly a separate class. The king gave his barons lands and estates, on condition that they should always be ready to attend him in battle. The barons let out many or most of their estates to persons of inferior rank, on the same condition; and these again had others under them, who held by a *similar tenure*—this is by the same rule—not to pay for the land, but to follow the lord to battle whenever he should require their services

Whenever the baron marched to war, those tenants, who thus held their estates by the condition of military service, marched with him; and though, after a time, it was allowable to *compound*, or for people to pay money to excuse themselves from actual service, yet the obligation still remained; and this sort of bond between the king and his barons, and the barons and their retainers, was called the *feudal system.*

Every great baron's dwelling in that age was a fortification, and every family lived in dread of some neighboring chief. The cause of this principally was the unsettled state of property. In what are called the *middle ages*, from the tenth to the sixteenth century, wars in Europe deprived conquered nations of their lands, and the victorious military chiefs took whole provinces, as Rollo took Normandy, and William I. took England. The lands seized by these military chiefs were divided among the officers of the chief; and the followers of that chief, and the former occupants of the soil, became the vassals of the great lord.

These poor people were not acquainted with the useful arts or comforts of life that we enjoy, but they could take care of cattle, cultivate the soil in a rude and imperfect manner, could help to erect the castles and churches of their masters, and could follow him to battle. This later service, together with a great part of the cattle and corn which

---

Who were the soldiers and what was the *Feudal system*?
What was every baron's dwelling in the middle-ages, and what was the cause of this state of society?
What was the condition of *vassals* under this system?

they could procure from the cultivation of the soil, they gave to their lords.

The lords always kept many of their vassals in their houses or castles, and usually went out with a considerable number of them as attendants. This was partly for show, and partly for safety. These followers were called Retainers, and when they went abroad with their master formed his Retinue. The more people a great lord had about his person, the better was he guarded, and the more was he feared.

In the present happier age of the world, when every man has his own business, and property, and leisure, and enjoyments, no great man has any right to the services of so many of his fellow-men; nor has he any need of them, for he has nothing to fear from the violence of others—he is protected by the laws of his country, and what is better, by the humanity of all men, who have learned, in some measure, to respect one another's lives and property; and to know, in order that all may be happy, all must be safe, and protected by each other.

But a thousand years ago men lived very differently The lands had been seized by the great lords of Europe, and the owners of property which lay together often claimed the same. These rude men would not wait for courts of justice to inquire into and settle their rights, but they and their vassals fought about them. Many of the richer and more powerful lords, wanting to become still more rich and powerful, and having no sense of religion, of justice, or mercy—none of the fear of God or love of man—murdered their neighbors, set fire to their houses, carried off their property, and seized their lands: on these occasions the ladies were often treated in a barbarous manner.

A remarkable instance of this may be found in Shakspeare's Tragedy of Macbeth. Macbeth, a Scottish no-

---

What was a great lord's retinue?
What is the reason why people in the present age do not live in this manner?
What was the *moral character* of the middle ages?
What example of the insecurity of life and property does Shakspeare give?

bleman, invited Duncan, king of Scotland, to his castle, and there murdered him, that he might be king instead of Duncan. On the murder of the king, his two sons fled from Scotland in fear of their lives. Macduff, a Scotch lord, followed Malcolm, one of the young princes, into England, upon which the usurper Macbeth was so enraged, that he vowed to revenge himself upon Macduff for this desertion.

In order to do this, Macbeth resolved upon killing Macduff's innocent family, which he had left behind, and he accordingly gave orders for this cruel act. It is described nearly thus;—After the bloody work was done, Rosse, a friend of the unfortunate family, escaped into England to inform Macduff of it. He found him talking to Malcolm, and after preparing his mind, relates the event.

"*Rosse.* Your castle is surprised, your wife and babes Savagely slaughtered!

Malcolm. Merciful heaven!

Macduff. My children too?

Rosse. Wife, children, servants, all
That could be found.

Macd. And I must be from thence!—
My wife kill'd too?

Rosss. I have said.

Mal. Let us make *medicines of our great revenge,*
To cure this deadly grief.

Macd. He has no children!—All my pretty ones?
Did you say all!

Rosse. All.

Macd. What, all my pretty chickens and their dam?'
Macbeth, Act IV. *Scene* 3.

You will observe that Malcolm proposes to make amends for this cruel injury by some "great revenge," that is by some act of equal cruelty to the murderers of Macduff's wife and children. This was the way in which people at that time usually endeavored to satisfy themselves, but they only continued a strife which the descendants of both parties felt bound never to forget nor forgive, and which

---

How was the violence and cruelty of Macbeth related to Macduff?
How did people in that age regard injuries?

many long years after the first offence was given, caused fresh quarrels, murders, and destruction of property.

In this state of violence and danger, many people lived in constant and great fear, and were always prepared to expect, and to defend themselves against an enemy. The rich lived in strong castles, surrounded by walls and gates, a watch was kept to look out for the approach of their foes, and, before the discovery of gun-powder, and the use of fire-arms, the knights—that is, the gentlemen-soldiers—used generally to wear *armor*.

Then, as at all times, there were good men—some who were not weak and timid, or ferocious and cruel, who could not see the acts of these barbarians without indignation against them, and compassion for the unfortunate victims of their cruelty. The distress of the ladies, above all, inspired the just and the generous with a desire to serve them, and to save them from the dreadful calamities to which they were exposed. Many noblemen and brave soldiers devoted themselves to the redress of injuries inflicted upon all good persons, and particularly upon the young and beautiful of the female sex. These formed what is called the order of Chivalry.

The young men who composed the order of Chivalry could not be admitted into it, unless they possessed strength and courage, and were distinguished by truth and honor; and this being known, made ambitious youth desirous to be so distinguished, that they might be worthy to assert justice, and to defend innocence, that they might become objects of admiration and praise, and form at once the protectors and ornaments of society. To be all this, it was necessary that they should not only be fearless and powerful, but that they should also be pleasing and interesting, that they should perfectly understand the use of arms to prevail over their enemies, and be masters of every graceful acomplishment to inspire the affection of their friends.

Many arts of little use at this time were *then necessary*, and these arts exhibited much grace and skill. The management of fiery horses, the throwing of the pike, (a sharp

---

What were the domestic circumstances of the English in the 12th century?
Who formed the order of Chivalry?
What education was bestowed on the knights of the middle ages?

instrument used in ancient war,) and the exercise of the bow, were taught to young men with as much and more pains than dancing, fencing, and music now require. Horsemanship, archery, &c. require great presence of mind and strength of body, and show elegance of person and quickness of thought to the utmost advantage.

For a long time Chivalry did much good, but at length it went out of use, because laws were made and enforced that compelled people to live peacefully together, so that the arts that belonged to Chivalry only served for amusement, and Knights or Champions used to practice a sort of mock fighting, as a mere trial of strength and skill, not intending to kill one another, but to spare the life of him who should be proved the weakest; and the most beautiful lady present at the encounter, used to give a prize to the victorious knight. These public spectacles were at last given up, but not all at once, for so late as the year 1600, and afterwards, we read of young gentlemen who were taught all the exercises of Chivalry

---

No nobleman, let his rank have been ever so great, could be considered a complete soldier till he was knighted, or acknowledged to be a knight—that is, a member of the *order* of Chivalry. There were many different orders of knighthood, in each of which different ceremonies and vows were used: but the chief formality was the kneeling down before some elder knight, who, giving a slight blow with his sword on the left shoulder, said: " In the name of God and St. George, rise up, Sir John!" or " Sir Thomas!" or whatever else the name might be. Amongst the different sorts of knights, were the knights-errant.

This order was first introduced in England in the time of king Stephen, by some young men, who, abhorring the tyranny of the lawless barons, bound themselves by solemn vows to devote themselves to the protection of the injured and helpless. The knights-errant were quite independent

---

Why did Chivalry go out of use?
How were knights created?
When did Chivalry commence in England?

of one another, and traveled about from place to place for the purpose of redressing grievances. This order of knight-errantry was of infinite service in softening the ferocious manners of the times. The spirit of chivalry seemed to belong wholly to the Norman character, no traces of it having been found amongst the plain and rustic Saxons.

Females in that age had not the liberty they enjoy in our time, but they were beloved and cherished by their families, and honored extravagantly by the knights. The daughters of noblemen were commonly educated in nunneries till they married: they then lived in their husband's castles, and were very often besieged, and taken prisoners, according to the chances of war. One of their occupations was that of surgery; and it was their office to make salves, and attend on the wounded; but their principal employment was embroidery and needle-work; and they used to sit in the great hall, surrounded by their damsels, working with them, and setting them their tasks.

When these ladies made a visit, they were furnished with a guard to protect them, lest they should be killed or carried off. But they had no want of society at home; for, besides the menials belonging to the castle, every lady had a number of damsels attendant on herself, who were the daughters of inferior knights and barons, or perhaps her own relations. And every castle was a sort of school for young nobles, where, first in quality of *pages*, and as they grew older, in that of *squires*, they learned the arts of war and hunting, which were the chief requisites for a gentleman.

What were the occupations of ladies in the middle ages?
Who were the companions and attendants of ladies?

CHAPTER IX

STEPHEN

[Years after Christ, 1136—1154.]

All the precautions which Henry had taken to secure the crown to his daughter were but vain. An usurper sprang up where he would least have expected one, in his favorite nephew Stephen, who was the second son of his sister Adela and the count de Blois. To him Henry had invariably shown the utmost kindness, and a preference above all his other relations. He had given him a large estate in Normandy; and had married him to the heiress of Boulogne, whose mother was Mary of Scotland, sister to his own queen, Matilda. But all these kindnesses could not inspire Stephen with gratitude. As soon as he heard of the king's death, he hastened to England; and though he met with a little opposition at first, yet he soon procured himself to be crowned at Westminster.

Stephen's deportment was popular and engaging, and he had much pleasantry in his conversation. He was a great favorite with the people; and to this, more than to any other cause, is attributed the success of his attempt on the crown. This usurpation had been so totally

---

Who succeeded Henry I.?
What immediate effect had Stephen's usurpation?

unexpected, that no preparations had been made to guard
against it; and the empress Maude, as she is commonly
called, and her friends, were so unprepared for the event,
that they knew not what to do. This gave Stephen time
to strengthen himself, before any attempts were made to
check his operations.

The first person who took up arms against him was
David, king of Scotland, who marched an army into England to vindicate the rights of his niece. But Stephen
contrived to win him over by ceding to him the greater
part of the four northern counties of England, and giving
to his son the earldom of Huntingdon. The wisest and
most powerful baron then in England was the earl of Gloucester, a son of the late king. He was warmly attached to
his sister; but as the other nobles acknowledged Stephen,
he also was obliged to submit. For the next three years
Maude appears to have made no direct attempt; but to have
been lying in wait for an opportunity to assert her rights.

A. D. 1139. Stephen raised great discontents by his
severity to some of his barons. This encouraged Maude and the earl of Gloucester, who had joined
his sister in Normandy, to come to England. They were
received in an evil hour into Arundel Castle, by the dowager queen Adelais: and from this time, for several years,
England was desolated by one of the most calamitous wars
it ever knew. The barons sided with the two contending
parties as their feelings, or rather as their interests, prompted them.

But, instead of an open war, it was a miserable vexatious
kind of hostility, and displayed all the worst evils of the
feudal system. Each baron, shut up in his own castle
with his own retainers, kept up a sort of petty war with
his nearest neighbor of the opposite party, to the destruction of all domestic comfort and civil order. "All England," according to an old historian, "wore a face of desolation and misery; multitudes abandoned their beloved
country, and went into voluntary exile: others, forsaking
their own houses, built wretched huts in church yards,

Who vindicated Matilda's rights?
Why did Matilda come to England?
What sort of war was carried on in England in Stephen's reign?

hoping for protection from the sacredness of the place Whole families, after sustaining life as long as they could by eating herbs, roots, and the flesh of dogs and horses, at last died of hunger; and you might see many pleasant villages without a single inhabitant."

A. D. 1141. After this contest had gone on for some time, without any decided advantage to either party, the earl of Gloucester, who commanded the empress's army, appeared before Lincoln, where a fierce battle took place on the 2d of February, 1141, Stephen was taken, and carried prisoner to Bristol Castle.

Upon this great victory, Maude was acknowledged queen, and on the 1st of June entered London in triumph. But instead of acting with prudence, or even with gratitude, despising the counsels of her uncle, the king of Scotland, and of her brother, the earl of Gloucester, to whom she owed so much, she treated her friends ungraciously, and her enemies insolently. She insulted the citizens of London, instead of granting any of their requests; and disgusted all orders of people so entirely, that, even while she was making preparations for her coronation, she found herself compelled to leave London, and fly to Winchester.

Here she was soon besieged by Stephen's youngest brother, Henry, bishop of Winchester. With the utmost difficulty she escaped on a swift horse, to Devizes; but the earl of Gloucester, in endeavoring to follow her, was taken prisoner, and carried to Rochester Castle. He, however, was soon after exchanged for Stephen. Thus, by both being taken prisoners, they both regained their liberty.

Stephen, about this time, was seized with a fit of illness, and was disabled, for a time, from taking advantage of this turn of fortune in his favor. As soon, however, as he regained his health, he pursued the empress. She escaped, borne in a litter, like a corpse, to Oxford; and took refuge there in the castle, during the absence of the earl of

---

Was Stephen defeated?
How did Matilda conduct herself after the battle of Lincoln?
How did Stephen obtain his liberty?
How did Matilda escape from Stephen?

Gloucester, who had gone into Normandy to bring prince Henry, Maude's eldest son, to England.

Stephen continued before Oxford for three months, having sworn not to raise the siege till he had taken the empress prisoner. At last the garrison was reduced to extremity by famine; but still Maude was too proud to surrender. The ground, it being now the middle of winter, was covered with snow. The empress, and three of her trusty knights, attiring themselves wholly in white, that they might be the less easily distinguished, opened by night a postern door, and got out of the castle; and after crossing the frozen river, and walking six miles, they reached Abingdon in safety, where they procured horses to convey them to Wallingford. At Wallingford, Maude was met by the earl of Gloucester, on his return from Normandy with prince Henry, a fine promising boy of eleven years of age; and she soon forgot all her late fatigues and alarms in the joy of that happy meeting.

The fatal and ruinous warfare between Maude and Stephen continued for some years longer, but in the year 1147 the empress had a severe loss, in the death of her faithful friend the earl of Gloucester. On his death, feeling herself, at length, wearied out with the struggle, she resigned her claims to her son Henry, who went into Normandy to collect an army which might enable him to renew the war. To that country Maude also retired, and spent there the remainder of her life; never interfering in public affairs.

A. D. 1153. The flames of civil war had latterly been subsiding, but they blazed up again on the arrival of prince Henry from Normandy. The two armies met at Wallingford, and faced each other for several days without coming to an engagement. Some of the barons, who deplored the miseries of the country had thus an opportunity of proposing an accommodation, to which Stephen the more willingly consented from having a short time before lost his eldest son, Eustace.

Did Matilda surrender to Stephen at Oxford?
Did Matilda ever make peace with Stephen?
Was civil war revived in England during Stephen's reign?

It was agreed that Stephen should keep the crown during his life, and that Henry should succeed to it at his death. The news of this treaty was received with the greatest joy all over the country, and the king and his people at last obtained some repose. But the following year, some disagreements ensuing between Stephen and Henry, the war seemed ready to burst forth again. Happily for the country, the death of Stephen put an end to the contest.

Stephen died at Dover, on the 25th of October, 1154

THE NORMAN LINE.

Began to reign.	Reigned Years.		
1066	21	William the Conqueror.	
		Robert,	
1087	13	William Rufus,	Children of William the Conqueror.
1100	35	Henry the First,	
		Adela, countess of Blois,	
		William, son of Robert,	
		William,	Children of Henry the First.
		Empress Matilda,	
1135	19	Stephen, son of Adela and the count de Blois grandson of William I.	

THE SAXON LINE RESTORED.

1154	34	Henry the second—son of the empress Matilda, and Geoffroy Plantagenet;—grandson of Henry the First and Matilda of Scotland, who was niece to Edgar Atheling, and descended from the Saxon kings.	

CHAPTER X.

HENRY II.

[Years after Christ, 1154—1189.]

Henry Plantagenet was the eldest son of Geoffry, earl of Anjou and the empress Matilda. It was the custom before family surnames were adopted, to call each person

---

What treaty was made between Stephen and prince Henry?
Who were the Norman princes, and how was the Saxon line restored?
Who succeeded Stephen?

by a surname of his own; as Harold *Harefoot*, William *Rufus*. Thus Geoffry got the surname of *Plantagenet*, from wearing in his helmet a sprig of the plant *genista*, or broom; and Henry, either because he liked the name, or from affection to his father's memory, retained it, and by this means it became established as the surname of his family.

Henry had had the great advantage of receiving a part of his education at Bristol Castle, under the superintendence of the earl of Gloucester, who was the most learned and virtuous nobleman of his age. Henry had possession of Normandy given to him when he was only sixteen years old. By his father's death, in 1151, he became possessed of Anjou, Touraine, and Maine. The year following he married Eleanor, heiress of Guienne and Poitou, who was many years older than himself, and had before been married to, and divorced by the king of France Thus he already possessed a very large domain in France, when the death of Stephen put him in possession of England also.

He was at this time twenty-one years of age; of the middle size, and remarkably strong and active. Whilst under the earl of Gloucester's care, he not only acquired all the common military accomplishments of the times, but also that uncommon one, a taste for study. He delighted in the conversation of learned men. He had an affectionate heart and an excellent understanding, and inherited all that was good and admirable in his grandfather Henry, without the alloy of his bad qualities.

The first act of Henry, on coming to the crown, was to send away all the foreign soldiers that Stephen had brought into England; and to order all the castles that had been built during the civil wars to be demolished. He also confirmed a charter of privileges to the people; and to use the words of one of the best historians,* " no king in so short a time, had done so much good, and gained so much

---

Who educated Henry II. and what were his circumstances?
What was the character of Henry II.?
What were the first measures of Henry II.?

* Henry

love, since Alfred." In 1155, he recovered from the king of Scotland that part of the north of England which Stephen had ceded.

Henry also carried his arms against the Welsh, who had been very troublesome neighbors; and though his army was once in some danger of being defeated, he, in the end, made an advantageous peace with them, and compelled them to give up some places which they had taken on the English border. From this time till the year, 1163, he was chiefly engaged in a war with the king of France, in pursuance of a claim he considered himself to have, in right of his wife, on Toulouse, and some other territories.

The fertile island of Ireland, was divided into five separate kingdoms. Very little mention is made of it by the English historians, till the year 1171, when Dermot, one of the five kings, being driven from the kingdom of Leinster, came over to England to implore the assistance of Henry, who gave him some money from the royal treasury and permitted him to enlist in his cause any of the English whom he could prevail on to join him.

Accordingly the earl of Pembroke, surnamed *Strongbow*, and a few other noblemen, returned with Dermot to Ireland, and with their assistance he soon recovered his kingdom. Not contented with this success, Dermot thought that, by the help of his English friends, he might also possess himself of the other four kingdoms. But Strongbow did not dare to engage in a plan for the conquest of the whole island without first soliciting Henry's consent.

The king's answer was for some time delayed; and the earl, meanwhile, hastening his preparations, collected in England an army of 1200 men; but when he was on the point of conveying them to Ireland, he received Henry's positive commands not to proceed. He was, however, now too much bent on the enterprize to give it up; so putting life and honor to the hazard, he set sail.

At Waterford Strongbow was joined by Dermot, and there married his daughter Eva. He then proceeded to the

---

In what wars did Henry engage?
What is the early history of Ireland?
What were the achievements of earl Strongbow?
Did Strongbow follow the king's orders?
How came Strongbow king of Ireland?

attack of Meath, which was soon conquered. The year following Dermot died, the earl Strongbow, in right of his wife, succeeded to his possessions, and thus became king of a great part of Ireland.

Henry had been exceedingly displeased with the earl for having disobeyed him; nor was he appeased till Strongbow came over to England, and resigned to him all these great acquisitions. Henry allowed him to retain part of Leinster, and went over himself in 1172, with a fleet of 400 vessels, to take possession of his new dominions. The petty princes, overawed by such a powerful force, immediately submitted; and Roderick, the supreme king of the island, consented to become tributary; and thus was this important conquest effected without bloodshed.

Thomas à Becket, was at this time a very distinguished person, and his quarrels with king Henry were a subject of concern and interest even to many foreign potentates. Thomas à Becket was the son of a citizen of London, and was the first Anglo-Saxon who had arrived at any kind of eminence since the conquest. Becket had early been remarked for his great abilities, and for his attachment to the cause of the empress Maude.

When Henry came to the throne, he selected Becket as his favorite and companion; and at length made him his chancellor, thus placing him in the highest dignity in the kingdom next to that of the archbishopric of Canterbury. He also confided to him the education of prince Henry, his eldest son.

Becket now indulged himself in every kind of luxury and magnificence. He never moved without a numerous train of servants; his dress was splendid in the extreme; he was profuse in his gifts; the luxury of his table and of his furniture was greater than had ever been seen before; and Fitzstephen, who was his secretary, and wrote the history of his life, states, as an instance of his extreme de

---

Did Strongbow surrender Ireland to Henry II.?
Who was Thomas à Becket?
What favor did Henry show Becket
How did Becket live?

licacy, "that in winter his apartments were every day covered with clean hay and straw, and in summer with green rushes, or boughs, that the gentlemen who paid court to him, and who could not, by reason of their numbers, find a place at table, might not soil their fine clothes by sitting on a dirty floor."

Though Becket had been ordained a deacon, he considered himself more a *layman* than an *ecclesiastic*, and employed his leisure in hunting and hawking, and similar diversions. He also engaged in military affairs, and conducted 700 knights, at his own charge, to attend the king in his war in France. His house was a place of education for the sons of the chief nobility, and the king was often present at the entertainments he gave.

As an instance of the familiarity with which the king treated Becket, Fitzstephen, an historian of that age, relates the following story:—One day, while they were riding together in the streets of London, they met a poor beggar shivering with cold. The king made the observation, that it would be a good deed to give that poor man a warm coat. The chancellor agreed, and added, "You do well, sir, in thinking of such a good action." "Then he shall have one presently," said the king, and seizing on the chancellor's cloak, which was of scarlet lined with ermine, he tried to pull it off. The chancellor, not liking to part with it, held it fast, and the king and he were near pulling each other off their horses in the scuffle. At last, Becket letting the cloak go, the king gave it to the beggar, who, was much astonished at such a scene, and such a gift, from such a man.

The bishops had, at this time, encroached so much upon the privileges of both the king and the people, that the king was hardly master of his kingdom, or the people masters of their own consciences. One great cause of this evil was, that the clergy were not amenable to the common laws of the country, but were governed by laws among themselves, called *ecclesiastical laws*. Henry, feeling the inconvenience of this church tyranny, had long meditated the put-

---

Had Becket the manners of an ecclesiastic?
What familiarity with the king did Becket enjoy?
Did Henry encourage the tyranny of the clergy?

ting a check to it. And, on the death of the archbishop of Canterbury, he promoted Becket to that dignity, believing that he would be ready to forward the design of lowering the pride and power of the clergy.

But no sooner was Becket established in his new dignity than he seemed changed in character, as well as in condition. He renounced all his gay and active amusements, and was always seen with a book in his hand, or else absorbed in deep meditation. He affected the greatest austerities; he wore sackcloth next his skin, and never changed it till it was full of dirt and vermin; he ate nothing but bread, and drank water in which fennel had been steeped to make it nauseous; he lacerated himself with continual scourging; and he every day washed the feet of thirteen poor beggars. In short, the ostentation of affected sanctity made him take a satisfaction in inflicting on himself the severest penances.

His conduct towards the king was not less changed than his personal deportment and way of living. He withdrew from the intimacy with which Henry had treated him, and resigned the office of chancellor, saying he must now devote himself wholly to his spiritual functions. And so far was he from giving any aid to the king's plans of reform, that he set himself up as a strenuous supporter of the usurpations of the clergy. In all this conduct he was encouraged by the pope; and Henry was thus kept in a continual ferment for eight years.

Henry was so much disappointed and exasperated by the conduct of Becket, that forgetful of all his former regard for him, he certainly treated him both unjustly, and, on some occasions, severely. At last, in a moment of great irritation, he unhappily exclaimed, "Is there nobody that will rid me of this turbulent priest?" Henry probably had no sooner said these words, than he forgot them. But they were not forgotten by some of those who heard them, and who thought they should do the king an acceptable service by executing what they imagined to be his wishes.

Did Becket resist the encroachments of the clergy?
Did Becket aid the king's purposes?
How did Henry regard the priestcraft and disloyalty of Becket?

Four gentlemen of his household set out immediately with the utmost speed from Bayeux in Normandy, where the king then was, to England. When they arrived at Canterbury, they demanded admittance into the archbishop's palace. The servants, apprehensive of some evil design, obliged their master to fly into the cathedral, thinking the sanctity of the place would protect him. But the assassins followed him; and, because he would not submit to be their prisoner, they slew him on the steps of the altar, as he knelt before it.

When Henry heard of this murder, he was so much shocked and concerned, that he shut himself up for three days, and refused to let any body come near him. At last his attendants forced open the door of his room, and persuaded him to take some refreshment. The king afterwards, caused a magnificent tomb to be erected for Becket in Canterbury cathedral, he walked barefoot to the shrine, and permitted himself to be lashed by scourges as he knelt before it; and thus considered himself as fully absolved from all guilt he might have incurred by being accessory to his death.

A. D. 1173. Henry was sovereign of England, Ireland, and of a third part of France. All his dominions were in a state of tranquility. But it seems as if princes were destined to pay for their royalty the high price of that domestic happiness which their subjects often enjoy. The Queen, whom he had married for the sake of her rich dower, was of an unamiable and jealous temper, and not only gave him much vexation by her own conduct, but also encouraged her children to behave undutifully to him.

Henry, the eldest of them, had been crowned by his father, when he was about fifteen years old; it being not uncommon at that time for the heir to be crowned in his father's lifetime. He soon became impatient to reign in reality, and entered into a conspiracy with the kings of France and Scotland, and other princes who were jealous of king Henry's power, to dethrone him.

Who killed Becket?
How did Henry receive the intelligence of Becket's death?
What were the king's domestic circumstances?
What was the conduct of Prince Henry?

The king perceived that his son was less dutiful and respectful than formerly, and therefore removed from about him some persons who gave him bad advice. On this the prince, and his brothers Richard and Geoffry, whom he had persuaded to join him, fled to the court of the king of France; and even queen Eleanor, in the disguise of a man, tried to escape there also, to the very same king from whom she had formerly been divorced, on account of her ill-conduct. She was, however, discovered, and brought back to Henry, who shut her up in strict confinement.

The rebellion which had been preparing now broke out. On the side of Normandy, Henry was beset by the king of France and the earl of Flanders, while William king of Scotland marched into Cumberland, where he was joined by all the discontented barons of England. But in no part of his reign did Henry act with more wisdom and vigor than in this great emergency. The united forces of so many enemies were unable to do him any serious injury, and in the following year, 1175, all their schemes were frustrated by the capture of William king of Scotland, who was taken prisoner at Alnwick Castle.

When the news of this event was brought to Henry, he was in bed; but he instantly rose, and called his attendants about him, that he might tell them the happy tidings. The king of France was now glad to make peace. Henry's generosity to his defeated enemies is much to be admired. He gave liberty without ransom to above nine hundred noblemen who were made prisoners: and he gave the king of Scotland his liberty, on condition that he and his successors should thenceforward swear fealty to the king of England. He pardoned his sons, on the score of their youth; and to keep his son Henry for the future out of the way of bad advisers, he made him accompany him in a tour round the kingdom.

But though Henry behaved to his son in the kindest and most paternal manner, the young prince who seemed

---

Did the mother, and brothers of Henry conspire against the king?
Who were the king's foreign enemies, and did they prevail against him?
Was Henry a generous man, and to whom did he show generosity?
Did Henry reform his undutiful son's heart?

to be quite devoid both of affection and gratitude, grew weary of the constraint he was kept in, and importuned his father, under different pretences, to let him quit England. This at last the king very unwillingly agreed to, and the prince returned immediately to his former companions, and spent his time in all kinds of idle amusements, and gave the king continual vexation by his headstrong and obstinate conduct.

At last, the prince having a quarrel with his brother Richard, and the king seeming to take Richard's part, the prince, in the violence of his passion, broke through all restraints, and was actually leading an army against his father, when the tumult of his mind threw him into a fever. Finding himself dying, he sent a repentant message to his father, entreating forgiveness for all his undutiful behaviour, and beseeching that he would come and see him.

This the king would not do, apprehending his illness to be only pretended; but he sent him his ring in token of forgiveness. The prince received it with thankfulness, and a little before his death desired to be laid on a heap of ashes with a halter about his neck, to testify his deep humiliation and contrition. This was done, and in this state he died. Henry's grief when he heard that his son was dead, was very great indeed. He bitterly reproached himself for having refused to go to him, and forgot, in sorrow for his death, all his faults and misconduct.

Prince Henry died in the twenty-ninth year of his age, and as he left no children, his next brother, Richard, became heir to the throne. Richard also was of a turbulent disposition, and on many occasions behaved very ill to his father. In the year 1186, Henry's third son, Geoffry, was killed in a tournament at Paris. He left one daughter, called the Damsel of Bretagne; and soon after his death, a posthumous son was born, who was named Arthur.

A. D. 1188. The news arrived in Europe of the taking of Jerusalem and the defeat of the Chris-

---

Did this unworthy prince ever repent?
Did prince Henry die in a hardened state?
Who became heir to the crown of England on the death of Prince Henry?
What princes of Europe engaged in a crusade, A. D. 1188.

tian army by Saladin, sultan of Egypt. The consternation this news occasioned flew from country to country, and fired all the warriors of Europe with a desire of driving the infidels from the holy city. Philip, king of France, and Richard Plantagenet were among the first to take up the cross.

Richard, jealous of the favor which John, his youngest, and now only surviving brother, had with his father, wanted to take him with him to the Holy Land; but this his father would not consent to; and Richard, whose fiery temper could not brook the least contradiction, then joined Philip, who indeed had probably drawn him on, in making war upon Henry; instead of carrying his troops to Palestine.

Henry, being totally unprepared for such an attack, was obliged to subscribe to a humiliating treaty; but what afflicted him most of all was the conduct of John, his favorite son, who forgetting every tie of duty and gratitude, had joined in the rebellion. This seemed to weigh down the king's heart more than any other affliction of his life; and he fell ill of a fever, occasioned by anxiety of mind. Feeling himself dying, he desired to be carried to a church. He was laid at the foot of the altar, and there expired, on the 9th of July, 1189, in the 57th year of his age, and 35th of his reign.

He married Eleanor, the heiress of Guienne. Their children were—William, who died when a child; Henry who married Marguerite of France, and died in 1182: Richard, surnamed Cœur de Lion: Geoffroy married Constance of Bretagne, died in 1186, leaving a son, named Arthur, and a daughter; John, surnamed Lackland; Maud, married Alphonso of Castile; Joan, married William, king of Sicily.

One of Henry's institutions, which still remains, is the division of the kingdom into circuits, in which justices appointed by the king travel round to decide causes and

---

Why did not prince John accompany his brother Richard to Palestine, and what followed the king's refusal?
What event hastened the death of Henry, and when did he die?
Who were Henry's children?

administer justice. This at that time was a most necessary protection against the tyranny of the barons, who often took the administration of the laws into their own hands. It was during this reign that the distinction between Saxons and Normans began to wear away, and that they learned to consider themselves as one people.

Learning advanced considerably in England during the reign of Henry II. His grandfather, Henry the First, was a great encourager of learning; and in the reigns of Stephen and Henry II. there were many learned men, both poets and historians, to whom we are much indebted for the knowledge of the events of their times, and of the times before them. Of these the most eminent are, William of Malmsbury, Henry of Huntingdon, and Giraldus Cambrensis; the last of whom wrote an account of a journey through Wales, and also a description of Ireland, with the history of the conquest of that island. All the writers of this time were monks and priests. Few of the laity could write; it was remarkable if they could read.

The invention of paper, the art of making which was discovered in the 12th century, was of infinite advantage to the progress of learning. Books could now be multiplied at less expense, and a library was become essential in every monastery. Every monastery had also a room called the writing room, where the younger monks were employed in transcribing books: for printing was yet unknown.

About the time of Henry II. many Jews came over and settled in England: but they were treated with great indignity, and to distinguish them from Christians, were obliged to wear a square yellow cap.

Family surnames were unknown before the Conquest and appear to have been then introduced from the circumstance of many of the Normans who came over to England being called by the names of the places they came from in Normandy. Their children, willing to

---

What existing institution may be traced to the wisdom of Henry II.?
What was the state of learning in England in the reign of Henry II?
What invention facilitated learning?
When were the Jews first settled in England?
When did surnames first become common in England?

preserve the remembrance of their Norman origin, also called themselves by the same names.

The present noble families of Seymour (anciently St. Maur,) and Sackville, and many others, derive their names in this manner from places in Normandy. It was soon found that family names were not only honorable, but also convenient. Family names have now become universal; but they were once only assumed by distinguished families; and it was a long time before thay were adopted by the lower orders of people.

It was related in the preceding chapter that Ireland was conquered by the Earl of Pembroke, and that little was known previously by the English concerning Ireland. This much, however, is generally admitted, that in the fifth century, St. Patrick, who was a native of Cornwall, or as some say of Wales, was carried by pirates to Ireland, and that he converted the inhabitants, who till then professed the religion of the Druids, to Christianity. From that time Ireland was a place of refuge for learned men of all countries; and religion and science flourished there till the eight century, when the country was overrun by the Danes, who destroyed most of the churches and monasteries.

When the Danes were expelled, the Irish not having an Alfred to govern them, sank into great barbarism, and it was not till many years after earl Strongbow's time that they assimilated themselves in any degree to the manners and habits of other civilized nations.

Have surnames become general?
What Irish tradition is generally believed?
Why is it presumed that the Irish degenerated?

CHAPTER XI

RICHARD I

[Years after Christ, 1189—1199.]

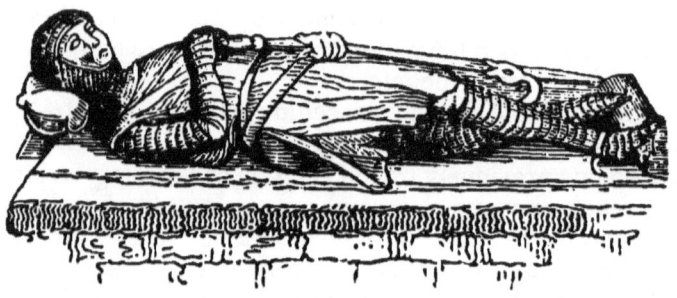

Monument.

Richard, surnamed Cœur de Lion, from his undaunted courage, had received from nature a very generous disposition. His faults were those of a lofty spirit, and were, perhaps, too suitable to the unruly temper of the time he lived in, to be then considered reprehensible or dangerous For his father's death he felt extreme sorrow; and on seeing his dead body, expressed an agony of remorse for his own undutiful conduct towards him.

One of the first acts of Richard's reign, was to release his mother from her long confinement. He bestowed many kind but ill-judged gifts on his brother John, which, instead of inspiring him with any affectionate feeling, only put it the more in his power to show his ingratitude. Richard soon turned his whole mind to the crusade. He sold the royal castles and demesnes, in order to raise money, and had recourse to many unjust and unworthy methods of extorting it from his subjects. He also, for the sum of ten thousand marks, absolved the king of Scotland from his oath of doing homage to the kings of England.

A. D. 1190. At length the armament was ready; and Richard, accompanied by a number of the

---

What sort of man was Richard Cœur de Lion?
What were the first acts of Richard's reign?
When did Richard go to Palestine, and with whom did he go?

English barons, all as eager in the cause as himself, arrived at Messina on the 14th of September, 1180. Here he was joined by Philip, king of France; and the season being too far advanced for them to proceed immediately to Palestine, it was agreed that they should pass the winter in Sicily. There could not be a greater difference of character than that which existed between these two kings.—Richard, though proud and domineering, was brave and generous. Philip was equally proud, but was sly and deceitful.

It will not appear surprising that two such opposite characters should quarrel before their six months' residence in Sicily was over; and it must be acknowledged that the first aggression came from Richard. He had long been contracted to Adelais, sister of the French king; but Henry, his father, had repented of the engagement, and would not permit it to be fulfilled while he lived: and now Richard, having become enamored of Berengaria, daughter of the king of Navarre, broke off his engagement to Adelais.

A. D. 1191. King Richard prevailed with his mother, queen Eleanor, to bring the princess Berengaria to Messina. They arrived the day before he was obliged to sail; but, it being Lent, the marriage, according to a regulation in the Roman Catholic Church, could not then take place. Eleanor returned to England, and the princess, accompanied by the queen of Sicily, Richard's sister, embarked for the Holy Land. During the voyage the ship the two princesses were in was in great danger from a violent storm; and the king of Cyprus refusing to admit the ship into his harbors, Richard laid siege to that island, and in a short time obtained entire possession of it. Here he and Berengaria were married; and after leaving a governor in the island he sailed for Acre, where the king of France, who had some time before left Sicily in great displeasure with Richard, was already arrived.

Acre was a town on the coast of Palestine, in possession of the Saracens, and had been besieged for the last two years by an army of Christians collected from all

---

What cause of offence was given by Richard to Philip of France?
Where, and to whom was Richard I. married?
Where was Acre, and when did that town surrender to Richard?

parts of Europe. The Christians were now in their turn surrounded and besieged by a large army of infidels, under the famous Saladin. The arrival of Richard, whose valor was well known, revived the courage of the Christians; and the town, being attacked night and day, was obliged to surrender on the 12th of July.

Soon after the capture of Acre, the king of France returned home, pretending that the climate disagreed with him; but in reality because he was jealous of Richard, and had not forgot his quarrel with him at Messina. Before he went he solemnly engaged not to make any attempt on the territories of Richard, though at this very time he entertained the full intention of attacking them as soon as he got back. He also gave secret orders to the duke of Burgundy, the commander of the troops he left behind, to omit no opportunity of thwarting and mortifying the English king.

In the meantime, Richard, unsuspicious of these designs, thought only of his open and declared enemies. He displayed extraordinary bravery and skill; and in a battle near Joppa, which lasted from morning till night, gained a great victory over Saladin. The victorious Christians then entered Joppa, or rather the ruins, which were all that was left of the town, which had been wholly dismantled by the Turks.

Richard's intention was immediately to have pursued Saladin, who had re-assembled his scattered forces at Ascalon; and had he done so, his success would in all probability have been complete: but the duke of Burgundy, agreeably to the instructions he had received, insisted on staying to rebuild the walls of Joppa. Richard was unwillingly obliged to submit, and a delay of seven weeks was caused by that useless work.

When they at last set forth again, the rains and natural impediments, to which were added those that the duke of Burgundy still threw in the way, prevented their getting to Jerusalem till the end of the year 1191: and, when at last they had arrived in sight of it, the French troops, and some

---

Did Philip of France act with generosity towards Richard?
What victory over Saladin was achieved by Richard?
Who retarded Richard's designs in Palestine?
What compelled Richard to retire from Jerusalem?

others, refused to advance to the siege; and Richard, to his bitter mortification, was obliged to retreat to Ascalon.

This march is described as the most painful of all that the army made; and when, at last, worn out by fatigue and famine, it arrived at Ascalon, the place was found such an entire ruin, that it became necessary to set to work immediately to repair it. Richard set the example by working with more ardor than any common laborer. Soon after, the duke of Burgundy, and all whom he could entice to follow him, separated from the army, and went to Tyre.

In the meantime the affairs of England had gone on very ill. Prince John, and the bishop of Ely, to whom the chief authority had been given, soon disagreed, and the whole kingdom was in a state of disturbance. At last the bishop was obliged to abandon the country; and delegates were appointed, who acted more prudently. When the king of France got home, he lost no time in inviting John to unite with him in seizing on Richard's territories.

A. D. 1192. John was only prevented from doing so by queen Eleanor, who appears to have acted like a wise and good woman at this juncture. Philip then would have invaded Normandy with his own forces; but he was obliged to give up this design, all his barons refusing to accompany him in so unjust and ungenerous an attempt. The news of these transactions reached Ascalon about the middle of April, and Richard then resolved to return to Europe.

But while Richard was preparing for his return, he heard that Saladin was besieging Joppa, and that the Christians there were reduced to the last extremity. Giving up, therefore, his design of immediately embarking, he went directly to Joppa, and defeated the Pagans in a furious battle, in which he performed prodigies of valor. Soon after this he fell ill, and, being unable to pursue his advantages, concluded a truce with Saladin for three years, three months, three weeks, three days, and three hours.

Amongst the many causes that had from the first impeded

How did Richard conduct himself at Ascalon?
What was the state of affairs in England during the absence of Richard?
What determined Richard to return to Europe?
What circumstance detained Richard in Asia?

the progress of the Christian army in the East was the division that arose in it from the rival interests of Conrad, marquis of Montferrat, and Guy of Lusignan, who each contended for the empty title of king of Jerusalem; while the substantial part, the kingdom itself, was in the possession of the Turks. The kings of France and England had taken opposite sides in this contest, Philip taking the part of Conrad, and Richard that of Lusignan. Richard, before he quitted Palestine, was called on by the whole army, to decide this question.

Richard decided in favor of Conrad; but, to compensate the disappointment to Lusignan, bestowed on him the kingdom of Cyprus, a far more substantial gift than that which his rival obtained; for Cyprus remained in the family of Lusignan during a period of three hundred years. In the year 1471, Cyprus was annexed to the Venetian dominions, and long remained the only territory that was gained to Christendom by all the devastation and bloodshed of the crusades. It is now again subject to the Turks.

On the 9th of October, the two queens having sailed for England previously, Richard commenced his disastrous voyage. After many storms at sea, he was shipwrecked near Aquileia. He then attempted to pass though Germany in the disguise of a pilgrim. Unfortunately he had made the duke of Austria his bitter enemy by some personal affront at the siege of Acre; and having betrayed himself by a profuseness more suitable to the king he was, than to the pilgrim he wished to appear, he was discovered and made prisoner by his unforgiving enemy, who, afterwards, on condition of receiving a share of the ransom, gave him up to the emperor of Germany.

The news of his imprisonment caused the greatest sorrow to all his subjects, who had been anxiously watching for the return of their brave king. John alone rejoiced at his misfortune; and by spreading a report of his death, endeavored to obtain the crown for himself. The king of France also made an attack on Normandy; but the barons remained faithful to Richard, and successfully defended their country.

On whom did Richard bestow the island of Cyprus?
What happened to Richard in his voyage to England?
Did Richard's subjects adhere to him faithfully?

Richard, meanwhile, was treated by the emperor with every possible indignity, was confined in a dungeon, and loaded with chains. His cheerfulness and gay humor did not, even under these circumstances, forsake him, and after a time he was taken to the town of Worms, where a meeting of the princes of Germany, called *a Diet of the empire* was to be held.

When Richard arrived at Worms, the emperor, by way of justifying his own ungenerous behavior, accused him before the diet of having driven away the king of France from Palestine, of having affronted the duke of Austria, and of having made peace on too easy terms with Saladin, and added many other equally unfounded charges. But Richard defended himself so eloquently and pathetically, that many persons shed tears on hearing him, and all were convinced of the malice of his accusers. After this, the emperor agreed to set him at liberty on the payment of 100,000 marks of silver, and on his giving hostages for the future payment of 50,000 marks more.

When this treaty was made known in France, it threw Philip into the greatest consternation, and he sent a message to prince John, bidding him " take care of himself." Philip and John then tried to bribe the emperor to keep Richard a year longer in prison. The emperor, who was exceedingly avaricious, longed to accept their offer; but he dared not do so, for the pope, Celestine the Third, considering Richard as the champion of Christendom, threatened the emperor with excommunication, if he refused to fulfil his engagement.

Queen Eleanor, and all Richard's friends in England, used every means to raise the sum required for his *ransom* A general tax was levied to procure it; but, this not being found sufficient, the nobles voluntarily contributed a quarter of their yearly incomes, and the silver that was in the churches and monasteries was melted down. When the money was collected, queen Eleanor took it herself to Ger-

---

How did Richard support adversity?
How did the emperor of Germany justify his treatment to Richard?
Who persuaded the emperor to detain Richard a prisoner, and who prevented him?
Who procured Richard's ransom?

many, and had the happiness of receiving her son, and bringing him to England.

A. D. 1194. Richard landed at Sandwich on the 20th day of March, after an absence of four years, fifteen months of which he had been a prisoner. He was received with overflowings of joy; and in London with such a display of wealth, that the Germans who had accompanied him exclaimed, "If our emperor had known the riches of England, your ransom, O king, would have been much greater."

After Richard had settled some affairs in England, and been a second time crowned, that he might wipe off the stain of his captivity, he embarked for France to defend Normandy against an attack which Philip was preparing to make. The morning after his landing at Harfleur, prince John suddenly rushed into his apartment, and, throwing himself at his feet, implored his forgiveness, which the king immediately granted, though he could not feel any cordial affection for such a brother. Indeed, he soon after said to some of his attendants: "I wish I may forget my brother John's injuries, as soon as he will forget my pardon of them."

The four following years were passed by Richard in a succession of wars and truces with the king of France. At last, by the meditation of the pope, a truce for five years was agreed upon, to enable the kings to undertake another crusade. But the death of Richard prevented. It had been rumored that a considerable treasure had been found on the lands of the viscount of Limoges. Richard claimed this, as of his right as sovereign; and, on the viscount's refusing to give up more than a part, declared positively that he would have the whole, and immediately laid siege to the castle of Chalus, where the treasure was supposed to be lodged.

A. D. 1199. The garrison offered to surrender the castle, and all that was in it, provided they might march out with their arms. Richard vindictively refused their offer, protesting he would take their castle by

---

How was Richard received in England?
How did Richard and Prince John meet?
What transaction was Richard engaged in during four years?
When and where was Richard fatally wounded?

force, and put them all to death. On the 28th of March, 1199, as he was taking a survey of the castle, and giving directions for the assault, he was wounded by an arrow from the cross bow of Bertrame de Gourdon. The wound appeared trifling at first, but it soon turned to a gangrene, and in a few days his life was despaired of.

Before Richard died, the castle was taken, and all the garrison were instantly hanged, excepting Bertrame, whom the king ordered to be brought into his presence. "What harm have I done to you?" said he to him, "that you should thus have attempted my death?" "You killed my father and brother with your own hands," replied the man. "and intended to have killed me, and I am ready to suffer any torments you can invent with joy, since I have been so happy as to kill one who has brought so many miseries on mankind."

Richard, conscious of the truth of this bold reply, bore it with patience, and ordered the man to be set at liberty: but this command was not obeyed, and Bertrame was put to death as soon as the king had expired.

A. D. 1199. Richard died on the 6th of April, 1199, in the forty-second year of his age, and tenth of his reign. He left all his dominions to his brother John. He had at one time appointed Arthur of Brittany his heir; but on his death-bed he altered his will. When he was dying, he remembered with bitter anguish his undutiful conduct to his father, and desired to be buried near him. He had no children.

During this reign (only four months of which the king passed in England) the disorders of that country arrived at a pitch that had been before unknown. No man's life or property was secure; and there was at one time a regular band of robbers, which, till their leader, William Fitzosbert, was taken and hanged, threatened London itself with destruction.

How was Richard reproved on his death-bed?
Were Richard's last commands obeyed?
Who was Richard's successor?
What was the condition of England in this reign?

CHAPTER XII.

JOHN

[Years after Christ, 1199—1216.]

John came to the crown of England without having one heart in his favor. His perfidiousness, cruelty, and rapacity were already well known; and he had neither personal bravery, nor mental ability, to make up for his faults. He had early shown his incapacity for government. For his father, Henry the Second, intending that Ireland should be his inheritance, sent him there, to accustom the people to him. But he insulted the Irish chiefs, ridiculed their customs and habits, and behaved with so much folly and levity, that his father thought fit to alter his purpose.

At the time of king Richard's death, Arthur of Bretagne was of an age and temper to feel the disappointment of being excluded from his inheritance. His mother was a woman of violent temper; and by her advice he placed his cause in the hands of the king of France, who was glad enough to have an opportunity of interfering with the affairs of England. John, however, found means to persuade Philip that it would be more to his advantage to abandon Arthur; and the two kings entered into a treaty, in which it was settled that Philip's son Louis should marry Blanche of Castile, John's niece; and that Arthur should be given up to John, who would have immediately put him to death, had he not found means to escape.

A. D. 1202. Three years afterwards, Arthur married a daughter of Philip, who then undertook his cause, and assisted him to besiege the castle of Mirabel, in Poitou, where his grandmother, queen Eleanor, who had always been his enemy, lived. He had nearly got possession of the castle, when John, acting with a vigor quite unusual to him, came suddenly to his mother's rescue, and took the unfortunate Arthur prisoner, with his sister the

---

Was John prepared to be a good king?
What was John's treatment of his nephew, prince Authur?
What misfortune overtook Arthur?

damsel of Bretagne, who was carried to England, and kept in perpetual imprisonment in Bristol castle. Arthur was taken to the castle of Falaise, where the king gave orders to Hubert de Burgh, the governor, to put him to death.

Hubert, desirous to save the unhappy young prince, placed him in concealment; and, pretending that he was dead, had the funeral service publicly performed for him. But the Bretons were so much exasperated at the supposed murder of their prince, that Hubert found it necessary to inform them of his being alive. But no sooner did John hear of it, than he had Arthur removed to Rouen, where he himself resided; and it is generally believed that he murdered his unfortunate nephew with his own hands.

This barbarity filled every mind with horror, and John became an object of universal detestation. And, partly because his barons refused him assistance, and partly from his own sloth and cowardice, he made but little opposition to the wily Philip, who drove him step by step out of Normandy, and severed that province from the crown of England, after it had been for three hundred years in the possession of the descendants of the Norman Rollo. His mother's inheritance also, and nearly all the rest of John's territories in France, yielded themselves up to Philip.

A. D. 1208. John had a quarrel with the Pope, Innocent III., about the choice of an archbishop of Canterbury. Innocent insisted on the election of Stephen Langton, an Englishman, whose superior abilities had raised him to the dignity of cardinal; and John refusing to confirm his choice, the pope laid the kingdom under an *interdict*. This, however, John did not much regard.

John occupied himself during the next two years in expeditions against the Irish and Welsh, and in extorting money from his own subjects, and from the Jews especially, by many unjust and cruel methods. One of his contrivances was to assemble all the abbots and abbesses of the religious houses in London; and when he had col-

---

What was the death of Arthur?
Who separated Normandy from the dominions of the king of England?
What quarrel between king John and the pope broke out A. D 1208?
How did John treat the Jews and the religious houses?

lected them together, he kept them prisoners till they had paid him a large sum of money.

The pope, finding that his interdict was of no avail, now resolved on a more effectual way of bringing John to obedience. He *excommunicated* him, absolved his subjects from their oath of allegiance, and published a sort of crusade against him, exhorting all Christian princes and barons to unite in making war upon and dethroning him. To the king of France the pope applied particularly; and Philip, who was not slow in availing himself of the opportunity thus offered, assembled a numerous fleet and army at Boulogne for the invasion of England.

The dread of being conquered by the French overpowered the dislike the English had to John. They flocked to him in great numbers on this emergency and a large army was soon collected at Dover. While affairs were in this state, the pope, who only wished to humble John, and not to increase the power of Philip, sent his legate Pandulf to England, and promised John that if he would receive Langton as archbishop of Canterbury, he would recal the sentence of excommunication.

When John had agreed to this, the legate required him to resign his crown to the pope, and promised that the pope would restore it to him again, on condition of receiving a yearly tribute; and would forbid Philip to invade the realm of England. John agreed to these ignominious terms; and it is said that when he took his crown, and laid it at the feet of the *legate*, the pope's representative, that haughty cardinal spurned it with his foot, and that it was some time before he consented to replace it on the king's head.

Philip, when he heard of these arrangements, and was ordered by Pandulf to withdraw his forces from the coast, was enraged beyond measure. But, as he did not dare to make the pope his enemy, he found himself obliged to submit. Unwilling, however, that his great preparations

---

Did the Pope persevere in his hostility to John, and who aided him?
Did the Pope offer conditions of reconciliation to John?
Did John disgracefully submit to these terms?
What caused a battle between the French and English?

should be thrown away, he determined to attack the territories of Ferrand, earl of Flanders.

In this extremity Ferrand applied to John, who sent to his assistance the fleet that had been collected for the defence of England. A battle ensued between the English and French fleets, and the English were completely victorious. Philip, on the loss of his fleet, returned home with his army in disorder.

John was so much elated by this victory, that he wanted to follow it up by the invasion of France ; but his barons refused to accompany him. He therefore entered into an alliance with Otho, emperor of Germany, and some other princes, who engaged to enter France on one side, while John, with some foreign troops that he had collected, attacked it on the other. Otho accordingly entered the Netherlands ; and John landed an army at Poitou, and penetrated into Anjou and Bretagne.

The army of the emperor being completely defeated at Bouvines, John made a five years truce with Philip, and hastily returned to England. There a most unwelcome reception awaited him. His barons, tired out by his weakness and wickedness, had been long conspiring together against him. They were now joined by Stephen Langton, the new archbishop, who, having discovered a concealed copy of the charter granted by Henry I., drew up from it a bill of rights and privileges, which the barons, in full assembly, approved of.

A. D. 1215. This the king, on his return from France, was called on to sign : but he refused to do so. At last, finding himself abandoned by every body, and in a most desolate condition, he sent the earl of Pembroke, a nobleman distinguished for virtue and ability, to propose a conference with the barons. A meeting accordingly took place on Friday, the 15th of June, 1215, in a large meadow, between Windsor and Staines, called Runimede, which means the *meadow of council*, and which was so called because it had been used by the Saxons as a

---

Did John continue the war with France, and how did the war terminate ?
Who opposed the arbitrary measures of king John ?
What measure was proposed by the English barons to king John ?
When and where was the great charter signed ?

place for public meetings. At this meeting was signed the famous *Magna Charta.*

Under the feudal system, the power of the kings was very oppressive, and had become more and more so, till no subject could act in the commonest affairs of life without the king's consent, which could be obtained only for money. No person among the higher classes could marry without the king's consent; and he could oblige heiresses to marry whom he liked. Widows often paid fines, to save themselves from being compelled to marry again. We read of a countess of Chester, who paid king Stephen five hundred marks, that she might not be obliged to marry again for five years; and of a countess of Warwick, who paid king John five hundred marks that she might not be obliged to marry till she pleased.

The Magna Charta was a writing declaring the people of England exempted from certain oppressions, and entitled to certain privileges; and it contained sixty-three different clauses: only the most vexatious tyranny which kings could exercise over the people, could make such clauses necessary. These, for instance: that the goods of every free man shall be disposed of, after his death, according to his will: that if he die without making a will, his children shall succeed to his property: that no officer of the crown shall take horses, carts, or wood, without the consent of the owner: that no free man shall be imprisoned, outlawed, or banished, unless by the judgment of his peers, or the law of the land: that *even* a rustic shall not, by any fine, be deprived of his carts, ploughs, and implements of husbandry. This last was the only article in that great charter for the protection of the laboring people.

Laws there were before this time, but they were very ill kept. Till men are civilized, the will of the strongest is the law, to which the weakest must submit. While the

---

Did the first kings of England interfere in the private concerns of their subjects?
Did the Magna Charta improve the condition of the English people?
Were aws of much efficacy previously to the grant of Magna Charta?

Romans were in Britain, the island was governed by the Roman law; but when they departed, every vestige of government and their language departed with them. The Saxons brought in their own laws, or rather customs; for there were no written laws till the time of Ethelred, who was the first Christian king of Kent.

The code of Ethelred still exists, and strongly shows the simplicity of manners in those ancient times. Alfred, and after him Edward the Confessor, also made codes of laws, many of which are still in force. From the number of laws for the preservation of the peace, which are to be found in those ancient codes, it would appear that the Saxons were a most quarrelsome race. Indeed, scarcely any meetings were held in those rude ages, either for business or pleasure, without ending in rioting and bloodshed.

King John, as soon as he quitted Runimede, retired sullen and out of humor to the Isle of Wight, where he spent three months in planning schemes for revenging himself on the barons. He sent agents to raise an army of Brabanters, promising them the plunder of the barons' estates. Meanwhile the barons, too much despising the king to believe him capable of any vigorous measures, had made no preparations against him, and were amusing themselves with feastings, tournaments, and bear-baitings, the usual diversions of the times; when John, starting from his concealment, appeared before Rochester castle at the head of an army of foreign soldiers.

A. D. 1216. The barons were now reduced to great extremities; and in their distress resorted to the worst and weakest measure that could have been thought of. They invited Louis, eldest son of the king of France, to come to their aid, promising him the crown of England, in right of his wife, who was the king's niece. Louis landed with his army at Sandwich, on the 23d of May; he then retook Rochester castle, and entered London

---

What sort of people do the old codes show the Saxons to have been?
Did a civil war follow the grant of Magna Charta?
What king of France entered London in triumph?

in a sort of triumph, the citizens doing homage to him as their proper sovereign.

It was now king John's turn to fly, and the baron's turn to pursue. Every place submitted to them till they came to Dover. Hubert de Burgh was governor there, and defended the castle so well, that Louis swore a solemn oath that he would not quit its walls till he had taken it, and hanged all the garrison. This oath was the preservation of England; for the delay of the French prince before Dover castle, gave the barons time to reflect on their error in having called in his aid; and many of them abandoned his party, and joined the king.

A. D. 1216. John by this means mustered once again a considerable army; but meeting with some disasters in his march into Lincolnshire, fatigue and anxiety threw him into a fever. With great difficulty he reached Newark, where he died on the 19th of October, 1216, in the forty-ninth year of his age, and the eighteenth of his reign.

John was twice married. By his first wife he had no children. He had two sons and three daughters by his second wife: Henry, who succeeded him; Richard; Jane, married to Alexander, king of Scotland; Eleanor, married first to the earl of Pembroke, secondly, to the earl of Leicester; Isabella, married to Frederick II., emperor of Germany.

I. is extraordinary that the reign of the worst king and the worst man that ever wore the crown of England should be the one that has brought the most lasting good to the nation The Magna Charta has consecrated the reign of king John to all succeeding ages. Besides this great charter, he had, in the early part of his reign, granted one to the citizens of London, conferring on them many of the privileges they at this day enjoy.

An *interdict*, was forbidding, or interdicting, divine ser

What circumstance disposed the English barons to abandon the French king?
What was the death of John?
Who were John's family?
What great benefit to the English nation derived from John?
Was John generous, or selfish—superstitious, or religious—pusillanimous, or courageous? (Ans. *the pupil's judgment.*)
What was an interdict?

vice to be publicly performed. When a nation was under an interdict, the churches were shut; the bells were not rung; the dead were buried in ditches and holes, without the performance of the funeral service; diversions of all kinds were forbidden; and every thing wore an appearance of mourning and gloom.

Excommunication was a worse sentence still, and was levelled at persons, as an interdict generally was at nations. A person who was excommunicated, was considered as unholy and polluted; every one was forbidden to come near him, or to render him any friendly offices. Thus, if the sentence could have been fully enforced, it was possible for the most potent monarch to become, by a single mandate of the pope, a miserable outcast.

In this age, robbery was common. Robin Hood lived in the reigns of John and his successor. He died in the year 1247. He is said to have been a man of birth and fortune, and to have squandered his patrimony. He then, as the story goes, betook himself to the woods and forests, and became, if such a phrase be proper, a sort of *gentleman robber;* and pacified his conscience by robbing only the rich, and by being beneficent to the poor. But his fame is more owing to the ballads that have been made on him, than to any of his own good or bad deeds.

CHAPTER XIII.

HENRY III.

[Years after Christ, 1216—1272.]

When King John died, his eldest son Henry, called Henry of Winchester, from the place of his birth, was only eight years old. The Earl of Pembroke, who was a wise and good man, was made protector of the kingdom,

---

What was excommunication?
Who was a famous robber in king John's time?
Who succeeded John, and who was the *protector?*

and governor of the young king; and while he lived, the youth and incapacity of Henry were of no material disadvantage to the country. Pembroke, by renewing the great charter, and seeing that the articles of it were duly executed, brought back most of the rebellious barons to the royal cause.

A. D. 1217. Louis continued in England some months after the death of John, but without being able to increase the number of his partisans; and on the 19th day of May, he encountered the royal army at Lincoln, and was so completely beaten in a battle which was fought in the streets of that town, that he was glad to make peace with the protector, and to withdraw with the remnant of his army into France.

The earl of Pembroke governed the kingdom with honor, wisdom, and success, till 1219, when, to the misfortune of England and its king, he died. Hubert de Burgh, and Peter de Roches, a native of Poitou, were appointed to succeed him.

A. D. 1223. When the king was sixteen years old, he was declared of age to govern by himself. In 1224, Philip, king of France, died, and his son Louis succeeded him; but *he* also died soon after, and left an infant son, Louis the Ninth, under the guardianship of his mother, Blanche of Castile. Henry thought this would be a good opportunity to attempt the recovery of Normandy, and led an army there in 1230; but he so misconducted the expedition, that, instead of obtaining any advantages, he returned in a few months to England, covered with disgrace.

A. D. 1236. Henry married Eleanor, daughter of the earl of Provence, and immediately raised her friends and relations to some of the highest offices of the state, which gave great offence to the English nobles. This king's most hurtful folly was the weakness with which he attached himself to strangers, particularly to foreigners, and the fickleness and caprice with which he cast off old favorites to set up new ones.

On what account did the French king make peace with England?
When did the earl of Pembroke die, and who succeeded him?
What happened to Henry in Normandy?
What was the principal folly of Henry's government?

And he was also so profuse to his favorites, that his treasures were soon exhausted, and he was often obliged to apply to parliament (as the great council of the nation began about this time to be called) for a supply of money. By these proceedings he made himself every year more and more despised, and many plans were formed for deposing him.

The pope, profiting by Henry's imbecility, made many and great encroachments on the rights of the church of England. The benefices were by his means filled with Italians, and he contrived to intermeddle on all occasions. In 1255 he led the king into much expense, by conferring on his second son Edmund the title of king of Sicily, which he did in the hope of revenging a quarrel of his own with Mainfroy, king of Sicily, by drawing on Henry to invade that island. All the English barons refused to give the least assistance to this project.

The king, finding every method fail of extorting money from his subjects for this expedition, resorted to one that was till then unknown. He gave to Italian merchants bills of exchange to a great amount, for money pretended to be advanced by them for the Sicilian war. These bills were drawn on the prelates of England, who at first refused to pay the demands thus made on them: but through the remonstrances of the pope they at length submitted.

A. D. 1258. The absence of the king's brother, who went to Germany, and of many nobles who were attached to the royal cause, gave an opportunity to the disaffected barons of bringing about the rebellion they had planned. Simon De Montfort, earl of Leicester, who had once been one of the king's favorites, took the lead in this rebellion. The barons assembled at Oxford on the 11th June, 1258, and obliged the king, and his eldest son, then eighteen years of age, to agree to a treaty, by which twenty-four of their own body, at the head of whom was De Montfort, had authority given them to reform all abuses.

Did the Pope continue to meddle in the affairs of England?
Did the English barons engage in an expedition planned by the Pope?
When were *bills of exchange* invented?
Did the imbecility of Henry induce a rebellion in 1258?

The barons, under this pretext, assumed a right to govern the kingdom: but the people scarcely acknowledging such rulers, or not knowing whom they were to obey, paid no respect to the laws, and it seemed as if all government was dissolved. This state of things lasted for six years. The king and the barons were continually making treaties the conditions which were broken as soon as made.

The king of France, Louis the Ninth, with a very different policy from that which had actuated his grandfather Philip, tried to make peace between Henry and his barons, but Henry was too weak, and De Montfort too ambitious, to listen to reason, and all Louis's endeavors were unavailing.

A. D. 1264. At last prince Edward, who inherited more of the capacity and courage of the Plantagenets than either his father or grandfather had possessed, became old enough to stand forward and assert his own and his father's rights; and many barons, disgusted with the conduct of the twenty-four self-appointed rulers, joined the royal standard. The armies of the king and of the earl of Leicester met at Lewes, in Sussex, on the 14th of May, 1264.

The result of this encounter was the complete discomfiture of the prince. Edward, finding himself surrounded by Leicester's troops, without the possibility of escaping, was obliged to submit to any terms that might be imposed: and he and his cousin prince Henry were detained, and sent strongly guarded to Dover castle, under the color of being hostages for their two fathers, who were still, in effect, kept prisoners.

Leicester now could do whatever he liked. He used the king's name for his own purposes, seized on the property of many of the royal barons, and took possession, in the king's name, of some of the royal castles. He also formed plans of raising himself to the throne. But his ambition caused his ruin. The earl of Gloucester, his

---

Did the usurpation of the barons produce confusion in England?
Did Louis of France promote peace in England?
Did prince Edward maintain the rights of the crown?
How did Leicester treat the king and prince Edward?
How did the earl of Leicester conduct himself?

former associate, and now his rival, seeing himself eclipsed by Leicester's greatness, secretly planned his ruin.

Leicester, perceiving himself an object of suspicion, tried to regain the good opinion of the people, by pretending to set Edward at liberty, and restore him to his father; but as Henry was in reality a prisoner also, the prince only changed his place of confinement, and Leicester became the more hated for this deceit. In the meantime Gloucester had retired to his estates on the borders of Wales, and put his castles in a state of defence. He was proclaimed a traitor in the king's name by Leicester, who came to Hereford, bringing the king and the prince with him.

The earl of Gloucester, being anxious for an opportunity of getting the prince out of Leicester's hands, was very much pleased at this. He formed a plan which he contrived to communicate to him for his escape, and sent him a horse of extraordinary fleetness. The prince, according to Gloucester's plan, pretended to be very ill, and in a few days, appearing a little better, he obtained Leicester's permission to ride out for the benefit of his health

Riding slowly, the prince after some little time, persuaded the gentlemen who were his guards to ride races with one another. When he thought that their horses were sufficiently tired with this exercise, he raised himself erect in his saddle, and telling his guards "he had long enough enjoyed the pleasure of their company, and that he now bade them adieu," he put spurs to his horse, and was soon beyond the reach of pursuit. He was joined immediately by the earl of Gloucester; and, as soon as his escape was known, all the loyal barons flocked to him, and he was thus at the head of a considerable army.

Leicester, having the old king still in his power, obliged him to issue a proclamation, declaring the prince a traitor. He also sent for his own eldest son Simon from London, who accordingly set out to join him with a great reinforcement. But the prince intercepted and defeated Simon at Kenilworth; and, before Leicester could hear of his son's

How did Leicester endeavor to gain the favor of the people?
Who assisted prince Edward to escape from the custody of Leicester?
How did the prince make his escape?
Did prince Edward gain any advantage over the barons?

defeat, Edward's army appeared in sight, bearing in front the banners taken from young De Montfort at Kenilworth.

This made the earl at first suppose that the reinforcement he was expecting had arrived; but, when the prince advanced near enough for him to find out his mistake, he exclaimed, "Now God have mercy on our souls, for our bodies are prince Edward's!" The battle soon began, and king Henry was dragged into the midst of it by Leicester, and was near being killed by one of prince Edward's soldiers; but he called out, as the soldier, not knowing him, was going to strike him down, "I am Henry of Winchester, thy king; don't kill me."

A. D. 1265. The soldier then led Henry out of the battle; and the prince, being informed where to find him, flew to put him in a place of safety, and then returned to the fight, which ended in his gaining a complete victory. Leicester and his son Henry were killed. This important battle was fought at Evesham, on the 4th of May, 1265, and put an end to the confederacy of the barons. Simon, De Montfort's eldest son, and a few others, still made, indeed, some ineffectual struggles; but these were only like the subsiding of a storm.

On the 4th of May, 1270, prince Edward embarked at Portsmouth for the Holy Land, meaning to join the king of France (who had set out on a crusade, the sixth and the last,) at Tunis; but, on his arrival there, he found that Louis, who has acquired the surname of Saint, had died of the plague. On his death, the French troops returned to Europe; but Edward resolved still to pursue the enterprise with his own little army.

Edward conducted himself with great skill and valor; and the Saracens, who found him a very powerful enemy, employed an assassin to murder him. Edward wrenched the dagger from the man's hand, and killed him in his attempt, not however before he had himself been wounded

---

Was the king's life in imminent danger in a battle between his con's and Leicester's troops?
When were the barons finally defeated?
Did prince Edward engage in the last crusade?

in the arm with the poisoned weapon. The wound, we are told, might have proved fatal, had not his affectionate wife Eleanora, who had accompanied him to Palestine, prevented the effect of the poison by sucking the wound. He set out on his return to Europe soon afterwards.

A. D. 1272. Whilst the prince was thus exposing himself to unnecessary perils abroad, the royal family was suffering great affliction at home. Prince Henry, son of the *king of the Romans*, (as prince Richard, the king's brother, was entitled,) was basely murdered in Italy by the exiled sons of the earl of Leicester, and his father died of grief at Berkhamstead. King Henry was become old and feeble; and his government, never much respected, was now totally despised; and riots, robberies, and excesses of all kinds, were perpetually committed.

Henry III., worn out by infirmities, died at Westminster on the 16th of November, 1272, in the sixty-fourth year of his age, and the fifty-seventh of his reign. The longest reign in British annals, with the exception of that of George III.

He married Eleanor of Provence. His children were, Edward; Edmund, titular king of Sicily; Margaret, married Alexander III., king of Scotland; and Beatrix, married to the duke of Bretagne.

The state of society in England during the long reign of Henry III., deserves some notice. It has been mentioned that under the feudal system, the whole territory of the country, except a certain portion reserved to the king for his own uses, and the church property, was bestowed by the king upon the nobles; and that they held their immense estates upon condition of supporting the king, and affording him assistance to fight his battles, no other army existing, than that afforded by the nobles or barons of their dependents.

The nobles held courts and administered justice, each in

What remarkable circumstance happened to Edward in Palestine?
What was the condition of England in the last days of Henry III?
Whose was the longest reign in England?
How did the feudal system divide the territory of England?
What was the king's council?

his own domain; though Henry II. had divided the kingdom into circuits, and judges were appointed to travel through the circuits, to see the laws enforced. When the king required advice, the barons were called from their castles to the capital to give him counsel. The assembly of the barons was called the "King's Council."

In the course of time, certain *free men*, left the baron's estates and carried on arts and commerce in towns, and formed what were called *corporations*—that is, companies with certain privileges. The barons, perhaps sold or gave estates to some of their favorite retainers, so that besides, barons and vassals, tradesmen and merchants, there came to be in England, Franklins or freemen—independent possessors of small estates.

The richer and more intelligent of these last-mentioned classes formed what is called the *gentry* of England, that is the gentlemen and ladies distinguished from the nobility, and the inferior classes. The latter were the mechanics, laborers, and house servants. This order of gentry was, perhaps, a long time in forming, but it came to be acknowledged as very respectable in the reign of Henry III.

It appears that when the barons resisted the despotism of the king of England, and proposed to restrain the abuses of power, they thought it expedient that the gentry as well as the nobility should have some share in the government, and therefore they proposed that besides the king's Council to deliberate upon public affairs, another body should be summoned to legislate or make laws for the country.

The first certain information we have of a parliament, like the parliaments of the present time, is in 1265, when the earl of Leicester, in the king's name, sent writs, or written orders, to the sheriffs, to send "two discreet knights from each county" to serve in parliament. Every city and borough was also ordered to send "two of its wisest citizens and burgesses."

At first the nobles and the representatives of the counties

Who became independent orders in England?
Who formed the gentry, and who the lower classes?
Were the middle classes admitted to the legislature of England?
What is the first information we possess of the origin of the English parliament?
Do the lords and commons assemble together?

and towns assembled in one house ; but afterwards they divided themselves into two : and hence arose the House of Lords, and the House of Commons; the one composed of noblemen who attend there in right of birth, and the other of gentlemen who are elected by the people.

Before laws were written, and lawyers contended for law to be enforced, and judges were appointed to explain the law and what it demanded, it has been stated, that nobles settled disputes, or wars decided them; but besides those modes of deciding the right, trials by *combat* and ordeals were admitted.

The trial by *combat* was a *duel*, or trial of arms. Two angry persons fought together and the disabled person was pronounced the offender, and the conqueror the justified man. The *ordeal* required an accused person to walk over burning ploughshares, or hot irons blindfold, and if he escaped burning he was pronounced innocent, and discharged from punishment of the imputed crime. In the reign of Henry III. trials by ordeal were abolished.

A license was granted in this reign to the people of Newcastle, allowing them to dig for coals, the first mention we find of that useful mineral. In this reign, though the class of gentry arose, the condition of the lower orders remained unchanged; and slaves were bought and sold like brute animals at the fairs. There were no regular shops, and the merchants and traders travelled from place to place to dispose of their goods.

Roger Bacon was the most eminent man of the age of Henry III. This extraordinary person was a monk at Oxford, and was the most learned man of his age. He applied his learning to the discovery of useful knowledge. He invented telescopes, reading glasses, microscopes, and many other astronomical and mathematical instruments. He discovered gunpowder, though he considered it as an object of mere curiosity, rather than as an invention that could be applied to the destruction of human life.

How were disputes settled before laws were written, and courts of law established?
What was the trial by combat, and what the ordeal?
What circumstances are memorable in the reign of Henry III. ?
Who was the most eminent man of this age in England, and for what?

Bacon's genius soared so far above all his contemporaries, that he was looked upon as a magician, and thrown into prison, where he was kept for many years. He at length returned to Oxford and died there, a very old man in 1292.

CHAPTER XIV

EDWARD I.

[Years after Christ, 1272—1307.]

A. D. 1274. On receiving news of his father's death, Prince Edward set out for England, but he delayed so long on the road, that he did not arrive there till the 2d of May, 1274. His first business was to restore the police of the kingdom, and he made many excellent laws and regulations. His expedient to fill his coffers was not so commendable. He employed commissioners to examine into the titles by which all persons held their estates; and if any one had not a *legal title*, that is, a writing which recorded that the estate was given or sold to the proprietor, or his ancestors, he was compelled either to pay a great fine, or to forfeit his land to the king.

When the commissioners came to earl Warrenne, and desired him to produce the title by which he held his estate, he drew an old rusty sword out of the scabbard, and said, "This is the instrument by which my ancestors gained their estate, and by which I will keep it as long as I live." When this answer was reported to Edward, he became sensible of the hazard he was incurring, and put an end to the commission.

When did Edward I. come to the throne, and what was his policy?
How did Earl Worrenne assert the *title* of his estate and what is a *title* to landed property?

A. D. 1282. The Welsh, under their Prince Llewellyn, had long been very troublesome neighbors to the English. They had joined in Leicester's rebellions, and did not keep the terms of peace which Edward made with them on coming to the throne. Perhaps Edward was not sorry to have this pretext for making war on them; and they, presuming too much on their own strength, attacked his army on the 11th of December, 1282, and were totally defeated.

The Welsh king, Llewellyn, was killed in the battle, and his brother David was taken prisoner, and beheaded like a common traitor. His head was put on the walls of the tower of London, and his limbs were quartered, according to the barbarous custom of those times, and were hung up in four different places, at York, Winchester Bristol, and Northampton.

David being the last branch of that family of ancient kings, Edward took undisputed possession of Wales, and promising the people a prince of their own country, who could speak no English, presented to them his own eldest son, born a few days before in Carnarvon castle, who was thence called prince of Wales, as all the eldest sons of the English kings have been called since.

The kings of England and Scotland had lived in singular harmony, during the last two reigns, in which the intermarriages between the royal families of Scotland and England had made a family as well as a national union. Alexander the Third had married king Edward's sister who died leaving only one child, Margaret, who afterwards married the king of Norway, and died, leaving a little daughter about three years old. Alexander himself died in 1286, and his infant grand-child became heiress of his dominions.

Edward proposed to the king of Norway that the prince of Wales should marry his daughter, the little queen of

---

On what pretext did Edward make war with the Welsh?
How did Edward treat the Welsh princes?
Whom did Edward offer the Welsh for a king?
Was the royal family of Scotland connected with that of England?
What hindered the marriage of the prince of Wales with the queen of Scotland?

Scotland. Such early marriages were then not uncommon. Indeed Alexander and his queen had been *betrothed*, or promised to each other, when neither of them was a year old. The king of Norway and the parliament of Scotland having consented to this match, the young queen was on her way to Scotland, when, being taken ill, she was obliged to be landed at the Orkneys, and there she died.

The death of a little girl of three years old was never before so much lamented, nor has ever since produced such disastrous consequences. But her death prevented the union between the two nations, and plunged Scotland into long and bloody private feuds and public wars. No fewer than thirteen competitors for the throne sprung up. Robert Bruce and John Baliol were the two whose claims were the strongest; and they agreed to refer the decision to Edward, who was so much looked up to by the princes of Europe, that he had before been applied to, to determine a competition for the crown of Sicily. In that case, where his interest was not concerned, he had given a wise and equitable decision. Happy had it been for both England and Scotland, would he have done so now: but the temptation offered was too great for him to resist.

Edward came to Norham, on the border of Scotland, with a numerous army; and first insisted that his supremacy over Scotland should be admitted; which the Scots agreed to after much hesitation. He then required that the royal castles, and places of strength should be put into his hands; and, when this was done, he gave judgment in favor of Baliol, who was proclaimed king of Scotland. But the mere name of king was all that he obtained, for being of a weak capacity, he could make no resistance to the encroachments and exactions of Edward, who treated him like a child, and was disposed to treat the Scots like slaves.

On their refusing to submit tamely, he marched into Scotland, and defeated at Dunbar the army of Baliol.

What event threw the Scots into a state of civil warfare?
Why did Edward I. interfere in the affairs of Scotland?
How did Edward treat the Scots?
What was the end of John Baliol?

Baliol then threw himself into the hands of the king of England, who obliged him to make a solemn renunciation of his crown, and detained him a prisoner for three years. He was then allowed to retire to France, where he died at an advanced age, having been nominally a king for four years.

While Edward was thus endeavoring to increase his dominions in one quarter by injustice and violence, he lost part of them in another by an artifice more contemptible, but not more unjust, than those he himself practised. Guienne, the inheritance of the old queen Eleanor, had still remained to her posterity, when almost every thing else they had possessed in France was gone.

Some disputes arising with Philip the Fair, king of France, about the ceremony of doing homage for that duchy, Edward, by way of a form of acknowledgment of the feudal superiority of the king of France, was persuaded to surrender the duchy to Philip, who promised, on the word of a king, to restore it immediately; but when that wily monarch had got possession, he would not resign it, and Edward was too deeply engaged in the affairs of Scotland to be able at that time to avenge himself.

In 1291 Edward had the affliction of losing his queen. She died at Harby, in Nottinghamshire, and Edward accompanied her body from thence to its burial place at Westminster, and, to commemorate her worth, and his own grief, he caused a stone cross to be erected at every place where the body stopped in this melancholy journey.

A. D. 1296. After the imprisonment of Baliol, Edward treated Scotland like a conquered country. Earl Warrenne was appointed governor of the kingdom, and all the offices of state were given to Englishmen. The Scots groaned bitterly under this degradation; and, in 1297, William Wallace, whose name will never be forgotten, stood forth, though only a private gentleman of small estate, to rescue his fallen country.

By what right was Guienne retained by the English?
How did the king deceive Edward I.?
How did Edward express his grief for the death of his queen?
What Scots gentleman resisted the aggressions of Edward I.?

Wallace was soon joined by several of the nobility; and, notwithstanding the many impediments he met with from the jealousies of some of the nobles, he maintained the struggle for eight years, but with various success. At one time he pushed his victorious arms into England; but at another his cause was nearly ruined at Falkirk, where Edward obtained a complete victory. At last, in 1305, he was betrayed into the hands of the English, who put him to death.

A. D. 1305. John Baliol had died in France the year before, and Robert Bruce, son of the former competitor, now stood alone as claimant of the throne of Scotland. He collected a small army; and the countess of Buchan, in whose family the right of crowning the king had been hereditary, placed the crown upon his head; her brother, who ought to have done it, being in the English interest. When Edward heard of this, he was enraged beyond measure, and vowed the destruction of *The Bruce*, whose escapes and adventures were very extraordinary; and are related in an interesting manner by Sir Walter Scott in his Tales of a Grandfather.

Edward's next and last expedition began with a solemn oath, that he would march into Scotland, and never return till he had brought it into entire subjection. And he kept his vow; but not in the way he had intended, for he did not subjugate Scotland, and he never returned. He spent many months in a vain pursuit of Bruce and his adherents, who contrived to conceal themselves in the fastnesses amongst the mountains, watching for favorable opportunities of coming forth from their hiding-places, and annoying the English.

A. D. 1307. At last Edward, exasperated by disappointment, sent for all the forces in his dominions to meet him at Carlisle. Before the army could arrive, the king became so ill as to be confined to his chamber. It was reported that he was dead, and to show the falsehood of the report he set out from Carlisle: but when

---

What became of Wallace?
Who laid claim to the crown of Scotland A. D. 1306?
What was the king's last expedition?
Where did Edward I. die?

he had advanced a few miles, to a place called Burgh on the Sands, he was obliged to stop. He there expired in a tent by the road-side, on the 7th of July, 1307.

Edward was seventy years old, and had reigned thirty-five years. He was twice married; first to Eleanor of Castile, by whom he had fifteen children; and, secondly, to Marguerite, sister of the king of France, by whom he had two sons. Edward, before he died, charged his eldest son to send his heart to the Holy Land: to carry his body with the army into Scotland, and not to bury it, till he had made a complete conquest of that country; and never to recall Piers Gaveston, a wicked favorite of the son, whom the father had banished.

In the relations of son, husband, and father, Edward I. was exemplary: and yet this man, with all these fine and noble qualities, was the occasion of infinite misery to many thousands of people. The desire of possessing himself of the whole island had so beset his mind, that every other consideration gave way to it. To attain this end, he turned courage into mad ferocity, and prudence into deceit and craft, and instead of doing good to his subjects, and mankind, inflicted the evils of war to the utmost extent of his power.

Amongst the many violent acts of Edward was the banishment of the Jews. He drove them out of the country, and leaving them only money enough to enable them to reach some foreign land, seized on all the rest of their property.

The first commercial treaty to which England was a party, was made between Henry the Third and the king of Norway. The trade of England was chiefly carried on by Germans. The principal commodities were wool, lead, and tin. These were brought to certain towns in different

---

What was the king's age, &c ?
How did Edward I. treat the Jews?
What was the state of commerce in England during the reign of Edward I.?
By whom was the most considerable trade of England carried on?

parts called the staple towns, where the collectors of the king's customs were appointed to receive the *duty*, which is a tax paid to the custom-house for the use of government on all articles brought from foreign countries.

The goods were then sold to the German traders, who were called the merchants of the staple; and these people exported them abroad, and imported gold, silver, and various goods in return. The Lombards also were foreigners who settled in England. Their business was chiefly to lend money on interest. Lombard-street in London, was so named from them.

In respect to their pleasures the people of England imbibed something of the spirit of their monarch. Their very amusements were all of a martial sort; and the learning the use of arms was a necessary, perhaps may be added, a principal part of the education of a gentlemen. To every castle belonged a paled court called the tilt-yard, where the young men used to practise all the exercises and manœuvres requisite to make them good warriors.

These exercises, and the mock combats in which they engaged, were always practised with blunt spears, and it was thought very dishonorable for them to wound each other. They had also many games in these tilt-yards which were excellently calculated to improve their strength and agility. Riding at the ring was one of these; the object of which was, while riding at full speed, to run the point of a spear through a small ring that hung suspended from a high post.

The Tournament was a favorite spectacle of the English nation. A *tournament* was a public meeting of knights, to display their skill and courage in mock combats. These meetings were commonly proclaimed for a long time before hand, that knights from a distance might be able to attend. They were in general held by kings and princes; and queens, and the wives and daughters of the nobles, were among the spectators; and the most beau-

---

What were the favorite amusements of the English people at this time?

Were *mock combats* safe, and what other games were practised by the English of the 14th century?

What was a Tournament?

tiful lady, or the one of highest rank, commonly bestowed a scarf, or some such prize, on the knight who acquitted himself best

CHAPTER XV

EDWARD II.

[Years after Christ, 1307—1327.

Queen Isabella going to Paris, 1325.

The reign of Edward the Second, is nothing but a detail of follies on the part of the king, and of violences on that of the nobles. The king began his reign with disobeying all the dying commands of his father. He recalled Gaveston from banishment; and, abandoning the invasion of Scotland, gave himself up to frivolous and idle amusements. He resembled his father in the beauty of his person, but not in the qualities of his mind. He was weak, passionate, and irresolute, fond of trifling diversions, and, if we may believe historians, was addicted to the ig-

---

Was Edward II. a weak or a wise man?

noble vice of drinking to excess. He was devotedly attached to his favorites, who were with no exception, ill-chosen and unworthy persons.

A. D. 1307. Edward married Isabella, daughter of Philip the Fair, king of France; a most unfortunate marriage for him, though at first the queen had the greater cause for complaint, as the king neglected her society, and spent all his time with his favorite Gaveston.

Piers Gaveston was a native of Gascony; and his elevation to riches and honors above the old nobility of England made him an object of general dislike; a dislike which was greatly increased by his own conduct; for he treated the nobles with the utmost insolence, and used to divert himself and his royal master by turning them into ridicule, and giving them contemptuous nicknames.

This treatment they so highly resented, that they entered into a confederacy against him, at the head of which was the king's cousin, the earl of Lancaster, a very rich and powerful baron. The demand of the confederate nobles was, that Gaveston should be sent out of the country. Edward affected to comply with their demand; but instead of sending him back to Gascony, as they had meant, he made him lord deputy of Ireland, and the year after recalled him.

A. D. 1312. The nobles, and indeed the whole nation, were so completely exasperated against the king and Gaveston, that a civil war broke out. The earl of Lancaster, who was the leader of the barons' army, hearing that Gaveston was in Scarborough castle, despatched the earl of Pembroke against that place, who took Gaveston prisoner, and brought him to his own castle of Deddington in Oxfordshire.

One day when the earl of Pembroke was absent from his castle, it was beset by a party of troops, headed by Guy, earl of Warwick, who took Gaveston to Warwick, where Lancaster and the other confederate nobles were assembled. The next day they carried him to a neighbor-

---

Whom did Edward II. marry?
Who was Piers Gaveston?
How did the English nobles regard Gaveston?
Who took Gaveston prisoner?
In what cruel manner was Gaveston killed?

ing hill, called Blacklow Hill, and there they put him to
leath, satiating their savage hatred by looking on while his
head was severed from his body.

When the king heard of the murder of his favorite, he
was thrown into agonies of grief, and made unwonted exertions to revenge his death; but he had so completely lost
the affections of his people that he had not the power to
make his resentment felt, and was obliged to smother it
and accept of peace on the terms the barons chose to offer.

A. D 1314. While England was thus distracted by its
own internal broils, Robert Bruce by his
courage and intrepidity, had established himself on the
throne of Scotland. He drove the English out of that
country step by step, till nothing remained to them but the
castles of Stirling, Dunbar, and Berwick. At last Edward
resolved to rouse himself and his people, and to reduce
Scotland to the English yoke by a single blow. He entered Scotland at the head of the largest army that had
ever marched out of England; and, arriving on the 24th
of June within three miles of Stirling, he there saw the
Scottish army drawn up on the banks of the little river
Bannock.

Bruce had only been able to muster about 30,000 men
to oppose the immense host of the king of England, but
he chose his position with great judgment, and neglected
nothing that could facilitate his success. He placed his
army on a rising ground, with the river in front, and a bog
on one side; and to make the approach still more difficult,
he caused pits to be dug, and filled with sharp stakes, and
the tops covered over and concealed by turf and leaves.

The English halted for the night; and, confident in their
numbers, and despising the little army opposed to them,
spent the night in feasting and merriment; while the Scots
whose very existence as a nation depended on the result
of the coming day, passed their time in devotion, and in
mutual exhortations to conquer nobly, or to die. The
young earl of Gloucester the king's nephew, who com-

Did Edward II. resent Gaveston's death?
Did Robert Bruce attack the English in Scotland?
How did Bruce encounter the English at Bannockburn?
Did the Scots imitate the insecurity of the English at Bannockburn?

manded the cavalry, was the first to advance from the English army, and falling into one of the covered pits, was the first to die on that disastrous field.

The cavalry, having lost its leader, was thrown into confusion; and being attacked by sir James Douglas was put to the rout. The infantry astonished by the defeat of the cavalry, and mistaking some boys and wagoners of the Scottish army, who were furnished with banners, for another army, fled without striking a single blow. So great was the panic of the flying multitude, that Edward found it impossible to rally his forces, and was himself obliged to fly to avoid being taken prisoner.

The number of the slain was very great, and would have been still greater, had not the Scots been more intent on plundering the English camp than on pursuing the fugitives, who had eighty miles to go before they could reach a place of security. And thus ended the battle of Bannockburn, a battle which established Bruce on the throne of Scotland, and which is remembered by the English as the most signal overthow they have sustained since the Conquest.

When Edward returned to England after this discomfiture, he found his power more curtailed than ever. The country was torn in pieces between two parties, the royalists, and the partizans of the earl of Lancaster. The king, whose infirm mind was unable to support itself without the prop of an exclusive favorite, weakened his own cause, and drove from him many loyal hearts, by the injudicious choice he made of a new favorite, a Welsh gentleman called Hugh Spenser, a man of an insolent temper and a rapacious disposition. The king loaded Spenser and his father with honors and riches, which soon made them as much objects of jealousy and hatred as Gaveston had been.

A.D. 1322. In March the earl of Lancaster was taken prisoner at Boroughbridge, and carried to Pontefract. After a short trial he was condemned

---

What was the success of the Scots in the engagement at Bannockburn?
Was Bruce established on the Scottish throne?
Who became the favorite of the king of England?
What was the end of the earl of Lancaster?

to death; and on the 22d of March this once powerful nobleman, placed on a miserable horse, and clothed in a shabby dress, was led out of Pontefract, which had been his own chief place of residence, and taken to a hill near the town, and there beheaded with the same circumstances of savage cruelty which had taken place when he himself put Gaveston to death. Eighteen other noblemen were also beheaded, and many estates were forfeited to the king most of which he bestowed on his avaricious favorite.

A. D. 1325. In this year a quarrel arose between the two kings of France and of England, about doing homage for Guienne, which had been restored to the English king. Queen Isabella was sent to accommodate matters between her husband and brother. But she cared little for the interest of her husband, and at length conspired with his enemies.

Isabella collected all the nobles who had been exiled on account of Lancaster's rebellion; and placing one of them. Roger Mortimer, a man of infamous character, at the head of her councils, set herself up in rebellion against Edward The Spensers were so much detested, that, out of hatred to them, many nobles joined the queen, and set out with a numerous army in pursuit of the king.

The king, abandoned by every body, fled into Wales, in hopes of raising an army there. In this hope he was disappointed; and he next embarked for Ireland, in the belief that he should there find a place of refuge: but being driven about by adverse winds he was obliged to re-land. He then sought to conceal himself and a few followers in the monastery of Neath; but his retreat was soon discovered; and Henry, earl of Lancaster, (son to the earl who was executed at Pontefract,) made him a prisoner, and carried him to Kenilworth. Both the Spensers were taken with the king, and fell sacrifices to the hatred of the people.

In the meantime, the King's eldest son, Edward, prince of Wales, a boy of fourteen years old, had been placed by his

---

On what pretence was a quarrel excited between France and England in 1325?
Who joined queen Isabella in rebellion against the king?
Under what circumstance was Edward II. taken prisoner?
After the imprisonment of Edward what was the condition of England?

mother and Mortimer at the head of the rebel army, and had been declared regent. But as the authority he possessed was a mere name, the kingdom was in a deplorable state. There was no government, the courts of justice were shut, and the people committed all kinds of violence without control. The mobs of London and other cities committed robberies and murders with impunity, and were called by the name of *the Riflers.*

The queen and Mortimer having got the king into their power, declared him incapable of governing, deposed him and proclaimed the prince king in his stead. But the prince refused to be king in his father's lifetime without his consent. To remove this scruple, the parliament sent a deputation to Kenilworth, to intimate to the king the sentence of his deposition, and to procure his consent to the coronation of his son.

As soon as the miserable king saw the deputies, he fainted; and when he recovered, and was told their errand, he said to them that he was in their power, and must submit to their will. Judge Trussel, one of the party, then, in the name of the people of England, renounced all fealty to Edward of Carnarvon; and sir Thomas Blount, high steward, broke his staff, and declared all the king's officers discharged from their service.

Thus ended the reign of Edward the Second, a period of nearly twenty years of public disgrace and private calamity. But his own miseries did not end with it. After his deposition he was put under the care of the earl of Lancaster: but the queen and Mortimer, thinking that Lancaster treated the king too humanely, removed him to the custody of Lord Berkeley, John de Maltravers, and sir Thomas Gournay, who were to keep him each a month by turns.

Lord Berkeley behaved kindly to the unfortunate Edward; but it seems as if the other two were desirous to kill him by ill-usage. They hurried him about from castle to castle, in the middle of the night, and but half clothed.

Who demanded the coronation of the prince of Wales?
Did the king submit patiently to his enemies?
Did king Edward's miseries terminate with the loss of the crown?
What indignities were offered to Edward II. during his imprisonment?

One day Maltravers ordered him to be shaved with water out of a dirty ditch, and refused to let him have any other The king shed tears at this usage.

These varied insults and cruelties did not satisfy the savage hearts of the queen and Mortimer, who, therefore, ordered Gournay and Maltravers to despatch him without delay. And they, taking the opportunity of Lord Berkeley's absence, murdered the king at Berkeley castle, with circumstances of great cruelty. He was murdered on the 21st of September, 1327, in the forty-third year of his age. He was called Edward of Carnarvon, from having been born there.

It appears from the historians of this age that little of the present refinement of the English nation was then known. Froissart, a French historian, tells us in his Chronicles, that "the English were so proud and haughty, that they could not behave to the people of other nations with civility." Nor does he give a more favorable account of the Scots; for he says of them, "they are naturally fierce and unpolished, and in Scotland there is little or no politeness, the people being a herd of savages, envying the riches of others, and tenacious of their own possessions."

Erse or Gaelic was the original language of the Scots; but great part of the Lowlands of Scotland being conquered by the Saxons, about the time when they made themselves masters of England, the Saxon became the language of that part of the country. The Saxon, so introduced into Scotland, continuing afterwards unmixed with the Norman, remained much purer there than in England. In England there arose, in different districts, so great a difference of dialect and pronunciation, that one half of the kingdom did not understand the other.

The domestic manners of the English were very different in the fourteenth century from those of our age.

At whose instigation was Edward II. murdered?
What says the historian Froissart of the English and Scots of the 14th century?
What was the language of the British at that time?

Though famine sometimes followed war, and the neglect of agriculture, the nobles lived gluttonously and wastefully This extravagance was checked at one time by interference of the king.

Edward the Second issued a proclamation forbidding the people of his realm to have at dinner more than two courses. 'Whereas, by the outrageous and excessive multitude of meats and dishes which the great men of our kingdom have used, and still use in their castles, many great evils have come upon our kingdom, the health of our subjects has been injured, their goods consumed," &c. &c.

The usual hour of dinner amongst the higher classes was eleven o'clock in the morning. They had no meal equivalent to our tea; but early in the evening had a supper. And, in great houses, before the company retired to bed, cakes and spiced wines were handed round.

The houses of the nobility had commonly some sort of garden or "pleasance" attached to them; and all the monasteries had orchards and gardens, including a "herberie," or physic garden, the chief medicinal nostrums of the times being preparations from herbs.

We do not hear of ornamental gardening till many years afterwards; and the list of *culinary vegatables* at this time cultivated was very scanty, there being few besides carrots, parsnips, and cabbages, in general use There was then, not such a thing as a potato in Europe.

CHAPTER XVI.

EDWARD III.

[Years after Christ, 1327—1377.]

Edward III., at the commencement of his reign, not being more than fifteen years old, was only a tool in the

---

Was luxury known in England in Edward the second's time?
How were meals regulated in England?
What was the *horticulture* of England in the 14th century?
What was the conduct of Isabella and Mortimer after the death of Edward II.?

hands of the queen and Mortimer, who confiscated the property of the Spensers, and appropriated it to their own purposes. They caused the late king's brother, the earl of Kent, to be executed under a false charge of treason; and by their revengeful and rapacious conduct made themselves so much hated by the people, that the nation would soon have been thrown into internal confusion, had not a foreign foe appeared, and drawn the public attention to a more pressing danger.

Robert Bruce thought this a favorable time to retaliate on the English the sufferings they had brought on Scotland, and began hostilities on the border. Edward immediately took the field against him, and though no important action was performed on either side, showed Bruce that he had roused a far more formidable antagonist than the late king had been. Bruce was glad to put a stop to the war by entering into a negotiation with the queen for the marriage of his infant son with her daughter Jane.

A. D. 1328. Edward married Philippa of Hainault, a queen of the highest and most irreproachable character, and no less distinguished for her sense and intrepidity, when the occasion called these qualities forth, than for her benevolence and gentleness to all whom she could benefit by her kindness.

Edward also is esteemed one of the greatest of English kings, though he has been more commonly admired for his bravery and military skill than for his better qualities. He was majestic in his figure, and his countenance bore a very noble expression. His address was pleasing; he was well versed in the learning of his time, and had an excellent understanding; but, unfortunately for his country, all the powers of his mind were early engrossed by one ruinous desire, that of making conquests.

His mother had had three brothers, who were all kings of France one after the other, and who all died leaving only daughters. There is a law in France, called the Salique law, which excludes daughters from inheriting the crown. Consequently, when Charles, the last of the three

---

What disposed Edward and Robert Bruce to make peace?
What was the character of Philippa of Hainault?
What was the character of Edward III.?
Upon what account did Edward III. claim the throne of France?

brothers, died, Philip of Valois, his uncle's son, became king, as being the next male heir. But Edward affirmed himself to be the next male heir, being nephew to the late king, and contended that though his mother, according to the French law, could not be queen, still he might be king as inheriting through her.

But before Edward could be master of France, it was necessary for him to shake off the bondage in which his mother and Mortimer still kept him. He had soon an opportunity of doing this. Isabella and Mortimer (now earl of March) resided at Nottingham castle. Edward, by the assistance of the governor, contrived to get through some subterranean passages into an apartment where Mortimer and the queen were; and in spite of the entreaties of the queen, who called upon her son "to have pity on the gentle Mortimer," he seized, and had him carried away prisoner to Westminster. Mortimer was soon after hanged on a gibbet at Tyburn. The queen-mother was deprived of all her ill-gotten riches, and was confined during the remainder of her life a sort of state prisoner at Rising.

A. D. 1331. The king now took the administration of affairs into his own hands, and by his wise regulations gave early proof (for he was very young) of his great capacity: but unhappily his love of war soon called him off from the arts of peace. He renewed hostilities with Scotland, where David, son of the brave Robert Bruce, was now king, a child of only seven years old.

David in less than a year was driven from the throne his father had so hardly won, and was conveyed into France; and the son of John Baliol was recalled from his retirement and made king of Scotland, if king he could be called, who was only a tool in the hands of Edward, and who was placed on the throne and displaced from it, as the party of the English or of The Bruce prevailed.

At last, Edward, tired of this unprofitable war, determined to abandon it, and to apply all his strength to a project

---

How did Edward punish his mother and Mortimer?
How did Edward manifest his disposition for war?
What happened to young David Bruce?
When did Edward prosecute his pretensions to the dominion of France?

he had long harbored against France. He was occupied during two years in raising money and making preparations. In 1338 he landed with an army at Antwerp, but found himself unable then to proceed. In 1340 he sailed again, and encountering the French fleet off Sluys, completely defeated it, after a most bloody and obstinate fight.

This defeat was so entirely unexpected on the part of the French, that no one dared to tell Philip of it, till at last it was hinted to him by his jester, who said in his hearing. "Oh! what dastardly cowards those English are!"—"How so?" said the king. "Because," rejoined the jester, "they did not jump into the sea, as our brave men have done." The king then demanded an explanation, and heard from his courtiers the whole disastrous story.

A. D. 1340. After the victory of Sluys, Edward disembarked his men, and advanced as far as Tournay: but here he found himself obliged to make a truce with Philip. He returned to England, where his absence had produced many inconveniences. He was at this time involved in great difficulties. All his allies deserted him: he had drained the country of money, and was obliged to pawn the crown, and even the queen's jewels.

A. D. 1346. Nothing could divert this warlike prince from his inordinate ambition to possess himself of the crown of France; and he continued to make many unavailing attempts on that country. At last, success seemed likely to crown his efforts. He landed at La Hogue in Normandy on the 12th of July, with an army of thirty-two thousand men, in which was his oldest son, who has been called the Black Prince; so called, it is supposed from the color of his armor.

Philip, hearing of this invasion of the English, assembled a large army to oppose them, and, breaking down all the bridges as he passed, came in sight of them on the banks of the Seine, near Rouen. The two armies marched for

---

Who informed the king of France of the defeat of his fleet?
Did any misfortunes result from Edward's attempt on France?
When did the king of England renew the war with France?
What hindered the king of England from coming to battle with the French troops on the Seine?

some time on opposite sides of the river; the English on the left or western, the French on the right or eastern side. Edward wished to cross over, but could not, on account of the bridges being broken. At last he contrived to cross by means of a stratagem. He made preparations for repairing the bridge at Poissy, and then suddenly decamped as if to march further up the river.

The French also set off in the same direction, which Edward no sooner perceived, than he hastily turned back to Poissy, and repairing the bridge with the utmost expedition, crossed over it, and turned off towards Flanders, while the French were keeping along the side of the river. But when he reached the banks of the Somme he found himself in a still worse dilemma. Here also the bridges had been destroyed, and Gondemar de Faye was on the opposite side to prevent his crossing, and the king of France was behind him with 100,000 men.

Edward offered a hundred marks to any one who would show him a ford, and a peasant was tempted by the promised reward to point out a place at Blanchetaque, between Abbeville and the sea, where it was possible to cross at low water. Edward first plunged into the water, calling out, "Let him who loves me follow." The whole army instantly followed, and before Philip could arrive at the same place, the rising of the tide made it impossible for him to cross over, and obliged him to go round by Abbeville.

Edward, after he had crossed the ford, surprised Gondemar and defeated him; and the next day, the 5th of August, had time to post himself in an advantageous position on the plain of Cressy, before Philip and his army came up with him.

It was about three o'clock in the afternoon when Philip's advanced troops came up with the English, and the battle soon became general. At the first onset, the part where the Prince of Wales was posted, was furiously beset: and

---

What retarded the English troops at the passage of the Somme?
How were the English enabled to cross the Somme?
Where did the English king finally post his army?
How did the king of England regard the Black Prince at the battle of Cressy?

the king, who had taken his station on the top of a wind mill, from whence he could overlook the whole field, was importuned to go to his succor; but he refused, saying "He would not deprive his son, and those who were with him, of the honor of the victory."

These words being repeated to the prince and his companions, inspired them with extraordinary courage. After fighting till the close of the evening, the French army was completely discomfited. The king fled, accompanied by only five knights and about sixty soldiers, leaving on that bloody field eighty bannerets, and forty thousand dead and dying men.

When the battle was over, Edward rushed to his son, and embraced him with great affection, while the prince fell on his knees before his father, and craved his blessing Edward stayed three days at Cressy to bury the dead, and then marched to Calais, with the intention of laying siege to it; but, finding it too strong to take by storm, he determined to subdue it by famine. He stationed his fleet directly opposite the harbor, and built huts for his soldiers all around the town, so as completely to invest it, and prevent it from getting assistance either by land or sea. He then sat down patiently waiting the result.

John de Vienne, the governor, seeing himself shut out from all succor, determined to hold out to the utmost, in hopes that Edward's patience would be tired, and that he would raise the siege. And, to make the provisions that were in the town last the longer, he turned seventeen hundred old people, women, and children out of it. When Edward saw all these forlorn wretches thrust out from Calais, and the gates locked upon them, he had compassion on them, and gave them food and money, and let them pass through his army in safety.

After the siege had lasted eleven months, the garrison were in so much distress for want of food, that they were reduced to eat horses, dogs, and cats, till even this failed,

---

How did the battle of Cressy terminate?
In what manner did the English attack Calais?
Did the hard-hearted Edward ever manifest compassion?
On what unworthy conditions did the king of England offer succor to the citizens of Calais?

and John de Vienne found himself obliged to *capitulate* Edward agreed, after some hesitation, that on condition that six of their principal citizens should come to him barefooted, with ropes about their necks, and bring him the keys of the town, he would spare the lives of the rest.

The people of Calais were greatly distressed, when they heard the terms the king of England insisted on. While they were deliberating on what was to be done, Eustace de Pierre, one of the richest merchants of the town, offered himself as the first of the six victims. His example inspired five others with equal courage, and after a sorrowful parting with their friends (for they all expected to be hung), they appeared before Edward.

The king affected, for it is supposed he was not in earnest, to be so much enraged against the people of Calais for holding out so long against him, that he ordered these six men to be executed. Queen Philippa then fell on her knees before him, and besought him to pardon them.

A. D. 1347. The king granted the queen's request, and she had the citizens of Calias conducted to her apartment, where she entertained them honorably, and sent back to the town, bestowing on them rich presents. Edward took possession of Calais on the 4th of August, and turning out all the old inhabitants, peopled it entirely with his own subjects.

The extreme cruelty of Edward's conduct to the people of Calais, and the folly and selfishness of his invasion of France, demonstrate the inhumanity and vain glory of military renown, and the superior wisdom of those who aim at the improvement, and not the aggrandizement of a country. Edward would have shown himself more wise and virtuous, had he remained in England, and promoted the welfare of his subjects at home.

What example of greatness of soul was exhibited by Eustace de Pierre the surrender of Calais?
Who interposed in behalf of the citizens of Calais?
How did Edward III. eventually treat the inhabitants of Calais?
Which is the wiser policy of statesmen, to promote the improvement of a nation within itself, or to extend its *physical power* by foreign conquests?

While these things had been going on in France, David Bruce had been recalled to Scotland, and took the opportunity of Edward's absence to invade England. But queen Philippa acted with such vigor, that an army was speedily raised, and he was taken prisoner near Durham, and afterwards brought to the Tower of London. The queen hastened over to France to carry this good news to Edward, and had arrived just before the surrender of Calais.

Edward's successes in France were suspended for the next six years by a pestilence; so terrible as to be called the Black death, which raged throughout Europe, and proved a greater scourge to the people than even the calamities of war.

A. D. 1350. Philip de Valois died, and was succeeded by his son John. And in 1352 the animosity between the French and English revived with such fury, that neither the pestilence, nor the truces which had been made (but ill kept,) could restrain them from renewing hostilities. The English had generally the advantage, and during the next four years greatly extended their territories in France.

Of those who distinguished themselves in these wars none surpassed the Black Prince. On the 6th of July, 1356, he marched from Bordeaux with an army of 12,000 men, and after taking and burning many towns and villages, he encamped on the 17th of September within two leagues of Poitiers. The same evening the king of France with an army of 60,000 men, encamped within a mile of the prince, who, when he saw the French army advance thus unexpectedly upon him, exclaimed, "God help us! it only remains for us to fight bravely."

The cardinal of Perigord, who was with the French army, was very desirous to prevent an engagement, and rode backwards and forwards several times between John and

---

By whose energetic and useful interference was David Bruce made prisoner?
What greater calamity than war afflicted Europe in the middle of the 14th century.
When did the war between England and France break out?
With what army did the king of France meet the English forces?
What instance of moderation was exhibited by the Black Prince before the battle of Po'tiers?

the prince, in hopes of being able to make peace. The prince said to him, "Save my honor, and the honor of my army, and I will readily listen to any reasonable conditions."

John would consent to nothing, unless the prince and a hundred of his knights would surrender themselves prisoners of war. The reply of the prince to this was, that "he would never be made a prisoner but with sword in hand." The cardinal, finding his endeavors unavailing, retired to Poitiers, and the two armies made themselves ready for battle. The next day, Monday, the 19th of September, the prince drew up his army in excellent order, and riding along the lines, exhorted his men to fight valiantly; saying that he himself was resolved that England should never have to pay a ranson for him.

The king of France formed his army in three divisions, but after engaging with the English and suffering great loss, the commanders of two divisions, misapprehending their danger, fled precipitately from the field of battle. Thus were two-thirds of the French army conquered more by their own fears than by the arms of the enemy.

The king's division, meanwhile, which was alone much superior in numbers to the whole English army, resolutely maintained its ground. The English, encouraged by seeing victory within their grasp, and the French, perceiving that it was now necessary for them to exert their utmost valor, fought desperately; but at length, three of the French generals being killed, the cavalry gave way, and the king, who had shown great personal bravery, was left towards the end of the day with a few followers on the field of battle; and being surrounded by English and Gascons, he and his youngest son were taken prisoners.

The Black Prince, being overpowered by excessive fatigue, had at this time been persuaded to take some rest in a little tent On being informed that John had been tak-

---

How did the Black Prince prepare his army for the encounter with the French?
What happened to two divisions of the French army?
What misfortune overtook the king of France?
Did the Black Prince bear his victory with moderation?

en prisoner, he sent the earl of Warwick to conduct the royal prisoner to his tent. The king was surrounded by soldiers who were clamorously disputing for the possession of him, when the earl arrived, and rescuing him from their turbulence, led him to the prince, who received him with every mark of respect and sympathy.

The prince soon ordered a magnificent supper to be served up, and would not *sit* in king John's presence, but stood behind his chair, trying to soothe and comfort him. The king, much affected by this generous treatment, burst into tears, and declared, that though it was his fate to be a captive he rejoiced that he had fallen into the hands of the most generous and valiant prince alive.

A. D. 1356. The loss of the French in this battle was very great. Besides those who were taken prisoners, there were above 6000 men at arms left dead on the field. The prince, after returning thanks to God for the victory, praised his troops for their conduct, and gave rewards and dignities to those who had more particularly distinguished themselves. He remained at Bordeaux till the 24th of the following April, when he sailed with his royal prisoners to England.

On the approach of the victorious prince and his distinguished prisoners to London, they were met by a train of a thousand citizens in their best array, who conducted them with great state to Westminster. The Black Prince, in a plain dress, and on a little palfrey, rode by the side of the king of France, who was clad in royal robes, and mounted on a beautiful horse. When they arrived at Westminster, king Edward met them, and embraced the captive king with every mark of respect and affection.

The French king and his son were treated, during the three years they remained in England, more like visiters than prisoners. Edward had now two captive monarchs in his kingdom: but on the 3d of October David Bruce regained his liberty, and returned to Scotland, after a captivity of eleven years

---

How did the Black Prince treat king John ?
How did the Black Prince conduct himself towards his army, and when did he return to England?
What was the reception of the Black Prince in England ?
Which two kings were prisoners in England ?

France was thrown into the greatest confusion by the misfortune of her king. The dauphin was appointed regent; and the necessities of the country were so great that he was obliged to enter into a treaty with Edward, by which he gave up to him in full sovereignty a large tract, containing several provinces, to which Edward's town of Bordeaux formed a sort of capital.

John's ranson was fixed at three millions of gold crowns, and forty noblemen were to be sent over to England as hostages till the money should be paid. This treaty, after many tedious negotiations, was at last completed. Edward accompanied John to Calais, and the two kings, with many expressions of affection and regard, parted on the 24th of October, 1360.

Edward then returned to England, after bestowing all his newly acquired French provinces on the Black Prince, who went to hold his court at Bordeaux with the Princess Joan his wife, the beautiful daughter and heiress of the earl of Kent. She had before been married to Sir John Holland, by whom she had two sons.

A. D. 1364. The duke of Anjou, one of the hostages for the payment of John's ranson, having escaped, and the dauphin making some difficulty in fulfilling the articles of the late treaty, John, who felt that by this breach of faith his own honor was impeached, returned to England to put himself again in Edward's hands; and, falling ill of a fever, he died at the palace of the Savoy early in the year 1364.

The Black Prince is among the chief favorites of the English nation. His warlike qualities and achievements are accounted the glory of his times. But the wars in which he engaged were not just, therefore we can only admire the qualities of his heart. These would have adorned any condition of life, and would have induced good and great enterprises if he had lived in a better age, and had he been bred

---

What became the capital of the English possessions in France?
When did John return to France?
When did king Edward return to England?
Where did the king of France die?
How ought the character of the Black Prince to be regarded?

to the services of peace instead of the unhappy profession of arms.

After having made himself lord of a considerable portion of France, the Black Prince engaged in the affairs of Spain. Pedro the Cruel, and his half-brother, Henry of Trastamare, contended for the throne of Spain. Pedro's was the hereditary right, and Henry was the better man, and more desirable king. Pedro implored the assistance of the Black Prince and he heartily engaged in the cause of the dethroned monarch, and, accompanied by his brother John of Gaunt, duke of Lancaster, marched an army of 30,000 men into Spain.

Henry of Trastamare met them with a force of more than 100,000 men; and the battle of Najara was fought between these two unequal armies on the 3d of April, 1367. In this battle the skill and valor of the prince and his well-disciplined troops overthrew the immense host of Spain; and, against the wishes and endeavors of the whole nation, replaced a hated tyrant on the throne.

Pedro no sooner found himself thus re-established, than he forgot his obligations to the Black Prince, and treated him with great ingratitude. Many of the English soldiers fell victims to the unhealthiness of the climate: the health of the prince also suffered exceedingly, and, in great disgust at the conduct of Pedro, he returned with the shattered remains of his army to Bordeaux.

Henry of Trastamare, as soon as he knew that the English had withdrawn from Spain, returned there, and, by the assistance of the king of France, attacked and defeated Pedro in a pitched battle, and slew him with his own hand. Henry then peaceably ascended the throne, and the two daughters of Pedro fled to Bordeaux, and again claimed the protection of the Prince of Wales.

These two princesses soon after married two of the English princes, the third and fourth sons of king Edward Constantia, the eldest, married John of Gaunt, whose first

---

In the cause of what Spanish prince did the Black Prince engage?
Did the Black Prince serve a good or a bad cause in Spain?
What were the unhappy consequences of the Spanish enterprise to the English army?
What was the end of Pedro the cruel?
Who married the daughters of Pedro?

wife had been daughter and heiress of the earl of Lancaster. Isabella, the other sister, married Edward, duke of
York. The duke of Lancaster immediately on his marriage assumed, in right of his wife, the title of king of
Castile.

The Black Prince, from the time of his return from
Spain, became subject to continual ill health. After some
months of constant suffering, he became unable from weakness, to mount his horse, and was obliged to give up the
command of his army. From this time the power of England on the continent declined; every expedition was unsuccessful, and the fleet suffered a signal defeat off Rochfort.

The prince returned to England, as a last hope, for the
recovery of his health; but after lingering some time, he
died on the 8th of June, 1376, in the forty-seventh year of
his age. His death was felt throughout England, both as
a private and as a public loss. And though the parliament was at that time much displeased with the king on the
subject of raising subsidies, it expressed the utmost sympathy in his grief at his son's death, and showed its respect
for the memory of the prince by attending his remains to
Canterbury, where his monument is still to be seen.

The loss of his son, broke the heart of the old king, who
did not long survive him, and died at his palace at Shene,
June 1, 1377, in the sixty-fifth year of his age, and the fifty-
first of his reign. Queen Philippa is mentioned by all
historians in the highest terms of praise. She and Edward
lived together in uninterrupted harmony forty-two years.

Their sons were: Edward the Black Prince; Lionel,
duke of Clarence, who died in 1368, leaving an only daughter, married to Edmund Mortimer, earl of March; John
of Gaunt; Edmund, duke of York, married Isabella of
Castile, by whom he had Richard, who married his cousin
Anne Mortimer, and was the father of Richard duke of
York; Thomas of Woodstock, duke of Gloucester; and

From what time did the Black Prince decline in health, and what
was the state of the English power abroad?

When did the Black Prince die, and what effect was produced by his
death?

Did Edward III. long survive his son, and how long did he live after
his marriage?

Who were the children of Edward III.?

three other sons, who died young, and four daughters
The five sons of Edward III. were all made dukes by
their father. They were the first persons who bore that
title in England. The Black Prince was the first duke of
Cornwall.

Edward III. founded the order of the Knights of the
Garter. He rebuilt and enlarged the castle of Windsor.
He also rebuilt St. Stephen's chapel at Westminster, where
the house of commons held its assemblies till 1834, when
it was consumed by fire. Its first assemblies were held in
the chapter-house at Westminster.

The division of the house of parliament into lords and
commons, the exact commencement of which is not
known, was thoroughly established in this reign.

The laws and statutes were in this reign commanded to
be written in English, having been written in Norman
French ever since the Conquest.

It has been supposed that Edward owed the first of his
victories to the use of gunpowder, which was first used,

What order of knights was founded by Edward III. ?
What edifices were built in this reign ?
What was thoroughly established in this reign ?
When were English laws first written in the English language ?
When was gunpowder first used by the English, and by whom was it
invented ?

it is said, in war, in the battle of Cressy. Gunpowder was first invented by Friar Bacon, as some say, though Schwartz, a German, also claims the merit of the discovery.

Among the customs of European courts and great families was that of keeping a professed *jester*. Kings and nobles amongst the number of their attendants, had one whose business it was to play the fool, and who was privileged to say or do any thing that was ridiculous for the sake of diverting those about him.

The fool's dress was motley; that is, made of different colors. He also wore a cap made with two great ears, to resemble asses' ears, and he had little sheep-bells fastened to different parts of his dress.

All the diversions of the English, whatever they may be now, were formerly of a noisy and tumultuous kind. When a nobleman opened his castle to his guests, on occasions of public festivity, the courts and halls were crowded with minstrels, mimics, jugglers, and tumblers; and there was a confusion and mixture of feasting, drinking, dancing, singing, tumbling, and buffoonery, which would appear very disreputable now in any nobleman's mansion.

There was not at that time a playhouse in the whole kingdom. Jugglers, &c. used to travel about the country, and, when they were not received into private houses, they exhibited their tricks in carts in the open streets. The streets used then to be scenes of great gaiety; for we are told that the servants of the citizens of London were accustomed on summer evenings to dance before their masters' doors.

Queens and persons of high rank were occasionally conveyed in horse-litters. These litters were like a bedstead fastened by shafts before and behind to two horses. Over the litter there was a canopy held, supported on four long poles, each pole carried by a man on foot; so that this mode of travelling was not a very expeditious one.

Who were professed jesters and how did they dress?
How did the English divert themselves in the 14th century?
Were there houses for jugglers, &c. to exhibit in?
What carriages were used by people of rank in the reign of Edward III.?

CHAPTER XVII.

RICHARD II.

[Years after Christ, 1377 1399.]

Richard of Bordeaux was the only surviving child of Edward the Black Prince, and was proclaimed king on the death of his grandfather. There was no regent appointed; but the young king's three uncles took the direction of affairs upon themselves. John of Gaunt, the eldest of the three had a high spirit, and great ambition. Being a man of activity and exertion, he had had, even in his father's lifetime, great authority in the state. The duke of York was well meaning but indolent, and of slender capacity. The duke of Gloucester was turbulent, bold and meddling; but John being the oldest, had the chief sway in their councils. Yet he soon showed himself ill qualified to be the leader of affairs, and plunged the country into great distresses by several unprofitable expeditions both into France and Scotland.

A. D. 1381. A poll-tax of a shilling a head, levied on all persons throughout the kingdom above the age of fifteen, raised the discontents of the lower orders of the people to the greatest pitch. This tax was very oppressive in that age, when a shilling would buy ten times as much food as it will now buy, and was therefore equal to ten shillings at present, and very few poor people could earn a shilling.

One of the persons employed to collect this tax having been killed in a quarrel with a tyler at Deptford, called Walter, a crowd collected; and from this small beginning a serious disturbance broke forth. Wat Tyler, as he is called, took upon himself the command of the insurgents and sent messages into the neighboring counties, inviting

---

Who was Richard II., and who were directors of English affairs during his minority?
What tax was levied upon the English people in 1381, and why was it very oppressive?
Who instigated the oppressed people to rebellion?

the common people to join together, to shake off the yoke of servitude, and to take vengeance on their oppressive masters.

The people willingly obeyed the summons, and leaving their employments, hastened to Blackheath, the place of rendezvous, burning the houses and plundering the estates of the nobility and gentry as they passed. The mob, when assembled at Blackheath amounted to 300,000 men. Wat Tyler and another man, called from his business as a thresher, Jack Straw, were appointed leaders, and they all set off towards London. The king's uncles were absent from the kingdom; and this insurrection was so sudden, that no preparations had been made for checking it. The king, with his mother, and a small number of the nobility, took refuge in the Tower of London.

It is needless to repeat all the violences of this mob, but it is but justice to the courage of the young king to relate that he determined to meet these enraged people and hear their grievances. The next day, June the 14th, the king, with a few unarmed attendants, left the tower, and proceeded to the appointed place, where he found about 60,000 persons assembled. The king, in a gentle manner, asked them what they wanted. They replied, " they wanted the freedom of themselves and children."

The king promised that their desire should be granted, and that, if they would return to their homes, he would give them charters for their *freedom*. Immediately thirty clerks were set to work to write these charters, which were given to all who demanded them, and immediately the mob dispersed, and every one returned peaceably and contentedly to his home.

The freedom for which they asked was, probably, exemption from certain services to the superior classes, and from the slavery from which the people of England were not then entirely exempted.

In the meantime Wat Tyler, with Jack Straw, and the most desperate of the party, instead of going with the

---

How did the insurgents proceed?
Did Richard manfully meet the insurgents?
Did the king satisfy the insurgents?
What was the *freedom* which the English people demanded?
Did all the insurgents meet Richard II.?

others to meet the king at Mile-End, had broken into the Tower of London, and murdered the archbishop of Canterbury, the lord chancellor, and many other persons whom they found there. Their design was to seize on the young king, to murder all the nobility, and to plunder and then burn London.

On the following day, June 15, these desperate men were stopped in their mad career. The king was passing through Smithfield, attended by the lord mayor and about sixty horsemen. Wat Tyler met them with 20,000 of the insurgents, and, riding up to the king, behaved with so much audacity, that Walworth, the mayor, unable to endure the sight of this clown's insolence to his sovereign, drew his sword, and felled him to the ground with a blow.

The rioters seemed for a moment stunned with surprise by the loss of their leader; and before they had time to recover themselves, the young king, with astonishing presence of mind, rode up to them, and said: "My friends, be not concerned for the loss of your unworthy leader I will be your leader." And turning his horse, he rode into the open fields at the head of the multitude, who seemed to follow him unconciously, and without knowing why.

A cry, meanwhile, had arisen in the city, that the king had fallen into the hands of the rebels, and instantly some thousands of brave men flew to his rescue. When they appeared, the mob, seized with a panic, fell on their knees before him, imploring his pardon, which he granted them, on condition that they dispersed and returned to their homes. This they all did: and thus the insurrection melted away, like snow in a sudden thaw.

Richard's conduct during this disturbance naturally led his people to imagine that he had inherited the courage and vigor of mind of the Plantagenets: but the fair promise which he had thus given was soon blighted. He betrayed, as he advanced in age, a weakness and frivolity which made him totally unfit for the government of a kingdom.

What happened at Smithfield, June 15th, 1381?
What admirable presence of mind was exhibited by Richard II.?
What was the end of the insurrection?
Did Richard II. sustain the character he manifested in his youth?

Richard's person was extraordinarily beautiful: he loved pomp and show, hated business, and was very fickle When the ferment of the insurrection was over, and the country was restored to tranquillity, he revoked all the charters of freedom which he had given, and compelled the bond-tenants to return to their state of villainage, and perform all their accustomed services to their lords.

During the next five years nothing material occurred, and the chief business of the parliament was to keep a check on the duke of Lancaster who wanted to drain England of men and money to prosecute the claim on the crown of Castile which he possessed in right of his wife, the daughter of Pedro the Cruel. It was long before he could prevail on the parliament to grant the necessary supplies.

A. D. 1386. Lancaster raised a large army, and, taking the duchess and his three daughters with him, sailed for Spain. He landed at Corunna, and his troops were suffered to overrun the province of Gallicia without much opposition; for the king of Castile, who was son of Henry of Trastamare, trusting that the same causes would destroy the forces of the duke of Lancaster which had formerly been so fatal to those of the Black Prince, avoided meeting him in the field.

This enterprise did not obtain the crown of Castile, but after much fruitless fighting, Lancaster withdrew his claim, and married one of his daughters to the king of Portugal, and another to the prince royal of Castile, the son of Henry Trastamare. The duke was well pleased at having thus secured the crown to his posterity, and returned to England in 1389.

During the three years of Lancaster's absence, Richard, by his abuse of the royal power in displacing the officers of the government, and putting in their places his own idle favorites, had made himself exceedingly unpopular. The parliament had also made great stretches of power; had

---

From 1381 to 1386, what occurred in England?
What army, for the conquest of Castile, was raised by John of Gaunt?
What was the result of Lancaster's expedition?
Did Richard II. lose his popularity with the English nation?

condemned and imprisoned one of the king's chief favorites, Michael de la Pole, earl of Suffolk, and obliged the king to sign a commission of regency to fourteen noblemen, thus divesting himself of all authority.

The duke of Gloucester was at the head of the party against his nephew, and, not contented with reducing him to be a mere cypher, determined to destroy every friend that remained to him. Richard, though he had assembled around him so many vicious characters, still preserved his respect for sir Simon Burleigh, a good and venerable old man, who had been appointed his tutor by the Black Prince by whom he had been greatly esteemed.

Neither that circumstance, nor Burleigh's age and virtue, could preserve him from the malice of Gloucester, who procured his condemnation on a pretended charge of high treason. And though the queen, Anne of Bohemia, remained on her knees three hours before the inexorable Gloucester, entreating for his life, he was executed as a common traitor. De la Pole and a few others saved their lives by a timely flight. The rest of the king's favorites were put to death.

A D. 1388. In this year was fought the battle of Otterburn, between the English and Scots, in which Lord Douglas was killed, and Henry Percy, better known as Harry Hotspur, was taken prisoner. It was an engagement of no material consequence, but Shakspeare has made it celebrated.

After a quiet submission of about a year and a half to his uncle's tyranny, Richard suddenly roused himself into exertion, and asserted his own right to hold the reins of government. He took the great seal from archbishop Arundel, a creature of the duke of Gloucester, and gave it to William of Wykeham, and acted with so much sense and vigor, that Gloucester, and his party were thunderstruck, and relinquished their assumed authority. The duke, however, was not of a character to submit patiently:

Who plotted the destruction of Richard, and who was his best friend?
How was sir Simon Burleigh treated?
What battle was fought by the English in 1388?
Did Richard ever act with energy?

and though the king conferred on him grants of immense value, in hopes to purchase his friendship, was continually engaged in factious schemes.

Gloucester at length retired to his castle of Pleshy, in Essex, where frequent meetings were held by the discontented nobles. The king hearing that his uncle had a design of seizing his person, determined to be beforehand with him, and caused him to be seized by surprise, and conveyed to Calais. His chief associates, the earls of Warwick and Arundel, were committed prisoners to the Tower. The duke of Gloucester was then accused of high treason, and a parliament was summoned at Westminster, Sept. 17th, 1397, to proceed on his trial.

When the day of trial arrived, the governor of Calais was summoned to produce his prisoner: but instead of producing him, he sent word that Gloucester had died in prison. The exact particulars of his death were never known; but there is every reason to believe that he was murdered by the king's orders. The king is supposed to have acted on this occasion by the advice, advice he lived bitterly to rue, of the earl of St. Paul, a French gentleman.

The following year a quarrel arose between Henry Bolingbroke, John of Gaunt's only son, and the duke of Norfolk. It seems that the duke had spoken of the king as having instigated the murder of Gloucester; and that Bolingbroke, indignant at the charge, took it up as a personal offence. Richard, whose guilty conscience did not dare to have the matter openly discussed in a court of justice, adjudged it to be determined by a *single combat*, which was to be fought between Norfolk and Bolingbroke, on Sept. 16th, 1398, at Coventry.

The nobles and the parliament were already assembled to see the fight, and the combatants had entered the lists, when the king forbade them to engage, and banished Hen-

---

How did the king proceed against the duke of Gloucester?
What became of the duke of Gloucester?
What dispute arose between Henry Bolingbroke and the duke of Norfolk?
How was the quarrel of Bolingbroke ordered to be settled?
How was the quarrel of Bolingbroke concluded?

ry Bolingbroke for ten years, and the duke of Norfolk for life; who both left the kingdom highly dissatisfied with the sentence.

It is apparent by this arbitrary sentence of banishment, without any offence against the laws being proved, by the trial by combat, and many executions upon frivolous pretences, that life was held cheap, and that the will of the prince was superior to law in England in this rude age.

A. D. 1399. John of Gaunt died, and Richard seized on all his great estates. Bolingbroke was at the court of France when he was informed of this injustice done to him. He resolved immediately to reclaim his rights; and oeing assisted with ships and soldiers by the duke of Bretagne, he came over to England, and landed July 4, 1399, at Ravensburgh, a town in Yorkshire, near the mouth of the Humber, which has been long washed away by the encroachments of the sea. The king was at that time in Ireland, where he had taken a considerable force, for the purpose of quelling an insurrection, and his uncle the duke of York, was left regent during his absence.

It is probable that when Bolingbroke first landed, he had no view beyond that of getting back his inheritance: but finding himself joined by the earls of Northumberland and Westmoreland, and by other powerful noblemen, he soon began to entertain designs upon the throne itself. The duke of York was preparing on the king's part to make resistance; but he too being persuaded by Bolingbroke, in an interview which he had with him at Bristol, that he was only come to claim his own inheritance, joined him with the forces under his command.

Richard himself soon after landed at Milford Haven, and finding that his uncle, instead of having an army ready for his service, had gone over to the party of Bolingbroke retired with a few friends to Conway. After some short negotiations, he imprudently agreed to a personal conference with his cousin at Flint Castle: but as he was on his

---

Was *law* or the will of princes more powerful in the fourteenth century?
When did John of Gaunt die, and what course was taken by his son?
What part did the duke of York take in regard to his nephew?
How did Henry Bolingbroke treat Richard II?

way there with a few attendants, he was met by Bolingbroke, who conveyed him to London, and sent him prisoner to the Tower.

Bolingbroke at first told the king he only intended to assist him to the government of the kingdom; but as soon as he found him completely in his power, he openly declared his own design upon the crown, and obliged him to sign a paper containing his resignation of the kingdom. This paper was read before the parliament, and approved of by them. A list of crimes and errors of which the king had been guilty was read, and he was then declared solemnly deposed; and the archbishops of York and Canterbury led Bolingbroke to the empty throne, and placed him on it.

Richard was conveyed a prisoner to Pontefract Castle, and there, it is supposed, was put to death in the beginning of the year 1400. in the thirty-fifth year of his age and the twenty-fourth of his reign. He married, first, Anne of Bohemia; and, secondly, Isabella of France. and left no children.

In this reign the reformation of religion made some advances. It has already been told that the Catholic religion was the christianity of England. It continued to be so till what is called the Reformation took place in the sixteenth century. John Wickliffe, a priest who held the living of Lutterworth, in Leicestershire, became known, in the latter end of Edward the Third's reign, by a controversy with the begging friars. He afterwards attacked the corruptions of the whole body of the monastic clergy; and though he might not, perhaps, be the first who discovered the fallacy of many of the doctrines of the church of Rome, he was the first who dared to invegh against them publicly.

Did the English parliament repose Richard II. ?
Where did Richard die .
What was the state of religion in England during the reign of Richard II ?

During Wickliffe's life no positive step was taken to bring about the reformation of the church; yet he prepared the way for that which afterwards followed, by awakening the people to the conviction that the Romish church had gone far astray from the purity of the Christian religion. Till the time of Wickliffe, there were none but Latin bibles, which were only to be found in possession of the priests; so that the mass of the people were kept in total ignorance of the scriptures.

A. D. 1380. Wickliffe undertook and completed a translation of the bible into English This, though highly acceptable to the laity in general, was universally disapproved of by the bishops, and all who were attached to the Roman church; and a bill was brought into the house of lords to suppress the English translation. But the bill was rejected, in consequence of the warm remonstrance of John of Gaunt, who concluded by saying, " We will not be the dregs of all, seeing that other nations have the law of God, which is the law of our faith, written in their own language."

Wickliffe was not the first who gave the English a translation of the bible. The old Saxon bishop Adhelm translated the book of Psalms into Saxon in the year 706. The venerable Bede also made a translation of the whole Bible; but when the popes began to rule the affairs of the English church, none but Latin bibles were allowed to be used, in order to keep the people in ignorance, and that the priests and monks might make them believe what they pleased. The followers of Wickliffe were called Lollards, a name given them by their adversaries out of derision.

It was mentioned that the mob in the time of Richard II. destroyed the Temple. The Temple is the name of a building that was once a monastic house, belonging to the Knights Templars, an order of monkish knights, who instead of living in monasteries, and wearing cowls, put on armor, and devoted themselves to the protection of those who went on pilgrimages to the Holy Land. They also

---

What influence had Wickliffe upon the people of England?
How was Wickliffe's translation of the bible regarded?
Was Wickliffe's translation the first English bible?
What was the Temple and who were the Knights Templars?

took on themselves the vow of celibacy, and observed other monastic rules.

This order was after a time dissolved; and Edward the Third granted their house, which from them was called the Temple, to the students of the common law, by whom it is still inhabited. The Temple church, built by the Templars, after the model of that of the Holy Sepulchre, is one of the most curious in London, as well on account of its antiquity and architecture, as for the monuments it contains of the old knights.

The begging friars were people who, because our Saviour and the apostles avoided worldly riches and honors, pretended to imitate them by going about begging; and who seemed to think that poverty and beggary were the essence of religion.

The exceedingly ferocious manners of the age are strikingly exemplified in the following anecdote. King Richard marched into the north in 1385 to check an incursion of the Scots, and halted some days at Beverley by the way. His army was too numerous to be lodged in the town, and part was, therefore, dispersed in the neighboring villages. A poor German knight who was one of those who were so dispersed, was looking for a lodging, and trying, in very bad English, to make himself understood.

A squire belonging to the king's half brother, Sir John Holland, began to abuse the poor German, and laughed at him; but an archer of sir Ralph Stafford's took part with the German, and shot the squire. When sir John Holland heard of his squire's death, he made a vow that he would neither eat nor drink till he had killed the German knight, the innocent cause of the affray; and riding furiously about the lanes in search of him, till it was dark, he met sir Ralph Stafford in a narrow lane, and struck at him with his sword as he passed. The blow was fatal; but sir John Holland rode on, without knowing perhaps at the moment whom he had killed.

What building in London is now called the Temple?
Who were the begging friars?
What disregard of life, and rudeness, are illustrated in a circumstance which occurred in 1385?
By whom was sir Ralph Stafford killed?

When men in that age had committed crimes they fled to a church, and there they could not be taken, because the law forbade to violate the sanctuary. This afforded impunity to many violent acts. Sir John Holland would have been hanged for the murder, had he not taken refuge in the sanctuary of St. John of Beverley. The king was exceedingly angry with him, and refused to pardon him; and his mother, the widow of the Black Prince, was so miserable that she died of grief. Holland afterwards obtained the king's pardon, and was made duke of Exeter, and married John of Gaunt's youngest daughter.

Though the preceding instance exhibits lawless and inhuman manners, the history of that age will show that virtuous men manifested themselves in the midst of crime. The following example of self-discipline is extraordinary, and is a proper sequel to the anecdote of sir John Holland: Sir Ralph was a very accomplished young man, and the only son of an old lord Stafford, who was then with the royal army. Lord Stafford, as soon as he had recovered from the first burst of grief at his son's shocking murder, went to the king and told him, that as he was on his road to fight the Scots, he would not let his grief prevent him from serving his country in the hour of need. "And," added he, "during this expedition, I shall not think of my affliction: for I like not that the Scots be rejoiced at the misery of the earl of Stafford."

The afflicted old man accordingly accompanied the army into Scotland, and performed all the duties of a soldier and commander, as if he had had a heart free from sorrow: but as soon as the expedition had ended, he went to the Holy Land, on account of his son's death, and did not live to return

---

The fourteenth century, in relation to England, was a

Why was not sir John Holland punished for killing sir R. Stafford?

Did many virtues flourish among the crimes of the fourteenth century?

How did lord Stafford bear his son's murder, and where did he die?

What was the intellectual character of the fourteenth century in England?

period of ignorance, slavery, and superstition; but ignorance in this period obviously gave way to progressive knowledge; slavery to political liberty; and superstition to the influences of true religion.

A great improvement in the English language was attained in this century. The language used under the Saxons in England was the Anglo-Saxon; that introduced by the Normans and afterwards extensively written and spoken, was the Norman French; and that used in the prayers of the churches was the Latin. Anglo-Saxon, Norman, and Latin make up the present English.

The first histories and poems known in England were written in these primitive languages, but in the latter end of the fourteenth century there had been formed a proper English language. The laws were written in it, the scriptures were also translated into it, and poetry was written in English.

Liberty of thought is a right which all men have, to examine, each for himself, what is right and wrong, and what is true or false. Most persons believe what those who are older than themselves say; but when we are grown to be men and women, it is proper to inquire what is right and wrong, true and false, as if we had never been informed, and then each man will gain wisdom for himself.

In rude ages, poor and very ignorant people are not allowed to determine what is right and wrong, and what is true and false—the powerful determine for them. Thus it was in the fourteenth century. The barons told their vassals they had no rights of their own, and the priests told all people they could not understand the scriptures without their explanations, and the vassals and people submitted.

But in that very age, *liberty of thought* began to assert itself; the poor people said, We are *men* and not brutes—we ought not to be bought and sold like cattle; and Wickliffe and his followers said to the people, The Roman Ca

---

What was the progress of language in England?
What was first written in English?
What is liberty of thought, and how should it be used?
Who restrained the poor people of England from improving their minds?
How are the poor gradually enlightened?

tholic priests deceive you—you can understand the Scriptures if you will read them. You must be taught to read. Here is the bible in your own English language.

Those who claimed freedom from Richard II. only demanded their natural rights. They exerted natural and political liberty not known before in England. Wickliffe demanded a still more valuable liberty—the liberty to seek and to declare truth, which makes men free from ignorance and prejudice.

The poets of this age were reformers, and enlightened men. The first poem of any considerable length in the English language was written by Robert Langlande, a priest. It describes the Christain life, and the abuses of religion under the popes. Geoffrey Chaucer was another poet of that age who reproved the vices of the clergy.

John of Gaunt, though he undertook some unjust wars, was a great man, a lover of religious freedom, and a companion of wise men: he honored Wickliffe, and was the friend of Chaucer. He married for his last wife, Catharine Swynford, the sister-in-law of Chaucer. Chaucer is called the father of English poetry—he died in 1400.

What were the just demands of the English people during the reign of Richard II.?
Who were he English poets?
Was John of Gaunt an enlightened man?

CHAPTER XVIII

HENRY IV.

[Years after Christ, 1399—1413.

Rustics of the 15th century.

Henry IV., only a few months before he obtained the crown, was wandering about, a banished man, in a foreign land. His success was the more surprising, because he had no personal qualities, except the kingly quality of courage, to attach the people to him. Nor had he, even after Richard, the next right of inheritance; for the undoubted heir was Edmund Mortimer, earl of March, whose grandmother was daughter of Lionel, duke of Clarence, elder brother of John of Gaunt. Mortimer was at this time a child of seven years old: and though the parliament passed him by, and settled the crown on Bolingbroke and his heirs, yet Henry thought him too dangerous a rival to be at large, and kept him a prisoner at Windsor.

The king himself was in no enviable condition. His life was made miserable by continual apprehensions of plots

---

Was Henry IV. the hereditary successor to the crown of England?
What disturbed the tranquility of Henry IV., and how did his reign commence?

and conspiracies, apprehensions not without cause. He had possessed the crown only a few months, when a dangerous conspiracy against him was entered into by some nobles attached to Richard, which soon after broke out into an open war, but a division ensuing between the leaders of the party, it was soon and easily crushed. All the nobles who were taken in arms were beheaded, and thus a bloody beginning was made to this distracted reign.

In the year 1401, the king had a very narrow escape. One night he perceived concealed in his bead, just as he was stepping into it, a steel instrument with three sharp points, which would either have killed him, or wounded him severely, had he lain down on it. The author of this attempt was never discovered.

Besides his secret enemies, Henry had a formidable open foe in Owen Glendower, a Welsh gentleman of high spirit and courage. Glendower proclaimed himself prince of Wales, and his countrymen crowded to his standard. Favored by the mountainous nature of the country, he was able to maintain himself for seven years against all the endeavors of Henry to subdue him, and frequently made incursions into the English border, and plundered and killed the inhabitants.

A. D. 1402. The Scots commanded by earl Douglas, entered England with 10,000 men. They were defeated at Homildon Hill by the earl of Northumberland and his son, Henry Hotspur. Douglas, with many others, was taken. Immediately on the news of this victory, Henry sent to prohibit Northumberland from ransoming any of the prisoners; a command the Percies resented violently, and the more so, as it was chiefly by their means that Henry had been enabled to ascend the throne.

Northumberland, with his brother the earl of Westmoreland, and his son Hotspur, in talking over this business together, more and more inflamed their mutual resentments; and Hotspur, who had that name from his fiery temper,—urged on his father and uncle till they resolved

---

Were any attempts made to kill Henry IV.?
Who rebelled against Henry in Wales?
What occurred in 1402?
With whom did the Percies conspire against Henry IV.?

8

to dethrone Henry. To strengthen their cause, they gave Douglas his liberty, and engaged him to assist their enterprise. They also admitted Glendower into their confederacy who undertook to join them on the borders of Wales, with 10,000 men.

A. D. 1403. Douglas and Hotspur, leaving Northumberland to follow him with the main army, reached Shrewsbury early in July, but before they could be joined by Glendower the king's army approached; and on the morning of July 21, the great battle of Shrewsbury was fought. The king commanded the main body of his army, and displayed the utmost prudence as a general, and courage as a soldier.

Prince Henry, the king's eldest son, began on this day his career of military glory; and, though he was wounded by an arrow in the face, would not quit the field. On the other side, young Hotspur and the earl of Douglas performed prodigies of valor. The two armies were nearly equal in numbers, each consisting of about 14,000 men, and the victory remained some hours undecided.

The king had caused several of his attendants to wear armor resembling his own, and Douglas, who ardently desired to engage with him personally, sought him over the field of battle, and often thought he had fought with him, and slain him; but he as often found himself deceived, and was at last himself taken prisoner. Hotspur was killed, and the royal army at length remained master of the field, on which six thousand men lay dead.

When Northumberland heard of his son's death, he disbanded his army, and retired, almost broken-hearted, to Warkworth. But when Henry proclaimed a pardon to all the rebels who would return to their allegiance, the earl, encouraged by these gentle measures, came to York, where the king then was, and threw himself at his feet, to implore his mercy and forgiveness. At first the king received him with a frown; but, remembering how much he owed to his former services, and pitying the poor old man's bereaved

---

When was the battle of Shrewsbury fought?
What courage was displayed in the field of Shrewsbury?
What happened to Douglas and Hotspur at Shrewsbury?
What generosity to Northumberland did Henry IV manifest?

condition, he granted him his life, and soon after restored to him almost all his honors and estates.

A. D. 1405. Notwithstanding the attempts Henry had made to conciliate the people, they became more and more discontented; and another formidable insurrection broke out, of which Scroop, archbishop of York, and Thomas Mowbray, earl marshal, were the active movers. They soon assembled a body of 15,000 men, and encamped on Skipton Moor, expecting to be joined by the earl of Northumberland, who had again taken arms against the king.

To suppress this sudden and formidable rising, the king sent Ralph Nevil, earl of Westmoreland, into the north. Nevil, finding the insurgents more numerous than he had expected, had recourse to stratagem. He sent to inquire of them what were their grievances, that if reasonable, they might be redressed.

Nevil next invited the archbishop and the other leaders of the party to a conference, in which they stated their demands. To all of these Nevil agreed, and solemnly pledged himself to procure the king's ratification. When he had thus completely lulled into security, Nevil persuaded them to send messengers to their troops, to tell them that peace was made, and that they might return to their own homes; promising, on his own part to do the same.

But while the archbishop, unsuspicious of any fraud, sent orders to his men to disband, the wily Nevil gave his own message to a person whom he had previously ordered not to deliver it: and, as soon as he had perceived that the insurgents' camp was broken up, and the men dispersing, he caused a body of his own soldiers to come suddenly to the place of conference, and carry off the archbishop, and all those who had accompanied him, prisoners to Pontefract. They were every one beheaded even Scroop himself, which was the first instance in England of a capital punishment being inflicted on a bishop The deceitful conduct of Nevil cannot be too much detested.

Did Northumberland show gratitude to his king?
By what deceitful transaction did the earl of Westmoreland mislead the archbishop of York, &c.?
What terms did Nevil offer the insurgents?
How were Scroop and his adherents betrayed?

A. D. 1408. Northumberland, on hearing of the death of his friends, fled first into Scotland, and afterwards into Wales, where he wandered about for some time. He afterwards returned into the north, and made a last attempt to overthrow the power of Henry: but his party was defeated, and himself slain, in a battle on Bramham Moor, in Yorkshire.

The repeated ill-success of these rebellions at length subdued all the king's enemies. Even the Welsh, despairing to establish their independence, abandoned Glendower, who wandered about in various disguises, till he died at his daughter's house at Mornington, in Herefordshire, in 1415

A. D. 1415. A most unexpected chance threw into the hands of Henry, the only son of Robert III., king of Scotland. David Bruce, having no children, had been succeeded by his sister's son, Robert Stuart, who died in 1390, leaving two sons. The eldest, Robert III., succeeded his father, and was a prince of a very feeble character; the other son was duke of Albany, a restless and ambitious man, who got the affairs of the nation into his hands, and ruled them imperiously, and even imprisoned and starved to death the elder of his brother's two sons.

Robert, anxious to save his other son, James, (afterwards king James I. of Scotland,) from falling into the hands of his cruel uncle, was desirous to send him to France, and committed him to the care of the earl of Orkney, whom he directed to conduct him to that country. They embarked secretly, and set sail, but their vessel was taken off Flamborough head by an English privateer; and the prince and his attendants were conveyed to Henry who, on being told by the earl of Orkney that the young prince was going to

---

What became of Northumberland?
How did the rebellion terminate in this reign?
Who reigned in Scotland in 1415?
How did Prince James of Scotland fall into the custody of Henry IV.?

France to learn French, said, "I understand French, and therefore ought to be entrusted with his education."

Henry then committed James and his attendants close prisoners to the Tower. When the poor old father heard the news, it threw him into such agonies of grief that he died in three days. James remained a prisoner till he was twenty-eight years old, the duke of Albany being in the meantime regent in Scotland; but Henry made some amends for his unjust conduct towards the young prince, by giving him the best education the times afforded, so that he proved, when restored to his kingdom, the most accomplished monarch that ever sat upon the Scottish throne.

This prince's history is very affecting. He remained in England eighteen years, but he was not kept in close confinement all that time. He had an excellent tutor appointed to superintend his education; he learnt tilting, wrestling, archery, and all the exercises then usually practised by young men of rank; and excelled in these exercises, as well as in the more refined studies of oratory, jurisprudence, and the philosophy of those times.

James had an extraordinary talent for music and poetry. Indeed some say that he was the inventor of that sweet and plaintive style of music which is peculiar to Scotland; but others assert with more probability, that he merely reduced the wildness of Scottish melody to the rules of composition. His poetry is extraordinary, considering the time and circumstance, in which it was written.

When the duke of Albany died, the people of Scotland paid their king's ransom, and he returned home. After reigning fifteen years he was assassinated. His whole life was not, however, unfortunate, for he lived to do much good to his native country. He made excellent laws, and reformed many abuses; and conducted himself with so much firmness, justice, and good policy, that the name of James the First of Scotland is still held in reverence. While at

---

What effect had the capture of the prince upon his father, and how was the former treated in England?
How was prince James educated?
Was prince James possessed of extraordinary genius?
What is the sequel of prince James's history?

Windsor, he became attached to Jane Beaufort, granddaughter of John of Gaunt, whom he married as soon as he was restored to his own country.

At last Henry had some respite from his enemies, but he suffered greatly from bad health; and soon after the death of archbishop Scroop he became afflicted with a loathsome eruption in his face, which the common people considered as a punishment for the death of that prelate, who was much beloved by them.

The king's happiness was also much embittered by the wildness of his eldest son, who, when not engaged in military exploits, in which he displayed great courage and ability, passed his time in a very licentious way. One of the prince's companions was once committed for a robbery, and brought before the chief justice, Gascoigne. Gascoigne refusing to release the offender, the prince drew his sword, and behaved in a very violent manner, on which the chief justice ordered him to be taken to the King's Bench prison. The prince, conscious of the impropriety of his own conduct, submitted to the punishment; and when this incident was related to the king, he exclaimed, "Happy the monarch who possesses a judge so resolute in the discharge of his duty, and a son so willing to submit to the laws!"

In the last year of Henry's reign he sent a body of troops to France, under the command of his second son, the duke of Clarence, to join the duke of Burgundy in a civil war which he was carrying on against the duke of Orleans. He, no doubt, hoped that, by fomenting the distractions of that unhappy country, he might be able to regain some of those possessions in France which were now lost to the English. But both parties dreading the admittance of a large body of English troops into the country, prevailed on Clarence, by the promise of a sum of money, to retire into Guienne.

Was Henry IV. happy in his private condition?
What anecdote is related of prince Henry?
Did Henry IV. renew hostilities in France?

The king's health now rapidly declined, and he became subject to epileptic fits. It is said, that one day, when he was in one of these fits, the prince, who believed him to be actually dead, carried the crown, which was placed by the king's bedside, out of the room. When the king came to himself, he instantly missed it, and sternly asked, who had taken it away?

The prince made a dutiful apology, which pacified the king, who said with a sigh, "Alas! fair son, what right have you to the crown, when you know your father had none?" "My liege," answered the prince, "with your sword you won it, and with the sword I will keep it." "Well," replied the king, "do as you please; I leave the issue to God, and hope he will have mercy on my soul."

A. D. 1415. Not very long afterwards, while he was performing his devotions in Edward the Confessor's chapel at Westminster, Henry was again seized with a fit. He was conveyed to the abbot's lodging, and there expired, on the 20th of March, 1413, in the 46th year of his age, and the 14th of his reign. His first wife was Mary de Bohun, by whom he had four sons and two daughters: his second wife was Isabella of Navarre, widow of the duke of Bretagne, by whom he had no children.

Several Lollards were in this reign condemned to death for their opinions. The Lollards put no faith in the pardons and indulgences granted by the pope, not thinking that the souls of men were in the keeping of any sinful and mortal man like themselves: and this opinion was very displeasing to the Roman Catholic clergy, who made a great profit by the sale of those indulgences. The Lollards disbelieved also in *transubstantiation*.

Transubstantiation is the belief that the bread and

Did Henry IV. suspect the prince of undutifulness to himself?
Did the king bestow his crown on prince Henry?
What was the state of religion in England during the reign of Henry IV., and what were the opinions of the Lollards?
What was meant by transubstantiation?

wine taken at the sacrament actually becomes, by the priest's blessing, the *real* body and blood of our Saviour, the *very substance*, instead of considering them, as Protestants do, to be solely a memorial of Christ's last supper, and to be taken in remembrance of him.

There were other points in which the Lollards differed from the then established church, such as the praying to images and relics, doing penance, saying masses for the souls of the dead, and many more: but that of denying transubstantiation was considered the most material difference, or rather was made a sort of test of faith, by which heretics were to be distinguished.

Arundel, archbishop of Canterbury, was the chief persecutor of the Lollards, and caused many of them to be condemned and executed. One of them, of the name of Badby, was sentenced to be burnt at Smithfield. He was tied to a stake, and faggots were piled around him, which were just going to be set on fire, when the prince of Wales rode up to him, and besought him to renounce his opinions and save his life, promising to give him enough to live comfortably upon, if he would do so.

The poor man thanked the prince with many expressions of gratitude; but said that, as he firmly believed his opinions to be true, he would not sacrifice his conscience to save his life. When the faggots were set on fire, the prince came again, and entreated him to recant; but he continued steadfast as before, and was accordingly burnt.

These are the first instances of the burning for *heresy* mentioned in English history. This cruel practice was followed from that of the Catholics of Italy, France, and Spain.

How did the Lollards differ from the Catholics?
How were the Lollards persecuted?
Were the Lollards firm in suffering for their doctrine, and who commenced burning for *heresy*?
What is *heresy*?

ENGLISH HISTORY 169

CHAPTER XIV

HENRY V.

[Years after Christ, 1413—1422.]

A gentleman and ladies of rank of the fifteenth century.

Henry, as soon as his father had breathed his last, retired to his own room, and spent the remainder of the day in prayer and privacy. On the following morning he is said to have sent for the low companions of his youthful follies, and to have told them that he was now going to lead an altered life, and to enter on new and important duties; at the same time forbidding them to appear in his presence, till they, like himself, should have reformed their conduct.

The young king possessed, in an eminent degree, the qualities most calculated to make him a favorite with the people. Even in the midst of his wildest excesses, he had always given proofs of a good and feeling heart. He had already distinguished himself for military courage, and his deportment was at once commanding and ingratiating. His

---

Did Henry V. abandon his youthful follies when he came to the throne?
By what qualities did Henry V. commend himself to the English nation?

person was tall and slender, his hair dark, and his features exceedingly beautiful; and in the general joy with which he was received as king, *the defect in his father's title to the crown,* seemed to be forgotten.

It must be remembered that the succession was through the oldest, and *next oldest* of the royal family in order. The *defect in Henry's title,* was, he had set aside the heirs of his grandfather's *second* son, and being a son of a *third* son, had taken the place of the legitimate heir; this heir being the earl of March, a great grandson of Lionel, duke of Clarence, the elder brother of John of Gaunt, Henry's grandfather.

Henry, confiding in this his general popularity, set at liberty the earl of March, (who had been kept in close confinement during the whole of the last reign) and treated him with an unsuspicious frankness, which more effectually secured his fidelity than bars and bolts could have done. This young nobleman, in the following year, was made a party to a plot against Henry, which had for its object to place himself on the throne; but he discovered the whole plot to the king, who put to death all the ringleaders of the conspiracy.

To show his respect for the memory of the unfortunate Richard, who had knighted him, and from whom he had, when a boy, received many kindnesses, Henry caused his remains to be removed from Langley, where they had been buried, and re-interred at Westminster with great pomp.

Amongst many other generous acts, Henry recalled the son of Hotspur from exile, and restored to him the estates and honors of his family. In short, his conduct fully justified in all respects, except in that of his persecution of the Lollards, the high opinion the nation had formed of him. But in that instance we may suppose he was actuated by a mistaken zeal for what he considered the true religion

One of the most distinguished followers of the *new doc-*

Why was the title of Henry IV. defective? (*title* signifying legal right to reign.)
How did Henry V. treat the earl of March?
What respect was shown to the remains of Richard II.?
What instances are given of opposite traits in the character of Henry V.—generosity in one case and cruelty in another?
Who was lord Cobham?

trine was lord Cobham. He had been in the early part of his life very wild and ill-conducted; but from the time he adopted the reformed opinions, he had led a moral and religious life. Henry, thinking highly of him as a wise and virtuous man, attempted to reason with him on what he himself thought the fallacy of the new opinions.

The king, however, after a long conversation, became so much provoked by Cobham's perseverance in the defence of his tenets, that he turned him over to an assembly of bishops, by whom he was committed prisoner to the Tower. From thence he made his escape, and secreted himself in Wales in the year 1417; when a particular search was made for him, on suspicion of his having excited a popular tumult; and being taken, he was condemned and burnt as a heretic.

Meanwhile the miseries of France were extreme. Civil war raged with the greatest fury; the nobles seemed to have caught the frantic madness of their monarch, and to be actuated by the desire of exterminating each other. Towns were taken and destroyed, the open country was desolated by fire and sword, and all to gratify the hatred and revenge of the dukes of Orleans and Burgundy. This sad condition of that unhappy country added fuel to the ambition of the English king.

A. D. 1415. The military ardor of Henry induced him to revive the claim to the crown of that country which had been made by Edward III. He accordingly made preparations for asserting it; and the leading parties of France were so intent on their own internal quarrels, that they saw not the gathering tempest, till it was ready to burst on their heads, and Henry, with thirty thousand men, had already crossed the Channel.

Henry had time to besiege and capture the town of Harfleur, while the dukes of Orleans and Burgundy were at Paris, contending who should command the army which was to be sent against him. This contest being at length decided in favor of the duke of Orleans, he marched from

---

Was lord Cobham treated as a wise and virtuous man deserved?
What was the condition of France in 1415?
Upon what pretence did Henry V. make war upon France?
What town in France did Henry capture, and what army marched against him?

Paris with 100,000 men, meaning at one blow to annihilate the English army, which, by the heat of the weather, and by disorders brought on by eating too much fruit, was now reduced to 10,000 men.

Henry, after repairing Harfleur, and placing an English garrison in it, designed to return to England. He departed from Harfleur in October, 1415, proceeding by easy journeys, and enforcing the strictest discipline. He paid the country people liberally for every thing he had of them; and they consequently brought him supplies of provisions, notwithstanding the orders they had received to the contrary. During the march, the king fared no better than the meanest soldier, and encouraged his men by the cheerful and friendly manner in which he conversed with them.

On October 24th, they arrived near the village of Azincourt, where they beheld the whole French army drawn up at some distance before them. Henry took an attentive survey of the country from a rising ground, and saw that it was equally impossible to retreat or to advance without a battle. He, therefore, resolved to hazard one the next morning; and sent his faithful Welsh squire, David Gam, to reconnoitre the number of the French army. Gam's blunt account was, that "there were enough to fight, enough to be killed, and enough to run away."

The evening was dark and rainy; but, as soon as the moon was risen, the king took advantage of its light to examine the place with great care. He chose his position on a small rising ground, surrounded on every side by brushwood and trees. He then placed guards and lighted fires, and the army, with the exception of some who passed in prayer what they supposed would be the last night of their lives, retired to rest.

While these things were passing in the English camp the French passed the night in noisy festivity; and, confident of victory on the morrow, it was agreed among them that all the English should be put to the sword, excepting the king and the chief nobility, who were to be saved for the sake of their ransoms.

How did Henry demean himself in France?
Where did the English come in sight of the French army?
How did the English pass the first night at Azincourt?
What preparation did the French make for battle?

When morning dawned, Henry summoned his men to
attend mass, and then prepared for the battle. He disposed
his little force in such a manner as to make it appear to
be more numerous than it really was. In front he placed
sharp stakes pointed with iron, a contrivance which was
of great service in keeping off the enemy's calvary. He
then rode along the line, clad in shining armor, with a
crown of gold, adorned with precious stones, on his head,
and addressed an animating speech to each corps as he
passed.

The two armies were now drawn up nearly opposite to
each other; but for want of space, the French were not
in such good order as the English, who were waiting,
every man in his place, with his bow ready bent, for the
moment when the charge should be sounded. That instant, the archers who were in front discharged such a flight
of arrows as threw the French line into some confusion
As soon as they had expended all their arrows, they
rushed on the enemy with their swords and battle-axes,
and defeated the first line.

The second French line, commanded by the duke
d'Alençon, then advanced, and encountered the second
line of the English, led on by Henry. The conflict was
close and furious; and the duke of Gloucester was wounded and unhorsed, and would have been slain, had not
Henry defended him till he could be borne off the field.
On this the duke d'Alençon, who had made an oath to
kill or take the English king, forced his way to Henry,
and, aiming a furious blow, cleft the crown on his helmet;
but was immediately overborne and slain without doing
him any farther injury.

Eighteen other French knights had also taken the same
vow; and, like the duke, lost their lives in attempting to
fulfil it, being all killed by the king's faithful squire, David
Gam, and two other Welshmen, who defended their master
at the cost of their own lives. Henry knighted these his
brave defenders as they lay bleeding to death at his feet.

When the second line of the French army knew that

Did Henry exhibit excellent management in his preparations?
What threw the French into confusion?
How did the duke of Alençon come by his death?
What French and English were killed in this battle?
How did the battle of Arzincourt end?

their leader the duke d'Alençon, was killed, they made no more resistance, and the remaining division of the army fled without having struck a blow. Henry, after a conflict which lasted only three hours, obtained a complete victory in circumstances that scarcely seemed to allow him any hope of escape from his enemies. The loss of the French, both in killed and prisoners, was immense.

Amongst the killed were the dukes of Orleans and Bourbon; and it is remarkable that the principal loss fell upon the nobles of the two factions; and that comparatively few of the common men were slain. Henry returned to England in great triumph with his prisoners; and the people were in such ecstacies of joy, that when he approached Dover, many of them plunged into the sea to meet his barge.

The circumstances of the battles of Cressy, Poitiers, and Azincourt, have a singular resemblance to each other. In each we see a powerful prince plunging, without any adequate object, into the midst of an enemy's country, and surrounded and in danger of being destroyed. And in each we see, at the head of an immense host of French, a commander who commits the same error of despising, through vain glory, a handful of desperate men: and that these handfuls of desperate men should each time obtain a complete victory, is, doubtless, very extraordinary.

The cabals amongst the nobles of France, instead of being checked by the late national calamity, only became the more violent. The king of France, Charles the Sixth, was mad; the dukes of Orleans and Burgundy, contended for the kingdom; and the queen took part with the Burgundians. The Orleans party were called the Armagnacs.

Such was the state of things, when Henry landed with a considerable army in Normandy, on the 1st of August, 1417. No preparations had been made for opposing him; and he marched forwards, taking possession of all the towns in his way; little resistance being attempted, except at Rouen, which sustained a siege of nearly six months, and was at last only reduced by famine.

Who were slain at Azincourt, and how was Henry received in England?
What battles were much alike?
What was the state of the French nation at this time?
What reception awaited Henry in France 1417?

In the meantime the factions of France, as on Henry's former invasion, were too much occupied in their mutual contests to observe the progress of the English king. The queen and duke of Burgundy had sent secret orders to their friends in Paris to put every one who was known to be an Armagnac to death. It is said that in consequence of this bloody mandate 14,000 persons were massacred: and while the streets were actually streaming with blood, the queen and duke made their triumphant entry into Paris!

When Henry at last had conquered the whole of Normandy, the contending parties began to look about them, and to consider, when too late, what was to be done. The queen and the duke of Burgundy, invited Henry to a personal interview, where many points were discussed, but nothing finally concluded. The dauphin, alarmed by the duke of Burgundy's alliance with Henry, contrived to detach him from it, and to induce him to make peace with himself.

This apparent reconciliation was celebrated throughout France with every demonstration of joy; joy, however, which was but of short continuance, for the reconciliation was only pretended on the side of the dauphin, who inviting the duke to a personal conference on the bridge of Montereau sur Yonne, caused him to be assassinated, and even stood by and witnessed the murder.

Nothing could exceed the fury of the Burgundians at this dreadful tragedy: and Philip, the son and successor of the murdered duke, forgetting every other consideration in the desire of vengeance, entered into a treaty with Henry, which went to confer on him the regency of France during the life of the present king, and, at his death, the succession to the crown, in exclusion of the dauphin, against whom England and Burgundy agreed to unite their forces. The king of France was at this time in the power of the Burgundians, and was made a party to their treaty.

A. D. 1420. One of the articles was, that Henry was to marry the princess Catharine, the king's

---

What atrocities were committed at this time in France?
What was Henry's success in France?
What alliance did Henry make, and how was it observed on the part of the Dauphin of France?
What subsequent treaty was made between the French and English?
When was Henry V. married?

youngest daughter This marriage was accordingly solemnized; and the two kings and their queens made a triumphant entry into Paris. The title of the new regent was ratified by the states general, (a kind of parliament,) and the union of the two crowns was celebrated with great outward demonstrations of joy.

The duke of Burgundy presented himself to the assembly of the *three estates*,—the nobles, the clergy, and representatives of the other orders,—clothed in the deepest mourning, to demand justice on the murderers of his father; and a sentence of excommunication was pronounced on the dauphin and his accomplices, who were declared incapable of succeeding to any honor or dignity. The dauphin did not submit tamely to be thus disinherited; but appealing to God and his sword for the maintenance of his title, he assumed the title of regent, and vigorously defended himself and the few places that still adhered to him.

Early in the following year, Henry, with his young queen, came to England, leaving his brother, the duke of Clarence, behind him as his lieutenant; but after a few months' absence, he returned hastily to France, on hearing that the duke of Clarence had been killed in an engagement with some Scottish soldiers in the dauphin's service. Henry took with him the captive king of Scotland, in the hope that the presence of their king would detach the Scots from the dauphin.

This project did not succeed, for the Scots remained steady to the side they had taken. In May, 1422, Henry with the queen and his son, who had been born a few months before, made a triumphant entry into Paris, to show the people their future king. But though the magnificence of the show might amuse the Parisians for a moment, it could not stifle the discontent they in secret felt at the humiliation of their country.

After this, Henry rejoined his army, and reduced several towns which had adhered to the dauphin: but, while besieging Cosne he was taken ill, and was obliged to give up the command of his army to his brother, the duke of Bed-

---

Did the Duke of Burgundy demand redress for the murder of his father?
Why did Henry V. return to England in 1421?
Did the French nation regard Henry V. with cordiality?
When was Henry V. taken violently ill?

ford. He then retired to Bois de Vincennes, near Paris where he grew rapidly worse. He soon felt himself at the point of death, and sent for the duke of Bedford and the earl of Warwick, to come to him, and receive his last directions.

Henry appointed the duke of Bedford regent of France, and the duke of Gloucester regent of England; and his infant son he committed to the care of the earl of Warwick. He also gave a particular charge that the prisoners taken at Azincourt should not be set at liberty till his son was of age. After he had given his final directions, he asked his physicians "how long they thought he might live?" And when they told him, "about two hours," he shut out from his thoughts every earthly care, and spent his remaining moments in devotion.

A. D. 1422. Henry V. died Aug. 31, in the thirty-fourth year of his age, and the tenth of his reign. His death is said to have been hastened by the unskilfulness of his physicians. His funeral procession was conducted with prodigious pomp through France, and afterwards from Dover to Westminster, where he was buried. Tapers were kept burning day and night on his tomb for nearly 100 years, and might be burning still, perhaps; if all customs of that kind had not been abolished at the Reformation.

Henry married Catharine of France, and left one son, Henry, born at Westminster, December 6, 1421. The queen afterwards married Owen Tudor, a Welsh gentleman, by whom she had three sons: Edmund, earl of Richmond, married Margaret, daughter of John Beaufort, duke of Somerset, and was the father of Henry Tudor, afterwards king Henry VII.; Jasper, earl of Pembroke; and Owen.

Manners and customs of the reign of Henry V. were improving in England, but the conveniences of life were still far behind ours of the present age. The nobility at

---

What were the last appointments of Henry V.?
What were the *obsequies* of Henry V.?
Who were the family of Henry V.?
What was the domestic architecture of Henry the Fifth's time?

that time no longer lived shut up in gloomy castles; but began to inhabit large mansions, built of timber, and covered with plaster. The outside wood work was very much carved, and the windows were large and wide. The principal apartment was the hall, which was two or three stories high, and commonly had an entrance porch. The floor of the upper half of the hall was raised about a foot higher than the rest, and called the *dais*, and there the lord of the mansion sat with his guests. The lower part was common to the menials of the family, of whom there were in every house a great number. The furniture of these halls was not very sumptuous, and usually consisted of only a long table fastened to the floor, three or four wooden benches for the gentlemen, with some low stools for the ladies, and perhaps a corner cupboard.

The walls were covered with large pieces of tapestry, hung on tenter-hooks, and taken down in summer. Some houses had chimneys; but in many the fire-place was in the middle of the floor, and, unless when a hole in the roof was made for it, the smoke found its way out through the rafters.

In the halls, while the nobles and their guests sat at table, they were entertained by singers, minstrels, and dancers. Over their heads were the perches for their hawks, and at their feet the pavement was crowded with dogs, gnawing the bones that were thrown to them: and besides all this, was the bustle and confusion of the numerous and noisy attendants, who, it should appear, were allowed to bawl and shout, and talk to each other.

When the master of the house and his guests had eaten what they chose, the serving men took their share, and what remained was given to the poor, who, at the hour of dinner, stood in crowds about the gate to receive it.

Accommodations for sleeping were not very comfortable. In the reign of Henry V. a flock bed, and a chaff bolster, were considered extraordinary luxuries, and pillows were only made for sick people. Feather beds, however, were used by kings and princes. The beds of the middle classes of people, were straw pallets covered with a sheet, and a log

---

Describe the hall, the *dais*, the furniture, the chimneys?
What were the manners of the old barons in their country houses?
What sort of bedding was used in this age in England?

of wood for a bolster, with a blanket and coverlet, like what is now used for horse-cloths. Servants had very seldom any sheets at all, and the sleeping in night-clothes was an extravagance they did not indulge in. And in war even such accommodations as these were sometimes denied to princes themselves.

CHAPTER XX.

HENRY VI.

[Years after Christ, 1422—1461.]

The duke of Bedford, who was appointed to the regency of France by the late king, was not his inferior either in valor or wisdom, and was much superior to him in the excellent virtues of clemency and command of temper. The earls of Warwick, Salisbury, Arundel, and lord Talbot, who held high offices in the state and army, were all men of distinguished abilities; so that the death of Henry made no immediate change in the situation of affairs in France.

Charles VI. ended his unhappy reign a few months after the death of Henry. The dauphin, Charles VII., immediately assumed the name of king, and lost no opportunity of trying to regain his kingdom: but Bedford did all that a wise and politic man could do to support the interests of his nephew. He agreed to the ransom of the king of Scotland, and made a seventeen years' truce with that country which prevented Charles from obtaining any farther assistance from it.

A. D. 1428. The earl of Salisbury, with a powerful army, laid siege to Orleans, which still adhered to Charles. At the second assault a small tower which defended the bridge was taken. At the top of this

---

Who were the chief men in England at the time of Henry the Fifth's death?
What was the state of affairs in France?
Where was the earl of Salisbury killed?

tower was a grated window, which overlooked the town; and while the earl of Salisbury was taking a survey from it, he was perceived by the master gunner of the enemy who aimed a gun at the window, which shivered the iron bars of the grate and wounded the earl so desparately that he died a few days afterwards.

The siege was continued under the direction of the earl of Suffolk and lord Talbot, who completely defeated the army which had been sent to the relief of the town, and Charles now thought it impossible to save it; when one of the most extraordinary circumstances that has ever been recorded in history occurred, and not only preserved Orleans from the English, but also greatly contributed to their being deprived soon after of all their late conquests in France.

There was a young woman of the name of Joan d'Arc, who was servant at an inn at Neufchatel in Lorraine. The accounts she was continually hearing from the travellers who came to the inn, of the distress the people of Orleans were reduced to, and of the little probability there was that Charles would be able to preserve that town, or any other that remained to him, worked up her mind to such a pitch of sympathy for the sufferers, and of enthusiasm for the cause of her king, that she fancied herself delegated by God to raise the siege of Orleans, and restore to Charles the kingdom of his ancestors.

Joan imparted what she considered her high commission to the governor of a neighboring town, and desired him to send her to the king. At first the governor treated her as an insane enthusiast; but at last, being overcome by her importunities, he allowed some of his attendants to conduct her to the royal presence. It was two days before she could gain admittance; but when she appeared before the king, and announced her errand, he and his courtiers were so much astonished by her appearance and manner, that they declared themselves convinced of her being commissioned by Heaven to expel the English from

---

Did an extraordinary circumstance preserve the city of Orleans?
Who was Joan of Arc?
How did the French king and his nobles regard Joan of Arc?

France, and an escort was ordered to conduct her to Orleans.

A. D. 1429. The hardships to which Joan had been inured had qualified her to bear the fatigue of a soldier's life. It having been part of her business at the inn to tend the horses, she was already an expert rider: and when she got admitted into the town, she headed the troops, and made several sallies against the English, in which she was always victorious.

The belief of her sacred mission, while it revived the low spirits of her countrymen, depressed those of the English soldiers, who joining in the general superstition imagined, when they were combatting with her, that they were fighting against Heaven: and Suffolk was obliged to raise the siege of Orleans, May 8, 1429.

The French, improving this advantage, laid siege to several of the towns which were held by the English; and in all these sieges the Maid of Orleans, as Joan was now called, behaved with the intrepidity of an experienced soldier. On one occasion, when scaling a wall, she was wounded in the head, and fell from the top of the ladder into the ditch; but without regarding the hurt, she exclaimed with a loud voice, "Advance, advance my countrymen! the Lord hath doomed the English to destruction." —Another time she was wounded in the neck by an arrow, and drawing out the arrow herself, she retired to have the wound dressed, and then returned to lead on the troops.

In the month of June, the French and English armies met. So much discord and confusion prevailed among the English, that the French obtained an easy victory. These successes greatly increased the fame and influence of Joan: and now, having raised the siege of Orleans, she insisted on being allowed to attempt the object which she had next at heart, that of crowning Charles at Rheims; and in this attempt also she succeeded, although the country about Rheims was for the most part in possession of the enemy

---

What had been the occupation of Joan of Arc?
What were the achievements of Joan of Arc?
Were the French armies victorious under the influence of Joan, and how did she crown her enterprise?

When the ceremony of the coronation was over, Joan announced that she had fulfilled her mission: and falling at the king's feet, besought him to permit her to return to her former station. The king denied her request, and constrained her to remain with the troops; but as a reward for what she had done (being too poor to give her a more substantial one,) he ennobled her and her family by the name of "Des Lys."

During these events the duke of Bedford was not idle: out his military skill and policy could do little to stem the torrent that was now rapidly leading back the French from their foreign conquerors to their rightful king. He hoped, by having the young Henry also crowned, to counteract the effect of Charles' coronation: but, though the ceremony took place at Paris with great parade and pomp, it had no effect upon the hearts of the French people, who were only drawn the more towards their own king by seeing another assume those honors that ought to have been his.

On the first unexpected turn of fortune, the French commanders had been willing to give all the honor of their success to Joan; but after a time they became jealous of her fame: and one day, when some troops under her command were repulsed near Compeigne, and obliged to retreat into the town, the governor admitted all the party except poor Joan, who, it is said, was purposely shut out. Being thus left alone amidst a host of enemies, she was pulled from her horse and taken prisoner.

It is with sorrow that we retrace the short remainder of this heroic woman's life. The treatment she received from the duke of Bedford and his council is a lasting stain upon the memories of men, who, as soldiers, Englishmen, and Christians, should have shown humanity and justice towards her. She was burnt alive in the market-place at Rouen; and Charles, who owed so much to her services, made no effort to save her.

How did Charles VII. recompense Joan?
How did the duke of Bedford concert measures on the part of the English?
Did Joan of Arc fall into the hands of the English?
Did the duke of Bedford treat Joan with humanity?

A. D. 1435. The duke of Burgundy withdrew from his alliance with the English, and a solemn peace was ratified between him and Charles at Arras; an event that was celebrated throughout France with transports of joy, but which caused such deep vexation in the duke of Bedford as to occasion his death.

His death was a serious loss to the English, and not only in regard to their affairs in France, but also in regard to the government at home; as he had often quelled, by his influence and authority, the disagreements between the duke of Gloucester, who was the regent of England, and the cardinal Beaufort, who had now the principal care of the young king.

The duke of Bedford's death opened a fresh subject of contention, in the choice to be made a new regent of France, and while the English council was disputing who should be appointed to that office, Charles got possession of Paris, and of many other important places. The duke of York was at last appointed to the regency.

The duke, when he arrived in France, found affairs there in a very declining state, and only supported by the bravery and exertions of lord Talbot, who was now the sole survivor of Henry the Fifth's brave band of warriors. In 1438, a dreadful famine and pestilence raged at England and France, and almost occasioned a cessation of hostilities: and a negotiation for peace was entered into, which the duchess of Burgundy, from truly Christian motives, labored heartily to promote.

This good princess was daughter of the king of Portugal, and grand-daughter of John of Gaunt: but some trifling difference on the subject of doing homage, made her good offices of no effect, and prevented an end being yet put to a war, which had desolated France and exhausted England for twenty-five years.

A. D. 1440. After some little interval the war was renewed with vigor on both sides, but the

---

When did the duke of Bedford die?
Was the death of Bedford a loss to the English nation, and why?
Who was made regent of France?
What circumstances led to overtures of reconciliation between France and England?
What prevented peace at this time?

duke of Orleans, after a tedious and melancholy captivity, which had lasted ever since the battle of Azincourt, regained his liberty and returned home; and, in 1444, he and the duchess of Burgundy procured a truce for six years between the two countries.

Hitherto Henry VI. has been almost entirely out of sight. In fact he would have been very glad to have remained so: for, being of a timid and quiet disposition, he was unfit for the cares of royalty. He was of a gentle and humane disposition, but from the inferiority of his understanding was only fit to be a passive instrument in the hands of others.

Henry was in his twenty-fourth year, when cardinal Beaufort, chiefly for the sake of thwarting the duke of Gloucester, who wished the king to make some more advantageous alliance, contrived his marriage with Margaret of Anjou. Gloucester, as if he had forseen the miseries which this fatal union was to bring upon the country, did all in his power to prevent it. But his efforts only made Beaufort and his party the more eager to bring it about, and the marriage took place in 1445. Instead of the king's receiving any dower with his bride, he agreed to give up a large tract of Maine and Anjou to her father.

Margaret was a woman of a high spirit and a vindictive temper. She never forgave the duke of Gloucester for the opposition he had made to her marriage, and came to England vowing vengeance against him in her heart. She found willing associates in cardinal Beaufort and the duke of Suffolk, who had already, by their machinations, involved Gloucester's wife, Eleanor Cobham, in a charge of witchcraft, and caused her to be sentenced to perpetual imprisonment in the Isle of Man.

Beaufort and Suffolk entered with the queen into a wicked confederacy to accuse Gloucester of high treason but found it impossible to substantiate any actual charge against him. He was, notwithstanding, imprisoned, and soon afterwards was found dead in his bed.

What was the character of Henry VI. ?
Who promoted Henry's marriage—with whom, and with what result ?
What were the disposition and conduct of the queen of Henry VI. ?
Into what conspiracy did Margaret enter ?

If Margaret was really accessary to this horrid deed, she was fully punished. Gloucester's death, was in fact, her greatest misfortune: for, had he lived, his ability, his integrity, and his great popularity, would probably have preserved the royal family from those calamities that afterwards befel them. Cardinal Beaufort did not live to see the evils he had helped to bring on the country, and died soon after Gloucester, in 1447.

The queen and Suffolk now managed every thing their own way, and by their violent and rapacious conduct made themselves more and more abhorred. While Gloucester lived, they had not ventured to acknowledge the agreement that had been made to give up Maine and Anjou to Margaret's father. And knowing that the duke of York, who acquitted himself with great wisdom and prudence in the regency of France, would never consent to the execution of a measure so ruinous to the English cause, they recalled him, and gave the regency to Beaufort, duke of Somerset, nephew to the cardinal.

Suffolk and Margaret had soon reason to repent of this unwise measure. For York, who had hitherto been a man of strict loyalty, feeling himself greatly injured, now meditated on a high revenge, that of asserting his own right to the crown. By his father he was descended from Edward the Third's youngest son. From his mother, who was the last of the Mortimers, he inherited the claim of that family from Lionel, *second* son of the same king. John of Gaunt, from whom Henry the Sixth was descended, was Edward's *third* son. Therefore York, in right of his mother, had certainly a superior claim to the throne. He kept his design secret for some time, lying in wait for an opportunity of forwarding them.

A. D. 1450. The Queen and Suffolk, by their mismanagement, lost the whole of Normandy; and the popular indignation against them became so great, that the parliament committed Suffolk to the Tower,

---

Was the duke of Gloucester's death a misfortune to Queen Margaret?
Why was the duke of York recalled to England?
In what enterprise did York engage?
What was the death of Suffolk?

and tried him for high treason. The queen contrived that he should be only sentenced to a five years' banishment But the resentment of his enemies was not to be so easily satisfied. He was pursued from Harwich, where he had embarked, and overtaken before he had reached the opposite shore. Being brought to Dover his head was struck off on the side of a small boat, and his body was left on the beach, where it was found by his chaplain, who conveyed it to be buried at Wingfield in Suffolk.

The unsettled state of the country now showed itself in tumults and insurrections. The most formidable was one that broke out in Kent, headed by a man named Jack Cade, who defeated an army of 15,000 of the king's troops at Sevenoaks; and, elated by this victory, advanced to London. Entering the city, he put to death the sheriff and several nobles, and striking with his staff what is called London stone, said, "now am I master of London."

Cade's triumph did not last long, for lord Scales with a strong body of men, soon drove out both him and his rabble; and, a pardon being offered to all who would return to their homes, Cade soon found himself without a single follower. For a short time he wandered about in disguise but was at last found lurking in a garden at Rothfield in Sussex, where he was killed by Alexander Eden, a gentleman of Kent.

A. D. 1451. Calais was all that remained to the English in France. The venerable Talbot, now in his 80th year, obtained permission to make a last effort for the recovery of Guienne. He landed at Bordeaux, Oct. 17, 1452, and for a time success attended him : but on July 23, 1453, this brave veteran was killed in an attack on the French camp at Chatillon; and his son, Lord Lisle, refusing to comply with his father's entreaties that he would fly and save himself, was slain fighting by his side.

The duke of Somerset now returned to England, and became the queen's adviser and favorite. His misconduct in France had made him very unpopular, and all eyes naturally looked up to the duke of York, who had acquit-

---

What rebellion broke out at this time ?
What was the end of Jack Cade ?
What possessions in France remained to the English in 1451 ?
Who was made protector of England, and why ?

ted himself so well during his regency. In 1454, the king sunk into a state of total bodily and mental weakness. The duke of York was on this made protector of the kingdom; and the first use he made of his power was to put Somerset in prison. The king soon after recovered his reason, and then Somerset was set at liberty, and York displaced from the protectorship.

A. D. 1455. The animosity between these two nobles soon afterwards threw the whole nation into a ferment. They both assembled their friends and vassals, and met at St. Alban's, where a desperate battle was fought, in which Somerset was killed, and the duke of York was completely victorious. The king, whom Somerset had dragged much against his will into the battle, was wounded, and took refuge in the house of a tanner. Here the duke of York found him, and falling upon his knees before him, declared himself his loyal subject, and ready to obey his commands. "If so," said the king, "then stop the pursuit and slaughter."

The use which was made by the duke of York, of this single victory was marked with the greatest gentleness and moderation. He conducted Henry to London, and treated him with every mark of submission and respect. However, notwithstanding York's professions of loyalty, under pretence of freeing the king from evil counselors, he continued to carry on a civil war against him; and the battle of St. Alban's was followed by many others, which were fought with various success between the two parties.

At last the duke declared his secret views on the crown itself, and on this many who had joined him because they supposed him to be contending solely for the public good, deserted his standard. He, seeing himself suddenly abandoned, retired for a time into Ireland. Nevil, earl of Warwick, a very powerful nobleman, and brother to the duchess of York, assembled a body of 25,000 men, and obtained

---

What nobleman engaged in hostility, and how did the duke of York treat the king?
Does it appear that the loyalty of York was sincere?
How did York prosecute his design to obtain the crown of England?

at Northampton so great a victory over the royalists that they fled in all directions.

The queen and her son, the prince of Wales, were obliged to fly with a few attendants, and escaped with difficulty into Scotland, where they were received with great kindness, by the young king, James III., and were soon after joined by the duke of Exeter and others of the king's friends, who now began to be called *Lancastrians*, and the wars that ensued between the Yorkists and Lancastrians are called in history, the wars of York and Lancaster. The earl of Warwick, after the battle of Northampton, had found the king sitting alone in his tent, and carried him in triumph to London.

The duke of York now returned to England, and laid before the parliament his claim to the crown. That he was the direct heir of Edward III. could not be denied, but the principle of keeping the succession in the direct line was not invariable, or, at least, was not always strictly attended to; and the parliament was unwilling to dethrone the reigning king. It was therefore determined, after many warm debates, that Henry should continue on the throne during his life, but that, on his death, the duke of York and his heirs should succeed instead of the prince of Wales, the king's only child.

Margaret was not of a disposition calmly to see her son thus set aside. By great exertions she contrived to collect a body of 20,000 men, consisting chiefly of borderers, whom she enticed into her service by the promise of giving them the plunder of the fertile lands of England. With this army she proceeded towards London, and at Wakefield was met by the duke of York, who, not aware of the number of her forces, had with him only 5000 men

A. D. 1460. York wished to have remained on the defensive in Sandal Castle, near Wakefield till his son Edward should arrive with a reinforcement but by the advice of the earl of Salisbury he changed his

---

What became of the king and his family at this time?
How did the parliament of England settle the succession to the crown?
Did the queen submit to the parliamentary decision?
Where was the duke of York killed?

plan, and on the 30th of December, marched in order of battle to meet the enemy;—a fatal determination, for his little army was totally defeated. He himself was among the first who fell, and the spot where he was slain is still fenced off in the corner of a field near Sandal.—Richard, duke of York, had many great and good qualities, and his death was sincerely lamented by all those who had taken up his cause.

York left three sons, Edward, George, and Richard, and three daughters. Another son, Edmund, who was earl of Rutland, a beautiful boy of twelve years of age, was killed on the same day with his father, being butchered by lord Clifford on Wakefield bridge, where a small chapel, which is still standing, was afterwards built, to perpetuate the memory of that bloody deed.

Margaret, equally merciless in victory as she had been undaunted in defeat, sent the earl of Salisbury, and many other knights and gentlemen, to Pontefract, where they were beheaded without a trial. She caused the head of the duke of York to be stuck on the gates of York, with a paper crown on it. The queen then set forwards to London; and the borderers fully availed themselves of their license to plunder, for they pillaged and burnt every church and dwelling, marking their way by fire and devastation.

A. D. 1461. The earl of Warwick hastened to meet the queen, taking with him the poor passive king. The two armies met at St. Alban's, which was a second time the scene of a bloody battle. The Lancastrians obtained the victory, and Warwick fled from the field, leaving the king behind, who rejoiced to be restored to the queen and his son. Margaret, however, notwithstanding this victory, finding, as she advanced nearer London, that the party of the Yorkists was stronger than she had expected, was obliged to retreat again into the North.

Edward, the young duke of York, after obtaining a victory over the Lancastrians at Mortimer's Cross, near Hereford, entered London on the 3d of March, and was proclaimed king with the loudest acclamations of the popu-

---

What children did the duke of York leave?
How did Margaret conduct herself at this time?
What occurred at the second battle of St. Albans?
Who was crowned king of England in 1461?

lace. The next day he went in solemn procession to Westminster Hall, where he took his seat on the throne, and received the homage of the nobles who were present. —Henry the Sixth lived many years after this event.

Henry VI., notwithstanding the feebleness of his character, was not without moral worth, and his imperfect virtues entitle his memory to respect while his misfortunes excite pity. Though Henry VI. was a very insignificant king, he was, as a man, amiable, well-meaning, and pious. Indeed, an old historian says of him, that "there never was a more holy, nor a better creature; a man of a meek spirit, and a simple wit, preferring peace to war, and rest to business, and honesty before profit. He was governed of those he should have ruled, and bridled of those he should have sharply spurred."

History treats of something besides wars; the wisdom and folly, the virtues and vices of a nation appear in domestic manners, in religious faith and worship, and in the transaction of civil affairs. Belief in witchcraft and love of war were among the follies of the age we are describing. There are no witches in reality; but it was one of the vulgar superstitions of those ignorant times to believe that God permitted his all-wise decrees to be influenced by the malevolent feelings of particular persons, who were called *witches* and *sorcerers*, and were falsely supposed to have the power of destroying life and health by their spells or artifices.

It appears in the history of all nations, that during seasons of the greatest ignorance and public calamity there are causes at work to make men wiser. Thus, when innocent persons are burnt by ignorant and cruel men for the imputed crime of *witchcraft*, those who witness the punishment, naturally inquire if there is such a crime in reality, and they discover that there is not, therefore they cease

---

What were the virtues of Henry VI.?
What besides war does history treat of?
What is witchcraft?
Does Providence appoint natural means to enlighten ignorance and reform error, and what example may be given?

from persecuting supposed witches, and indeed disbelieve
entirely that there are any.

In the same way, when a country is desolated by a
bloody war the thinking people inquire, which is better—
Peace or war?—and at length they come to the conclusion
that peace is better, and should be cherished. Also, when
arbitrary, or feeble princes misgovern a nation, " the
thoughtful and the free" deliberate, and determine that
many men, the representatives of a whole people, are wiser
than one man, and can rule a nation better than one, and
others, the mere tool of tha. one—so wise government, and
civil order grow up out of despotism. Notwithstanding
the foreign wars, and civil discord of England, the principles of better government were always in operation, as the
progressive power of the English parliament will serve to
show.

In the reign of Edward the First, the parliament had
little else to do but to grant supplies for the purpose of
carrying on the king's wars. As the necessities and importance of the nation increased, so did the power of the
parliament; and succeeding kings, whatever laws *they*
might make, could not establish them till they were ratified by the parliament. In Richard the Second's reign,
these functions were reversed: the parliament made the
laws, and the king sanctioned them.

The reigns of the Lancastrian kings proved favorable
to the liberty of the people; for the first two monarchs of
that family, conscious of the weakness of their own title,
and how much they owed to the good will of the people,
were naturally inclined to make concessions to them; and
it was during this period that the power of the parliament
became confirmed.

Though the constitution, government, and laws of England had not then arrived to that degree of perfection which
they have since attained, yet they were even then better

By what natural cause do men come to seek peace rather than war,
and free rather than despotic governments?
What was the primitive function of the English parliament, and when
was it a.tered?
Why did the Lancastrian kings confirm the power of parliament?
Was the political constitution of England favorable to the happiness
of the nation in the fifteenth century?

than those of any other country in Europe; at least, if we may believe Philip de Comines, a French writer, who wrote the memoirs of his own times, (which are the times we are now speaking of,) and who says : " In my opinion, of all the states in the world that I have seen, England is the country where the commonwealth is best governed, and the people least oppressed."

During the civil wars, the sufferings of many thousands of individuals, must doubtless have been very great; but the laws and constitution remained unchanged: and the cause of freedom having once taken root, strengthened by degrees, till the liberty of the people, the power of the nobles, and the dignity of the crown, became at length happily balanced.

The progress of the British navy is an important cause of the national power and prosperity. Henry IV., who was in many respects a politic ruler, strengthened his navy, and checked the depredations of the privateers, which had become so troublesome, since the time of Edward the Third, as greatly to impede the commerce of England. His son, Henry V., was as victorious by sea as by land; and while he and the duke of Bedford lived, England maintained the dominion of the narrow seas. Then Beauchamp, earl of Warwick, for a while, kept up the honor of the English navy.

These wars of York and Lancaster are sometimes called "wars of the Roses," because the Lancastrians used a red, and the Yorkists a white rose, as the badge of their respective parties.

During the long wars of York and Lancaster, the navy declined; but again revived under Edward the Fourth, who not only was an encourager of commerce, but was also a sort of merchant himself; for he had many trading vessels of his own. In his reign the fisheries also began to be much attended to, so that, about this period, many different kinds of ships were employed.

Did the civil wars overthrow the laws of England?
Did the English navy flourish under the Lancastrian kings?
During the civil wars and in the reign of Edward IV., what was the prosperity of naval affairs and commerce in England?

CHAPTER XXI.

EDWARD IV.

Years after Christ, 1461—1483.]

THE EARL OF SALISBURY,
Who was killed at the siege of Orleans, 1428.

Edward was scarcely nineteen years old, when he found himself, almost beyond his own expectations, thus suddenly placed upon the throne. He was brave, active, and enterprising, with a capacity far beyond his years, and was exceedingly handsome. But these attractive and brilliant qualities were blackened by the worst vices. In peace he revelled in every kind of self-indulgence, and in war, was sanguinary beyond all who had gone before him. He told Comines, a writer of that time, that he had been in nine battles, in eight of which he fought on foot, and had never been defeated.

The first battle which was fought after he became king was at Towton, a village between Ferry-bridge and Tad-

---

What was the character of Edward IV. ?
Was the Lancastrian contest continued, and what occurred near Tadcaster?

caster. Never did two mighty armies encounter each other with more inveterate hatred; and the orders of the commanders on each side were to take no prisoners, and give no quarter. The battle lasted from early in the morning till late in the evening, and was one of the most bloody ever fought in Britain.

The snow fell thickly, but the Yorkists had their backs to the storm, while the Lancastrians, who faced it, were greatly incommoded by it. The latter, after a desperate struggle, at length gave way, and, flying from the field, were pursued with great slaughter. When the news of this defeat reached York, Henry and his family, who were there waiting the result, fled with the utmost precipitation to Scotland.

A parliament, which was now summoned to settle the government, confirmed Edward's title to the throne. The new king satiated his revengeful temper by many bloody executions, and every Lancastrian who fell into his hands was condemned as a traitor. To strengthen his own party, he conferred honors and titles on all his friends Indeed it was doubly expedient for him to make new peers, since the late exterminating wars, and the executions which had been made by his own order, had greatly reduced the numbers of the nobility. He created his brother George, duke of Clarence, and his brother Richard, duke of Gloucester.

In the meantime queen Margaret made two voyages to France, in hopes of obtaining aid from thence. At length Louis the Eleventh, who had succeeded his father Charles VII. in 1460, supplied her with a small body of troops, on condition that she should give Calais up to him, if she ever regained the crown of England. With these troops she advanced from Scotland, and took the castles of Alnwick and Bamborough, in Northumberland. But her success was of short duration.

Lord Montacute, brother of the earl of Warwick, gained a victory over Margaret at Hedgeley Moor, April 25th

---

What was the result of the battle of Towton?
Did Edward consult parliament, and how did he administer government?
How did queen Margaret proceed?

1464 and three weeks afterwards he gained another at Hexham, which was so decisive that Henry was only saved by the swiftness of his horse from being made prisoner. The queen and her son sought to conceal themselves in a wood; but there, losing their way, they fell amongst a gang of robbers, who took from them every thing they had that was valuable. The robbers then luckily began to quarrel about the division of the plunder, which gave Margaret and the prince an opportunity of escaping from them.

As they were wandering about bewildered in the wood, they encountered another robber. The queen, knowing that both flight and resistance were impossible, went boldly up to him, and presenting her son, said, "Behold, my friend, the son of your king! I commit him to your protection;" which appeal so wrought upon the man, that he led them to a place of concealment, where they remained till the pursuit was over. He then conducted them to the seacoast, from whence they made their escape to France.

Henry, meanwhile, had fled into Lancashire, where he was with difficulty protected by his friends for more than a year, and where he suffered many hardships and privations in his wanderings from one place of concealment to another. In July, 1465, as he was at dinner in Waddington Hall, he was betrayed by a monk to sir James Harrington, who conveyed him to London, and resigned him into the hands of his great enemy the earl of Warwick.

Warwick treated him with the utmost indignity, and tying his feet in the stirrups, as if he had been a criminal, compelled him to ride in that manner three times round the pillory, while the populace were by proclamation forbidden to show him any marks of respect or compassion.

The extreme savageress of this treatment, serves to show the inhumanity of the age—a great nobleman could inflict it without self-reproach; and a civilized people could witness these indignities offered to a man, and a king

---

What became of Henry VI., and his queen after the battle of Hexham?
What presence of mind was exhibited by Margaret, and whither did she escape?
What happened to king Henry?
How did Warwick treat his prisoner?
What is shown by the indignities put upon Henry VI.?

without displeasure. Mankind are better now. Henry was committed to the Tower.

The Lancastrians were now reduced to so much distress, that many of the most distinguished nobles of that party were absolutely begging their bread in foreign lands, while the Yorkists were revelling in their forfeited estates. These estates were bestowed so as to create the most superfluous wealth to the new proprietors, while the rightful possessors were suffering in want—one among many instances of the miseries inflicted by arbitrary princes.

Edward enriched his two brothers with many of these estates. The earl of Warwick had also a very large grant. This nobleman inherited great estates from his ancestors, and had married the heiress of the old Beauchamp, earl of Warwick, so that he became the richest subject in the kingdom. On his different estates he maintained 30,000 people, a number which must be considered the more extraordinary, as the whole kingdom did not, probably, at this time, contain much more than 2,300,000 souls, not the fifth part of its present inhabitants.

Edward indulged himself in all the luxuries and pleasures to which his disposition strongly inclined him. Sometime before, he had become attached to Elizabeth Wydville, the widow of sir John Grey, by whom she had two sons. Edward privately married this lady, though he did not at first venture to declare his marriage. The court was soon filled by the new queen's relations. Her father was created lord Rivers. Her three brothers and five sisters were all raised to the rank of nobility, and married into the greatest families, and her eldest son was married to the king's niece, daughter of the duke of Exeter.

A. D. 1469. The earl of Warwick, who had been desirous to connect the king with some powerful foreign family, was exceedingly indignant at his impolitic marriage, and could with difficulty conceal his dislike of the queen and all her relations. The king's two

---

What was the condition of the two parties of York and Lancaster?
What instance is given of the wealth bestowed by Edward on his favorites?
Whom did the king marry, and how did he favor the queen's relations?
With whom did Warwick conspire against the king?

brothers also, seeing themselves supplanted by these new favorites, felt a growing antipathy to them all. The duke of Clarence, who had married Isabella, Warwick's eldest daughter, conspired with his father-in-law against the king. They at first retired into France, where they were soon joined by all the scattered friends of the house of Lancaster.

Queen Margaret, who with her son had been living in retirement in Lorraine, seized this opportunity of again coming forward, and cemented the union she now made with Warwick, who had before been her most inveterate enemy, by the marriage of the young prince, her son with the earl's youngest daughter Anne. And it was concerted amongst them to dethrone Edward, and that Warwick should be regent of England during the life of Henry, or till his son prince Edward should be of age, and that in case the prince should die without children, Clarence should be king after him.

A D. 1470. While these plans were forming, Edward was giving himself up to a succession of diversions. When Warwick landed at Dartmouth, Sept. 13, and was joined by numbers of disaffected persons, he was taken by surprise. With great hazard he and the duke of Gloucester escaped in a trading vessel to Friesland. They had embarked with so much haste that they were unprovided with money enough to pay for their passage, and the king was obliged to recompense the captain of the ship by giving him his cloak. The queen remained in England, and with her daughters took refuge in the Sanctuary at Westminster, where her son, afterwards Edward V., was born.

A. D. 1471. Edward being gone, and the Yorkists stunned as it were by so sudden a blow, the earl of Warwick carried all before him. The poor forgotten Henry was now dragged from his prison, and once more made a king. This restoration lasted only a few months; for the Yorkists recovering from their consternation, Edward returned to England, and regained possession of London, and again committed his helpless rival to the

---

How was it resolved to restore the house of Lancaster?
Was Edward IV. obliged to leave England?
Was Henry VI restored?

Tower. Warwick collected all his forces, and marched in haste against Edward, who, aware of his movements, advanced to meet him.

The two armies approached each other near Barnet, April 12th, and in the night time the fickle Clarence deserted to his brother with 12,000 men. The next day the fight began, and the advantage was undecided, till the soldiers of Warwick attacked by mistake a party of their own friends, who, thinking they were betrayed, immediately fled. This threw the Lancastrians into confusion, and Edward, improving the advantage, became entire master of the field. The great earl of Warwick died covered with wounds, and many other nobles fell with him.

Queen Margaret and her son had embarked for England on March the 4th, but had been tossed about by contrary winds, and did not land till the evening of the day on which the battle of Barnet was fought. When instead of the triumphant return they had anticipated, they found that all their hopes were blasted by the catastrophe of that fatal day, the queen's undaunted spirit forsook her for the first time. She sank to the ground and fainted.

When she revived, she fled with her son to the Sanctuary at Beaulieu; and intended to have returned immediately to France. But some of the dispersed Lancastrians gathering around her, she was persuaded to stay and make one more effort to regain the kingdom: a fatal resolution, which cost the lives of many brave men, who were defeated and slain in a battle that was fought at Tewkesbury, on the 3d of May.

The queen and the young prince were soon after taken prisoners, and thus an end was put to the bloody contest between these two rival families, a contest which had lasted eighteen years, and had cost the lives of sixty princes of the royal family, above one half of the nobles and principal gentry of the kingdom, and 100,000 of the common people.

After the battle of Tewkesbury, the young prince Ed-

What was the result of the battle of Barnet?
How did Margaret bear the defeat of Barnet?
What was the consequence to the Lancastrians of the battle of Tewkesbury?
What became of Margaret and her son?

ward was brought into the king's presence, who asked him how he dared to come into his kingdom in arms. He boldly replied, "I came to recover my father's kingdom:" upon which Edward struck him on the face with his gauntlet, and the dukes of Clarence and Gloucester, with their attendants, instantly fell upon him with their swords, and killed him. Margaret survived her son nine miserable years, five of which she was kept prisoner in the Tower. Louis XI. then ransomed her, and she returned to France, where she died in 1480.

Edward, after the murder of the prince, returned in triumph to London, and the next day Henry VI. was found dead in the Tower. The manner of his death will probably ever be a secret; but there is a suspicion of his having been murdered by the duke of Gloucester. By the death of prince Edward, Anne, daughter of the earl of Warwick, was now a widow.

Gloucester, though his hands were stained with the blood of her husband, resolved to marry Anne: but Clarence, who had married her eldest sister, wished her to remain single, that he might secure to himself the whole of earl Warwick's vast estates, and contrived to secrete her. Gloucester, however, discovered and immediately married her.

A. D. 1475. Edward made preparations for a war with France, and landed at Calais with 30,000 men. But while the English at home were expecting great conquests from this powerful armament Edward, who was now grown indolent, and fonder of pleasure than of war, suffered himself to be cajoled, by the cunning of Louis the Eleventh, into a disgraceful peace, and accepted of a large sum of money as the price of his return to England. Louis also corrupted the integrity of many of the English nobles, and bribed them by rich presents and pensions to be favorable to the interests of France.

The king now led a life of self-indulgence and luxury;

What instance of cruelty was exhibited by Edward IV. and his brothers?
Would princes act thus at the present time?
What was the death of Henry VI.?
Whom did the duke of Gloucester marry?
What expedition was attempted by Edward, and how did it terminate?

but he had one secret care which corroded all his enjoyments. Although the family of Lancaster had been in a manner extirpated, one distant branch still remained Henry Tudor, earl of Richmond, a grandson of Owen Tudor, and descended, by his mother, from John of Gaunt was the only person now left alive, in whose veins ran any of the blood of the Lancasters. He was, therefore, considered as the representative of that family.

Richmond had been brought up in the court of the duke of Bretagne, who protected him from every attempt the king of England made to get him into his power. Edward promised to marry the young Richmond to his eldest daughter, and thus to unite the two houses of York and Lancaster; and by this promise the duke was prevailed on to send him to England. But no sooner was he set out, than the duke, beginning to doubt the sincerity of Edward's intentions, sent after Richmond and brought him back: he thus probably saved him from destruction.

A. D. 1478. Clarence having spoken with imprudent freedom of the king, Edward appeared glad to seize the opportunity of getting rid of a brother whose fickleness and petulence were continually giving him offence. Clarence was impeached and condemned to die by the parliament; but, as a royal and brotherly favor, the king allowed him to choose the manner of his death. It is difficult to believe historians when they gravely tell us that he desired to be drowned in a butt of malmsey. He left a son, who had the title of Warwick from his grandfather, and a daughter, afterwards countess of Salisbury.

A. D. 1483. Edward was chiefly employed during his latter years in making negotiations with foreign princes, most of which came to nothing. In his private life he was sunk in sloth and vice. He died April 9, in the forty-first year of his age, and the twenty-third of

---

Was one of the Lancasters living?
Where was the earl of Richmond, and why was he prevented from going to England?
On what account was the duke of Clarence impeached and condemned?
When did Edward IV die and what was his family?

his reign. He married Elizabeth Wydville, and left two sons and five daughters.

It is proper to mention in this place that the most important benefit ever conferred by these useful arts upon mankind, was, during the reign of Edward IV., extended to England from the continent. This was nothing less than the art of printing.

The invention of printing is of uncertain origin, but is generally conceded to John Faust or Faustus, a citizen of Mentz in Germany. The first book known to be printed by him was a bible in 1450.

The honor of introducing it into England is ascribed to William Caxton, an honest citizen and mercer of London, who, while following the business of his trade in Holland, had heard and seen much of this new discovery. Being very solicitous of making so valuable an art known in England, he established himself for some time at Cologne, for the purpose of learning it.

Though Caxton was in his fifty-seventh year, he applied himself so diligently to his new undertaking, that in 1471 he printed a book, entitled "The Recule of the History of Troy." He then came to England, and set up a printing press. Caxton lived till 1491, and printed nearly fifty different books, most of them translations by himself from the French. Caxton says of himself that he was a "rude and simple man." Surely he was the greatest benefactor of his age and country!

It is delightful to think that while all the princes and nobles of the land were murdering each other without remorse, there was this excellent person, regardless of these destroyers and plagues of men, patiently introducing among that evil and unthankful generation, the greatest blessing divine Providence could grant them.

What important benefit was conferred upon England in the reign of Edward IV.?
Who invented printing, and when?
Who introduced printing into England?
What were the labors of Caxton, where did he die, and how should his memory be regarded?

CHAPTER XXII.

EDWARD V.

[Years after Christ, 1483.]

We are now come to the shortest reign and the most pathetic story in the annals of England. When Edward IV. died, his eldest son was about thirteen years old, and was at Ludlow castle, under the care of his uncle, lord Rivers, and his half-brother, lord Grey. The title of the family of York to the crown was now completely established, and no objection was made to the young Edward's being proclaimed.

But though the public willingly acknowledged the young prince, there was amongst his nearest relatives, one who had long marked the innocent boy for destruction. This person was his uncle Richard, duke of Gloucester, a prince of great bravery and ability, but a man of most execrable selfishness, deceitfulness, and cruelty. It was to him that the victories of Towton and of Barnet were principally ascribed.

Richard had long formed the project of usurping the crown, and had cloaked it with the most profound dissimulation. His first step, soon after his brother's death, was to impart to lord Hastings a wish to remove the lord Rivers and Grey from about the person of the young king. Hastings, a loyal and honest man, but who wore a bitter enmity to the queen and her relations, willingly agreed to second this design; and Richard accompanied by Hastings and by the duke of Buckingham, who was still deeper in his secrets, set out with a numerous train to meet the king, who was on his way from Ludlow to be crowned at London.

Who was the acknowledged successor of Edward IV.?
Who had plotted the destruction of the prince, and what sort of man was he?
Who were the *complotters* of Richard's criminal designs?

They met the king and his little party at Stony Stratford, where the lords Grey and Rivers waited on the duke of Gloucester, and passed the evening with him in convivial mirth and pleasantry, unsuspicious of the coming evil The next morning, they and two other gentlemen of the king's retinue were seized and sent to Pontefract, and all the rest of Edward's attendants were dismissed, and forbidden cn pain of death to come near the court.

The young king, finding himself alone, and in the power of his uncle, whom he had been early taught by his mother to dread, was struck with grief and terror; but Gloucester falling on his knees, assured him with strong professions of loyalty and affection, that what he had done was for his preservation. Edward then suffered himself to be soothed into composure, and set off with his uncle towards London.

There the news of these violent measures arrived before Gloucester and the prince, and occasioned great alarm, for no one knew what to expect from such a strange beginning. The queen, fearing the worst, instantly fled into the Sanctuary at Westminster, taking with her the duke of York, then about seven years old, and her five daughters.

On the 4th of May, Gloucester conducted his nephew into London, riding before him bareheaded, and saying to the people, " Behold your king!" Two days after, a great council was held, in which the artful duke was appointed Protector of the king and kingdom. Preparations were begun for Edward's coronation on the 22d of June: but on the 13th of May, during the meeting of the council at Westminster, the door of the hall was suddenly opened, and a party of armed men, the tools of the cruel duke of Gloucester, rushed in, crying out, " Treason! treason!"

The archbishop of York, Morton, bishop of Ely, and the lords Stanley and Hastings, who were all now hurried off to the Tower, and committed to close custody, except lord Hastings, whom Gloucester pronounced a traitor, and com-

---

How were the young king and his relations treated?
Did Gloucester dissimulate with his nephew?
Whither fled the young king's mother and her children?
How were preparations for the coronation commenced and interrupted?
How was Lord Hastings treated?

manded to be immediately put to death. He was only permitted a few moments' delay to confess himself to a priest, and his head was cut off on a log of wood which happened to be on the spot.

On the same day, sir Thomas Ratcliffe, one of Richard's chief confidants, entered Pontefract with 5,000 men, and without any trial, beheaded lord Rivers and lord Grey, and their two fellow prisoners. The death of lord Rivers caused much lamentation, for he was the most accomplished nobleman of his time.

Gloucester, while committing these acts of violence, still kept on his mask of loyalty. He declared in council that it would be highly indecent to suffer the duke of York, during the ceremony of his brother's coronation, to remain in the Sanctuary, a place where thieves and murderers found refuge. The archbishop of Canterbury was in consequence sent to require the queen to surrender her young son.

Having now got both the young princes into his power Gloucester declared to the people, that the late king had been married to another lady previously to his marriage with lady Elizabeth Wydville, therefore her son was not the legitimate king; and the citizens of London were thus persuaded to offer him the crown.

Richard at first affected to decline it, and said "his love of his brother's children was greater than his love of a crown:" but when the duke of Buckingham urged the suit, Richard pretended to overcome his reluctance, and accepted the offered gift. He was the same day proclaimed king, and was soon after crowned. The same preparations that had been made for the coronation of Edward V. served for that of Richard III.

It was long before the fate of the two unfortunate young princes was known with certainty, but they never appeared more. Some years afterwards two people owned themselves to have been concerned in their murder, and said that

---

What were the next violent measures of Richard's adherents?
Upon what pretence did Gloucester get the young king into his possession?
By what falsehood did Gloucester lay claim to the crown?
Did Richard pretend to refuse the crown, and when was he crowned?
What became of the young princes

the two princes had been suffocated in their bed, and buried at the foot of a staircase in the Tower.

Edward was in his thirteenth year when his father died, and reigned not quite three months

Mummeries. From a MS. of Edward the Third's reign.

The troubled times of England it seems, did not much interrupt the popular amusements. It has been mentioned that the English nation were fond of noisy sports. We have seen the early Saxons entertained with the bards and minstrels; and the Normans with jousts and tournaments and we have heard that the baronial halls and courts abounded with the tricks of jugglers and buffoons.

Dramatic entertainments, representations of stories by assumed characters, came slowly into fashion in England, and did not take the form of an elegant and moral enter ainment till the age of Shakspeare (1580,) or thereabouts.

There were theatrical entertainments long before there were theatres. The first public representation that was any thing like a play was exhibited as early as 1378, and was called a *miracle*. It was the history of St. Catharine and was performed by the priests of Dunstable. The actors were attired in the holy vestments belonging to the abbey of St. Alban's. In Richard the Second's reign the clergy of St. Paul's enacted a miracle before the king and

---

What were the amusements of the English people at different times?
What was the progress of the drama in England?
What was a dramatic *miracle?*

queen which lasted eight days, and in which was represented the greater part of the history of the Bible.

These *miracles* were succeeded by *mysteries*, in which sacred subjects were strangely jumbled with mimicry and buffoonery. By degrees, some little moral allegory crept into these entertainments, and miracles and mysteries gave way to *moralities*, which consisted of long elaborate speeches from allegorical personages, as Theology, Adulation, Admonition, &c. These plays were all performed in churches and chapels, and the actors were almost always ecclesiastics. Besides these church plays there were *secular* plays and interludes performed in private houses and in the streets, by jugglers, tumblers, and jesters, whose business it was to rove about and exhibit their talents.

In the time of popery there were so many saints' days, and holidays, the lower orders of people had a great deal of time for their amusements. Christmas was the chief time of sports; and in the king's courts, and probably also in private families, a leader of the sports was elected, who had for the time the pleasant title of *lord of misrule*.

When there was so much play, of course there was less work. The country was miserably cultivated: there were frequent famines; the dirt and wretchedness of the poor was extreme: hunger and idleness made them always ready to raise tumults and disturbances. Their condition is now better, though poor laborers of England do not dance and sing so much as their ancestors did, they enjoy more comforts, and fewer of them are killed in broils, or die of hunger.

What were Mysteries and Allegories?
What effect had the Catholic religion upon popular amusements in England?
Is too much diversion conducive to the well being of a people?

CHAPTER XXIII

RICHARD III.

[Years after Christ, 1483—1485.]

RICHARD, DUKE OF GLOUCESTER, AFTERWARDS KING.
From a MS. in the Royal Library.

I. must not be supposed that the citizens of London solicited Richard to accept the crown entirely from the love they bore to him. He had caused the city to be surrounded by numerous bodies of troops, and would have proceeded to violent measures, had not the citizens acted as they did.

The new king, soon after the coronation set out with his queen, and only son, then about eight years old, on a royal progress through the kingdom. When the court arrived at York, the king, to gain popularity amongst the people, who flocked there in great numbers to see him, entertained them with the ceremony of a coronation, and was crowned in the cathedral at that city a second time.

But while Richard was thus making a parade of his

How were the citizens of London constrained to offer Richard the crown?
Where was Richard III. crowned?
What conspiracy was formed against Richard?

royalty, a plot was already brewing to deprive him of it. Morton, bishop, of Ely, had been committed to the custody of the duke of Buckingham. That shrewd prelate soon saw that though the duke had received great rewards from the king, he yet wanted more, and that resentment and discontent were rankling in his mind. Morton accordingly found no difficulty in persuading him, notwithstanding he had so greatly contributed to the exalting of Richard, to join in a conspiracy formed for deposing him, and for placing Henry Tudor, earl of Richmond, on the throne.

The friends of Richmond were desirous of supplying the defects of his title by marrying him to Elizabeth, daughter of Edward IV., who certainly, now that her brothers were gone, seemed to have the best right to the crown. Having formed their plan, they sent messengers to the young earl, entreating him to come to England immediately; and they made preparations at the same time for a general rising on the 18th of October. But Richard, whose vigilance had not let this tempest gather unperceived, assembled an army rapidly at Northampton, to be ready to march to that part of the country where the storm should burst.

Buckingham was prevented from acting against Richard being betrayed to him for a reward of a thousand pounds. He was taken to London, and begged earnestly to see the king, and plead his cause before him; but Richard refused his request, and ordered him to be immediately executed. The other conspirators, discouraged by this disastrous beginning, dispersed, but were many of them taken, and the execution of some of the ringleaders terminated this formidable insurrection.

A. D. 1483. Richard made a triumphant entry into London, and all things now seemed to prosper to his wishes. But he, whose heart was too hard to feel for the affliction of others, was himself vulnerable in his paternal affection. Edward, his only child, died April 9 1484; and we are told that the king's grief was so excessive that he almost "run mad." The grief of the queen was

---

What plan was formed for the exclusion of Richard, and how did he prepare to frustrate that plan?
What happened to the conspirators against Richard?
What domestic misfortunes happened to Richard?

not less violent; and her death a few months afterwards is generally ascribed to it.

Richard, notwithstanding all his spies, and the secret intelligence he kept up in the country, does not seem to have been aware that, while Richmond was supposed to be in France, soliciting aid from foreign princes, he in fact passed great part of the time in Wales, making himself friends among his countrymen; for the Tudors were a Welsh family. Once, when at Tremostyn, in Flintshire, he was so near being discovered by one of Richard's spies, that he only escaped by jumping out of a back window, and getting through a hole, which is still called the *king's hole*.

Richmond, on his return to France, heard a report of Richard's marriage with the princes Elizabeth. On this, hastily collecting all the English exiles, and a few French soldiers, he mustered a body of 3000 men, and with this small army he landed at Milford Haven, August 7, 1485, trusting to the co-operation of his friends in England.

When Richard heard how small a number of persons accompanied the earl, he despised so weak an enemy. But when he found that enemy to be presently joined by some Welsh troops that had been sent against him, and that his numbers were fast increasing, he began to think the danger more urgent. His spies either could not or would not give him true information; and he began to suspect and distrust all about him.

Richard at this juncture adopted the only measure he could devise, to prevent the defection of the army in his cause. Lord Stanley, to whom Richard had given the chief command in his army, was in secret league with Richmond, whose mother he had married. Richard though he knew not exactly what to apprehend, seized on Stanley's son, and kept him as a hostage for the fidelity of his father, who was thus prevented from openly appearing in Richmond's cause.

Richard being desperate, at length roused himself, and collecting what troops he could, marched from Notting-

---

Where was the earl of Richmond 1485?
When and where did the army of Richmond land in England?
How did Richard prepare for his adversary?
What measure did Richard take in respect to lord Stanley?
Where did Richard encounter Richmond's army?

ham, where he was keeping his court, to Leicester. August 22d, he left Leicester with great pomp, wearing a crown on his helmet, but with a countenance indicating a troubled mind, and encamped at the abbey of Merivalle, not far from Bosworth, where Richmond had arrived the night before. The two armies were placed so near together, that during the night many deserted from the royal army and joined Richmond.

The next morning the forces on both sides were drawn out in line of battle. The battle began, but no vigor or spirit was displayed in the royal army; and, when lord Stanley suddenly turned and attacked it, Richard saw that all was lost, and exclaiming "Treason! treason! treason!" rushed in the madness of rage and desperation into the midst of the enemy, and made his way to the earl of Richmond, hewing down all before him.

The earl rather shrunk back at the approach of such a desperate antagonist; but his attendants gathered round Richard, who fought like a wild beast at bay, till at last he fell covered with wounds. His helmet was so beaten in by the blows it had received, that its form was quite destroyed. Scarcely any persons of note fell on this memorable field.

Richard reigned little more than two years, and was slain in the thirty-fifth year of his age. He fell near a brook which runs through Bosworth field. The dead body of the king was treated like that of a malefactor, and thrown neck and heels across a horse, and carried to Leicester, where it was buried in the church of the Grey Friars. But his bones were not permitted to rest in this humble bed; for at the destruction of the religious houses by Henry VIII., they were torn from their burying-place. His coffin was afterwards used as a drinking trough for horses at an inn in Leicester.

The consequences of the battle of Bosworth were of great importance, not only to the individuals who were engaged in it, but to the whole nation. Indeed, no battle

---

How did Richard demean himself in the battle of Bosworth field?
How did Richmond meet Richard, and how fell Richard?
How long did Richard III. reign, and how was his dead body treated?
What were the consequences to the English nation of the battle of Bosworth?

since that of Hastings, had been productive of such material changes. The battle of Hastings brought in the feudal system in its most oppressive form; and the battle of Bosworth put an end to it, and also to the long line of Plantagenet kings, who had governed England for 330 years.

There were fourteen Plantagenet kings: Henry the Second, and thirteen descendants. Four of these, John, Henry III., Richard II., and Henry VI., were feeble monarchs. The rest inherited all the abilities and bravery of their great ancestor: but they were one and all of them ignorant of what may be called a Christian policy,—ignorant that it is the duty of princes to seek the improvement and happiness of their subjects, rather than the increase of territory, or the triumph of arms. But, in despite of the false notions of their kings, the English nation was gradually becoming more free, intelligent, and virtuous, during these successive reigns.

THE PLANTAGENET LINE

Began to reign	Reigned Years.	
1154	35	Henry II. Plantagenet.
1189	10	Richard I. Cœur de Lion, } sons of Henry II.
1199	17	John Lackland,
1216	56	Henry III. son of John.
1272	34	Edward I. son of Henry III.
1307	20	Edward II. of Carnarvon, son of Edward I.
1327	50	Edward III. son of Edward II.
1377	22	Richard II. of Bordeaux, grandson of Edward III.
1399	14	Henry IV. of Lancaster, cousin to Richard II. grandson of Edward III.
1413	9	Henry V. of Monmouth, son of Henry IV.
1422	49	Henry VI. of Westminster, son of Henry V.
1461	22	Edward IV. of York, third cousin to Henry VI. great great grandson of Edward III.
1483	3m.	Edward V. son of Edward IV.
1483	2	Richard III. Crookback, uncle of Edward V. and the last of the Plantagenets.

Who were the Plantagenet kings and what their general character?

CHAPTER XXIV.

HENRY VII.

[Years after Christ, 1485—1509.]

HENRY VII. AND HIS QUEEN.
(From an old picture by Mabuse.)

King Richard was the last man slain on the field of Bosworth, and his death was the signal victory to Henry of Richmond. The soldiers who had engaged in pursuit of the fugitives were recalled by hearing the shouts of "Long live King Henry!" and, returning to the field of battle, they saw sir William Stanley placing on Henry's head the battered crown that had been struck off from the helmet of Richard.

Henry was at this time thirty years old, and two ruling passions, swayed his conduct from the first hour of his reign, to the end of his life. These were his avarice, and his hatred to the house of York. The first command he issued, even before he had left the bloody field where he had been proclaimed king, was that persons should be sent into Yorkshire, to seize young Edward Plantagenet,

---

When was Henry of Richmond crowned king of England?
What were the ruling passions of Henry VII.?

earl of Warwick, the son of the duke of Clarence, and to convey him to the Tower.

But, notwithstanding Henry's rooted dislike to the house of York, he soon found he could not maintain himself on the throne without allying himself to it He therefore renewed an agreement he had formerly made to marry the princess Elizabeth; but his reluctance to the marriage was so great, that he put it off till the following year. He had so much jealousy of its being supposed that he derived through her his right to the crown, that he would not permit the queen's name to be mentioned in the act of parliament that was passed for settling the succession.

A. D. 1487. Henry's conduct towards all those who had been connected with the late royal family naturally irritated them against him, and a scheme was contrived, which, though it failed in the end, had many abettors, and gave him for a time much trouble and vexation. Lambert Simnel, the son of a baker of Oxford, was instructed to personate the young earl of Warwick, who, it was pretended, had made his escape from the tower.

Richard Simon, a priest, had the chief management of this plot. He took Simnel into Ireland, where the house of York had many friends; and there, the credulity of the people coinciding with their wishes, he was proclaimed at Dublin by the title of Edward VI. When Henry heard of this pretended earl of Warwick, he caused the real earl to be taken from his prison, and carried in procession through London.

This measure, though it satisfied the people of England, did not convince those of Ireland, who asserted that Henry had exhibited an impostor, while they were in possession of the true Plantagenet. Whether the duchess of Burgundy was really of the same opinion, or whether she was glad of an opportunity to disturb Henry, does not appear; but she certainly assisted Simnel with a body of troops under the command of Martin Swartz, an experienced leader

---

Whom did Henry marry, and how did he regard the queen?
What impostor appeared in England 1487?
What measures did Henry take to expose this impostor?
Who assisted Simnel?

The earl of Lincoln, son of the countess de la Pole eldest sister to the duchess, also joined Simnel in Ireland. Leaving Ireland with a force of eight thousand men, they landed in Lancashire, expecting to be joined by the inhabitants. But they were mistaken in this expectation, and penetrated as far as Stoke, near Newark, without receiving any addition to their numbers. Here they were met, June 16, 1487, by Henry, with a considerable force, and defeated after a fierce engagement.

Lord Lincoln and Swartz were slain. Simnel, and his protector Simon, were taken prisoners, and received better treatment than they could have expected; for Henry contented himself with imprisoning the priest for life, and with degrading the new-made king to be one of the scullions of his kitchen.

A. D. 1493. Another impostor started up, in a youth called Perkin Warbeck, who had been secretly instructed to personate Richard duke of York, the young brother of Edward V., who, it was pretended, had escaped from the Tower, by the connivance of the ruffians who had murdered his brother. This youth had a strong resemblance to the Plantagenets, and acted his part so well that many persons were actually convinced that he was the prince.

Warbeck presented himself at the duchess of Burgundy's court at Brussels, and claimed her protection, as being her brother's son. The duchess appeared at first to doubt his story, and then, as if suddenly convinced by his answers to her questions, she embraced him with a transport of joy, exclaiming that he was indeed her long lost nephew. She then appointed a guard of soldiers to attend him, and treated him as the head of the house of York.

The news of this extraordinary circumstance brought numbers of people to Brussels : and the answers of Warbeck were so extraordinary, that all who saw and conversed with him were persuaded of the truth of his story

---

- Where was Simnel defeated ?
- What became of Simnel and his chief abettors ?
- Who pretended to be the duke of York ?
- What princess encouraged Warbeck ?
- How did Henry prove the imposture of Warbeck ?

Henry now became anxious to publish to the world the certainty that the real duke of York had been murdered, and he obtained the confession of two persons who owned themselves to have been accessary to the death of the two young princes.

Amongst those who flocked to see Perkin Warbeck were two men sent by Henry, who were commissioned to insinuate themselves into his confidence. In this they succeeded so well that they became acquainted with his secrets, and sent regular information of his plans to the king, who was thus enabled to know what persons in England were in correspondence with him. These persons were all seized in one day, and were immediately tried, condemned, and executed. Sir William Stanley was beheaded for having been heard to say, that " if he was sure Perkin Warbeck was the real duke of York, he would never bear arms against him."

These sanguinary measures deterred people from venturing to own themselves friends or favorers of Warbeck, who made two unsuccessful attempts to land in the realms which he claimed for his own. His first attempt was in Kent, and his second in Ireland. He then tried his fortune in Scotland, and having convinced the king, James IV., that he was a true Plantagenet, that young monarch received him with the utmost kindness.

James entered into Warbeck's cause with all the warmth of a generous mind, regardless of the danger of making an enemy of so powerful a monarch as the king of England, with whom it was greatly his interest to remain at peace. He gave Warbeck in marriage to the lady Catharine Douglas, one of the most noble and accomplished ladies in Scotland, and published a manifesto, inviting the English to repair to the standard of their rightful sovereign, Richard IV.

A. D. 1496. James also raised an army, and, in October, invaded England. The Scots immediately began to plunder, as was their custom; and War-

---

Did Henry punish the friends of Warbeck?
Where did Warbeck successively try to advance his cause?
How did James IV. of Scotland assist Warbeck?
What regard for human life and the right of property was manifested by Warbeck?

beck expostulated with James on this barbarous manner of carrying on the war, declaring that he had rather lose a crown than obtain it by the ruin of his subjects.

While Henry was preparing to repel the Scots, a still more pressing danger assailed him in an insurrection of the men of Cornwall, who came in a numerous body towards London. They got to Blackheath, but were there defeated by the king's troops. Their leaders were taken and executed. The rest, on paying two or three shillings each into the king's coffer, received a pardon, and returned home.

Warbeck was soon deprived of the assistance which the king of Scotland had for a time afforded him. Henry, who was at all times a better negotiater than a soldier, preferred entering into a treaty with James to the meeting him in the field; and a truce was made between the two monarchs. Upon this Warbeck, after thanking James for the protection and kindness he had shown him, went to Ireland with about 120 followers, and his amiable wife, who would not forsake him.

Warbeck remained in Ireland some months, and on receiving an invitation from the Cornish men, who were still in an unsettled state, he landed at Whitsand Bay in that country. Warbeck was joined at Bodmin by 3000 men, with whom he marched forward and laid siege to Exeter.

A large body of the king's forces marched against him, and Warbeck left his companions to take care of themselves, and fled in the night to the abbey of Beauley. The Abbey was soon surrounded by the royal troops, and Henry would gladly have forced open the gates and seized on his victim, but was persuaded to try to entice him out of his sanctuary by the promise of his life.

Warbeck on receiving this promise, yielded himself up, and was carried prisoner to the Tower. He contrived to elude the vigilance of his keeper, and made his escape; but being soon taken, and brought back again, he was com-

---

What insurrection was quelled in 1496?
How did James of Scotland and Warbeck part?
Did Warbeck abandon his enterprise?
Where was Warbeck taken?

pelled to mount a scaffold at Westminster, and to read a paper by which he confessed himself to be an impostor. Warbeck afterwards contrived to have some communication with the earl of Warwick, his fellow prisoner, and a plan was concerted between them for their escape; but the plan being discovered, they were both executed. Perkin Warbeck was hanged at Tyburn, Nov. 23, 1499, and the earl of Warwick was beheaded on Tower-Hill three days after.

Henry, from this time till his death, was undisturbed either by tumults at home or by wars abroad. He made many treaties of alliance and commerce with foreign countries, but he chiefly employed himself in amassing wealth which he did in every possible way. He made many arbitrary and vexatious laws, and obliged those who infringed them in the slightest degree to pay heavy fines, or suffer imprisonment.

These rapacious schemes Henry carried on chiefly by the assistance of two lawyers, of the names of Empson and Dudley, whom he employed to entrap the rich and unwary. By these means, as well as by taxes, and *benevolences*, he acquired immense wealth, not only in money, but also in plate and jewels. He kept it with the most anxious care, under his own lock and key, in secret apartments in the palace at Richmond.

A. D. 1500. The king's eldest daughter, Margaret, married James IV. of Scotland; and, in 1501, prince Arthur, his eldest son, married Catharine of Arragon, daughter of Ferdinand and Isabella, the king and queen of Spain; but in the following spring the young prince died, and Henry, unwilling to lose the marriage portion of the Spanish princess, married her to his other son, Henry, a boy of eleven years old. In 1503, the queen, Elizabeth of York, died.

A. D. 1506. The archduke Philip of Austria, who had married the eldest sister of Catharine of Arragon, being on his way to Spain with his duchess, was

---

Did Warbeck escape from the Tower?
For what was Warbeck hanged?
What was the character of Henry's administration?

driven by contrary winds to land in England: and Henry under pretext of showing him and the duchess extraordinary honor, detained them till he had extorted from Philip a promise to give him in marriage his sister, the duchess dowager of Savoy, with an enormous dower.

Henry also obliged Philip to make a commercial treaty, exceedingly advantageous to England, and prevailed with him to give up Edmund de la Pole a distressed nobleman of the house of York, who had taken refuge in the Austrian dominions. Philip complied most reluctantly with this last demand: and Henry, when he had got all he wanted, suffered him and his duchess to depart.

Henry had scarcely got de la Pole in his power, when he became sensible that all his schemes of revenge, avarice, and ambition, were drawing to a close. A violent attack of the gout gave him warning of his approaching end. He now devoted the remnant of his life to make preparations for the awful change he had to expect; but even his dying acts were tinctured by that money-loving spirit, which had governed his life. Amongst other things he ordered that two thousand masses should be said for him at sixpence a piece.

One or two of his bequests, however, exhibited something like a conscience. He ordered that restitution should be made to those persons from whom his agents, Dudley and Empson, had extorted more than the law could warrant. He also ordered the debts to be paid of all persons in London and Westminster who were imprisoned for 40s. or under. Having thus done every thing that fear and superstition suggested, he died at his palace at Richmond, April 21, 1509, in the 24th year of his reign, and the 54th of his age.

He married Elizabeth of York, and had two sons, and two daughters:—Arthur, married Catharine of Arragon, and died young; Henry, his successor;—Margaret, married, first, James IV. of Scotland, and, secondly Douglas,

---

What marriage did Henry propose to make?
Whom did Philip of Austria give up to Henry VII.?
What put a stop to all Henry's plans?
By what means did Henry amass wealth, and when did he die?
Who were Henry the Seventh's children?

earl of Angus;—Mary married, first, Louis XII. of France, and secondly, Brandon, Duke of Suffolk.

The reign of Henry VII. was the dawn of what may properly be called English liberty; for though the Magna Charta had fenced in the nobles from the tyranny of the king, yet the great mass of the people were for a long time after exposed to the oppressions of the nobles: but now, the power of the nobility being much diminished by the long civil wars, the people began gradually to emerge from slavery.

Henry's policy also was to depress the nobles. He restricted the number of their retainers; and thus that idle race of people who had before passed their lives in following some great lord to the wars, or in hanging about his gates in time of peace, were driven to apply themselves to more industrious modes of life, and from helpless dependants became useful subjects.

Commerce too began to make a great alteration in the condition of persons in middle life; and Henry greatly facilitated their rise into consequence by lessening the strictness of entails, and so enabling the nobles to sell their estates, many of which thus came into the possession of rich commoners. With the change of property came a great change in the condition of all classes of people.

The land-owners found it advantageous to commute the service of their *villeins* for money, and made them pay rent for their lands and cottages; and thus from *villeins* they became *tenants*. It is difficult to trace every step of the lowest orders of the people from villeinage, which at some periods was a mere state of slavery, to freedom. The progress was so various and so gradual, that the state of villeinage seemed to decline insensibly, and after this time we find no more mention made of it.

Military service to the great lords being abolished, the

Was civil liberty advanced in England during the reign of Henry VII.?
How did Henry diminish the power of the nobles?
Did Henry change the tenure of property in England?
How was service changed to rent?
Was the army establishment of England changed?

army of England became from this time an independent body. The officers and soldiers serving by their own consent, and being paid by the nation.

In this reign the Star Chamber was first instituted; an arbitrary court of law, in which the king used to attend in person as judge, and which was called the Star Chamber, from the decorations of the room in which the sittings were held.

Though Henry was a very unamiable man, yet in some respects his conduct as a king was beneficial to his country. His dislike to the nobles made him considerate of the lower orders, and his love of money made him encourage commerce, and the navy. He built some four-masted ships, of a larger size than had ever been seen before.

Intelligence of the discoveries made by Columbus in the western hemisphere, disposed Henry to similar enterprises, and he fitted out a small fleet of ships, and sent them on a voyage of discovery, under the command of John Cabot, a Venetian merchant.

Cabot sailed in a north-west direction, and the first land he saw was what we now call Newfoundland, but which he called Prima Vista (first seen :) he next saw the island of St. John's and sailed to the south as far as Virginia, and then returned to England, where the king received him with great honor, and knighted him.

What was the court of Star Chamber?
Were the English navy and commerce benefitted by Henry VII.?
Did Henry encourage maritime discovery.
How did Henry treat John Cabot?

CHAPTER XXV.

HENRY VIII.

[Years after Christ, 1509—1547

A soldier in Henry the Eighth's reign.

Henry VIII. was in his nineteenth year when he ascended the throne. His understanding was shrewd and clear; he had received what was then thought a good education, and had more learning than most princes of his time. The pretensions of the two rival families of York and Lancaster were united in his person, and he was the first king since Richard II. who had ascended the throne with an undisputed title to it. He enjoyed great popularity, his father had left him an ample treasure, and the country was free from both foreign and from domestic wars. In short, no king of England had ever begun to reign under more prosperous circumstances.

For the first two years of his reign the political affairs of England prospered. Henry appointed a council of men of approved wisdom. He brought Dudley and Empson

---

When and under what circumstances did Henry VIII. succeed to the throne of England?

What were the first measures of Henry's reign, and who became his chief counsellor?

to punishment for their exactions in his father's reign, and he made advantageous treaties with France and Scotland At the same time he was extravagant in his amusements, and soon squandered much of his father's hoarded wealth in tournaments and other expensive pastimes, to the great grief of his careful counsellor Fox, bishop of Winchester, who, finding his remonstrances unavailing, introduced at court the afterwards highly celebrated cardinal Wolsey, a man of inferior birth, but very shrewd and dexterous, by whose assistance he hoped to be better able to restrain the follies of the youthful king.

Wolsey soon acquired an unbounded influence over Henry, but he only employed it to flatter the king's follies and to promote his own advancement. He was soon made archbishop of York and chancellor; but his ambition did not rest satisfied with this; he even aspired to be pope of Rome.

A. D. 1513. Henry was drawn in by his father-in-law, Ferdinand king of Spain, the most artful man of his time, to make war on France. He landed at Calais with a numerous army, and defeated the French troops under the duke de Longueville. This engagement has been called the Battle of the Spurs, from the haste with which the French cavalry took to flight. Henry afterwards took Tournay, and thinking he had now done enough to establish his fame as a conqueror, amused himself with tournaments and splendid entertainments.

On the same day on which Tournay was taken, a battle was fought at Flodden, at the foot of the Cheviot Hills, between James the Fourth of Scotland, and the English army under lord Surrey, afterwards duke of Norfolk. In this battle the king of Scotland was killed.

Henry soon after made peace with France, one of the conditions of which was that Louis should marry Henry's young sister Mary. Henry then, after placing a garrison in Tournay, returned to England; and the princess Mary his sister was sent in the following August, with a splen-

---

To what dignities did Wolsey attain, and to what did he aspire?
What were Henry's enterprises in 1513?
What happened at Flodden Field?
On what conditions did Henry make peace with France?

did train of ladies and nobles to France, where her stay however, was very short, for Louis soon dying, she returned to England, and, after a widowhood of a few weeks, married Brandon, duke of Suffolk.

Louis was succeeded by Francis I., one of the most gallant princes of his age. Ferdinand of Spain died in 1517, and was succeeded by his grandson, Charles V., who soon after became also emperor of Germany. Thus were the principal countries in Europe governed by three young monarchs, all equally emulous of fame and power. Charles and Francis were decided rivals, and they each courted and cajoled Henry, whose blunt and open character was no match for either of them.

Henry and Francis had agreed to have a personal interview; and Charles, in hopes of preventing its taking place, came to England. He could not succeed in preventing the interview; but he flattered Henry, and bribed his chancellor Wolsey, till he had sufficiently detached them from the interests of France.

The projected meeting between Henry and Francis took place in June, 1520. Both monarchs arrived within the English pale near Calais. The French king and his court took up their quarters at Ardres, and the English king was lodged in a magnificent palace which Francis had caused to be erected for him at Guines. Two thousand eight hundred tents, many of them covered with silk and cloth of gold, were pitched in the surrounding plain; but even this number was insufficient for the multitude who flocked to this splendid festival; and many ladies and persons of rank were glad to obtain a lodging in barns and to sleep upon hay and straw.

The French and English vied with each other in the splendor of their dresses, and this meeting is celebrated by the name of "The field of the cloth of gold." It continued a fortnight, and was a succession of entertainments. Wolsey, who was now made cardinal, took upon himself

---

Who were the three greatest monarchs of Europe in 1517?
How did Charles V. interfere between the kings of France and England?
What occurred at Guines in 1520?
What was done at 'The field of the cloth of gold?'

to regulate all the ceremonials, and at first the two kings only met, attended by their trains, and passed the day together, according to the formal etiquette prescribed by the cardinal. But such dull parade did not suit the frank and ardent spirit of Francis, and after two or three of these interviews had taken place, he mounted his horse early one morning, and, attended by two gentlemen and a page, rode off towards Guines.

The English, who were on guard at the palace, were astonished to see the king of France at that hour, and so attended; but Francis desired to be conducted to Henry's apartment, and undrawing the curtains of his bed, awoke him out of his sleep. Henry was as much amazed as his guards had been; and from that time the intercourse between the two kings was conducted in a more free and confidential manner.

On June 25th the two kings separated, and Henry and the emperor exchanged visits at Gravelines and Calais. This occasioned a renewal of tournaments and splendid entertainments; but amidst them all, Charles never lost sight of his own interests, and sought to counteract the effect of the treaties of friendship and alliance that had been made between the two kings at the "field of the cloth of gold."

Soon after Henry's return to England, the duke of Buckingham was accused of some treasonable expressions against the king and was beheaded; but his real crime was the having offended cardinal Wolsey, whose haughty and overbearing conduct had raised a host of secret enemies around him. Wolsey's power over the king was so absolute, that Henry, without perceiving it, was merely his tool; and making himself agreeable as well as useful, he ruled for ten years with absolute sway one of the most capricious and passionate of men.

Did the kings on this occasion depart from the pomp of majesty?
Did Charles V. manifest any real friendship for Henry of England?
Was Wolsey's influence upon Henry of great importance?

A. D. 1521. Henry distinguished himself as an author, and wrote a Latin book against the heresies of Luther, an eminent reformer of religion in Germany. This book was presented with great ceremony to pope Leo X., who rewarded the royal author with the title of " Defender of the Faith ;" and sent him a letter praising his " wisdom, learning, zeal, charity, gravity, gentleness, and meekness ;" most of which epithets few people could have less deserved.—The following year Leo died, and Adrian VI. was elected pope, to the great mortification of Wolsey.

A. D. 1522. The emperor Charles visited England a second time, and was entertained with a variety of splendid shows. Charles, as usual, mixed politics with his festivities, and applied himself to win the favor of the English nobles. By his artifices Charles effectually dissolved the bonds of amity between France and England ; and Francis declared of his late dear friend the king of England, " that he held him for his mortal enemy from that day forth."

War was soon after declared, but nothing very material was done. Henry was no great warrior, and Francis was more intent on prosecuting a war in Italy with the emperor than on making any attack on Henry. At length Francis was taken prisoner by Charles at the battle of Pavia, and remained in captivity nearly a year.

Charles, having now gained all he wanted, treated Henry with little ceremony, neglected to repay some money he had borrowed of him, and refused to ratify a treaty he had made to marry his daughter, the princess Mary. Wolsey also, who found the popedom a second time vacant, and himself still forgotten, had reason to complain of the emperor's breach of faith. He therefore easily persuaded his already irritated master to break with Charles, and make peace with France.

But Wolsey's fall was near at hand. It must not be forgotten that Catharine of Arragon, when she married the

---

Why was Henry VIII. called ' Defender of the faith?"
When, and with what effect did Charles V. make a second visit to England ?
What misfortune happened to Francis I. ?
Did Henry and the emperor Charles quarrel ?

king, was the widow of his elder brother Arthur Henry, after the arrival of many years, pretended it was a crime and contrary to the laws, for a man to marry his brother's widow; and that consequently Catharine was not his lawful wife. These scruples were increased by the arrival at court of Anne Boleyn, who had accompanied the king's sister, Mary, when she went to France, and had been educated in the French court, and returned to England with all her English beauty adorned by French grace and vivacity.

The king was so much captivated by Anne Boleyn's charms, that in order to be able to marry her, he formed the project of divorcing the queen. In this project he was encouraged by Wolsey, and he sent to Clement VII. who was now pope, stating his scruples about his marriage, and suing for a divorce.

A. D. 1528. Clement unwilling to displease the emperor, who was nephew to the queen of England, declined giving a decided answer, and after keeping Henry in suspense for more than a year, sent cardinal Campeggio to England, to determine, in concert with Wolsey, the validity of the king's marriage.

Campeggio exhorted the king in private to give up the thoughts of a divorce; and finding his exhortations unavailing, he next applied to the queen, advising her to submit to the king's will, and retire into a nunnery; but with her also he was unsuccessful. After another year spent in delays and negotiations, the two cardinals proceeded to the important trial: but they both seemed unwilling to come to any decision, and the king's patience was nearly exhausted.

It was now visible to all the courtiers that Wolsey's favor was declining. It happened about this time that Gardiner and Fox, the king's secretary and almoner, accidentally fell in company with Thomas Cranmer, a young

---

Under what pretence did Henry VIII. seek a divorce from Catharine of Arragon?

Whom did Henry wish to marry, and to whom did he sue for a divorce?

Did the pope immediately satisfy the king of England?

How was the king's divorce procrastinated?

Who was Thomas Cranmer and what did he propose?

priest of Cambridge. The conversation fell on the subject of the king's divorce. Cranmer at first declined giving any opinion upon it, but being pressed, he said that, were he king, he would spend no more time in fruitless negotiations with Rome, but would apply to the universities, and to the most learned men of Europe, proposing to them this plain question, "Can a man marry his brother's widow?"

The two doctors were much struck with this hint, and mentioned it to the king. Cranmer was immediately sent for to court, and the king was so much pleased with him, that he retained him in his service, and engaged him to write a book in favor of a divorce.

From this time Wolsey's influence greatly decreased. Anne Boleyn, who suspected that he opposed her elevation to the throne, joined with Wolsey's enemies in plotting his downfall: but their schemes were so secret, that when the king was prevailed on to permit an indictment to be brought against him for having unlawfully procured himself to be appointed the pope's legate in England, Wolsey was quite stunned at the unexpected blow. The great seal was taken from him, and given to sir Thomas More, and he was ordered to retire to Esher, near Hampton Court.

Wolsey's house at York-place in London, which was furnished like a royal palace, was taken possession of by the king, who also seized on the remainder of his property, even on his clothes, and on a magnificent tomb which he had prepared for himself at Windsor. Wolsey on this immediately dismissed his train of attendants; but as he had always been a most indulgent master, some of his servants, amongst whom was his secretary, Thomas Cromwell, refused to leave him.

The king's resentment against his former favorite seemed to subside after he had stripped him of his wealth. He sent him a general pardon, and allowing him to retain a part of his revenues, sent him to reside in his diocese of York. He there conducted himself with the greatest kindness towards his clergy, telling them he was come to

---

In what was Cranmer employed by the king of England?
What happened to Wolsey 1530?
Was Wolsey entirely dispossessed of his wealth?
Did Henry ever relent in his displeasure against Wolsey?

live amongst them as a friend and brother. Still, how ever, adversity did not cure him of his love of magnificence and expense, which again drew on him the king's displeasure.

By Henry's order, Wolsey was at last arrested of high treason, and was first taken to lord Shrewsbury's house at Sheffield Park, where he was to remain till the king's further pleasure should be known. While he was there, anxiety of mind threw him into a violent illness; and when sir William Kingston arrived to conduct him to the Tower, he was little able to bear the journey.

Wolsey, though in a dying condition, set out. On the evening of the third day, they reached Leicester Abbey, and Wolsey said to the abbot, who came to the gate to receive him, "My father, I am come to lay my bones amongst you." He was lifted from his mule and carried to his bed, from which he never rose. He died Nov. 29, 1530.

A. D. 1532. Henry and Francis had another interview near Boulogne, and amidst the masques and entertainments which took place on this occasion, made new treaties of alliance with one another. At one of these masques, Anne Boleyn danced with the king of France, who presented her with a valuable jewel, and promised to do all in his power to promote the king's divorce and her marriage. Soon after the English court returned home, and she and Henry were privately married.

A. D. 1533. Cranmer was promoted to the see of Canterbury, and proceeded to try the validity of the king's marriage with Catharine. A sort of tribunal was assembled at Dunstable, and after a fortnight spent in hearing arguments, and reading opinions, sentence of divorce was pronounced, declaring the king's marriage with Catharine of Arragon null and void from the beginning, and her daughter illegitimate.

What effect had his misfortunes upon Wolsey?
Where did Wolsey die?
What occurred to Henry VIII. in 1532?
When and where was the question of Henry's divorce settled?

Henry's marriage with Anne Boleyn was declared valid, and she was three days afterwards crowned, and received as queen. The divorced queen firmly refused to allow the legality of the sentence against her. She led a melancholy and secluded life at Ampthill, near Woburn, till 1536, when she died.

The news of the sentence passed against Catharine excited the most violent commotion at the court of Rome. Clement could not at first determine what part to take At last he made an angry decree confirming the legality of the king's first marriage.

Henry, in a violent passion at the pope's decree, immediately upon it called a parliament, which declared the *king's supremacy* over the church of England and denying all authority of the pope in England, bestowed upon the king all the emoluments and revenues that had hitherto been paid to the see of Rome out of the ecclessiastical benefices in England. Two years afterwards another parliament passed an act to dissolve 376 of the small monasteries and nunneries, and bestow all their possessions on the king.

Commissioners were sent all over the kingdom requiring every one to subscribe to the act that had declared the king to be the head of the church. Sir Thomas More, who had resigned the chancellorship some time before, refused to take the oath required. Fisher, bishop of Rochester, refused also ; and both these men, whose learning and wisdom had made them ornaments of their country, were beheaded.

Anne Boleyn's enjoyment of a crown was of short duration. Her French manners and vivacity, though they had pleased the king on their first acquaintance, displeased him after she became queen; and soon after the birth of a daughter (afterwards queen Elizabeth,) he seems to have 'ost all his affection for her. He either believed, or affected to believe, that she had conducted herself with great impro-

---

Where did Catharine of Arragon end her days?
How did the pope receive the news of the king's divorce?
Did Henry assert the independence of the English church?
Did all persons in England admit the king's supremacy?
Did queen Anne Boleyn retain the king's affections?

priety; and on the 2d of May, 1536, she was committed to the Tower.

It would be a melancholy task to go through the history of this unhappy young creature. Accused of a crime of which she was innocent, denied the sight of her parents, and surrounded by her bitterest enemies, she paid very dearly for her temporary exaltation. She was tried without being allowed an advocate to plead her cause. Her marriage was pronounced void, and her child declared illegitimate. She was beheaded, and the king the next day was married to Jane Seymour, daughter of sir Thomas Seymour of Wiltshire.

The new queen's disposition was a happy medium between the gravity of Catharine and the volatility of Anne; and she might perhaps have retained the king's affections longer than either of her predecessors had done, if her death, soon after the birth of a son, had not dissolved her union with him in less than a year. Henry now looked about in foreign courts for a suitable partner.

On the death of Wolsey, Cromwell, his faithful friend and servant, had entered into the service of the king, and had risen in favor till he was at last made chancellor. He, being a zealous friend to the Reformation, was desirous that Henry should ally himself to one of the Protestant princes of Germany, and procured a portrait, painted by Holbein, of the princess, Anne of Cleves, to show to the king.

Henry was so much pleased with the portrait, that he sent to demand the lady in marriage. When she arrived in England, the king found her so unlike the picture, that he was with difficulty persuaded to marry her; and when he discovered that she was stupid and ignorant, and could speak no language but Dutch, he disliked her more than before, and resolved on being divorced from her.

But, as a first step, he beheaded Cromwell, because he had been the adviser of this unlucky marriage. He then summoned a parliament which pronounced the marriage

---

How was Anne Boleyn treated?
How long did Jane Seymour live after marriage?
Who commended Anne of Cleves to Henry VIII?
How did Henry divorce Anne of Cleves?

void, and that each party was at liberty to marry again. Anne, however did not avail herself of this permission. She had an ample income assigned her, and the palace at Richmond, and spent the remainder of her life in England, to all appearance very contentedly; glad, perhaps, to have got rid of her capricious husband without losing her head.

A fortnight after this divorce had been passed, Catharine Howard, niece of the duke of Norfolk, was presented to the court as queen; the king having already been privately married to her. Henry was so much charmed with the wit and agreeableness of his new wife that he caused a thanksgiving prayer to be made for his happy marriage. But his happiness was soon overcast. He discovered her conduct to have been very abandoned, and she was beheaded Feb. 12, 1542.

A. D. 1543. Henry seemed now tired of marrying for beauty, and he looked out in his next wife for sense and discretion, which he happily found in Catharine Parr, the widow of lord Latimer. To her he was married, and this lady by her extraordinary good sense and prudence, contrived to preserve the good opinion of the king till his death

---

The demolition of the monasteries and the dispersion of the monks and nuns was too violent a measure to be taken quietly. In 1534 a disturbance was excited in Kent by a woman who pretended to have revelations from heaven. Her name was Elizabeth Barton, but she is better known by that of the Maid of Kent. The imposition was soon discovered, and the insurrection quelled. A more formidable one broke out two years after in Yorkshire and Lincolnshire, but the rioters were soon dispersed. The spirit of discontent was, however, still in the country,

---

How did Anne of Cleves spend her life?
On what account was Catharine Howard beheaded?
Who was the last wife of Henry VIII?
Did the English nation willingly submit to the change in church affairs?
How did Henry VIII. attempt to suppress popular discontent in England?

and the king sought to crush it by severe punishments and numerous executions. In 1538 he entered into a friendly alliance with the protestant princes in Germany: but as their object was to promote the reformed religion, and Henry's only to spite and annoy the pope and the emperor, the king of England and his new allies could not act together with any real cordiality.

The pope on his side lost no opportunity of injuring Henry, and employed the cardinal de la Pole to foment disturbances in England. Pole was the king's second cousin. He had been educated at Henry's expense, and long experienced his favor, but forfeited it by joining warmly with the pope in condemning the king's divorce. Clement made Pole a cardinal, and sent him as a legate into Flanders, that he might with the more facility correspond with his friends in England, and carry on his plots against the progress of reformation in England.

These conspiracies were not carried on so secretly but that Henry obtained some hint of them; and the cardinal's two brothers were executed in consequence. Even Pole's aged mother, the countess of Salisbury, was not spared. This venerable and last remaining Plantagenet was beheaded for having received a letter from her son.

The rich spoils the king had got by dissolving the smaller monasteries had made him greedy of more; and in 1539 his obsequious parliament passed an act for putting at his disposal all the remaining religious houses, which either had been or should be surrendered to him. The king was not backward in forcing them, by all sorts of means, to surrender. In 1545 another act was passed, which even empowered him to seize the revenues of the universities. But these were spared (as some have said) by the intercession of queen Catharine Parr.

A. D. 1541. Henry, who was very fond of royal interviews, was now desirous of having one with his nephew the king of Scotland (James V.;) and a meeting was to have taken place at York. Henry and his court kept the appointment, and waited for some days; but

---

Did the pope endeavor to recover his authority in England?
By what cruel measures did Henry oppose Cardinal Pole?
Did Henry persevere in his dissolution of monasteries?
On what pretence did Henry VIII. make war with Scotland?

the king of Scots, having been prevented by his clergy never came, and Henry was so much enraged at this insult that he declared war against him. The English army obtained an important victory at Solway Moss, and James was so much overwhelmed when he heard of it that he sunk into a settled melancholy, and died December 14, 1542, leaving an infant princess only seven days old.

This princess was the celebrated Mary queen of Scots, whose unhappy life and death will be related in its proper place. Henry was desirous to procure a marriage between the young queen of Scotland and his son, Edward prince of Wales, and used both force and artifice to bring it about. He wanted also to be made protector of Scotland during the queen's minority; but the Scots were too bold to be frightened, and too wary to be ensnared.

After Henry and the emperor had been at open enmity many years a reconciliation took place between them; and Henry, who with all his violence of temper and self-conceit was generally the dupe of others, was drawn in to make war on Francis. Charles and Henry, at the head of their armies, joined each other near Calais; and though the latter was now grown fat and unwieldy, he appeared in person in the field and laid siege to Boulogne, which was soon taken.

The king of France now pretended to negotiate a peace with the two potentates. But while the ambassadors were going through their formal ceremonials, a Dominican friar who was in their train, and had secret instructions from Francis, concluded a separate peace with the emperor, who withdrew his army, and left his friend and ally to take care of himself. Henry returned to England, after leaving a garrison at Boulogne.

A. D. 1546. Peace was made between France and England; and it was agreed that Boulogne, which had been bravely defended against all attempts Francis had made to regain it, should remain in the possession of the English for eight years, after which time it

---

Who was the only daughter of James V. of Scotland, and what interest did the king of England take in her affairs?
Did Henry engage in a new war with France?
Did Francis I. deal deceitfully with Henry?
Did Henry make peace with France and Scotland?

was to be given up to France on the payment of a certain sum of money. Peace was also about this time made with Scotland; and Henry, being no longer troubled with foreign enemies, had the more time to torment his own subjects.

Henry required the people to make his opinion the standard of their faith, and was continually changing that opinion, and making contradictory laws, so it was scarcely possible for his subjects to steer a safe course among the difficulties which his tyrannical caprice laid in their way. Many were put to death for denying his supremacy. Towards the end of his life he became dropsical, which being added to his unwieldy corpulence, disabled him from walking, and made him "more furious than a chained lion."

These infirmities, indeed, so greatly increased the natural violence and irritability of his temper, that every body was afraid to come near him. Even the queen, though she was his most attentive nurse, with all her patience and discretion, very narrowly escaped being impeached for high treason, in consequence of having one day displeased him by expressing herself warmly in a religious argument. Indeed, his tyranny and caprice were such that none could feel themselves secure.

A. D. 1546. Among the instances of Henry's injustice and cruelty, the death of lord Surrey is as much as any to be detested. The duke of Norfolk and his son, lord Surrey, were committed to the Tower. The duke had been one of the king's earliest favorites, and lord Surrey was one of the most accomplished noblemen in England, and had by his talents and acquirements retained the king's regard for many years. Both these noblemen were supporters of the Roman Catholic cause

---

How did Henry manifest exceeding fickleness of purpose and violence of temper?
Was the king's violence ever expressed towards queen Catharine Parr?
Upon what pretence were the duke of Norfolk and sent his son to the Tower?

and some people thought that a fear lest they should disturb the peace of the young Edward's reign, when he should come to the throne, was the real cause of their ruin.

Whatever the cause was, the charges actually brought against them were frivolous. The chief charges against lord Surrey were that he had quartered in his coat of arms the arms of Edward the Confessor, which had been done by all his ancestors; and that he studied Italian, and was fond of conversing with foreigners, which made it probable that he corresponded with cardinal de la Pole. He was declared guilty of high treason, and was beheaded Jan. 19, 1547.

The duke of Norfolk seemed to cling to life with more solicitude than his accomplished son had done. He tried every concession that he could think of to soften the king: but Henry, as if he thirsted for his blood, hurried on the proceedings of parliament, and his death-warrant was signed Jan. 27, but before it could be executed the king expired, and thus his victim escaped.

Henry died in the 56th year of his age, and the 38th of his reign. He had been six times married, and left three children—Edward, by Jane Seymour, who succeeded him; Mary, by Catharine of Arragon, Elizabeth, by Anne Boleyn, who both were afterwards queens of England.

Though Henry had declared both his daughters illegitimate, he appointed them in his will, after their brother, to the succession of the crown. In case they all died without children, he left the succession after them to the children and heirs of his youngest sister, the duchess of Brandon, to the entire exclusion of his eldest sister Margaret, who after the death of her first husband, the king of Scotland, had married the earl of Angus, and had one daughter, wife of the earl of Lenox, and mother of Henry Darnley, of whom we shall hear more.

Wickliffe's opinions notwithstanding the early persecutions of his followers, had never been eradicated. During

---

Upon what charges was lord Surrey executed?
How did the duke of Norfolk escape?
At what age did Henry VIII. die, and who were his family?
How did Henry VIII. order the sucession?
Had the Lollards been eradicated in England?

the long civil wars the government had so many cares, that it attended but little to any affairs of religion. Consequently the Lollards increased in number; and in the early part of this reign their opinions gathered strength from the success of their protestant brothers in Germany, where Luther, a new reformer, had arisen, and drew people more and more from popery. Henry VIII. at first treated the Lollards with the utmost rigor, but relaxed towards them at the time of his quarrel with the pope.

This reign is generally considered as the *era of the Reformation* in England, and much certainly was at this time done towards it. The country was freed from subjection to the pope: the clergy were made amenable to the same laws with the laity. But the same caprice and violence of temper that had made the king do thus much prevented him from completing the great work he had begun. He abolished the religious houses with all their rules and observances, and yet appointed priests to say masses for his own soul. He forbade the worship of images, and commanded the church service to be read in English: and yet he burnt many persons for heresy.

Henry permitted the Bible to be translated, and then forbade it to be read except by particular persons. But notwithstanding all the impediments the king's inconsistencies put in the way of the Reformation, and the steadier opposition of the Romish clergy, the pure light of the new religion was still kept burning, chiefly through the firm perseverance of Cranmer, till in time it cleared away the darkness of superstition and popery.

The great men of this reign demand some consideration. Few characters known in history deserve more commendation than Cranmer. He was the only one of Henry's favorites who had no little selfish views of his own. His whole soul was placed on one great object—the reformation of religion; and to that all the powers of his mind were applied. Wolsey's great abilities were chiefly employed in raising himself to the highest worldly dignity. Cromwell, though a zealous reformer, was intent on enrich-

---

Did Henry VIII. promote the Reformation of Christianity?
By whose influence was the reformation advanced?
Who were the chief men of Henry's reign?

ing himself from the pillage of the religious houses. And the other courtiers, one and all, had their own narrow selfish ends to serve.

Such is the power of virtue over vice, that the overbearing Henry stood in awe of the gentle-tempered Cranmer. The king's regard for him was at all times sincere; and at one time, when Gardiner and the duke of Norfolk thought they had got the king's consent to have him sent to the Tower, Henry privately warned the archbishop of the plot, and advised him how to defeat the malice of his enemies, who were the chief supporters of the popish party.

Cranmer was very anxious that the public service of the church should be in English instead of Latin, but he knew that the king would violently oppose such a change. He therefore thought best to lead to it by degrees; and when a prayer was to be composed for the king's preservation in the expedition to France in 1544, Cranmer besought him that it might be composed in English, that the people might pray with more fervor from understanding what they uttered. By degrees Cranmer gained permission to have the Lord's prayer also, the creed, and the commandments, read in English in the churches; and the year before the king's death the liturgy was added.

Some few copies remained of Wickliffe's translation of the Bible, but Cranmer was desirous of obtaining a better translation. At last he got the king's permission to have one made, but it was four years before the work was completed. These Bibles, when they at length appeared, were received with thankfulness all over the kingdom: they were placed in churches, and secured by a chain to the reading desk. The people flocked to the places where they could hear the Bible read, and many persons learned to read, for the sole purpose of perusing it. But Henry, in the latter part of his life, withdrew this general privilege, and would not permit the Bible to be read by the lower orders of the people.

What influence had Cranmer over the mind of Henry?
What services did Cranmer render to religion?
Did Cranmer procure the scriptures to be translated, and did religion dispose the English to improve in learning?

It was cruel to deprive them of their Bibles yet by learning to read, they had gained something that the king could not take away from them. The increase of books, through the invention of printing, had already made the English much greater readers than formerly; but in regard to writing they do not seem to have been much advanced. In that art but a small number was then instructed.

Not all the learned men of that time were reformers. Two of the greatest ornaments of this reign were zealous papists, sir Thomas More, and lord Surrey. The latter was a poet, and a man of elegant literature. The former, besides his learning, possessed a sarcastic wit which he could not help indulging even when on the scaffold. Erasmus also, though a native of Holland, greatly aided the progress of learning in this country. He taught Greek at Oxford, till he was driven thence by the violence of the popish party, who, alarmed at the appearance of any thing new, thought the study of Greek a dangerous innovation.

Cardinal Wolsey, also a Catholic, was a great man. He began the building of Hampton Court, intending it for his own residence. He began also the building of Christ Church, in Oxford, meaning to call it Cardinal College · but after his disgrace Henry seized on the revenues with which Wolsey had endowed it, and completing the building, took upon himself the credit of founding it. On his death-bed he uttered these affecting words :—" Had I but served my God as diligently as I have served my king, he would not have left me in my grey hairs."

The trade in African slaves was first practised by the English nation in this reign.

Were the people of England generally able to write in the reign of Henry VIII. ?
Who were sir Thomas More, lord Surrey, and Erasmus ?
Had Cardinal Wolsey any loyalty and public spirit?
What inhuman traffic commenced in the reign of Henry VIII. ?

CHAPTER XXVI.

EDWARD VI.

[Years after Christ, 1547—1553.]

Edward was in his tenth year when his father died. He had already displayed a gentleness of character that endeared him to those about him. Henry had appointed sixteen executors and twelve counsellors, to whom he entrusted the care of the king and kingdom. But at the first meeting of the executors, they deviated from Henry's will, by making lord Hertford, Edward's eldest uncle, whom they created duke of Somerset, protector of the kingdom.

The protector, who was a favorer of the Protestants, was careful to entrust the education of the king to men of the reformed religion. Edward's young mind readily imbibed their opinions; and he showed a knowledge, zeal, and early piety, that was quite extraordinary in a boy of his age. The completion of the Reformation itself, which had been left in a very unfinished state at the death of Henry was Somerset's next care.

A commission was formed for drawing up a *book of offices;* that is, a prayer book, to be used in churches, for the general use of the church. Cranmer, and Ridley afterwards bishop of London, were at the head of this commission. They agreed to make every thing as near as they could to the practice of the pure and early ages of the Gospel. They retained many of the prayers that had been used in the service of the Romish church, and fixed the Liturgy nearly as it is now.

A considerable portion of the lower orders of the people were won over to the reformed religion; and many of the higher orders, some from conviction, and some for the sake of doing as others did, abjured popery. Those who had obtained grants of abbey lands, warmly supported the views of the protector. Thus the nation was in a great measure

---

Whom did the executors of Henry VIII. appoint protector during the minority of his son?
Did the protector regard the young king's education, and the interests of religion generally?
What commission was appointed to regulate the public worship?
Was the nation brought to conformity in religion?

brought to a seeming conformity in religion. Bishop Gardiner, however, still stood out, and opposed every new regulation that was made.

It appears that the Scottish nation did not consent to the marriage of their infant queen with the king of England. Perhaps they wished to preserve themselves a separate kingdom; and being generally Catholics, many did not like a king of the reformed religion. But Henry was prepared for opposition to his will in this matter, and left an injunction to his executors to compel the Scots to this marriage.

The protector, to fulfil the injunction of Henry, fitted out a fleet of sixty sail; and marched with an army of 18,000 men into Scotland, and advanced within four miles of Edinburgh; and the governor of Scotland summoned the whole force of the kingdom to repel this formidable invasion. The English gained considerable advantage in their encounter with the Scots; and had Somerset pursued his advantage, he might have conquered Scotland: but he had received intelligence of some cabals that were going on at home, which made him eager to return to England.

The Scots, having recovered from the consternation which this defeat had caused, were more than ever irritated against the English, and firmly resolved not to give their queen to Edward. Some declared, that, "though they liked the match, they liked not the manner of wooing:" and to place Mary beyond the power of the English, they sent her, when six years old, to be educated in the court of France, and betrothed her to the dauphin.

When Somerset returned to Westminster, he summoned a parliament, and repealed many oppressive laws, and passed others which were wise and moderate, and for which he is entitled to the respect of posterity. But, though he was well-intentioned, he was unfit to contend with the malice of those who were envious of his high station. Amongst his enemies, his own brother, lord Seymour, was the most inveterate.

Why did the Scottish nation object to the marriage of their young queen with Edward VI.?
How did Somerset attempt to accomplish the late king's will?
Did Somerset effect his purpose?
Was the administration of Somerset wise and beneficial, and who was his inveterate enemy?

Seymour had been appointed lord high admiral, but aspired to supplant his brother, whose superior in abilities he knew himself to be.

Seymour was indeed a man of great powers of flattery and address, and had won so much on the good opinion of the dowager queen, Catharine Parr, that she married him very soon after Henry's death. After living with him one year she died; and his ambition then aspired to the princess Elizabeth, who, it is supposed, would have listened to his suit, had it not been opposed by the other officers of the state.

Dudley, earl of Warwick, son of that wicked Dudley who was a judge in Henry the Seventh's reign, used every means to increase the disagreements between the protector and his brother, hoping to raise his own greatness on the ruin of theirs. He led on the admiral to commit many rash and violent actions, and persuaded Somerset to commit him for high treason. His condemnation and execution soon followed.

Somerset never lost sight of the affairs of the church, and many important changes were made. The law forbidding the clergy to marry, was repealed; and a law was passed which inflicted severe penalties on those who persevered in the old worship, and rejected the service which was now appointed. The princess Mary, who was a rigid papist, alone refused to conform to this law.

On this Mary's chaplains were imprisoned, and she herself threatened with punishment: but when she appealed to her cousin the emperor, and made an attempt to escape from England, it was deemed prudent to allow of her having mass performed privately in her house. But this concession cost the young king many tears, so criminal did he esteem the popish faith in which she persevered.

Although the destruction of the religious houses has probably been a great benefit to us who live in after ages, it must have been a very bad measure at the time. Many thousand people were reduced at once from wealth or com-

---

Who persuaded Somerset to prosecute his brother?
Did Somerset persecute the Catholics?
Was the princess Mary a papist?
What became of the monks and nuns who were expelled from the religious houses?

petence to absolute want. Some of the heads of the suppressed houses had small pittances allowed them for their lives; but the monks and nuns were turned adrift, a helpless race of creatures, who could do little towards their own maintenance.

It was a hard measure to those countrymen and farmers who had enjoyed the church lands at easy rents; and there remained also a still more numerous body of sufferers, the idle poor, who had been daily fed at the convent gates, and scarcely knew how to work. All these were now reduced to want and obliged to seek their bread by labor.

These causes, with others, made the year 1549 a period of insurrections and tumults all over England. The protector, who really compassionated the poor, did all in his power to relieve their distresses. But, while he was befriending them, he gave offence to the rich, by the great state and almost royal dignity which he assumed.

A confederacy, headed by the earl of Warwick, was formed against him. He soon saw himself deserted by all except Cranmer, and by Paget, his secretary; and, sinking into despondency, he resigned the protectorship. He was then committed to the Tower; and after a few weeks' imprisonment, was heavily fined, deprived of all his offices, and then restored to liberty. A new council of regency was appointed, and the earl of Warwick placed at the head of it.

Warwick, not satisfied with the degradation of Somerset, determined on his death, and accused him, in 1551, of a plot to raise a rebellion, and to assassinate himself and other privy counsellors. On these charges he was tried, condemned, and executed, to the sincere grief of the people, to whom his goodness of heart had much endeared him.

The work of the Reformation was still continued, but with more intemperance, under Warwick, than had been ever visible while the affairs of the nation were conducted

---

What effect had the destruction of the religious houses upon the condition of the poor in England?
How did Somerset regard the poor?
By whom was Somerset deprived of the regency.
By what false charge was Somerset degraded and destroyed?
Did the reformers commit any acts of injustice in the reign of Edward VI?

by the milder counsels of Somerset. Gardiner was deprived of his bishopric, and thrown into prison. Bonner, bishop of London, was also committed to the Tower; and many of the clergy were obliged to have recourse to trades for a maintenance, being reduced to poverty by the greedy courtiers, who seized on a large portion of the revenues of the church.

The earldom of Northumberland having some years since become extinct, Warwick, a short time before the death of Somerset, had prevailed with Edward to make him duke of Northumberland, and to bestow on him the estates which had belonged to the earldom, and which had been forfeited to the crown.

The young king was now entirely in the power of Northumberland, who placed his son, Robert Dudley, about his person. Edward's health declined from that time, and Northumberland formed the project of raising one of his own sons to the throne. He began by persuading Edward, that as both his sisters had been declared illegitimate, they could not possibly succeed to the crown, and that, therefore, by virtue of his father's will, the succession devolved on the children of Mary, the dowager queen of France, by her second husband the duke of Suffolk, whose eldest daughter, the duchess of Dorset, was the undoubted heir to the crown. The duchess, who had no son, was willing to resign her claim to her eldest daughter, lady Jane Grey, and Northumberland married her to his son, Guildford Dudley.

Edward felt no scruple about depriving his sister Mary of her birthright, fearing that her bigotry would be hurtful to the Protestant cause. But he felt many regrets in regard to the princess Elizabeth, whom he affectionately loved. He however, consented to settle the succession on lady Jane Grey; and the patent of settlement was signed by all the great officers of state.

The king, who had been for many months in a very delicate state of health, grew rapidly worse; and soon after

---

How was the earl of Warwick rendered more powerful than ever?
How did Northumberland overrule the succession, and what was Lady Jane Grey's title to the crown of England?
Upon whom was the succession settled?
Where did Edward IV. die?

died, on the 6th of July, 1553, in the sixteenth year of his age, and seventh of his reign.

Though during this reign the country was in a distracted and divided state on the score of religion, and though the officers of the state were not less divided and distracted by their own private jealousies and cabals, still there never had been any former time when the commerce of England flourished so much.

An expedition, consisting of two ships and a bark, was sent out by Edward VI. under the command of sir Hugh Willoughby, for the discovery of a north-east passage to India; but the attempt failed; and sir Hugh, and all the people both of his own ship, and of the bark which kept company with him, were frozen to death in a harbor of Lapland. Richard Chancellor, the captain of the other vessel, was more fortunate, and returned home after wintering at Archangel. This voyage first led the way to a lucrative trade with Russia.

A code of articles in relation to public worship having been thought advisable, the better to bring the people to a conformity in religion, Cranmer was appointed to make one; and he drew up forty-two articles, from which, with some slight alterations and retrenchments, the presen *Thirty-nine Articles* are formed.

The Thirty-nine Articles are articles of belief, which contain a short summary of the doctrines of the church of England. Besides the forty-two articles, Cranmer also drew up the church catechism, which he compiled in great measure from that used by the German reformers, making some additions of his own. The latter part of the catechism concerning the sacraments, was added in the reign of James I.

Cranmer, notwithstanding the natural moderation of his mind, was at times betrayed into the furious zeal of the age; and it must be lamented that he condemned two persons, if not more, to be burned, for being Anabaptists,

---

Did commerce flourish in the reign of Edward VI.?
What voyage of discovery was undertaken in this reign?
What articles of faith to be acknowledged by all members of the Church of England were promulgated?
What are the thirty-nine articles?
Were there any martyrs in the time of Edward VI.?

and this, notwithstanding the entreaties of the young king that they might be spared to live, and to be converted from their errors.

Edward's early promise was very great, and his abilities were of a high order. His Latin exercises have been preserved, and, if he was not much assisted by his masters, do him great credit. His chief study was theology, and his greatest delight was listening to sermons.

It will be interesting to know what became of all the old monasteries and nunneries. Some were leveled with the ground; others, stripped of their timber and lead, were left in ruin, and still remain objects of admiration to all who delight in the relics of antiquity. Many were given or sold to laymen, who converted them into dwelling-houses, and others were turned into hospitals.

Henry bestowed many of the religious houses on those who attended on his person. One of his attendants was rewarded with some abbey lands for having wheeled his chair farther from the fire; and a lady, whose name is not handed down to us, had a monastic house given to her for making the king a pudding which he liked.

In this reign the convenience of ladies' dress was very much assisted by the invention of pins. To serve the purposes for which we employ that article, there were previously to the invention of pins, a variety of contrivances, buttons, hooks and eyes, laces and loops; and ladies used even wooden skewers to fasten on their dress. A needle was a very valuable implement at this time. None were made in England till the next reign, when a Spanish negro came to London, and made some.

CHAPTER XXVII

MARY.

[Years after Christ, 1553—1558.]

As soon as Edward had breathed his last, the duke of Northumberland went to Sion-house, where lady Jane

---

What were the favorite pursuits of Edward VI. ?
What became of the religious houses sequestered by Henry VIII. ?
Were the useful arts improved in this reign ?
Who saluted lady Jane Grey as queen of England ?

Grey lived, and saluted her as queen: but she, far from being ambitious of this dignity, entreated that it might not be forced upon her, and pleaded the superior claims of the two princesses. But the duke had gone too far to be stopped by the scruples of a young creature of sixteen: and lady Jane, who was naturally of a timid and gentle disposition, was soon persuaded by her father-in-law, and suffered herself to be proclaimed. No applause followed the proclamation, and no one seconded this bold step of Northumberland.

Lady Jane, after a joyless reign of ten days, thankfully returned from the royal apartments in the Tower, in which she had been placed, to the privacy of her own house: and the princess Mary, arriving from her retreat in Suffolk, was welcomed by the people with the loudest acclamations. For though the consequences of her stern bigotry were dreaded by those of the new religion, they yet dreaded still more the unprincipled character of Northumberland.

When the duke saw his project entirely overthrown, he sought to save his own life by the meanest supplications. He fell on his knees before lord Arundel, who was sent by the queen to apprehend him; and while in that posture, a woman rushed up to him, and held a handkerchief to his face, which she told him was stained with the blood of his innocent victim the duke of Somerset. Northumberland was condemned, and beheaded on Tower-hill. His son Guildford, and lady Jane, were also condemned to death: but on account of their youth and innocence, their sentence was not then executed; but they were kept in prison.

Mary was in her thirty-seventh year at the time of her brother's death. Her person is described as having been very ordinary, and her manner unengaging. Her education had probably been much neglected, and she inherited her mother's gravity, with her father's violence and obstinate temper. She was old enough at the time of Catharine's divorce to feel keenly the king's injustice, and the being forbidden to see her injured mother, was a great aggravation of her wrongs. She and Anne Boleyn never concealed their mutual dislike.

When was queen Mary proclaimed?
What happened to Northumberland?
What was the character of queen Mary?

Mary invariably refused to give her sister Elizabeth the title of princess; and her obstinacy in this and other particulars, had often drawn upon her her father's displeasure and he had frequently put her under confinement. These early mortifications increased the natural sourness of her temper.

The first act of Mary's reign showed a compassionate feeling, which raised the people's hopes of her character. She restored to liberty the old duke of Norfolk, who had languished in prison, with his unexecuted sentence hanging over his head, ever since the death of Henry VIII. She released also Courtenay, son of the marquis of Exeter, a young nobleman whose youth and talents had been wasting in a prison from his childhood, but who, soon after he was restored to the world, acquired a degree of grace and accomplishment, that made him an ornament to the court.

The queen's next act was to release Gardiner, Bonner, and Tonstall, who had been deprived of liberty, and of their bishoprics, in the last reign; and she hastened, with their assistance, to overturn the Reformation, and to restore the old religion, and, as much as possible, to replace every thing on its former footing. She was greatly anxious for a reconciliation with the pope, who, at first, made some difficulty to receive within the pale of the church such a country of heretics as England was now become: but this difficulty was at length overcome, and cardinal de la Pole was appointed legate in England.

But Mary, though she could restore the mass, the praying to images, and all the other ceremonials of the Romish church, found it impossible to recover to their former uses the lands and buildings of the religious houses.

The foreign protestants, who had brought many useful arts into the country, now hastily left it, and were followed by many English gentlemen, who were glad to escape from the persecutions which they foresaw were at hand. Cran-

---

How did Mary regard her sister, and what soured her temper?
Did Mary ever exhibit any generosity?
Did Mary restore the Catholic religion in England?
Could Mary recover the church property?
How did Cranmer and other Protestants demean themselves in the present juncture?

mer was advised to fly; but he said he had been too much concerned in every measure of the Reformation to desert its cause. The queen had early marked him for destruction. She was not of a temper to forget an injury, and hated him for the share he had had in her mother's divorce; which many good offices he had done for herself could never atone for in her eyes.

A. D. 1554. A marriage was agreed upon between the queen and Philip of Spain, only son of Charles V. The match was exceedingly disliked by the English; but the archduke was made to agree, that the administration of the government should remain entirely with the queen and her ministers; and that no foreigner should be permitted to hold any public office.

Still so great was the alarm excited, that a formidable insurrection arose in Kent, which was headed by sir Thomas Wyatt, who having traveled in Spain, brought home such an account of Philip as added to the previous horror of him that had existed. The object of the insurrection was to dethrone Mary, and to place lady Jane Grey on the throne; and if her father, the duke of Suffolk, did not actually join, he at least showed some approbation of it.

Wyatt, at the head of 4000 men, entered London; but many of his followers, perceiving that no men of note joined his standard, silently left him. He was summoned to surrender; and having done so, he was tried, condemned, and executed: 400 of his unfortunate followers suffered with him; and 400 more were conducted to the queen, with ropes about their necks, and falling on their knees, received their pardon.

Soon afterwards, lady Jane Grey, whose fate it was always to suffer for the faults of others, was warned that she must prepare for death. The queen sent a priest of the Romish church to harass her last moments, by attempting to convert her; but her constancy was not to be shaken, and she employed the small portion of time that was left her

---

What marriage contract was made for queen Mary in 1554?
Who headed a rebellion at this time?
What became of sir Thomas Wyatt?
What sentence was passed upon lady Jane Grey?

In prayer, and in writing, in Greek, a farewell letter to her sister, in which she exhorted her to be firm in her faith.

Lord Guildford Dudley was also condemned to die, and entreated to have a parting interview; but Jane refused it lest the affliction of such a meeting should overcome their fortitude. She appeared on the scaffold with a serene countenance, and declared that she had greatly erred in not having more firmly refused the crown; but that filial reverence, and not her own ambition, had been the cause of her fault. Her father was beheaded soon after; and the queen became so suspicious of almost every body, that she filled the prisons with nobles and gentlemen.

A. D. 1555. The time now arrived that had been fixed for the archduke's coming to England; but the admiral of the fleet which Mary had sent to escort him, dared not take him on board, lest the sailors should commit some violence against him. Such was the detestation in which he was held. At last he arrived: the marriage was celebrated at Westminster; and Philip, by his distant and reserved behavior, increased the previous dislike of the English.

From this time the chief business of parliament was to guard against the encroachments of Philip; while Mary's only anxiety was to increase the power and influence of a husband, on whom she doted with a troublesome fondness, though he, on his part, could with difficulty conceal his own dislike to his unengaging partner. On one subject, however, they were perfectly agreed, namely, in the desire to *extirpate heresy*, by the most violent and sanguinary measures.

Gardiner willingly entered into the views of Philip and Mary; but finding this work of cruelty more arduous than he had expected, he made it over to Bonner, a man of such inhumanity that he even delighted to see the dying agonies of the sufferers; and would often take on himself the office of executioner, adding to the misery of the poor creatures who suffered, by a mockery and levity, which, had it not

---

What was the end of lady Jane and her husband?
Was Philip of Spain liked in England?
In what was Philip and Mary agreed?
Was the *extirpation* of *heresy*, as the bigots of this reign called persecution, attended with manifestations of cruelty?

been asserted by writers of undoubted credit, one would have thought impossible.

In the course of the next three years, nearly three hundred persons were burned alive, martyrs to their religion; many more suffered imprisonments, fines, and lesser punishments. Two venerable and pious men, Latimer and Ridley, were amongst the first who perished; and they died exhorting each other to faith and courage. They were burnt, in the year 1555, in the public street at Oxford, near Baliol College.

Hooper, bishop of Gloucester, was another martyr. When he was tied to the stake, and the faggots heaped about him, the queen's pardon was placed on a stool before him, and if he would have recanted, he might have stretched out his hand to take the pardon; but he rejected it on such a condition, and died without uttering a groan.

If these scenes fill us with horror at the wickedness of Mary and her ministers, they also make us revere the constancy of the sufferers, who, sustained by faith and hope, could thus abide, without a groan, the horrors of a death of extreme torture. Far from extirpating the Protestant religion, these barbarities only set the hearts of the people the more resolutely against a church which could sanction such cruelty. The English law in regard to heretics, was nevertheless too mild to satisfy the ferocity of Philip, and he made an attempt to introduce the inquisition into England, but happily without success.

At the time when these executions took place, Gardiner also died. He was succeeded as chancellor, by Heath, archbishop of York, a man of slender abilities, but of a furious zeal. Gardiner's death hastened that of Cranmer. The new chancellor made no opposition to the queen's wish that he should be put to death, and he was condemned to be burned at Oxford. In a moment of weakness the archbishop, hoping by such a measure to preserve his life, signed a paper, in which he avowed his belief in the pope's supremacy. But Mary sent him word this should not save him

---

Who were burned for heresy in England in 1555?
What fortitude was exhibited by Hooper, bishop of Gloucester?
Did the cruelty of Mary and her ministers extirpate the reformed religion?
What became of Gardiner, and of Cranmer?

and that he must acknowledge his errors in the church, before the whole people.

The strength of Cranmer's mind now returned; and, when he was brought forth to the church to make his public recantation, instead of doing so, he bitterly bewailed his momentary weakness, and asserted his firm belief in the Protestant faith. He was immediately led forth to execution; and, when the faggots were set on fire, he stretched out his right hand, with which he had signed the paper, and held it in the flames until it was totally consumed, without betraying any symptom of pain, saying frequently, " This hand has offended;" then, as if his mind was more at ease for having made this atonement, his countenance became full of peaceful serenity, and he appeared insensible to all worldly suffering.

The next day the cardinal de la Pole was made archbishop of Canterbury; and he showed so much lenity towards the Protestants, as to excite the displeasure of the pope.

Philip, who had soon became weary of England, went, in 1555, to Flanders; and the queen, seeing herself treated by him with indifference and neglect, spent her time in tears and lamentations, and in writing long letters to him, which he never answered, and, perhaps, never read. The more he slighted her, the more she doted on him; and to procure money, in the hope of winning him back by supplying him with it, she loaded the people with taxes.

A. D. 1556. The emperor Charles V., wearied with the toils of royalty, which his intriguing and ambitious spirit had made a greater burden to him than to the generality of monarchs, took the extraordinary resolution of retiring from the bustle of the world to the retirement of a monastery, and resigned all his dominions to his son.

Philip, who had his father's ambition, but not his talents, immediately declared war against France, and he expected England should do the same; but, the Spanish yoke being

---

Was the constancy of Cranmer shaken at the prospect of death
Who succeeded to Cranmer as Archbishop?
When did Philip of Spain leave England?
When did Charles V. resign his dominions to his son?
Did Philip induce the English to declare war against France?

more than ever disliked, the queen could not prevail with her council to give their consent to infringe the peace.

When Philip, however, came to London, and protested that he would never again set foot in England, unless war was declared with France, the queen, almost frantic pressed the matter so urgently, as to overcome the reluctance of the council. War was declared. Mary, who had already exhausted her resources in furnishing Philip with money, resorted to the most unjust and violent measures to extort the means of fitting out a fleet and raising an army.

A fleet and an army were at last provided; and the latter, under the command of the earl of Pembroke, joined Philip's army in Flanders, in time to take a part in the battle of St. Quintin, in which the duke of Savoy, the Spanish general, gained a victory over the French; but, while Mary was triumphing at this success, the French were preparing for her a severe mortification.

Though every thing else in France had long been lost to the English, they still preserved Calais, which had been guarded as the chief jewel of the crown by every English king since Edward III., who had won it. It was so strongly fortified, and had always been so well garrisoned, that the French had never even attempted to recover it.

In Mary's feeble reign, the monks and bigots who composed her ministry, thought more of burning heretics, than of any other concern of state. They had neglected to keep the fortifications in repair; and, to save the charge of what they supposed an unnecessary garrison, withdrew the greater part of it during the winter months. The governor had remonstrated seriously, but in vain, against this unwise economy.

The duke of Guise, general of the French army, being well informed of these circumstances, determined to attempt the recovery of the town. It was surrounded by

---

Did queen Mary overrule her council in the question of war with France?
What was gained at the battle of St. Quintin?
What then remained to the English in France?
Did the religious policy of queen Mary's reign preserve the foreign power of the British?
What French general attempted the recovery of Calais?

marshes which, during the winter, were totally impassable, and could be approached on the land side only by two raised roads, defended by two castles. The duke made an attack on these castles, and soon took them, and, in the meantime, the French fleet besieged the fortifications of the town, next the sea, and thus lord Wentworth, the governor, saw himself enclosed on every side.

Though Wentworth had only a few hundred men with him, he made a brave resistance; but the town being unprovided with every thing necessary for sustaining a siege, he was obliged to surrender; and thus the duke of Guise made himself master, in eight days, of a fortress that had been deemed impregnable.

The news of this event struck a universal dismay all over England; and the queen declared that when she died, the word *Calais* would be found engraved upon her heart. Mary's health visibly declined from this time. The neglect of Philip, and her own disappointment at having no children, a blessing she vehemently desired, all preyed upon her health. She dragged on a few miserable months, and died Nov. 17, 1558, in the 43d year of her age, and the 6th of her reign.

The cardinal de la Pole died on the same day with the queen, and left an unsullied name behind him.

Arts and commerce did not flourish in the brief and troubled reign of the bigoted Mary. The czar of Muscovy first sent an ambassador to England in this reign. Drinking-glasses were not made in England till the time of queen Mary, and were at first considered more precious than silver. Some few looking-glasses were used at the toilet; but they were probably very small, and were commonly either carried about by the ladies in their pockets, or hung to their girdles.

A French priest who visited England in the middle of

Who surrendered Calais to the French?
Under what circumstances, and at what time did queen Mary die?
Did commerce, &c. flourish in Mary's reign?
How did a French priest describe the English?

the sixteenth century, thus describes the English of that age :—" The people of this country have a mortal hatred to the French ; and in common call us France knave, or France dog. The people of this land make good cheer, and dearly love junketing. The men are large, handsome, and ruddy, with flaxen hair. Their women are the greatest beauties in the world, and as fair as alabaster. The English in general are cheerful, and love music.

" In this land they commonly make use of silver vessels, when they drink wine. The servants wait on their masters bare-headed, and leave their caps on the buffet (sideboard.) In the windows of the houses are plenty of flowers, and at the taverns a plenty of rushes on their wooden floors, and many cushions of tapestry on which travelers seat themselves.

" The English consume a great quantity of beer ; the poor people drink it out of wooden cups. They eat much whiter bread than is commonly made in France. With their beer they have a custom of eating very soft saffron cakes, in which there are likewise raisins. It is likewise to be noted that the servants carry pointed bucklers, even those of bishops. And the husbandmen, when they till the ground, commonly leave their bucklers, swords, or sometimes their bows, in the corner of the field."

This loquacious traveler visited Scotland also, and describes it as a barren and wild country. Some of the Scotch, he says, applied themselves to letters, and became good philosophers and authors, but the people in general were rude and churlish.

How did the same priest describe domestic arrangements in England?
What were the habits of the poorer sort of people?
What did the same writer say of the Scotch of that age?

CHAPTER XXVIII

ELIZABETH.

[Years after Christ, 1558—1603.]

When Mary's death was announced to the parliament, which happened to be assembled at the time, the members all sprang from their seats; and shouts of joy, and the words "God save Queen Elizabeth!" were heard to resound on every side. When the news was spread abroad, the transport of the people was so great, that they hurried in crowds towards Hatfield, where Elizabeth was then residing, and escorted her into London. Elizabeth was then twenty-five years old.

The new queen, from her first coming to the throne, seemed anxious to show an entire forgetfulness of all her former sufferings, and never testified any resentment towards those who had been instrumental to them. Even sir Henry Benefield, in whose custody she had been for a time, and whom she had found a severe gaoler, experienced from her no other punishment or rebuke, but that of

---

What demonstrations of joy distinguished the accession of queen Elizabeth?

Did Elizabeth manifest a generous disposition to those who had injured her?

her telling him that he should have the custody of any state prisoner whom she wished to be treated with peculiar severity. The cruel Bonner was the only one of her sister's ministers to whom she showed a marked dislike. She turned from him with horror, and would never speak to him nor look at him.

The first great anxiety of all the Protestant part of the nation was to have a settlement of the affairs of the church. In this important business Elizabeth proceeded with great prudence and caution, and yet with so much determination and steadiness, that she soon replaced every thing in the state it had been at her brother's death; and all without one drop of blood being spilt, or a single estate confiscated Bonner alone, for refusing to acknowledge her supremacy was punished by being imprisoned for life.

Philip, as soon as he heard of queen Mary's death, proposed himself to her sister in marriage. Elizabeth never for a moment thought of consenting to such a union; but, perhaps, for fear of making him her enemy, or perhaps, from her accustomed caution, she delayed to give a decisive answer as long as she could; and when she sent her refusal, she took the opportunity of declaring to the parliament a determination to lead a single life.

Notwithstanding this declaration, Elizabeth some years afterwards admitted the addresses of the duke of Anjou, the brother of the king of France. But partly through her fear of lessening her own authority, if she admitted another to share it, and partly, perhaps, from love to her people, which made her unwilling to give them a foreign king, she broke off the match, after keeping the duke long in suspense.

The pretensions of Mary, the young queen of Scotland were an early source of disquiet to Elizabeth. Mary was great niece of Henry VIII., and on the plea that Elizabeth had been declared illegitimate, she asserted her own right to the crown, and took upon her the arms and title of queen of England. And though this empty boast was not followed by any active attempt, it yet laid the foundation in Elizabeth's mind of a deadly hatred towards her.

How did Elizabeth settle the affairs of the Church?
Who made Elizabeth an offer of marriage?
What French nobleman made proposals of marriage to Elizabeth?
Who, and on what pretence, claimed to be queen of England?

Mary had been married to the dauphin, who, on his faher's death, became king of France, by the title of Francis II.; and she had thus been, for a brief season, the queen of the most splendid court in Europe, into all the dissipations of which she entered eagerly. When, on the early death of Francis, she was obliged to return to Scotland, the contrast between the country she left, and that which she was now come to inhabit, struck her with melancholy; and the rude manners of the Scots filled her with disgust.

This disgust was increased by difference of religion Mary had been brought up a bigoted Catholic; and the Reformation, which had now made great progress in Scotland, was not marked there with a mild and conciliatory spirit. The Scotch reformers were men of rigid zeal, and condemned all gaiety and amusements as sinful. *They* were as much shocked at the queen's levities, as *she* was displeased by their austerity.

While these discontents were growing in Scotland, the queen of England was busily employed in putting the affairs of her kingdom in order. She called in the old coin, which had been shamefully debased in the last three reigns, and replaced it by a coinage of the standard weight. She filled her arsenals with arms; she introduced the manufacturing of gunpowder into England; she frequently reviewed her militia, and put the country into a complete state of defence; she encouraged agriculture, trade, and navigation, and increased her navy so much that she has been called " the queen of the northern seas."

Elizabeth's wise government was respected abroad and prosperous at home. She was exceedingly fortunate in the choice of her ministers; particularly in her treasurer, lord Burleigh, and her secretary Walsingham, who were men of extraordinary abilities and integrity. While affairs were managed with so much vigor and success, the people were scarcely aware in how great a degree their queen kept gradually enlarging her prerogative, nor how much their own liberties were infringed.

How did Mary of Scotland regard her own subjects?
What was the state of religion in Scotland, A. D 1559
What were the first measures of queen Elizabeth's reign?
Who were Elizabeth's ministers?

In all cases in which her own authority was concerned, Elizabeth was always decided and peremptory: and as she had generally good reason for what she did, and, above all, was frugal of expense, the mass of the people, though kept in great subjection, regarded her with enthusiastic attachment.

In regard to her private friendships Elizabeth exhibited less wisdom than in political affairs. Her chief favorite was Robert Dudley, earl of Leicester, a man wholly undeserving of moral respect. He was the son of that unprincipled duke of Northumberland who was beheaded in the reign of Mary.

The great rival of Leicester in Elizabeth's favor was Ratcliffe, earl of Sussex, a plain rough soldier, who loved and honored his mistress in sincerity, while Leicester only used her favor as the ladder to his own ambition. The queen valued Sussex, and employed him in many affairs of importance: but the assiduities of Leicester were more pleasing to her vanity, and she was fond of keeping him about her court. He continued to retain his place in her favor till his death, in 1588.

Early in the year 1563 Elizabeth caught the small-pox, and for some days her life was considered to be in danger. The prospect of her death, joined to the probability of the queen of Scotland's succession, encouraged the popish party; and when she recovered, the parliament besought her either to change her resolution, of living unmarried, or else to name her successor. Both these requests were very displeasing to Elizabeth.

Elizabeth was afterwards beset with princely suitors; but she always avoided as long as possible the giving them a decisive answer, and kept all persons, both friends and enemies, who were anxiously watching her conduct, in entire suspense as to her real intentions.

How did the English nation regard their queen?
Who was the favorite of Elizabeth?
Did the English desire their queen to marry?
Did queen Elizabeth act openly and sincerely as to her purpose of marriage?

Mary of Scotland, in the hope of being named by Elizabeth as her successor, affected to treat her with great respect. Both queens indeed pretended extraordinary regard for one another, and styled themselves in their letters "loving sisters." Mary having been urged by her council to a second marriage, thought proper to apply to Elizabeth to choose a suitable match for her. Elizabeth's wish was that her "loving sister" should continue a widow.

It was one of the weaknesses of this great queen to have the utmost dislike of any person's marrying, and she persecuted many of her own subjects for no other reason than because they did not choose to live single like herself. At length, having proposed two or three matches for Mary, which she knew she would not accept, Elizabeth pretended to be exceedingly displeased with her, when she at last chose for herself, and married her cousin Henry Stuart, Lord Darnley.

Darnley was the son of Margaret Douglas, daughter of Margaret, sister of Henry VIII., by her second husband lord Angus. Thus, after Mary, he was the next in succession to the crown of England. But this union, which appeared so suitable, proved most unfortunate in the end.

Darnley was a man of inferior capacity, and soon became the object of Mary's dislike and contempt; and she on her part gave him just cause for displeasure by making a favorite and a confidant of an Italian musician of the name of David Rizzio.

One evening, when the queen was at supper with Rizzio and some of the ladies of her court, Darnley, with a band of armed men, rushed into the room, and one of them stabbed Rizzio, as he clung to the queen's knees for protection. As one crime usually gives occasion for another, so Mary, by this barbarous murder, was provoked into the commission, if possible, of a greater crime. She admitted the earl of Bothwell, a man of infamous character, into her

---

With what mutual hypocrisy did the queens of England and Scotland treat each other?
Why did Elizabeth affect to be displeased with Mary of Scotland?
Who was Lord Darnley?
By what foolish conduct did Mary displease her husband?
Of what outrage was Darnley guilty, and what became of him?

councils, and in concert with him contrived and effected the death of Darnley.

With Bothwell's consent to the scheme, the queen persuaded Darnley, for the benefit of his health, to sleep in a lone house near Edinburgh, called the Kirk of the field This house, at a time when the queen was absent, attending the wedding of one of her women, was blown up by gun-powder; and the unfortunate Henry Darnley perished, leaving a son by the queen seven months old.

Soon after the death of Darnley, Bothwell contrived to carry off the queen (probably by her own consent,) and detained her for some little time in a sort of imprisonment, To the astonishment of all persons, she was so far from resenting this outrage, that though Bothwell was universally believed to have been Darnley's murderer, she did not scruple to marry him. This marriage increased the suspicions that she also was concerned in that atrocious deed.

A. D. 1567. Nearly the whole country, in just abhorrence of this crime, headed by the lords Morton and Murray, rose in arms against her; and Mary, finding that even her own troops were unwilling to fight in her cause, gave herself up into the hands of her enemies, who imprisoned her in Lochleven castle, and compelled her to sign a resignation of her kingdom to her son.

This infant was accordingly crowned king by the title of James VI.; and Murray, who was half-brother to the queen, though not a legitimate heir of the crown of Scotland, was appointed regent to the kingdom. Bothwell meantime had fled the country; and, after leading a wandering and wretched life, supporting himself by piracy he was at last thrown into a prison in Denmark. He fell into a state of insanity, and lingered ten miserable years in that condition.

Mary, after a short time, found means to escape from prison; and, raising an army, she encountered Murray at

---

Where did Darnley perish?
Whom did Mary of Scotland take for a second husband?
What circumstances compelled Mary to resign her kingdom?
Who was crowned king of Scotland, and what became of Bothwell?
Did Mary attempt to recover the throne of Scotland, and with what effect?

Langside; but her troops were completely defeated; and she having watched the battle from a neighboring eminence, put spurs to her horse, and never stopped till she got to the bank of a little river on the boundary between Scotland and England.

There the bishop of St. Andrews, who had accompanied her flight, caught hold of the bridle of her horse, and on his knees besought her to turn back: but she, preferring to trust Elizabeth's generosity, rather than again to encounter the insults of her own subjects, rushed through the stream to the opposite side. She soon arrived at Workington in Cumberland, from whence she sent a messenger to inform Elizabeth of the step she had taken, and then proceeded to Carlisle to await the answer.

Elizabeth, on receiving the news of this extraordinary event, was in the greatest perplexity how to act. Her whole conduct to Mary was so capricious and unreasonable in the beginning, and so tyrannical and cruel in the end, that historians have found it difficult to account for it. Whatever her thoughts were on receiving Mary's letter, she concealed them with great dissimulation, and pretended the utmost friendship for that unhappy queen.

Elizabeth's conduct to Mary exhibited none of her avowed friendship. She declared, that before Mary could be received at the English court, it was necessary, both for *her* honor, that she should be cleared from the heavy charges which had been brought against her by the Scots. She returned an answer to this effect to the queen of Scots, and sent lady Scrope under pretence of attending on her, but in reality to detain her in a sort of imprisonment: and she had her soon removed from Carlisle to Bolton-hall in Yorkshire.

Mary consented to an investigation of her conduct, and despatched the bishop of Ross, and eight other persons, to meet at York the commissioners sent by Elizabeth. The regent Murray also attended there; and after a tedious successoin of letters and protestations, in which both parties

---

Did Mary go to England?
How did Elizabeth treat Mary?
Why did Elizabeth refuse to receive Mary at court?
Was Mary brought to a legal trial?

acted with great duplicity, and seemed equally afraid of arriving at truth, nothing was proved.

When the conferences, which lasted some months, were over, Elizabeth persisted that as Mary was by no means cleared by the investigation which had taken place, she was herself justified not only in refusing to see her, but even in detaining her still a prisoner : and she now placed her in the custody of the earl of Shrewsbury, a nobleman who had large possessions in the North of England. Shrewsbury had the care of her for sixteen years at one or other of his country houses.

At first the unfortunate queen was allowed to receive visitors, and her eloquence and insinuating manners made every one who conversed with her believe her to be innocent, however they might have been prepossessed of her guilt. The Papists all took her part, and thought that the jealousy of Elizabeth towards her was more on account of her religion than from any other cause.

The duke of Norfolk was one of those who were most devoted to her; and he offered to contrive her escape, and to place her on the English throne, on condition that she would consent to marry him. Mary, glad to catch at any hope of escape, promised to do so, if she could obtain a divorce from Bothwell.

In this plot most of the English Papists joined. It was soon discovered, and gave Elizabeth a pretext for holding Mary with a harder grasp, and for preventing her from having any future intercourse with all persons but those of lord Shrewsbury's household. The duke of Norfolk was committed to the Tower, and was afterwards liberated on his promise to give up all correspondence with Mary; but he broke his promise, and again sent letters to her, though so secretly that even the vigilant Cecil did not for some time find it out.

A. D. 1571. At last, Mary wishing to send some money to her partizans in Scotland, Bannister, a confidential servant of the duke, was the person fixed on

---

Under whose custody was Mary imprisoned?
Who befriended Mary?
What conspiracy was planned for Mary's deliverance?
Did the duke of Norfolk act honestly in regard to Mary?
How was Norfolk's treachery discovered?

to take it. This money, and a letter which was to accompany it, were sent to Bannister by a person not in the secret; and he, perceiving there was some mystery, took the letter to lord Burleigh, who thus discovered that the duke of Norfolk and the Scottish queen were again conspiring to dethrone Elizabeth.

Norfolk was brought to trial, and believing that some papers had been destroyed which he had ordered his secretary to burn, boldly denied the being concerned in the plot: but these papers, instead of being destroyed, had been hid by the secretary under the mats of the duke's chamber, and under the tiles of the house, and were produced on the trial, and so fully confirmed his guilt, that he was condemned to die. Elizabeth always declared that she would have forgiven him, if, instead of persisting in falsehood, he had made a free confession. He was beheaded in 1572.

The queen was strongly importuned by the parliament to put her rival also to death; but though she saw that so long as Mary remained a prisoner in England she herself should never be secure from plots and conspiracies, yet she could not at once bring herself to consent to so violent and unprecedented an act. She would gladly have sent her out of the kingdom, and probably heartily repented of her own policy, in detaining her a prisoner.

Elizabeth had gone too far to recede: and since she could not with safety to herself now restore the queen of Scots to liberty, she determined to keep her even more strictly guarded than before; and removed her from the care of lord Shrewsbury, who, she apprehended, was too indulgent to his prisoner, to that of sir Amais Paulet and sir Drue Drury.

Philip of Spain, and the queen dowager of France, Catharine de Medici, had for many years past been forming schemes for restoring the Romish religion in England, by dispossessing Elizabeth, and raising Mary to the throne. Mary herself was in all their secrets; and as she received a jointure from France, on account of her being widow of

---

How did Norfolk conduct himself on his trial?
Why did Elizabeth refuse to put Mary to death?
On what account did Elizabeth put a more strict guard upon Mary?
Who conspired to dethrone queen Elizabeth?

a French king, she had means of getting from thence private intelligence, and had money at her command to distribute amongst her partizans in England and Scotland.

Elizabeth, meanwhile, was well informed of all that was going on: but she felt such entire confidence in the affection of her people, that she did not express any fears at the machinations of her enemies, till the discovery of a scheme to assassinate her privately gave her some alarm. This plot, which was contrived by a Catholic priest, one John Ballard, when ripe for execution, was communicated to many Catholic gentlemen, who readily joined in it, though not so secretly but that Walsingham had information of the whole.

When Walsingham had obtained all the information he wanted, he thought it was time to secure the conspirators; and fourteen of them were taken up, condemned, and executed, before Mary had any knowledge that the plot was detected.

One day, as Mary was taking the air on horseback, she was met by a messenger from the queen, who informed her of the detection and death of her friends, and that she was to be removed immediately to Fotheringay castle in Northamptonshire. She was accordingly compelled to set out for that place instantly, with the messenger who brought these unwelcome tidings, without being suffered to return to make any preparations for the sudden journey.

In a few days, Mary's arrival at Fotheringay was followed by that of commissioners from Elizabeth, who were appointed to try her for the part she had taken in the late conspiracy, of which it was believed she approved, and in which she connived. The proofs against her were but too strong. The commissioners returned to London after the trial, and pronounced sentence against her in the Star chamber, Oct. 25, 1586.

Elizabeth affected the utmost reluctance to consent to Mary's death; and sir Robert Cary, in his account of the

---

What served to tranquilize the queen's mind, and what plot against her life was contrived?
What happened to the conspirators?
How was Mary removed to Fotheringay Castle?
On account of what charge did Mary receive sentence of death?
Did Elizabeth readily consent to the death of Mary?

scenes to which he was an eye-witness, certainly thought that her sighs and tears on this occasion were sincere.

When Mary's condemnation was known in Scotland, the young king sent an urgent remonstrance to Elizabeth on the unjustifiable conduct she was pursuing towards his mother; but one of James's ambassadors secretly advised Elizabeth not to spare Mary, and undertook to pacify his master.

At length, after some months of apparent indecision on the part of the queen, who kept her ministers uncertain as to her intentions, she signed the death warrant. But when she found it had been despatched to Fotheringay, she expressed the most violent displeasure at the hasty officiousness of her servants, in hopes by such an artifice to transfer to them the blame of Mary's death.

A. D. 1587. On the sixth of February, the warrant was brought to Fotheringay by the earls of Shrewsbury and Kent, who informed Mary that she must prepare for death the next morning. Mary received their message with composure, and employed herself during the remainder of the day in writing letters, in dividing the few valuables she had amongst her servants, and in taking leave of them. She retired to rest at her usual time, but arose after a few hours sleep, and spent the rest of the night in prayer.

Towards morning she attired herself in the only rich dress she still possessed. A white lawn veil was thrown over her head; and when she was summoned to the hall where she was to die, she took a crucifix and a prayer-book in her hand, and leaning on sir Amias Paulet, she walked with a serene and composed countenance. She was met by the way by her faithful servant, Andrew Melvil, who flung himself on his knees before her, and burst into an agony of grief.

Mary endeavored to console him with the utmost firmness; but on charging him with her last message to her

---

Did the king of Scotland interfere in his mother's behalf?
What paper did Elizabeth sign, and what is a death warrant?
How did Mary receive sentence of death?
How did Mary prepare for execution?
What firmness did the last moments of Mary exhibit?

son, she melted into tears. She then entered the hall in which the scaffold had been raised, and saw, with an undismayed countenance, the two executioners, standing there, and all the preparations for her death. The place was crowded with spectators who seemed to forget her former faults, in compassion for her present calamitous condition.

After some time spent in prayer, she began, with the aid of her women, to unrobe herself; and seeing them ready to break forth into tears and lamentations, she made them, by putting her finger to her lips, a sign to forbear. She then gave them her blessing: a handkerchief was bound round her eyes, and without any visible trepidation she laid her head upon the block, and with two strokes it was severed from her body. Thus perished this unfortunate princess, in the 45th year of her age.

Mary had been a queen almost from her birth. From the age of six to that of nineteen she had been trained to levity and dissipation in the French court. From her nineteenth to her twenty-seventh year she had lived in Scotland, in a succession of crimes, follies, and sorrows. The nineteen remaining years of her life she had passed in a melancholy captivity, a prey to all the miseries of restraint, suspense and impatience. But time and affliction had neither subdued her spirit, nor wholly destroyed her extraordinary beauty.

In a letter written to Lord Burleigh, by a person who was present at the execution of this unhappy lady it was said, that when the executioner held up Mary's head, after it was cut off, her "borrowed auburn locks" fell off, and the same face that had appeared but a few minutes before so beautiful in life, now was seen so much altered in death, that the spectators could scarcely believe it to be the same: the hair was quite gray, and the face appeared to be that of a woman of seventy. After her death it was found, by one of the executioners, that the queen's favorite little dog had concealed itself amongst the folds of her dress, and the poor little animal could with difficulty be removed from his dead mistress.

How did Mary comport herself at the time of her execution?
What were the leading circumstances of Mary's life?
What was Mary's appearance after death?

A fine lady of the age of Elizabeth.

When the news of the execution of the queen of Scots was brought to Elizabeth, she thought it necessary to assume the appearance of excessive grief; she wore mourning, and for some days shut herself up with only her women. The king of Scotland expressed great resentment at the murder of his mother, and threatened Elizabeth with a war: but it was so much the interest of both sovereigns to keep at peace, that James, who was not of a warlike disposition, suffered his indignation to subside.

A. D. 1588. Philip of Spain had long been meditating an invasion of England; and, having completed his preparations, and collected his forces, he felt so certain of conquest, that he called his fleet which was now assembled in the Tagus, the *Invincible Armada*. His land forces, to the number of fifty thousand men, under the duke of Parma, were marched to the coast of the Netherlands, where a sufficient number of transports were prepared.

This whole armament, by land and sea, was so very powerful, both in the size and number of ships, in the strength and discipline of the Spanish soldiery, and the gallantry and spirit of the numerous volunteers who flocked to serve

---

Did Elizabeth manifest grief for the death of Mary?
Who invaded England in 1588?

in it, that it seemed much more than sufficien' to conquer England.

Elizabeth, meanwhile, sure of the affection of her people, at least of all who were Protestants, was undismayed. She made every necessary preparation for defence: but the English fleet, when collected altogether, was so small in comparison with that of the Spaniards, that her chief reliance was in the superior skill and bravery of her sea men and officers.

The fleet was commanded by lord Howard of Effingham. Drake, Hawkins, and Frobisher served under him. The land forces, which were very inferior to Philip's, both in number and experience, were divided into several bodies. One, commanded by lord Hunsdon, was appointed to guard the queen's person. Another, under Lord Leicester, was stationed at Tilbury Fort. The rest were placed wherever it seemed most likely that the Spaniards would attempt a landing.

The chief support of the kingdom was the vigor and prudence of the queen herself, who, showing no alarms at the dangers that threatened her, gave her orders with decision, and omitted nothing that could infuse courage into her people, and increase the general security. This heroic woman appeared on horseback at the camp at Tilbury, and, riding through the ranks, made so animating a speech to the soldiers, that every one felt roused to an enthusiastic attachment to her person.

Amongst other things, Elizabeth said on this occasion: "I know I have but the body of a weak and feeble woman, but I have the heart of a king, and of a king of England too: and think foul scorn that Parma of Spain, or any prince of Europe, should dare to invade the borders of my realms: to which, rather than any dishonor shall grow by me, I myself will take up arms; I myself will be your general, judge, and rewarder of every one of your virtues in the field."

How did Elizabeth meet this emergency?
Who commanded the sea and land forces at this juncture?
Did Elizabeth encourage the army?
In what speech did Elizabeth remarkably manifest her spirit and capacity?

While these preparations were making in England, the Armada was on the point of sailing, but was a little delayed by the death of the admiral, whose place was supplied by the duke of Medina Sidonia, a man utterly inexperienced in sea affairs. At length on May 29, 1588, this mighty armament issued from the mouth of the Tagus; but a violent storm coming on the next day, so many of the ships were disabled that it was obliged to return into harbor to refit.

It again sailed with orders to proceed directly to the coast of Flanders, thence to convey the duke of Parma and his troops to the Thames. But the Spanish admiral learning from a fisherman that the English fleet was assembled at Plymouth, ventured, in the hope of annihilating it at one blow, to disobey his orders, and made for that port.

The Armada, as it approached the Lizard Point, was descried by a Scotch pirate, who was cruising in those seas, and he, hoisting every sail, hastened to give notice of the enemy's approach. Effingham had just time to get out of port, when he saw the invincible Armada coming full sail towards him in the form of a cresent, and stretching over a distance of seven miles.

Lord Effingham soon perceived how heavily the Spanish ships sailed, and that they were very ill-built and unmanageable; and his confidence in his own little fleet became much strengthened. He was at first fearful of advancing too near, lest the weight of the Spanish ships should run down his own.

Effingham, however, soon saw that the bulk of the ships was an advantage to him, as presenting a larger broadside for his guns to act upon, and that their cannon were placed so high that they shot over the heads of the English. A huge ship of Biscay, laden with money, took fire, and

---

When did the Spanish Armada sail from the mouth of the Tagus?
Whither did the Armada proceed?
Where did the English admiral first perceive the Armada?
What was the construction of the Spanish ships?
What was the achievement of sir Francis Drake in the first engagement with the Spanish?

another large vessel sprung her mast, and these two, falling behind the rest, were taken by sir Francis Drake.

The Armada, however, still sailed heavily up the Channel; and the English vessels, many of them fitted out by private individuals, poured forth from every port, and joined lord Effingham, who followed in the rear of the Spanish, and took many of the stragglers. At last the enemy cast anchor off Calais, in expectation of being there joined by the duke of Parma.

Effingham now filled with combustibles eight of his smaller vessels, and sent them into the midst of the enemy, who, fearful of being set on fire by them, cut their cables, and dispersed themselves in the greatest alarm. During this confusion the English fell upon them, and took twelve of their ships.

The duke of Parma, on seeing these disasters of the Armada, and the superiority which the English had gained refused to hazard his army by sea; and the duke de Medina, finding his fleet nearly disabled, while the English had only lost one small vessel, thought it best to return homewards. The winds being contrary, obliged him to sail to the north, to make the circuit of Scotland; but the English still pursued, and, had not their ammunition fallen short, would probably have taken every ship.

The tempestuous weather nearly completed the destruction of this vast armament. Many of the remaining ships, after beating about at the mercy of the winds, were wrecked on the coasts of Ireland and Scotland; and those Spaniards who lived to return home, gave their countrymen such formidable accounts of the bravery of the English, and the tremendous dangers of their coasts, as effectually repressed all inclination to attempt another invasion.

A. D. 1588. The earl of Leicester died, and the young earl of Essex succeeded him in the queen's

---

What was the progress of the Spanish invasion?
How did Effingham proceed against the Spanish?
How did the Spanish commanders encounter the English?
What was the end of the Spanish enterprise?
Who were the queen's distinguished favorites

favor. Essex was in many respects more deserving than Leicester had ever been. He and sir Walter Raleigh, who was a distinguished navigator, as well as an accomplished courtier, soon became deadly enemies. The queen, however, who did not perplex herself with any of their quarrels, delighted in the lofty and impetuous spirit of Essex, and permitted him, even when quite a youth, to speak to her with more freedom than she would allow to any of her old and faithful servants.

A. D. 1598 Essex was appointed governor of Ireland, under the title of lord lieutenant,—a very difficult post, for the Irish had been in an unsettled state during the whole of Elizabeth's reign; and it was with difficulty that sir Henry Sidney, and other wise and experienced governors, could keep them in subjection.

At this time an insurrection had broken out in Ireland, headed by a powerful chief, who had formerly, as a mark of royal favor, received from Elizabeth the title of earl of Tyrone. Many of his people had formerly served in the wars of Philip of Spain, and were very effective soldiers; so that the insurrection assumed a formidable appearance and required a steadier hand to stem it than that of the impetuous Essex, who nothing doubting of his own abilities, hastened to take possession of his government. But he soon found greater difficulties than he had anticipated.

After some months of harrassing warfare, in which his men suffered greatly from fatigue and sickness, Essex, in defiance of the queen's commands, entered into a truce with Tyrone. Elizabeth sent a sharp remonstrance on this and other points in which her general had been guilty of disobedience, and commanded him to remain in Ireland till further orders.

Essex, instantly on the receipt of this letter, set out for England, and arrived at court before it could be known that he had left Ireland. As soon as he reached the end of his journey, Essex rushed into the queen's presence

---

Whom did Elizabeth appoint governor of Ireland?
Was the government of Ireland at that time difficult?
Did Essex obey the queen's orders in respect to the government of Ireland?
How did Essex afterwards displease the queen?

without changing his dress, which seriously offended her, and her displeasure so affected him as to make him very ill.

The queen was, moreover, offended with Essex because he had disobeyed her orders by returning to England and commanded him to retire to his own house, where he was to remain under a sort of custody, and sequestered from all company. Lord Montjoy was then promoted to the government of Ireland, and, being a man of capacity and vigor, he soon retrieved the queen's affairs in that country.

Montjoy's prudent government made the inconsiderate conduct of Essex appear by comparison the more blamable; and Elizabeth, after a severe struggle between her affection for her favorite and her sense of justice, at last consented that he should be brought before the privy council to answer for his mismanagement of the Irish affairs. Essex did not attempt to excuse himself, but made a humble submission to the queen, by which he hoped to restore himself to her favor.

Elizabeth received his contrite messages with great complacency; but when he applied to her for a renewal of a grant she had formerly given him, she refused him with some contemptuous expressions. These contemptous expressions so stung the proud heart of Essex, that the violence of temper, which he had with difficulty restrained, now broke loose. He declared in his rage, "that the queen, now that she was an old woman, was as crooked in her mind as in her person:" which words being repeated to Elizabeth, incensed her more against him than any former part of his conduct had done.

Essex, indeed, was so completely driven mad by his passion, that he thought he could overturn the government. He entered into a treasonable correspondence with the king of Scotland; but his want of secrecy and caution made him a bad conductor of a plot. His scheme was discovered, and on this, furious with rage, he rushed into the streets, and made a wild attempt to raise a mob

---

What punishment did Elizabeth inflict upon Essex?
Why did Elizabeth bring Essex to a public trial?
How did Essex regard the queen's treatment of him?
To what extravagant conduct did Essex proceed?

amongst the populace. But, though the citizens were much attached to him, they were afraid or unwilling to join him.

Hearing himself proclaimed a traitor, and the streets being presently barricadoed against him, so that he could not advance, Essex fled towards the river, and getting into a boat, went back by water to Essex House. There he was seized and conveyed to the Tower. His trial soon followed, and his guilt was too clear to give the queen the least pretex for granting him a pardon. Still her former tenderness, and her late resentment, kept her in a most pitiable state during the painful interval which elapsed between signing his death-warrant and his execution.

It appears that the queen, aware of his impetuous temper, and how little guard he had over himself, had formerly given him a ring, telling him that whatever disgrace he might afterwards fall into, she would promise him, on receiving again that ring, to give him a favorable hearing This pledge she had fully expected to receive at this juncture of his fate, and she attributed it to obstinacy his not sending it. And when she had given him as she thought ample time for repentance, and yet there came not the important ring, she no longer delayed his execution, which took place February 25, 1601.

For a time her feelings of resentment supported her under the loss of her favorite. But this consolation, such as it was, was taken from her when, about two years after the death of Essex, the countess of Nottingham being on her death-bed, besought the queen to come to her, as she had something to reveal. She then confessed that Essex had entrusted her with the ring to restore it to her majesty, but that she had been prevailed on by her husband to withhold it.

Elizabeth, in an agony of grief at this disclosure, shook the dying countess in her bed, and said that "God might forgive her, but she never could." She then broke from her, and when she regained her own apartments, threw

---

Did the queen cordially consent to the the execution of Essex ?
Did the queen ever give Essex a ring, and on what condition ?
Who intercepted from the queen the ring belonging to Essex ?
Did Elizabeth forgive the countess of Nottingham ?

herself on the floor, and gave herself up to the most incurable melancholy.

For ten days and nights she lay on the ground, supported by cushions. She refused to go to bed, or to take any thing that her physicians prescribed. Her end visibly approaching, her attendants requested her to appoint her successor. Some authors say she actually named the king of Scotland. Others say that when he was named to her, she raised her hand to her head, which her ministers were willing to interpret into a sign of consent.

When she grew too weak to make resistance, she was laid in her bed. In the evening of the last day of her life, the archbishop of Canterbury came to pray by her : and when, after some hours, he left off from weariness, she made a sign to him to go on, and did so every time he ceased to speak. This lasted till towards four o'clock in the morning, when her attendants perceived she had ceased to breathe. She died March 24, 1603, in the 70th year of her age, and the 45th of her reign.

Although Elizabeth preserved the internal tranquility of the kingdom unbroken during the whole of her long reign, yet the perpetual warfare she carried on with Philip, together with the occasional assistance she gave to the Protestants in France, kept up a military spirit among her subjects. She chose her admirals far more fortunately and more judiciously than she did her generals, and consequently her expeditions by sea were in general much more successful than those she attempted by land.

In an expedition to the Low Countries, sir Philip Sidney was killed at the siege at Zutphen. He was considered the most accomplished gentleman in England; and the sorrow for his death was so great, that both the court and the city went into mourning.

Did Elizabeth name a successor ?
How, and when did Elizabeth die ?
Was the military spirit kept up in England during the reign of Elizabeth ?
Where was sir Sidney Philip killed ?

Elizabeth outlived her great enemy the king of Spain two years. The trade of England would have increased greatly in this reign had not the activity and industry of the merchants been fettered by the patents and monopolies which Elizabeth granted to her courtiers and favorites.

The Protestants, though their religion was now established, were yet unfortunately divided amongst themselves. Many who had been exiled in the reign of Mary had found refuge at Geneva, and had there learned the doctrine of Calvin, the Swiss reformer. These persons, when they returned to England on the accession of Elizabeth, were much shocked to find that she retained, not only many of the prayers, but also many of the outward observances of the Romish church.

The *Puritans*, for so they were called on account of their way of life, scrupled, amongst other things, to perform the service of the church in a surplice, and many of the Puritan clergy refused *benefices* rather than be guilty of what they considered so great an impiety. A benefice is a living in the *established*, that is, the Episcopal church of England.

The queen, during her whole reign, was constantly on the watch to keep down the Puritans; and they, on their side, were as constantly seizing every opportunity to advance their cause. Their public preaching and private exhortations had a visible effect on the manners of the age, particularly in regard to the employment of the Sunday, which, by their example, began universally to be observed with seriousness, instead of being made as heretofore, a day of pastime, and often of excess.

In the fifth year of this reign was enacted the first compulsory law for the relief of the poor, which is the foundation of the present poor laws in England, and by another act of parliament passed in 1601, the system as it now exists was nearly completed.

A trade between England and Turkey was begun about

Did trade flourish in England during the reign of Elizabeth?
Were the Protestants united? Who were the Puritans?
Did the queen favor the Puritans, and did they influence the manners of the time?
When were the present poor laws of England first enacted?
When was the English trade with Turkey commenced?

the year 1583. The fame of the English queen then first reached the ears of the Grand Signor, who till then had believed that England was a dependent province to France.

The character of Elizabeth is a very difficult one to comprehend. She had the courage and understanding of a man, with more than a woman's vanity and weakness. She was attached to her people, and imposed few taxes, and inflicted few punishments; but nevertheless, she was one of the most arbitrary of monarchs. She treated the house of commons with the utmost haughtiness, and more than once sent her commands to the members "to avoid long speeches."

CHAPTER XXIX.

JAMES I.

[Years after Christ, 1602—1625.]

James was thirty seven years old when by the death of Elizabeth he was raised to the English throne, and thus united the whole island under one sovereign. His character was an odd mixture of sense and folly. He possessed a natural shrewdness and sagacity, with a great share of vanity and conceit; and he made even his learning, which was considerable, appear ridiculous by his pedantry and pomposity. With all this he had a great deal of childish simplicity; and there was an openness of temper about him, which, though it may be reckoned a virtue yet made him quite unfit to control the jealousies which arose between his English and Scotch subjects.

His person was awkward, and his manners uncouth, and without dignity; and these defects, together with his broad Scotch accent, soon made him an object of contempt

---

Is the character of Elizabeth easily comprehended?
What was the character of James I.?
Did James command the respect of the English?

to those who had been accustomed to the stately majesty of Elizabeth.

James had married Anne, daughter of the king of Denmark, whose person and deportment are described as having been very homely and unprepossessing. They had three children at the time of James's accession. The eldest, Henry, was a promising boy of nine years old; the second child was named Elizabeth; and Charles, the youngest, was a boy of four years old.

James, though surrounded on his arrival in England by Scotch nobles, all greedy of English honors, still retained many of Elizabeth's ministers in their places. The most distinguished of these was Cecil lord Salisbury, son of the great lord Burleigh, who possessed much of his father's capacity, but without his integrity. One of the first acts of the king was to restore the family of Howard, and some others who had suffered in his mother's cause, to their estates and honors.

A conspiracy was soon afterwards formed to place on the throne the lady Arabella Stuart. This lady was the daughter of a brother of lord Darnley, the king's father; consequently she was his first cousin, and equally descended with himself from Henry VII. Her mother was an English lady of the Cavendish family, and she had been brought up amongst her mother's relations in great privacy.

Lady Arabella was neither qualified nor desirous to be a queen, and was totally ignorant of the conspiracy. The plot was soon discovered, and three persons were executed. Sir Walter Raleigh who had been accused of sharing in it, but whose guilt was not proved, was condemned to death, but reprieved, and afterwards remained in prison many years.

The Roman Catholics had expected great indulgence from James for his mother's sake; but they found, to their

---

What was James's family?
What were the first acts of James's government?
What were lady Arrabella Stuart's pretensions to the throne of England?
Who were engaged in the conspiracy in behalf of lady Arabella?
What plot was concerted by the Catholics?

great disappointment, that he was no less steady than Elizabeth had been to the cause of the Protestants; and to this disappointment was owing the well-known Gunpowder Plot, which had its first rise in 1604.

Catesby and Percy, two Catholic gentlemen, being in conversation on public affairs, Percy in great heat, said something about assassinating the king. The other replied that his single death would do them little good, and that they also must get rid of the lords and commons: he then suggested the possibility of laying a train of gunpowder under the parliament house, which would blow them up altogether.

Percy approved of the project: it was also agreed to communicate it to a few other persons; and they sent into Flanders in quest of Guy Fawkes, a man of known courage and zeal, then serving in the Spanish army, who they knew would be actively useful in the execution of their scheme.

This plot was in agitation all the spring. In the summer, the conspirators hired, in Percy's name, a house adjoining the house of lords, and began to undermine the wall between the two. After they had carried on their work some time, they learnt that a vault which had been used as a coal vault, and which was immediately under the house of lords, was to be let. Percy hired it, and secretly placed in it thirty-six barrels of gunpowder, and concealed them with faggots and billets of wood.

Every thing being ready, it was resolved that some of the conspirators should seize and kill the little prince Charles; and that others should get possession of the princess Elizabeth, and proclaim her queen, on the same day on which the king and queen, and their eldest son, were to be present at the opening of the parliament. Thus confident were they of destroying their victims.

This secret, though entrusted to above twenty persons, had been faithfully kept for near a year and a half; during

---

What was the Gun-powder Plot?
Who was Guy Fawkes?
What active measures were taken by the conspirators?
Did the conspirators intend to destroy the royal family?
Was the secret of the conspirators faithfully kept?

which period the execution was delayed from time to time by the repeated adjournments of parliament. The bigotry of the conspirators stifled all compunction at the thoughts of destroying so many of their fellow-creatures.

A few days before the meeting of parliament, lord Monteagle received a letter, very ambiguously expressed, which however, warned him of danger, and admonished him to go into the country instead of attending parliament. Monteagle knew not what to think of this letter, and showed it to lord Salisbury, who was no inclined to pay much attention to it, but who nevertheless, laid it before the king.

The king had sagacity enough to perceive, from its serious, earnest style, that something important was meant; and this forewarning of a sudden and terrible blow, yet with the authors concealed, made his suspicions come very near the truth. The day before the meeting of parliament, he sent the earl of Suffolk to examine all the vaults under the houses of parliament.

In that which was under the house of lords, Suffolk was surprised to see so many piles of wood and faggots, and was also struck with the dark and mysterious countenance of Guy Fawkes, who was found there, and who called himself Percy's servant. It was then resolved to make a more thorough inspection, and about midnight a magistrate was sent with proper attendance for that purpose. On turning over the faggots, the barrels of gunpowder were discovered.

Fawkes had been seized near the door, and matches, and every thing required for setting the train on fire, were found upon him. He at first appeared quite undaunted, but his courage afterwards failed him, and he made a full discovery of the plot, and all the conspirators. Catesby Percy and some others, hurried into Warwickshire, where one of their confederates, sir Everard Digby, not doubting but that the expected catastrophe in London had taken place, was already in arms.

What intimation of danger was sent to lord Monteagle?
What opinion did the king form of the letter to lord Monteagle?
What discoveries in relation to the plot were made by the earl of Suffolk?
How did the conspirators meet detection?

The country was soon roused against these wretches, who took refuge in one of those fortified houses which were common at that period, and resolved to defend themselves to the last. But the same fate awaited them which they had designed for so many others. Their gun-powder caught fire, and blew up, maiming and destroying several of them. The rest rushed out upon the multitude, and were literally cut to pieces, except a few who were taken alive, and afterwards executed.

The king showed more moderation on this occasion than was approved of by his subjects in general, who were wound up to such a pitch of horror at the greatness of the crime which had been attempted, that they would gladly have had every Papist in the kingdom put to death; and they were much displeased that James punished those only who were more immediately concerned in the plot

---

Soon after his accession, James employed himself in an unsuccessful attempt to bring about *a union* between his two kingdoms: but the parliament of England was so much swayed by old prejudices and antipathies against the Scots, that it would agree to nothing, except to annul the hostile laws that had formerly subsisted between the two kingdoms. The *union of the kingdoms*, meant the bringing the parliaments of both into one assembly, and making the same legislation serve for England and Scotland.

James's bad management of the finances, and his profuse generosity to his favorites, involved him in great difficulties. Amongst other ways of procuring money, he sold titles and dignities. The title of baronet, which might be purchased by any bidder for a thousand pounds, was now first created to supply his necessities.

One of James's greatest follies was an exclusive regard for some one favorite, who was generally chosen for his

---

How were the conspirators treated?
How did the English generally regard the papists at this time?
Did the English and Scots form a *union*?
Was James improvident?
Whom did the king create earl of Somerset?

agreeable exterior. One of these was Robert Carr, a youth of a good Scotch family, but of a neglected education. James undertook to be his tutor, and to teach him Latin. As he grew older, the king loaded him with dignities, and finally created him earl of Somerset.

This favorite had a sincere and wise friend, sir Thomas Overbury, who, on his wishing to marry the countess of Essex, strongly advised him against it. The countess, irritated at Overbury on this account, persuaded Somerset to have him put into the Tower, where he was soon afterwards poisoned. Somerset and the countess, the guilty contrivers of his death, then married: but he, being less hardened in wickedness, sank into a settled melancholy, and became so dull a companion, that the king, who liked gaiety and cheerfulness, grew weary of him.

Some time afterwards, the apothecary's apprentice, who had mixed the poison for Overbury, betrayed the secret. The guilt of Somerset and his wife was discovered, and they, and all who had been accessary to the murder, were tried; the accomplices, were hanged, but Somerset and the countess were only banished. They lived many years together, dragging on a miserable life; their former attachment, which had led them into guilt, being turned to the most deadly hate.

A. D. 1613. The earl of Salisbury died. He had been trained in the school of Elizabeth, and was by far the ablest of all James's ministers.

Some months before, the king had lost his eldest son, a prince of the highest promise. He was only in the eighteenth year of his age; but had already shown a spirit and nobleness of character, which had greatly endeared him to the English, particularly to many restless and ardent men, who, tired of the peace and inactivity of his father's reign, hoped to signalize themselves by military exploits under a prince of such a martial genius.

What is the history of sir Thomas Overbury?
What was the end of Somerset and his wife?
Was the earl of Salisbury an able minister?
What was the character of Prince Henry, son of James I?

13

Thirteen years of imprisonment had subdued Raleigh's pride and haughtiness. The people, admiring his accomplishments, and loving him for the fine qualities of his heart, were exceedingly desirous of his liberation. James, induced perhaps by the hope of obtaining a certain gold mine in Guiana, which Raleigh said he knew to be in existence, gave him leave to go and try his fortune; but still would not reverse the sentence of death which hung over his head.

Raleigh set sail with several ships, and directed his course to the river Oronooko; but the adventurers who had embarked with him in the hope of sharing in the expected gold mine were disappointed, and nothing was effected but the destroying of a small Spanish town, in the attack on which Raleigh's son was killed. The object of the expedition having failed, great murmurs arose against the commander, and he found himself obliged to return to England.

A particular inquiry into Raleigh's late conduct was instituted, and the king at length ordered the sentence of death which had been formerly passed on him to be put in force: he was beheaded, Oct. 20, 1618. This act of deliberate cruelty is the greatest blot in James's (in other respects) lenient reign, and caused at the time strong indignation amongst the people, who felt that they had lost the only man in the kingdom who had any reputation for valor, or any military experience.

Of all those men of brilliant talents who had encompassed the throne of Elizabeth, there was now only one left. This was lord Bacon, whose advancement had in the late reign been always opposed by lord Burleigh, who assured Elizabeth that, though he was a man of extraordinary genius, his head was filled with philosophy, and not with political knowledge.

James raised Bacon to the chancellorship, and his misconduct in that high post fully justified the sagacious Bur-

---

Why did king James liberate Sir Walter Raleigh?
Did Raleigh's last voyage procure any advantage to the English nation?
What impolitic and cruel sentence was passed upon Raleigh?
Who was lord Bacon?
Why was Bacon deprived of his honors?

leigh's opinion He was proved, if rot to have taken bribes himself, at least to have connived at his officers taking them; and being impeached on this heavy charge, and pleading guilty, he was dismissed from his office of chancellor, and sentenced to pay a heavy fine and to be imprisoned during the king's pleasure.

James, in consideration of his many merits, soon released him from prison, remitted the fine, and all the other parts of his sentence. He survived his disgrace five years, during which time he employed himself in prosecuting those philosophical studies in which he was naturally fitted to excel, and in which he has attained a higher and juster reputation than, perhaps, any other writer of any age or country.

A. D. 1619. James was strongly solicited to engage in a war for the support of the elector palatine, who had married his daughter, and had been made king of Bohemia by the free choice of the people of that country, who had revolted from the emperor of Germany. The elector's reign was of short duration; for his troops were defeated by the Austrians at the battle of Prague, and he thus lost not only his newly acquired kingdom, but also his hereditary principality, and was driven with his family to take refuge in Holland.

The elector made many efforts to regain the palatinate, and was assisted by the free services of a few valiant Englishmen: but he in vain solicited support from his father-in-law, whose reluctance to engage in war was so great that he refused to assist him in any other way than by entering into treaties and negotiations with other princes of Europe in his behalf. These took up a great deal of time, without producing any advantage.

One of James's schemes was to obtain the restoration of the elector, through the intervention of the king of Spain, with whom he had entered into a treaty for a marriage between the infanta and the prince of Wales. The thoughts

---

Why did James pardon lord Bacon?
Who was James's son-in-law and what were his misfortunes?
Did James enter into the concerns of the elector palatine?
What project did James form for the marriage of his son, and who encouraged him in it?

of this marriage were exceedingly disagreeable to the English people, who had not forgotten all that the nation had formerly suffered from a Spanish match: but James was determined on it, and in this determination he was greatly encouraged by George Villiers, duke of Buckingham, who had been for some time his exclusive favorite, and who had an unbounded influence both over him and the prince.

Buckingham, to gratify some fancy of his own, possessed the prince with the desire to undertake a romantic journey into Spain, to see the princess, and win her regard. It was with great difficulty that the king could be persuaded to give his consent to this project. At last, overpowered by earnest importunity, he agreed, entirely against his own judgment, to permit the departure of his son and Buckingham.

The prince and duke, persisting in their plan, left England disguised and undiscovered. In their way through Paris, they went to a court-ball, where Charles first saw the French princess Henrietta Maria, whom he afterwards married. When Charles arrived at Madrid, he made himself and his errand known. The king of Spain treated him with respect; but whether it was that Charles did not like the Spanish princess so well as the beautiful sister of the king of France, it is certain that, after an absence of some months, he returned to England wholly unwilling to pursue the treaty into which James had entered. James was afterwards persuaded to enter into another treaty with France for the marriage of the princess Henrietta Maria, and this at last he very unwillingly did.

James, finding all his attempts at an end to obtain assistance for his son-in-law by negotiations, at last resolved to pursue more vigorous measures, and embarked a body of troops for his succor, which were to act under count Mansfeldt, a celebrated German commander; but James had no genius for war, and the expedition was ill planned and came to nothing. This was the only warlike enter-

---

Who persuaded prince Charles to go to Spain, and who opposed that visit?

How was Charles treated at Madrid, and what princess did he desire for a wife?

What were James's warlike enterprises?

prise undertaken by England during this pacific reign, with the exception of sending to Holland, a short time before, a body of six thousand men, to serve under the command of Maurice, prince of Orange.

A. D. 1625. While the negotiation was still pending for the marriage of Charles and Henrietta Maria, the king fell ill of an ague. Finding his end approaching, he took an affectionate leave of his son, and died in the 59th year of his age, and in the 22d of his reign.

The conduct of James appeared to great advantage in his government of Ireland, which he found, at his coming to the crown, in a very disordered state. He endeavored to civilize the inhabitants, and to reconcile them to laws and industry: he abolished many remains of barbarism, and established English laws in that country; he declared the people free; and he did more in nine years to meliorate the condition of that island than had been done previously in the four centuries during which it had been subject to the English yoke.

To James I. we are indebted for the excellent translation of the bible now in use. Cranmer's bible, having been made from very defective Latin translations, was in many places not faithful to the originals. James, therefore, employed some very learned men to make a translation from the original languages,—the Old Testament, being in the Hebrew, and the New Testament in the Greek language. Nearly fifty persons were employed about it, and were four years in completing it. The excellence of the translation is universally acknowledged.

English books were at first printed in the German character. When Caxton brought the art of printing from Germany, he brought with him the types used in that country; and from these, and similar types, all English books

---

When did James die?
Did James attempt the civilization of Ireland?
What great benefit did James confer on all who spoke the English language?
Were English books first printed in the type we now use?

were printed, till the reign of James I. when the Roman character (the one now employed) was adopted, and soon entirely superseded the use of the old black letter.

In the reign of James the soldiers led idle lives, but the sailors were not without employment. The increase of trade and commerce, and the frequent voyages to America, gave them something to do: for in this reign may be dated the establishment of the first English colonies in America. James also took great pride in his navy, and built many large ships.

Though James's court was a continual scene of discontent and misrule, the mass of the people appeared to have lived very comfortably under his reign. By discouraging the thronging of the higher orders to court, he kept many of the principal families of the kingdom quietly at home where they lived both frugally and usefully amongst their tenantry. There were no expensive wars, and but few taxes

Riding at the Ring.

The farmers in James's reign were better off than the earls of Henry VII.'s. James himself was probably the poorest man in his dominions. Though not extravagant in his habits, he was always embarrassed from his extreme

---

What was the condition of the army and navy in James's reign?
What was the condition of the English nation generally in this reign?
Was James often in want of money and why?

ignorance of the value of money, and from his thoughtless profusion to his favorites. The queen also brought great expenses on him, by her excessive passion for *masques*, and all kinds of show and entertainments.—Masques were a kind of plays, generally performed by ladies and gentlemen in private houses.

It is proper to mention that Shakspeare, the greatest dramatic poet of England, lived in the reigns of Elizabeth and James. Ben Johnson and Edmund Spenser, also poets, were contemporaries with Shakspeare.

PRINCE HENRY.

Prince Henry is always spoken of as a very extraordinary young man. He showed such an early application to his studies, that even at the time when he was seven years old he wrote his father a Latin letter. And after he grew up, he constantly exercised himself in that language, by corresponding in it with his friend, sir John Harrington. Although he was fond of study, he did not neglect active and manly exercises, in all which he was extraordinarily expert.

But what was most admirable in him was his great judgment and discretion, of which, though he died so young, he gave many proofs. When he grew old enough to have a *separate establishment*, that is, a palace and servants of

---

Was Prince Henry a promising youth?
What was Prince Henry's moral conduct?

his own, he never would admit any one into his household whom he did not believe to be in all respects deserving of his good opinion. He was himself sincerely religious, and a strict observer of all pious duties.

Lady Arabella Stuart's history belongs to this reign, and a very melancholy one it is. It was her misfortune to be great-great-grand-daughter to Henry VII.; for being, after Mary queen of Scots and her son, nearest in relationship to the throne, she was an object of jealousy to both Elizabeth and James James, however, when he came to the crown of England, behaved kindly to her as long as she remained unmarried. At last she married a Mr. Seymour. For this offence both Mr. Seymour and she were imprisoned. Though confined in different prisons, they both of them contrived to make their escape at the same time; and hoped to join each other in some place of refuge abroad.

Mr. Seymour was so fortunate as to get safely into Flanders; but poor Lady Arabella was taken in Calais road, and brought back. This renewal of her captivity preyed so much upon her mind as to deprive her of her reason. She never recovered, and died in a few years. Some of her letters have been preserved, which show her to have been an amiable woman, naturally of a cheerful temper, and very far from having any ambition to be a queen.

TABLE.

Henry the Seventh's children.	Henry VIII., father of Edward VI., Mary, and Elizabeth; Margaret, married, first, James IV. of Scotland; secondly, Douglas earl of Angus. She was mother of James V. and of Margaret Douglas; Mary, married, first, Louis XII.; secondly, Brandon duke of Suffolk; and was mother of Margaret lady Dorset.
Henry the Seventh's grandchildren.	Edward VI.; Mary; Elizabeth; James V., father of Mary, queen of Scotland; Margaret Douglas, mother of Henry Darnley, and of Charles Stuart, who was father of lady Arabella Stuart; Margaret Brandon, married Grey earl of Dorset, and was mother of lady Jane Grey, and of two other daughters.

What were the misfortunes of Lady Arabella Stuart?
How did Lady Arabella end her days?

CHAPTER XXX

CHARLES I.

(PART I.)

[Years after Christ, 1625--1642.]

Charles was in the twenty-fifth year of his age when he ascended the throne. His features were regular, and he would have been handsome, if it had not been for the melancholy cast of his countenance. His deportment was exceedingly dignified. In the morality and regularity of his conduct he set a good example to his court and people: he was moderate in all his habits and his expenses, humane and gentle in his disposition, was a man of kind affections, and a most tender husband and father.

Charles's mind was cultivated, but he seldom acted as wisely as he could talk, and was often swayed by the counsels of men of far inferior capacity. His temper was somewhat hasty, but he was generous and forgiving. With all Charles's good qualities, he had unfortunately imbibed some prejudices, of education that proved fatal to him as a king. He had too high an idea of his royal prerogative and, with every desire to do right, had not the smallest notion of the true principles of government or policy.

From the very commencement of the new reign much popular dissatisfaction prevailed, chiefly because the king surrendered himself entirely to the control of Buckingham, who, implacable in his hatreds, fickle in his friendships, imperious and grasping in his desires, was regarded with universal dislike.

The king's marriage with Henrietta Maria, sister to the king of France, was also very displeasing to the people principally because she was a Papist, and their religious

---

What was the private character of Charles I. ?
Was the conduct of Charles equal to the wisdom of his discourse?
Under whose influence did Charles commence his reign ?
How did the English regard queen Henrietta Maria ?

feelings were shocked at her being allowed to exercise publicly her own form of worship. She also offended the more serious part of the nation, by the change her elegance and gaiety wrought in the manners of the court and the Puritans found less to dislike in the homely vulgarity of the late queen Anne of Denmark than in the grace and beauty of Henrietta.

It was a great error in James, and one into which Charles also fell, to be occupied with *abstract speculations*, that is, with thoughts of matters which did not concern his own business and duties, and not to see what passed under his eyes. Thus, while James was writing books on kingly government, he never perceived that the house of commons was no longer that subservient body it had been in all former reigns, but that it had at last found out its own strength, and that from being the slave of kings it was now able to be their ruler.

Charles also had been equally blind to this change, and was not aware of the difficulties which he was bringing on himself by his rash treatment of this great organ of the popular voice. The first year of his reign was spent by him in making attempts to extend his authority, and by the commons in trying to curb it. Provoked by this opposition, Charles hastily dissolved the parliament; and thus the king and the commons parted in mutual disgust and animosity, and, when the new parliament assembled, they met with feelings of suspicion and dislike.

A. D. 1627. Charles, by the persuasion of Buckingham, plunged into a war with France, and sent some troops to the relief of the French Hugonots at Rochelle. Buckingham had the command of this expedition, which was ill-planned and unskilfully executed; and in an attempt to land on the Isle of Rhé, he was repulsed with great loss. Another expedition for the relief of Rochelle was fitted out in 1628, and Buckingham went to Portsmouth to survey the preparations.

What change in the character of parliament took place in the reigns of James and his son Charles?
What conflict arose between Charles and the commons of England?
In what foreign enterprise did Charles engage in 1627?

At the same time with the duke a man by the name of Felton arrived at Portsmouth, a Puritan of a melancholy and enthusiastic turn of mind, who, hearing the universal complaints that were made against the favorite, persuaded himself that he should do his country a service by destroying him. His chief motive, however, was probably that of private resentment, at having been disappointed in his own hopes of promotion in the army.

Felton for some days followed the duke like his shadow, but without having an opportunity to effect his purpose. At last, as Buckingham was passing through a door-way, and turning to speak to sir Thomas Fryer, who was following him, an arm was suddenly stretched over sir Thomas's shoulder, which struck a knife into the duke's breast. All this passed in an instant. No one saw the blow, nor the person who gave it; but the by-standers heard Buckingham exclaim, " The villain has killed me!" and saw him pull the knife from the wound, and fall dead at their feet.

The confusion and alarm at this moment were very great, and every one rushed forwards in search of the murderer. He was rescued with some difficulty from the violence of the by-standers, who would have put him to death with their swords. Felton was afterwards tried and executed.

After the death of Buckingham, Charles placed his chief confidence in sir Thomas Wentworth, afterwards lord Strafford, and in Laud, archbishop of Canterbury. The first was a man of great talents and of a strong and unbending mind, but, unfortunately for himself and his master, his political opinions would have better suited the despotic times of the Plantagenets than the reign in which he was placed.

Laud's character was no less ill adapted than Strafford's to reconcile the wavering minds of those who were begin·

Who met Buckingham at Portsmouth?
How was Buckingham killed?
What punishment overtook Felton?
Who succeeded Buckingham in the favor of Charles?
Was Laud zealously attached to the church and government of England?

ning to fall off from the established church and government. He had an overweening opinion of his own dignity, and gave great offence to the Puritans by introducing into the church service some of the ceremonies of the Romish religion. He was, however, a man of eminent parts, and of great zeal in the king's service.

The supplies which the parliament had granted since Charles's accession had been both scanty and grudgingly given; and the late king, by his unthrifty management, had left the treasury in such an exhausted state, that his son, though frugal and regular, soon found himself greatly embarrassed, and wanted money to defray the necessary expenses of the government.

Charles had been provoked, by the unbending sturdiness of the commons, to dissolve the parliament a second time; and he now declared a determination to govern without one: but he was no gainer by this imprudent step, for his necessities soon drove him to procure money by many arbitrary and unjustifiable means.

The exactions of the Star Chamber were enforced with great severity. A duty called tonnage and poundage, which had been heretofore given to the reigning monarch as an especial grant from the parliament, Charles took upon himself to levy on his own authority. He also imposed a tax called ship-money, for the express purpose of maintaining the navy. But though the money was employed for the purpose for which it was demanded, and the navy put into a more serviceable condition than it had long been in, still, as it was considered an illegal tax, the people were highly irritated at its being levied.

Things were in this state in England, when Charles, with an indiscreet zeal, tried to introduce episcopacy, with the liturgy of the Church of England into Scotland: but the Scots, instead of submitting to change their own presbyterian form of worship, drew up a protestation, binding themselves to resist all religious innovation. This protestation they called the Covenant, and every person

---

Were the finances of Charles sufficient to defray the expenses of government?
Did Charles obtain money by unpopular and oppressive measures?
Did Charles introduce episcopacy into Scotland?

from one end of Scotland to the other, was required to sign it.

A number of these covenanters next formed themselves into an army, and placed themselves under the command of the earl of Argyle, seized on some of the king's castles, and hastily fortified the town of Leith. All ranks were so much inflamed by party zeal, that even ladies were seen mixing with the lowest rabble, carrying loads upon their shoulders, and assisting to complete the fortifications.

The king, to quell these disturbances, marched an army to Berwick, and negotiations were begun between him and the covenanters. Charles's visible unwillingness to make his native land, to which he was much attached, a scene of bloodshed, only served to encourage the Scots in their unyielding spirit. He was soon obliged to disband his troops for want of money to continue their pay, and he made many concessions to the Scots to induce them to return to their homes in peace.

This the Scots pretended to do, but they soon after appeared again in arms; and, in 1640, Charles found himself in such a distressed condition, that, after an interval of eleven years, he once more summoned a parliament, in hopes it would grant him some assistance. But, as soon as the commons met, instead of paying any attention to the king's affairs, it immediately entered on its own grievances.

This parliament, after it had sat only a few months, the king, in a moment of irritation, dissolved. This measure he had afterwards but too much reason to repent. His necessities were now so great, that he was obliged to borrow money of his ministers and courtiers. With the greatest difficulty he raised a body of troops, which he sent against the Scots, who were advanced almost to Newcastle. The two armies met at Newburn, and Charles's troops were defeated. He was thus reduced to greater difficulties than ever, and as a desperate resource, once more summoned a parliament.

What measures were taken by the Scotch Covenanters?
What at length led Charles to make concessions to the Scots?
Who summoned a parliament in 1640, and what were its measures?
Why was parliament dissolved and afterwards summoned by Charles?

The late events had not tended to put the commons in better humor with the king or his ministers; and their first measure was to impeach Strafford, who, having been formerly a Puritan, was more particularly obnoxious to that party, one of whom, Pym, an active leader in the house, had formerly said to him, " You have left us, but we will not leave you while your head is on your shoulders." And they so well remembered and kept their word, that he was brought to trial and condemned to death.

The king, knowing that Strafford's greatest fault in the eyes of the people was his attachment to himself, could not at first bring himself to assent to the *bill of attainder* that was passed against him, although the queen and some of his other advisers besought him to make that sacrifice to the public outcry. Juxon, bishop of London, alone advised him by no means to assent to the bill, if his conscience did not approve of it.

Strafford himself wrote to the king, entreating him, for the sake of public peace, no longer to defer his assent to it, and ended his letter thus:—" My consent will more acquit you to God than all the world can do besides. To you I can resign the life of this world with all imaginable cheerfulness."

Strafford perhaps thought that this letter would rather plead for his life than against it; and he seemed greatly surprised, and for the moment overcome, when he was informed that the king had actually consented to his execution. But he might have pitied rather than have blamed him, could he have known how much present grief, and after remorse he endured, from allowing his consent to the death of his faithful friend and servant to be thus extorted from him.

Charles, unwilling to give a personal assent to the bill which deprived him of his valued servant, sent a letter to

---

By whose orders was Strafford impeached, tried, and condemned for treason?
Did Charles readily assent to the death of Strafford?
In what terms did Strafford write to the king?
Did Strafford perhaps presume upon the king's interference in his behalf?

the peers, entreating them to confer with the commons for a mitigation of the sentence, or at least to obtain some delay. But the enemies of Strafford ware inexorable, and he was executed May 12, 1641.

A little before Strafford's death it had been resolved by the parliament to impeach archbishop Laud, and he was in consequence imprisoned on a charge of high treason. He was detained three years before he was brought to trial. The parliament confiscated his property, and notwithstanding his age, he was treated with great indignity, and his imprisonment made as uncomfortable as possible. Even the papers which he had prepared for his defence were taken from him.

While Strafford's fate was pending, and the king's mind was in a state of great agitation, a bill was brought him, the purport of which was, that the parliament should not be dissolved, prorogued, or adjourned, without its own consent. To this the king assented, and by this act he completely fettered himself. The next use the parliament made of its power was commendable. It abolished the oppressive court of the Star Chamber, and redressed some other grievances.

A. D. 1641. The king, for some months after these events, remained quite passive. Towards the end of the year he began to occupy himself with the affairs of Scotland, and went there in hopes to pacify the discontents of the people, by yielding to all their wishes While the king was thus employed, a dangerous rebellion broke out in Ireland, so that factions, cabals, and insurrections, surrounded him at once on all sides.

The disturbances in Ireland had been begun by Roger More, an Irish gentleman, whose object was to expel the English from that island; but the flame of rebellion being once lighted, raged more furiously than he had intended; and the Irish suddenly rose upon the unsuspecting English and massacred, without distinction of sex or age, all but

---

Did the king exert himself successfully in behalf of Strafford?
On what charge was Laud impeached?
Did parliament at this time enlarge its function and privileges?
What events marked the year 1641 in England?
What disturbances in Ireland occurred in the year 1641?

the few who could take refuge in Dublin. Shocked at these enormities, and finding himself unable to stem the fury of the rebellion he had raised, More abandoned his country and retired into Flanders.

Charles, in this emergency, was obliged to have recourse to the English parliament, who raised money and collected ammunition on pretence of the Irish service, but in fact kept the whole supply in reserve at home, in order to employ it against the king, in determined opposition to whose authority many parties of very different principles were now united.

One party was composed of men of moderate views, who, on account of the abuses of the prerogative which had taken place, thought it necessary to use strong measures to check the encroachments of arbitrary power. The party of the Puritans aimed at more than this, and insisted also on the destruction of the hierarchy.

Republican principles had also arisen, which sought the overthrow of the monarchy as well as the established church. Such being the state of the public mind, the king soon became involved in a labyrinth of trouble, from which he knew not how to extricate himself.

A. D. 1642. It will be impossible to enter into every particular of the unhappy differences between the king and the commons. Each party becoming more and more incensed, and things being likely to proceed to extremities, the king withdrew to York, taking with him his two eldest sons, Charles and James.

At York the chief nobility and gentry of the kingdom flocked to him, offering their services, and expressing their duty and attachment: for, now that it was become an open quarrel, many who had shown a disapprobation of his former measures condemned the violence of the parliament, and took part with the king. The peers, with the exception of lord Essex and a few others, adhered to the king, while the Puritans took the side of the parliament.

For what purpose did parliament raise an army?
What were the views of the moderate and of the puritan parties at this time?
Was there another party besides those last mentioned?
On what account did Charles retire to York?
Who adhered to Charles in this extremity?

The royalists, to show their contempt of the opposite party, and in ridicule of the formality of the close-cropped hair of the Puritans, gave them the name of *roundheads;* while they, on their side, gave to the royalists the titles of *cavaliers* and *malignants.*

It was now apparent that a civil war was inevitable; but each party hung back from commencing hostilities, in the hope that the other would incur the blame of being the first to draw the sword. At last, the king, having been refused admittance into the town of Hull by sir John Hotham, the governor, felt himself driven to the necessity of taking active measures; and, on August 20, 1642, he erected his royal standard at Nottingham.

It may not, however, be amiss in this place to give some account of that memorable parliament which so ably asserted the superior authority of a large legislative body over the single will of an arbitrary monarch. Pym and Hampden were two of the most active speakers in the house; and they were, perhaps, the persons who chiefly excited the people against the king. Hampden was a man of great abilities, of good private character, and probably acted from conscientious motives.

Sir Henry Vane was another promoter of the popular cause: he was a man of quick parts. He entangled himself much in theological discussions, and belonged to the Puritan sect. One of the most respectable of the parliamentarians was Sir Bulstrode Whitelocke, a man of great moderation and integrity, who took an active part in the politics of his time, from thorough conviction that he was acting for the good of his country.

Oliver Cromwell became in the sequel the most important man in the republican party, but at the beginning of the civil commotions was rather a follower than a leader of

---

What names were given in mutual contempt by parties of this age to each other?
When did Charles erect the royal standard at Nottingham?
Who were Hampden and Pym?
Who were Vane and Whitelocke?
Who was Oliver Cromwell?

faction. He was born at Huntingdon, and of the younger branch of a good family. Cromwell from a boy was remarkable for bodily and intellectual vigor. He first applied himself to the law; but it was too sedentary a study to suit his active disposition. He then took a farm near St. Ives; but, turning Puritan, distinguished himself more as a preacher and expounder of Scripture, than as a farmer.

Cromwell was first in parliament in 1626, and was a warm opposer of the crown. Finding his circumstances much impaired, he agreed with sir Arthur Hazelrig, Hampden and some other disaffected persons, to leave England, and establish a settlement in America on republican principles. They and their families were already embarked and the ships were on the point of sailing, when the king, was advised to issue a proclamation forbidding their departure.

Cromwell must have been a man of most extraordinary powers, to attain the wonderful influence over people's minds which he seems to have possessed; for he had none of that address or pleasing exterior which is generally necessary to obtain popularity. He was also a sloven in his dress, which was the more conspicuous at a time when gentlemen's dress was unusually graceful and becoming.

Sir Philip Warwick, a royalist, who wrote some memoirs, thus describes Cromwell:—" The first time that ever I took notice of him was in November, 1640. When I came one morning to the house, I perceived a gentleman speaking, very ordinarily appareled; for it was a plain suit, which seemed to have been made by an ill country tailor. His linen was plain, and not very clean, and I remember a speck of blood upon his hand; his stature was of a good size; his countenance swollen and reddish; his voice harsh and untunable, and his eloquence full of fervor."

Cromwell's appearance, however, was afterwards improved; for the same sir Philip Warwick says:—" I lived

---

What prevented Cromwell from going to America?
Was it Cromwell's extraordinary mind that commanded him to popular admiration?
How does sir Philip Warwick describe Cromwell?
Did Cromwell become more dignified in his appearance?

to see this very gentleman by multiplied good successes, and by real (though usurped) power, having had a better tailor, and more converse amongst good company, appear of a great and majestic deportment, and comely presence."

The Puritans, when they became inured to war, made very good soldiers: their officers were brave and determined; and the parliament had as good generals as the king. Lord Essex, and sir Thomas, afterwards lord Fairfax, had the chief command; they were both honest and well-intentioned men, and began by seeking to restrain the power of the crown, not to destroy it. But they found themselves hurried on at last by the fever of the times, to adopt measures which they would have shrunk from in the beginning.

The king's best generals were prince Rupert, the king's nephew, a son of that elector palatine who was so unfortunate, and the marquis of Newcastle. Prince Rupert was, perhaps, in some respects inferior to the marquis of Newcastle. Newcastle was a man of great powers, as well in council as in war. His high character, both public and private, induced many persons to join the king's army; and while he held the command of it the royal cause prospered. Seymour, lord Hertford, was another nobleman, who, although he never had any high command in the army, was yet a great accession to it.

On the 25th of August, 1642, on the evening of a very stormy day, the king set up his royal standard on the Castle Hill at Nottingham. It was soon blown down by the violence of the wind, and could not be raised again for some days. This trifling circumstance added to the gloom and sadness felt at that moment by all the king's friends. Yet many roused themselves to exertion, and prepared with alacrity for the hard and bloody conflict which lay before them.

The character of Charles seemed in many respects to have changed with the times. He now displayed a vigor

---

Did the Puritan party afford good soldiers?
Who were the king's best generals?
Was the king's army discouraged at the commencement of hostilities?
Did Charles seem to be effected by the emergency of his circumstances?

and address which astonished those who knew his former studious and inactive habits. Even the hastiness of his temper was abated; and he who had formerly shown an extreme impatience of injury or opposition, now submitted with exemplary resignation and cheerfulness to the necessities of his hard condition.

His greatest difficulty was to raise money; and what he could obtain was chiefly by voluntary contributions. The queen found means to get to Holland with her crown and the crown jewels, which she disposed of in that country; and she purchased with the money thus obtained, a small supply of arms and amunition. This was sent with all haste to the king; who, mustering his forces, appointed lord Lindsey general-in-chief, and prince Rupert general of the horse.

The parliament's armies were already in the field. Lord Essex commanded in the south; and lord Fairfax, and his son, sir Thomas, were generals in the north. From this time, for the next six years, England suffered all the horrors of a civil war. Garrisons were placed in all the towns and the people thought of little else but sieges and battles. There was scarcely any part of the kingdom that was not, at one time or other, the scene of some memorable action.

The first battle was fought Oct. 3d, at Edgehill in Warwickshire. At the onset prince Rupert bore down every thing before him; but before the day was ended, his rash imprudence lost all that his courage had gained. The two armies, after fighting all day, remained under arms during the night: but the next morning, after facing each other again, they retired from the field without renewing the fight. The loss on each side was equal, and neither gained a victory; though the parliamentarians considered themselves as somewhat entitled to claim it, because the king's general, lord Lindsey, was among the slain.

A. D. 1643. The siege of Reading, which was garrisoned for the king, occupied both parties for many months. It was at last taken by Essex, in the

---

How did the king obtain money, &c.?
Who encountered the king's army, and for how many years was England disturbed with this civil warfare?
What was the result of the battle at Edgehill?

month of April. During the summer the royalists were victorious in a battle at Lansdown, near Bath; and in another fought near Devizes: and the parliament had a great loss in the death of Hampden, who was mortally wounded in a skirmish at Chalgrave field, near Oxford.

Hampden was a man of such exemplary private character, that even his enemies were concerned at his death. The king, who had now made Oxford his head-quarters, was desirous, when he heard of his being wounded, to send his own surgeon to attend him: but in the interim Hampden died.

In reading the history of Charles I. it is necessary to discriminate between the virtues of the man and those proper to a king, and to remember that good dispositions do not make the wise ruler of a great people. "A man who will not hurt a fly will sometimes hurt a nation," says an able writer, Charles was such a man. He was doubtless amiable and humane, but he believed that nations ought to obey kings, because he thought kings had what he called a *divine right*, that is, that God appointed them to rule.

The opposers of Charles's arbitrary measures believed that the welfare of the nation was more important than the will, or pleasure of a king; that laws ought to govern the sovereign as well as the people; and that representatives of the people assembled in parliament ought to make the laws for the people, and give their sanction to the king's projects, instead of blindly obeying his commands.

To maintain these principles, not then generally acknowledged in Europe, there were brave and virtuous men in England ready to hazard their fortunes and lives; such a one was Mr. Hampden. He was a man of good education, and considerable property, and an example of every virtue. "He was," says the historian, Lord Clarendon, "of a most civil and affable deportment, his reputa

---

What were the actions of the spring and summer, 1643?
Did the king and the royal party show any generous feeling at the death of John Hampden?
Does mere humanity make a good king?
What notions were entertained by the patriot party concerning the rights of kings?
What was lord Clarendon's character of John Hampden?

tion for honesty was universal, and his affections seemed so guided towards the public good that no private ends could lead them astray."

Mr. Hampden was very temperate in diet, and the supreme governor over all his passions; he was of an industry and vigilance not to be tired out; of an understanding not to be imposed upon; and of a courage equal to his other qualities. Such was Hampden's moral courage that he dared at his own cost to question the right of the king to ship money, and brought the question before the courts of law.

This tax was known to be illegal;—indeed there was nothing which the people of England had for more than four hundred years better known, or more strenuously insisted upon than this—that the king had no right to lay a tax without the consent of parliament. But the judges before whom this violation of the laws was carried to obtain, if possible, a decision that might thoroughly expose it to the nation, decided that the king had a right, by his own royal authority to levy this tax or any other that he might think needful.

From that time Hampden's resolution to oppose the king, and all supporters of arbitrary principles and measures became more inflexible. In the beginning of the civil war he undertook the command of a regiment in the parliamentary army, and performed his duty faithfully till he was wounded in the battle of Chalgrave Field. He survived three weeks, and then gave up a life he had devoted to the cause of civil liberty.

In the beginning of the war, the royal army, which was chiefly composed of well-trained soldiers, under the command of officers who had many of them been accustomed to deeds of arms in the wars on the continent, commonly proved successful over the undisciplined forces of the par-

---

What great proof of moral courage did Mr. Hampden exhibit?
Did the English nation allow their kings to levy taxes?
What induced Mr. Hampden to take up arms, and how did he die?
Were the royal or the parliamentary troops most successful?

liament. But as these gained skill and experience, they became superior to any troops that the king could bring into the field; for every man of them was actuated by religious and political zeal, and entered willingly into the service.

Charles, during the course of hostilities, was often obliged to enlist almost any soldiers he could get, and amongst them many dissolute soldiers of fortune, who ridiculed the Puritans, and expressed their contempt for them, not by setting a better example of what was right, but by showing themselves to be deriders of all religion and virtue.

Nothing was so ruinous to the king's affairs as the conduct of these men, who committed all kinds of violence and excess. And the country people naturally liked that party best by which they were most humanely treated. Charles also, in his necessities, was glad to accept of the services of many Papists; and this was enough of itself to raise a great prejudice against his cause.

The war was now prosecuted with great vigor, and several battles were fought, with nearly equal success, in different parts of the kingdom. The parliament, finding it less easy than they had at first expected to crush the king, called in the aid of the Scots, and entered into what was entitled a solemn league and covenant with them.

The Scots gladly accepted the terms of friendly alliance offered by the English parliament, in the hope of being able, by thus connecting themselves with the Puritans, to overthrow the church establishment in England, and to set up their own Presbyterian form of worship in its place.

The king's supplies being gathered from the free-will offerings of his loyal subjects, were much more scanty than those of the parliament, who, having in their hands the power of levying taxes, used it without reserve. They also impressed soldiers, and these means enabled them, under continual defeats, to bring fresh troops into

---

Were many dissolute persons engaged in the royal cause?
What effect had unworthy adherents upon the interest of Charles
Whom did the parliament army call to their aid?
What motive influenced the Scots to take part with the English parliament?
What particular advantage had the parliament over the king?

the field. But it was not till the summer 1644 that they gained any decisive victory.

It happened that the marquis of Newcastle was then besieged in York by sir Thomas Fairfax. Prince Rupert came to the relief of the town, and, rejecting the advice of the marquis to wait for a more advantageous time, rashly led his forces against the besiegers. The two armies met at Marston Moor, about nine miles from York. Each party by turns had the advantage; but in the end, after a hard-fought battle, victory declared for the side of the parliament.

In the west of England, where Charles himself conducted his army in person, the campaign proved more favorable to him. He pursued Essex into Cornwall, where the people were highly zealous for the royal cause, and obliged nearly his whole army to capitulate. But this success availed but little to counterbalance the defeat at Marston Moor.

Meanwhile, the queen, who had returned to England, and had been with the king for some time at Oxford, believed herself in danger from the great dislike with which she knew herself to be regarded by the people. She therefore retired to Exeter, where her youngest child, the princess Henrietta, was born; and leaving her there, escaped into France.

A. D. 1644. During the winter, Charles remained at Oxford. Though there was not peace, there was at least a cessation of arms, and the country had rest for some months. In this interval a treaty was begun between the king and the parliament, called the treaty of Uxbridge; but as the parliament was rigid in its demands, and the king, perhaps, not altogether sincere in his concessions, it only ended in making both parties more distrustful, and more inveterate against each other.

A growing diversity of opinion, both in matters of politics and of religion, had for some time shown itself in the parliament; and a religious party now arose of men who

---

Which army was victorious at the battle of Marston Moor?
Was Charles as unfortunate as his generals?
What became of the queen during the war?
What were the events of the winter of 1644?

called themselves Independants, who rejected all qualifying measures that were proposed for the establishment of a limited monarchy, and declared themselves openly for a republic.

Cromwell was the chief leader of the Independents: he had greatly distinguished himself as a soldier and a general, and it was chiefly owing to him that the parliament's army had been at last so well disciplined and organized. Lord Essex, and many others, who had originally joined the parliament from an honest wish to redress grievances, and had been insensibly led on farther than they had intended were now anxious to make an accommodation with the king.

These men were overruled by the Independents; and Cromwell contrived by an act of parliament called the *self-denying ordinance*, to make Essex and many other generals resign their commissions. Cromwell also obtained that sir Thomas, now lord Fairfax, should be appointed general of the army, and himself his lieutenant-general.

On the return of spring, the two armies were again in motion, and many gallant deeds were performed on both sides. Scotland also had a share in the contest. A body of royalists was raised in that country by a young and gallant hero, the earl, afterwards marquis of Montrose, who performed many brave actions, but was defeated, after a short and brilliant career, and obliged to retire amongst his native mountains.

The king's affairs went now fast to ruin; and he lost, one after the other, almost all the towns he had garrisoned. He himself fled into Wales, and afterwards to Oxford, where he passed the winter.

Seeing his condition desperate, and dreading above all things to be made prisoner by the now triumphant parlia-

---

What party division showed itself in the parliament?
Who was the chief leader of the Independents?
By what measures did Cromwell obtain the chief command of the army?
What part did Montrose take in Scotland?
Where did Charles spend the winter of 1045?

ment, formed the unfortunate resolution of throwing himself into the hands of the Scots.

A. D. 1646. He accordingly set out from Oxford, and arrived on May the 5th at the Scottish camp before Newark. The Scottish generals were much surprised at the appearance of the king; and though they affected to treat him with respect, they put a guard upon him, and made him in reality their prisoner.

The Scots having now the king in their hands, required of him to send orders to the governors of Newark, Oxford, and all his other garrisons, to surrender. This he did, and the soldiers and officers all received honorable treatment from Fairfax.

As soon as the parliament knew that Charles was in the hands of the Scots, it began to treat with them for the possession of his person. The Scots, after some delays and hesitation, agreed, on condition of receiving 400,000*l.*, the arrears of their pay due from the parliament, to give up the king.

A. D. 1647. A private letter, communicating the information of this disgraceful bargain, was brought to Charles while he was playing at chess; and his self-command was so great that he continued his game, without betraying by his countenance or manner that he had received any distressing news. In a few days he was given up to the English commissioners, who were sent by the parliament to take him into their custody; and he was conveyed, in the month of February, to Holmby, in Northamptonshire, one of his own royal residences.

After the king had been at Holmby some weeks, Cromwell formed the design of carrying him thence by force, and sent cornet Joyce, with 500 men, to seize him. Joyce came armed with pistols into the king's presence, and told him he must come along with him.

What disposed Charles to trust himself to the Scots?
Where did Charles surrender himself to the Scots?
What did the Scots demand of Charles?
What conditions did the Scots make with the parliament?
Was the conduct honorable? (Ans. *the pupils own judgment.*
How did Charles receive the intilligence that he was given up to his enemies?
Who removed Charles from Holmby?

The king asked Joyce what warrant he acted, he answered by pointing to his soldiers, who were a fine body of men, drawn up in the court-yard. The king said, smiling, "Your warrant is indeed written in fair characters and legible;" and, knowing that resistance would be in vain, immediately consented to accompany him, and was carried to the head-quarters of the army at Triplo Heath, in Cambridgeshire.

The breach between the army and the parliament now came to an open rupture, and colonel Rainsborough marched to London, and completely reduced both the parliament and the city under the authority of Cromwell, who was become the acknowledged chief of his party. The king, meanwhile, remained with the army, and was far more comfortably situated than he had before been when under the rigorous confinement to which he had been subjected by the parliament, or under the insincere protection of the Scots. He was allowed to correspond with the queen; his friends and his chaplains were suffered to return to him and he was permitted the use of the Liturgy and the service of the church.

A. D. 1647. In the autumn the king was brought to Hampton Court, and was allowed to live there with some appearance of freedom. Having been at all times much beloved by his friends, he now, in his adversity became an object of respect even to his enemies. He retained all his former grace and dignity of manner, and had acquired a very winning gentleness and cheerfulness. His temper, instead of being ruffled by affliction, was calmed and moderated It seemed as if he had ceased to struggle with misfortunes, and piously resigned himself to the will of God.

While Charles was with the army, he was allowed to see two of his children, Henry and Elizabeth, who were under the care of lord Northumberland. At one time they were brought to him at Caversham: another time he was permitted to spend a day with them at Sion House, where lord Northumberland lived.

Did Charles resist Joyce?
Was Charles treated with humanity by the army?
How did Charles sustain adversity?
Was Charles permitted to see his children?

The king had also during this year the satisfaction of seeing his second son, the duke of York. The duke soon after made his escape to Holland, where his elder brother, the prince of Wales, had been sent some time before. Mary, the king's eldest daughter, had been married to the prince of Orange before the breaking out of the civil war, and the little princess Henrietta was still at Exeter.

An attempt was made, while the king was at Hampton Court, to renew the former treaties which had been set on foot between him and the parliament: but the terms of accommodation insisted on were such as the king would not accept, the Puritans strenuously insisting on the abolition of episcopacy, and the king as firmly contending for its support.

The Puritans were divided into a multitude of sects, and in the present interval of quiet, the soldiers employed themselves in religious discussions; and many of them set up as preachers and expounders of Scripture. Charles, having been told that some of these entertained designs against him, took a sudden alarm, and privately, with three attendants, left Hampton Court, with the intention of flying abroad.

Charles reached the coast of Hampshire; but not finding there the vessel he expected, he concealed himself for a short time at Tichfield, the house of the dowager lady Southampton. Here one of his attendants persuaded him to put himself in the hands of colonel Hammond, the governor of the Isle of Wight. Thus he prepared for himself a closer prison than any that his enemies had yet found for him

A. D. 1647. The king entered the Isle of Wight, Nov 13 For a short time he was persuaded by Cromwell into a renewal of the former treaty; but on

---

Where were four of the king's children at this time?
Did church affairs prevent any reconciliation between the king and the parliament?
What disposed Charles to fly from Hampton court?
Into whose hands did the king commit himself?

refusing to accede to the terms demanded, he was placed in close confinement in Carisbrook Castle. His situation was now very melancholy. All his attendants were dismissed, except Herbert and Harrington, men who had formerly been greatly prejudiced against him; but who now had become faithfully attached to him, and would willingly have sacrificed their lives in his service.

Colonel Hammond behaved with great compassion towards his royal prisoner, and allowed him every indulgence in his power. A part of the day the king constantly set aside for his devotions, and he spent much of his time alone writing in his bed chamber. The rest of the day he employed in reading, in exercise, and in conversing with his two attendants, who were both of them accomplished men, particularly Mr. Herbert, who had travelled much in Persia, and other countries of the East.

A. D. 1648. In the month of September, Charles entered into a new treaty with commissioners sent by the parliament, which had, for a time, regained some of its authority. Newport was chosen for the place of conference; and Charles left his prison, where he had now passed ten dismal months, and took up his residence in Newport, at the house of a private gentleman.

When the king met the commissioners, an affecting change was perceived to have taken place in his aspect since the preceding year. His countenance was pale and dejected; his hair was turned white, and it brought tears into the eyes of the spectators to see his "grey and discrowned head."

While the conference was going on, the king had permission to take the exercise of riding. He gave his word of honor not to quit the island, but he was so slenderly guarded, that it almost appeared as if the parliament wished him to seize some opportunity of making his escape. This he was importuned to do by his friends, who were now allowed to have access to him; but he rejected their

---

What was Charles's situation at Carisbrook Castle?
How did Charles employ himself?
On what account was Charles removed to Newport?
Did confinement produce upon Charles some of the effects of age?
Did Charles scrupulously keep his word?

advice, saying, he would not break the promise he had given.

The treaty consisted of several articles, to all of which, though tending to the abridgment of his prerogatives, the king agreed, two only excepted, one of which was for the abolition of episcopacy, and the other that all who had taken up arms in his cause should be declared traitors. After further debate, the king agreed to some modification in regard to episcopacy; but nothing could induce him to consent to the last article.

While the treaty between the king and the parliament seemed thus drawing towards a favorable conclusion, Cromwell, by one daring act, annihilated the whole power of the parliament, and destroyed all Charles's hopes of peace and security. He sent colonel Pride, with a body of troops to surround the parliament-house, a little before the time when the members were to assemble, with orders to permit those only to enter who belonged to the independent and republican party, and to exclude all the rest: and this he called "purging the parliament." The members admitted, who were between fifty and sixty in number, immediately elected themselves *governors of the kingdom*, and declared the treaty then pending with the king null and illegal.

The king, two days before this attack upon the house of commons by colonel Pride, had been once more seized by Cromwell's orders, and was removed from the Isle of Wight to a dreary fortress called Hurst Castle, which was situated on the coast of Hampshire and was nearly surrounded by the sea at high tide.

One night in the month of December, the king was waked out of his sleep by hearing the draw-bridge of the castle let down; and soon after he heard the clatter of horsemen in the court. At first he was much agitated; and when Mr. Herbert, whom he sent to inquire the cause of this noise, told him that major Harrison had

---

To what articles of treaty did the king refuse consent?
Who annihilated parliament for the time, and who usurped its powers?
Why was Charles removed to Hurst Castle?
What circumstance alarmed the king, one night at Hurst Castle?

arrived, he was the more alarmed, because he had some time before been warned that this Harrison was one of those who harbored the design to assassinate him.

At length, however, after spending some time in prayer he recovered his composure; and, having risen and dressed, he tranquilly awaited the event. He was soon informed that the purport of the major's coming was to convey him to Windsor; and he was glad to leave Hurst Castle even under such an escort.

Charles was four days on the road to Windsor, and during the journey received from all ranks of people many proofs of sympathy and respect, which greatly cheered him, but which were very displeasing to the governing faction. At Windsor, the king, though kept under great restraint, and though but few people were permitted to have access to him, was treated with civility.

A. D. 1649. All things being now prepared for the fatal catastrophe, the king, on the 6th of January, was impeached of high treason for having presumed to appear in arms against the parliament. When he was informed that he must prepare for his trial, he said little, but was heard uttering to himself—" God is every where alike in wisdom, power, and goodness." He then retired to his apartment, and spent some time alone and in prayer.

On the 18th of January, Charles was removed from Windsor to St. James's palace; and his guards and attendants were ordered to treat him as no longer possessed of royal dignity, and to call him merely Charles Stuart. His own attendants were forbidden to wait on him at table, and the common soldiers were appointed to bring him his meals. Charles was much shocked at this mark of disrespect; but soon recovering his composure, he merely said. " Nothing is so contemptible as a despised king."

The preparations for the trial were soon made. Crom-

Who conveyed Charles to Windsor?
How was Charles treated on his passage to Windsor, and after his arrival there?
Upon what charge was Charles impeached Jan. 6th, 1649?
What indignities were put upon Charles at St James's?
Was this treatment honorable and humane? (Ans. *pupil's own judgment.*)

well declared in a speech in parliament, that had any man voluntarily proposed to bring the king to punishment, he should have regarded that man as the greatest traitor; but, added he, " Providence and necessity hath cast it upon us."

On the 20th of January the king's judges, who were the persons called governors of the kingdom, assembled in Westminster Hall. Charles was brought three several days before the court which his accusers had created to try him, and each time refused to acknowledge its jurisdiction. On the last of these days, January 27th, he was pronounced guilty of having appeared in arms against the parliament, and was condemned to be beheaded on the third day after.

When he had returned to his apartment at St. James's he retired into his room with Dr. Juxon, and told Mr. Herbert to refuse admittance to all persons coming to take leave of him; adding, " My time is short and precious, and I am desirous to improve it the best I may in preparation. I hope those who love me will not take it ill that they have not access to me. The best office they can now do me is to pray for me "

A. D. 1649. A scaffold was erected in front of the palace at Whitehall, and on January 30, he was brought there, attended by Juxon and Herbert; but the latter was so much overwhelmed with grief, that the whole melancholy office of assisting the king in his last moments devolved on the aged bishop.

On the scaffold, the king spoke a few words: he declared himself innocent towards his people, doubtless he thought himself so—but acknowledged himself guilty in the sight of God; and that the consent which he had once given to the execution of an unjust sentence was now deservedly punished by an unjust sentence inflicted on himself.—So heavily did the death of Strafford still press upon his heart.

When and where was sentence of death pronounced upon Charles?
How did Charles sustain himself in his last hours?
Under what circumstances was Charles beheaded?
Though Charles was not a politic prince, does it appear that he was a good man in other relations?

Juxon then assisted him to unrobe. An executioner whose face was concealed by a mask, then struck off his head, and holding it up, said, "This is the head of a traitor!" This bloody spectacle seemed to cause a sudden revulsion in the minds of all the spectators, who felt as much surprised and shocked as if the catastrophe they witnessed had been unexpected.

Charles was in the forty-ninth year of his age, and the twenty-fifth of his reign. He married Henrietta Maria, daughter of Henry IV., king of France. Their children were three sons and three daughters

CHAPTER XXXI

THE COMMONWEALTH.

[Years after Christ, 1649—1660.]

The first act of that small body of men who chose to call themselves a parliament, was to abolish the house of peers as being useless and dangerous. A new great seal of England was made, the *legend* or *inscription*, round which was, "The first year of freedom by God's blessing restored 1648." All loyalists were treated with great severity, and it was made high treason to call the prince of Wales by any name but that of Charles Stuart. The forms of all public business were altered, and the new legislators gave to their government the name of The Commonwealth of England.

A. D. 1649. Cromwell went as lord lieutenant to Ireland, where he found every thing in a very distracted state: but in a few months he restored order in the island. He then left his son-in-law, general Ireton, as his deputy, the affairs of Scotland calling for his presence in that country.

Did the spectacle of Charles's execution distress those who witnessed it?
What was Charles's family?
What were the first measures of the Commonwealth?
How did Cromwell administer affairs in Ireland?

The Scottish Presbyterians had refused to acknowledge the English republic; and, resolving to adhere to the monarchy, had proclaimed prince Charles their king; and sent to invite him to come and take possession of the throne; but on such hard conditions, that those who were his best friends counselled him not to make such sacrifices for the empty title of king.

Charles, who entertained, probably, the dishonest intention of breaking through these conditions whenever he should be able, agreed to them, and returned with the commissioners. He was not suffered to set his foot on Scottish ground till he had signed the covenant: and the moment he was on shore, he was beset by the Covenanters. who strove to convert him to their own opinions.

He now found himself in a very comfortless situation. The Presbyterians kept the entire administration both of church and state in their own hands, and though they allowed him the name of king, they did not treat him even with the respect due to a superior. They paid so little regard to his feelings, that they obliged him to pass under the gates of Aberdeen, over which was hung one of the limbs of his faithful friend and servant, the marquis of Montrose, who had a little before been put to death for appearing in arms in his cause.

Under these circumstances, Charles secretly rejoiced on finding that Cromwell was on his march to Scotland with a powerful army for the purpose of driving him from his uneasy throne. The Scottish army, commanded by general Leslie, attacked Cromwell near Dunbar, and was completely beaten, with great loss; and Cromwell would soon have been entire master of the kingdom, had he not been attacked with a fit of illness, and been obliged to return to England.

A. D. 1651. Cromwell again entered Scotland, and marched so far into the country as to get behind the army of the Covenanters. Charles, who was with the army, which consisted of 14,000 men, seeing the

---

Did the Scots proclaim prince Charles king?
Who received Charles in Scotland?
How was Charles treated in Scotland?
Did Cromwell lead an army against Charles?

road to the English border thus opened to him, formed the bold resolution of marching forwards into England, falsely presuming, that all who were discontented with the Commonwealth would flock to his standard.

Charles marched forwards, in hopes at last to gather strength; but he arrived at Worcester with only his 14,000 Scots. Here he halted, and had a few days' rest after his long and fatiguing march. In the meantime, Cromwell, when he found that the king had slipped by him, left the command of the Scottish war to general Monk, and followed Charles with all possible expedition.

Cromwell raising the militia of the several counties as he passed, so that by the time he reached Worcester he mustered a considerable force. The next day, Sept. 4, 1651, he surrounded the town with his troops, and, falling on the royal army, soon destroyed it, the very streets being filled with dead bodies.

Charles after making a desperate resistance, was at last obliged to fly with fifty or sixty gentlemen in his company. They rode about twenty-six miles without stopping. It was then thought advisable for them to separate. Charles, by the advice of lord Derby, went to a lone house on the borders of Staffordshire, inhabited by a man of the name of Penderell, who with five brothers, were wood-cutters in the neighboring wood of Boscobel.

Charles committed himself to the care of these men, who showed themselves worthy of the confidence placed in them; for, though a high reward was offered to any one who would deliver up the prince, and it was declared certain death to conceal him, these honest rustics would not betray him.

On one occasion, fearing to be discovered by a party of soldiers who were searching the wood, Charles hid himself in a large oak tree; from amongst the branches of which he could hear the soldiers say, they wondered where he

---

What army adhered to Charles, and what expectations were formed by Charles?
Where did Charles halt in his march to England?
What was the result of the battle of Worcester?
Where did Charles take refuge in his flight from Worcester?
Did the protectors of Charles exhibit integrity and generosity?
How did Charles once conceal himself from his enemies?

could be, for they were sure he was somewhere in the wood.

Charles was wandering about not less than six weeks, from the time of the battle of Worcester without being able to get out of the country; and the risks he ran of discovery were very great. At last he arrived at a lone house, between Shoreham and Brighthelmstone, and found means to cross the water.

While Charles was thus wandering about, the party in power had been going on triumphantly. The victory at Worcester they chose to call their "crowning mercy." Monk had been successful in Scotland; Ireton kept every thing quiet in Ireland; and the government, elated by success, soon showed a desire to lord it over foreign states; and in 1652, declared war against the Dutch.

Holland was at that time regarded as the most considerable maritime power in Europe, and was supposed to excel all other states in the art of ship-building, and in the skill of her seamen. But now the English navy, which the late king had paid great attention to, and which was manned by sailors whom the circumstances of the time had made bold and hardy, was found a match for that of Holland; and admiral Blake was several times the victor in engagements with the Dutch admirals, Van Tromp, de Ruyter, and de Witt.

In the midst of all this success an ignominious fall was preparing for that comparatively inconsiderable band of men, who still called themselves a parliament. Cromwell, who now thought it time to drive them from the high station which he had suffered them to occupy, went, on April 20, 1653, to the parliament house, while the members were assembled, and placing a file of soldiers at each door, entered the hall, saying, "that he was come with a purpose of doing what grieved him to the very soul, and what he had earnestly besought the Lord not to impose upon him; but that there was a necessity for it."

He next sat down and heard the debates, and then

Did Charles escape to the continent?
How did the existing government of England proceed?
What was the naval power of Holland and of England 1652?
Did Cromwell disperse the republican parliament?

suddenly starting up, he exclaimed: " This is the time, I must do it." Turning to the members he loaded them with every term of reproach, and called them tyrants, oppressors, and public robbers. At last he stamped with his foot, on which signal the soldiers entering the hall, he ordered them to drive all the members out.

As the members took their compulsory departure, Cromwell said to them, " You are no longer a parliament; the Lord has done with you; he has chosen other instruments for carrying on his work." He then staid till the hall was empty; then ordering the doors to be locked, he put the keys into his pocket, and returned to the palace at Whitehall, where he and his family had taken up their residence.

Cromwell was now the sole head of the government, and no one attempted to dispute his power. To keep up the appearance of a Commonwealth, he summoned a parliament who set themselves to work to settle the affairs of the state. They considered the clerical office as being altogether a remnant of popery, and proposed that there should be no more clergy. The common law they deemed a badge of Norman slavery, and were desirous to set it aside They also voted that learning was heathenish, and the universities unnecessary.

This parliament had the name given it of Barebone's parliament, from the name of one of its chief orators. At last, the measures of the parliament became so utterly absurd, that Cromwell became ashamed of it, and suffered one only of their many proposed changes and regulations to be carried into effect. This one was in regard to the marriage ceremony, which was declared to be a mere civil contract, and was appointed to be performed for the future in private rooms, before a magistrate, instead of being solemnized in churches.

Cromwell had at this time the title of Protector conferred on him. The mass of the people were so tired of the tyranny and oppression of the parliament, that they were

---

How did Cromwell attack the parliament?
How did Cromwell justify this proceeding?
What absurd practices and notions were urged by Cromwell's parliament?
Did Cromwell fall in with the measures of this parliament?

thankful to get rid of their many masters, and to enjoy any thing like a settled government. And Cromwell, though he trampled on the laws of the country, would suffer no other person but himself to do so. He enforced justice and civil order, and made his government respected at home and feared abroad.

Cromwell kept up the power of the navy, and soon obliged the Dutch to sue for peace. He attacked the Spaniards because they interrupted the English in their traffic with Spanish America, and took from them the island of Jamaica in the West Indies, which is still retained by the English. The protectorship was not only confirmed to Cromwell for life, but was also settled on whomsoever he should choose to appoint after his death.

This proceeding alarmed both the republicans and the royalists, who began to fear that a power so well established would become permament, to the destruction of their different hopes. In 1655, a plan was formed for a general rising amongst the royalists. But Cromwell and his secretary, Thurloe, had full information of their designs, and before the appointed day of insurrection, many of the royalists were taken up; some were punished with death, and several others were sold for slaves, and sent to Barbadoes. This despotic act struck terror throughout the whole nation; and no other considerable attempt was made to overturn the protector's power.

Cromwell's government of Ireland was equally vigorous. Fleetwood, who had married his eldest daughter (Iretor's widow,) was his deputy, and carried many of his arbitrary measures into effect. Fleetwood was succeeded by the protector's second son, Henry, a young man of great abilities, and extraordinary goodness, who, pitying the condition of the Irish, did all he could to improve it.

Cromwell, in the latter part of his life, was under a continual dread of being secretly murdered. And though he had often braved danger in battle with intrepidity, he now betrayed a more than common fear of death; and every

---

How did Cromwell make himself acceptable to the nation?
Was Cromwell an able politician?
How did Cromwell treat the royalists who plotted against him?
Did Fleetwood and Henry Cromwell govern Ireland?
What disturbed the tranquility of Cromwell?

moment of his life was made miserable by the apprehension of losing it. In addition to these terrors, he had many causes of mortification in his own family.

Richard, Cromwell's eldest son, whom he meant for his successor, was a man of inferior talents and of no ambition. Henry Cromwell was a man of abilities, but had too much virtue to be willing to follow his father's footsteps. Cromwell's other daughters were zealous royalists; and Mrs. Claypole, the one whom he loved best of all his children, represented to him, when on her death-bed, and in terms which filled him with grief, her disapprobation of the conduct which he had pursued. From that time he was never seen to smile.

Cromwell's exertions and agitations were too great for his bodily frame to support. He found the exalted state to which he had attained, a burden too heavy to be borne, and died, a worn out old man, on September 3, 1658, in the 59th year of his age. He was buried with royal pomp in Westminster Abbey.

Cromwell's character is one of the most extraordinary in history. His talents were, in some respects, of the very highest order. In others, he was strikingly deficient. His government of Ireland; the manner in which he treated Holland and Spain, thus vindicating the independence and naval power of England, are undoubted proofs of the energy of his mind, and the wisdom of his policy.

Richard Cromwell was proclaimed protector in his father's place. But the nation soon found the difference between the strong hand of Oliver Cromwell, and the feebleness of his son, and showed a disposition to cast off his authority. But Richard quietly resigning a dignity which he had neither the power nor the inclination to keep, wisely saved himself from being dispossessed by violence He held the protectorship only a few months.

Henry Cromwell also resigned his command in Ireland

Did Cromwell's children resemble their father?
When did Cromwell die?
What was Cromwell's character?
Did Richard Cromwell succeed to his father?
Did Henry Cromwell enjoy a public station?

though his popularity in that country was very great, and he might have retained his power there if he had chosen to do so; but like his brother he preferred the tranquility of a private station to all the dangerous and uncertain enjoyments of ambition.

The country was now without any apparent ruler, and was split into a variety of factions. The republicans hoped to establish their long desired form of popular government and the royalists in their turn were full of expectations and projects.

Charles, meantime, on hearing of what was passing in England, left the Low Countries, where he had for some time past taken refuge, and came to Calais, where he staid, awaiting the event. For some time their seemed little chance of any turn in his favor; but, at last, what the efforts of his friends could not do, the rivalry of his enemies brought about.

Lambert and Monk had long hated each other; and Monk, partly perhaps to disappoint Lambert, who was secretly ambitious of the protectorship, formed the design of bringing back the king, and entered into a correspondence with him. But he kept his intentions so well concealed that he appeared to be only acting for the restoration of the parliament.

Monk collected several scattered regiments in Scotland, and marched directly into England. Lambert set forward to meet him, but found himself deserted by his own soldiers; and the parliament, being no longer held in terror by the troops, assumed once more the reigns of government arrested Lambert, and committed him to the Tower.

Monk and his army soon reached London. He appeared at first to acknowledge the authority of the parliament; but in a few days he openly avowed his contempt of that obtrusive body of men, and declared for a free parliament, he called together all the surviving members of the old or long parliament, who had been expelled by colonel Pride

---

Was England divided into *factions* after the death of Cromwell?
How did Charles regard the death of Cromwell?
Who formed a project to restore the monarchy?
How did Monk proceed to effect the restoration?
What measures were taken in respect of parliament?

in 1648. They met on February 21, 1660, and in a few days formally dissolved themselves, and issued writs for a new parliament, which assembled April 25.

On the 1st of May, Monk, having every thing ripe for his project, ventured to propose to parliament the restoration of the king. It is impossible to describe the joy with which this proposal was heard—a joy which soon spread from the house to the city, and from thence through the whole country. The peers, from all parts of the kingdom, hastened to reinstate themselves in their parliamentary rights: and on the 8th of May, Charles II. was proclaimed king, and a committee of gentlemen was sent to invite him to return and take possession of his dominions.

The king sailed from Scheveling, a small village on the coast of Holland, and was met at Dover by general Monk who conducted him to London, which he entered, amidst the joyful acclamations of the people, May 29, 1660.

In the time of the Commonwealth the business of banking was first practised. Before the civil war, the Mint in the Tower was the usual place of deposit for money; but after the commencement of the disturbances, the private property of individuals was no longer thought safe in the Mint, and the goldsmiths were employed by the rich merchants and tradesmen to take care of their money for them, and thus the goldsmiths became the first bankers.

Episcopacy had been abolished by the parliament during the war. In the time of the Commonwealth, most of the loyal and orthodox clergy were dispossessed of their livings, and allowed small pensions; and, instead of regular clergy, itinerant preachers were employed, who rode about the country to teach the people doctrines.

Charles the First appointed a post to carry letters once a week between London and Edinburgh. The system

---

Was the return of Charles to England acceptable to the nation?
When did Charles enter London?
When was banking first practised in England?
What was the state of the English church during the existence of the commonwealth?
When were mails first put in operation in Britain?

was afterwards much extended and improved during the Commonwealth: and the privilege of franking was then first allowed to the members of the house of commons. This was confirmed to them by Charles II., who extended the privilege to the peers also. *Franking* is the privilege of certain persons to send letters by mail, free of expense.

Newspapers were first circulated in England in the reign of queen Elizabeth, in order to apprize the country of the defeat of the Spanish armada. After this occasion had passed by, they were discontinued for many years. The date commonly assigned to their first publication in England is that of the year 1642

CHAPTER XXXII.

CHARLES II.

[Years after Christ, 1060—1685.]

CHARLES II. AND HIS QUEEN.

Charles was thirty years old, when, after sixteen years exile, he was so unexpectedly placed on the throne of his ancestors. He had a good figure, and though his features

---

When were newspapers first circulated in England?

were harsh, there was something agreeable in his countenance; and his cheerful, easy, and graceful deportment, made him altogether a very engaging person. He had a great deal of shrewdness and wit; and with common application, might have been any thing he pleased. But he loved amusement, and hated business, and to live idly and merrily was all he cared for.

The king began his reign by forming a ministry from amongst the best and wisest men of all parties, and he gave general satisfaction by the choice he made. An act of indemnity, or of general pardon, was then passed towards all those who had taken part against the crown, excepting only the judges who had sat on the late king's trial, and all those who had in any other way been immediately accessary to his death. About sixty persons had been concerned in that act. Of these many were dead, and others had left the kingdom.

Of those who could be brought to trial, ten only were executed: the rest were reprieved and placed in different prisons. Harrison, who had conducted Charles I. from Hurst Castle, was amongst those who suffered. He died justifying his conduct to the last. Hugh Peters also was executed. He had been one of Cromwell's fanatical preachers, and had not only been very active in stirring up the minds of the people against the king; but also, it was supposed, was one of the masked executioners who beheaded him.

General Lambert, and sir Henry Vane, though they were not absolutely regicides, were yet thought too guilty to be included in the act of indemnity. Vane was executed: Lambert was reprieved, and exiled to the island of Guernsey, where he lived thirty years, and from being a rigid Puritan, became a Roman Catholic.

This act of retribution being performed, the ministry applied themselves to the business of the state. The chancellor, lord Clarendon, who had attended the king during his exile, had the chief weight in the council, and by his inte-

---

What were the personal qualities of Charles II.?
How did Charles begin his reign?
Who of the late king's enemies were punished?
What became of Lambert and Vane?

grity and wisdom the government was carried on for a time with justice and moderation. The old standing army of the republicans was disbanded: the king retained only a few guards and garrisons; and most of the fortified places that had not been destroyed in the civil wars were dismantled.

Episcopacy was restored; nine of the old bishops, who still survived, were replaced in their sees, and all the ejected clergy returned to their livings. The Presbyterians saw these measures with dissatisfaction; but an insurrection of one of the sects among the repulicans gave the ministry a pretext to insist on the restoration of the church without any modifications. An *act of uniformity* was passed, which required the assent of all the clergy to several articles very obnoxious to the Presbyterians. Those who refused to sign these articles were disabled from holding their livings, and, in consequence, two thousand of them were deprived.

The Scots had joyfully seen the restoration of the kingly authority; but when Charles proceeded to settle the affairs of that country, he found the people altogether averse to receive the hierarchy, which he was exceedingly desirous to establish amongst them, perhaps the more desirous, because, in spite of his naturally careless temper, he could not have forgotten the indignities and insults which the spiritual pride of the Scotch Presbyterians had made him suffer when he had formerly been amongst them.

Charles won over Sharp, a Presbyterian leader, to accept the archbishopric of St. Andrews. Sharp was a vindictive and bigoted man, whose conduct only exasperated the people more against episcopacy. He was at last assassinated by a zealous fanatic of the name of Balfour of Burley; who, with a small party of men, chanced to meet him, as he was traveling with his daughter, dragged him out of his carriage and murdered him. This brutal assassination put an entire stop to the attempt to introduce episcopacy into the Scotch church.

Who was made Chancellor, and how was the army regulated?
How were church affairs regulated?
Were Charles's measures in regard to religion acceptable in Scotland?
How did Charles become unpopular in Scotland?
What stopped the introduction of episcopacy in Scotland?

A. D. 1662. Charles married Catharine of Braganza, daughter of the king of Portugal. The new queen had been educated in a convent, and was very formal and grave: she rejected the company of the English ladies, and would only have about her a set of old solemn Spanish duennas. The king found her and her court so dull, that he neglected her society, and spent most of his time with idle and dissolute companions, and unprincipled women.

A. D. 1664. Charles entered into a war with Holland, which afterwards led to a rupture with France and Denmark. This war was carried on wholly by sea; and the king's brother, James, duke of York, an active, enterprising man, commanded the fleet. Many well-contested actions were fought, and many fruitless victories gained. One of these engagements lasted four days, and is among the most memorable which are recorded in history.

The Dutch fleet consisted of seventy-six ships, and was commanded by the famous De Ruyter, and by Van Tromp, son of the great Van Tromp. The English fleet was commanded by prince Rupert, and by Monk, then duke of Albemarle, and altogether was nearly equal to the Dutch. The detail of the different engagements of the four days, would be little instructive. On the last day neither party had gained the victory.

The two fleets then retired to their harbors, but met again June 25th, at the mouth of the Thames, when the English obtained a decisive victory. De Ruyter, indignant at being obliged to fly, frequently exclaimed, "O God, amongst so many thousand bullets, is there not one to put an end to my miserable life!" The English were now incontestably masters of the sea; but they had been visited at home during this year by so many calamities, that they had no spirits to rejoice in any triumphs over a foreign foe.

In the preceding autumn a most violent plague had broken out, particularly in London. There, in a short time, ninety thousand persons are said to have died of that

---

Who was Charles's queen, and what was his domestic character?
What circumstances called forth the talents of James, duke of York?
Who were the commanders in the naval battle of 1666?

malady. While London was still suffering under this calamity, it was assailed also by another. On the 3d of September, 1666, a fire broke out near London Bridge, which spread with such rapidity that thirteen thousand houses were burnt down.

These dreadful scenes were not without some good effect on the king's disposition, and detached him for a while from the idle and dissolute habits he had sunk into; but his vicious companions soon got about him, and rallied him out of all his good resolutions; and he relapsed into his former way of life.

These vicious companions, the chief of whom was the duke of Buckingham, had long meditated the overthrow of lord Clarendon, whose integrity made him the particular object of their dislike. It happened that the Dutch fleet sailed up the Medway, and destroyed some ships in the harbor at Chatham. A peace was made with Holland soon afterwards. Buckingham and his party found means of turning both this peace itself, and also the disgrace at Chatham, to the particular discredit of Clarendon, insinuating that the latter could not have taken place, unless he had been negligent of the public security.

Charles, who had little gratitude in his nature, forgetting how faithfully this great statesman had served him in all his wanderings and necessities, and how much his wisdom had contributed to strengthen him on the throne, was not sorry to have a pretext for removing a man who was some check upon his vices. Clarendon was, therefore, impeached on various frivolous pretences, and was sentenced to banishment.

Clarendon retired into France, and employed the remainder of his life chiefly in composing his History of the Rebellion, and also in writing an account of his own life. His youngest daughter, Anne Hyde, married the duke of York soon after the restoration. She died young, leaving two children, the princesses Mary and Anne.

Were the plague and the fire of London great calamities?
Did the public calamities at all affect the king?
Who assailed the reputation of lord Clarendon?
How did Charles treat Clarendon?
Where did Clarendon end his days?

After Clarendon's disgrace, prince Rupert, the duke of Ormond, sir Orlando Bridgman, and other men of experience and high character, had for a time the chief weight in the council. But in 1670 their influence declined, and the king, whose carelessness about public affairs daily increased, committed the entire management of the state to five of the most unprincipled men in the kingdom, Clifford, Ashley, Buckingham, Arlington, and Lauderdale, who were called the *Cabal*, from the first letters of their names.

One of the nefarious measures of this administration was to shut up the *exchequer*, and to take possession of the money which private individuals had placed in it. Another and a still more generally unpopular measure, was that of entering into a new war with the Dutch, in order to gratify Louis XIV., one of the most ambitious, vain-glorious, and unprincipled kings that ever reigned.

Charles at first hesitated to take such an unpopular step: but he was, at length, persuaded into it by his sister Henrietta, duchess of Orleans, who was sent on a visit to him by the French king. It is even said that the restoration of popery in England, was made an article of a secret treaty between the two kings. Charles, if he had any religion at all, was in his heart a Papist; and the duke of York was a professed one.

The French and English fleets now joined each other. As they were at anchor in Solebay, De Ruyter came unexpectedly upon them. The duke of York commanded in chief, in the action between the Dutch and the combined fleets, and had his ship so shattered that he was obliged to remove his flag on board another. The battle lasted the whole day, and De Ruyter declared that, of the thirty-two actions he had been in, this was the hardest fought. The English and Dutch lost many ships and neither party gained any thing. The French took care to keep aloof during the engagement.

Another memorable naval action was fought on August

Who were the *Cabal?*
Did the English government at this time engage in the interests of France?
What was the influence of the king's brother and sister over him?
How did the naval battle of Solebay terminate?

11, 1673. The English fleet was commanded by prince Rupert, the Dutch by De Ruyter. In this battle too, as in many of the former, nothing was gained by either party.

A. D. 1674. By the death of Clifford, and the disgrace of Ashley, who had been created lord Shaftesbury, the *cabal* was broken up. More honest ministers came into place, and wiser measures were pursued One of these measures was to make peace with Holland but Charles still kept up with France a secret alliance on the most dishonorable terms. He received privately from Louis XIV. an annual pension of two millions of livres, as the price of his supporting the French interest in his own court.

Charles and his parliament were generally on bad terms. In 1678 the parliament, which had sat seventeen years, was dissolved. It had assembled in all the intoxication of joy, loyalty, and hope, which it was natural to feel on the king's restoration; and it separated with feelings of severe disappointment at his utter want of principle.

The following year another parliament was summoned, in which great struggles were made to exclude the duke of York, on account of his religion, from the succession, and to settle the crown, after the death of Charles, who had no legitimate children, on the duke's eldest daughter Mary who was now married to the prince of Orange. But this bill of exclusion could not be carried.

In this parliament the liberty of the subject was materially secured by the passing of what is called the Habeas Corpus bill, by which it is rendered illegal to detain in prison any individual who claims to be tried, and which thus affords a complete protection against all kinds of arbitrary imprisonment.

The people were now becoming more and more dissatisfied both with the king and his brother; and the quiet of the country was greatly disturbed by tumultuous meetings. One plot was formed in favor of the duke of Monmouth a

---

What was the result of the battle fought August 11th, 1673?
What was the state of public affairs in England, 1674?
What was the public feeling in 1678?
Was the duke of York excluded from the succession?
What is the act of Habeas Corpus?
What disturbed the public tranquility in England, A. D 1331?

son of the king, whom some of the more violent opposers of the Popish party were desirous to declare heir to the crown.

The papists, in their turn, had also a plot of their own to secure the duke of York's succession: and both parties were thus agitated by turns with various hopes and schemes. It was at this time that the names of Whig and Tory, names so often since used and abused, were made the appellations of two opposite factions.

While the country was thus filled on all sides with discontent and apprehension, the king was urged by the vindictive temper of the duke to exercise severities foreign to his nature; and many persons were taken up and executed on suspicion of being engaged in plots.

One of these persons was lord William Russell, a nobleman of high character, who was accused of being privy to what was called the Ryehouse plot, from the name of a house near Newmarket, where the conspirators held their meetings. The witnesses against him were men of infamous character; but, notwithstanding the want of proper evidence, he was condemned and executed.

Algernon Sidney, son of the earl of Leicester, was also tried and executed with as little show of justice. Nothing was proved against him, but he was known to be attached to republican principles, and for this reason was the more easily suspected of harboring designs against the king.

The king, though he permitted these things to be done, does not appear to have approved of them, and often opposed his brother's violent counsels. In the midst of a life of vicious indulgence, Charles was attacked by an apoplexy, and died, after a few days illness, February 6th, 1685, in the fifty-fifth year of his age, and the twenty-fifth of his reign. Charles II. married Catharine of Braganza, daughter of the king of Portugal. They had no children.

When were the terms Whig and Tory applied first to political parties?
What disposed Charles II. to severe measures?
On what charge was lord William Russell executed?
For what was Algernon Sydney executed?
Did Charles approve of these arbitrary measures, and when did he die?

Charles was a man of exceeding profligacy of manners; and the influence of his example, and that of his associates, was eminently corrupting to the nation. This infection spread from the court through the country; and the people, flying from one extreme to the other, gave up the appearances of gravity and saintliness to assume the opposite character of licentiousness. Even the public taste was corrupted. Many of the books written at that time were polluted with the same vicious spirit that so generally prevailed in society.

There were, however, some worthy exceptions to this degraded literature. Paradise Lost, a poem which for sublimity and purity has never been excelled, was published in this reign. Milton, the admirable author, was a man of great learning, and had been Latin secretary to Oliver Cromwell. He wrote many prose works, which are almost all political, and in favor of independent and republican principles.

Charles II. was not without sentiments of humanity. In the great fire of London, the people at first seemed to lose their senses in the greatness of the calamity. The king was the first to regain his recollection. He himself attended late and early to encourage and reward the workmen, and showed great presence of mind and activity.

Charles possessed talents, but made no good use of them. There was a lively epigram made on him by one of the wits of his court :—

> Here lies our sovereign lord the king,
> Whose word no man relies on;
> Who never said a foolish thing,
> And never did a wise one.

This was shown to Charles, and he said, in his pleasant way, that it was very true; for his words were his own, but his actions were his ministers.

What were the manners of Charles and his court, and what were the effects of these manners?
Who was the great poet of Charles's age?
Was Charles II. naturally humane?
What epigram was made upon Charles?

CHAPTER XXXIII

JAMES II.

[Years after Christ, 1685—1688.]

James was in the fifty-third year of his age when he succeeded to the throne of England. He had not his brother's talent and brilliancy, but he was a man of much perseverance and steady application to business. He had been by his mother brought up a Papist, and had acquired from his religion a harshness and bigotry which does not appear to have belonged naturally to his character. He meant to act rightly, and to be, according to his own ideas, a good king. But he mistook, or to speak more properly, he did not regard the feelings, opinion, or character of the people he had to govern.

As he was very young when the civil war broke out, he received no regular education. When James was about fourteen years of age, he was secretly removed from the charge of the parliament, and conveyed by one of the royalists into Holland, and afterwards to Brussels.

James was always glad to be with his brother, but towards the end of the year 1659, Charles was reduced to the utmost distress; and James was on the point of accepting an offer made to him by the king of Spain to take the command of the Spanish fleet, when his brother's restoration placed him at the head of the English navy; a situation that suited him well, for he was a man of great personal courage, and naturally inclined to an enterprising and active life.

James, as soon as he came to the throne, professed an intention to maintain the laws of the country both in church and state; and this declaration served greatly to tranquilize the minds of the populace, who were well disposed to rely on it, because James, notwithstanding his known bigotry, had hitherto preserved a high character

---

What was the character of James II. ?
What was James's education ?
Who placed the duke of York at the head of the English navy ?

for sincerity. Yet he soon after despatched a Catholic priest to Rome to negotiate a re-union with the papal see. The pope, Innocent XI., had more prudence than the king, and advised him to attempt nothing rashly.

The duke of Monmouth had found it necessary to leave England during the ferment of the real or pretended plots in the late king's time; but now, encouraged by the dread the people had of popery, and relying on his own popularity, he returned and landed at Lyme, in Dorsetshire, June 11, 1685, with only a hundred followers. He pretended that his mother had been privately married to Charles, and that he was the legitimate heir to the crown.

Monmouth soon assembled 6000 men, and was prevented only by want of arms, from raising a much greater number. Had he marched immediately to London he might, perhaps, have had some chance of succeeding; but instead of doing so, he wasted his time by staying to be proclaimed in the different towns he passed through. On July 5th, he encountered the king's army at Sedgemoor near Bridgewater, and was totally defeated.

Monmouth himself fled from the field of battle without stopping, till his horse dropped from fatigue. He then changed clothes with a peasant, and endeavored to conceal himself in the most sequestered places. At last he was found lying down in a wet ditch, hiding himself under the fern leaves that grew on the bank. Monmouth was taken to London, and besought an interview with the king, that he might try to move him to pity the favorite son of a brother whom he had tenderly loved.

But Monmouth's crime was too dangerous to be forgiven; and he neither had had no abettors, or was too honorable to betray them. He was beheaded in the 36th year of his age. Though this execution was seen by crowds of people, they could not bring themselves to believe that their favorite was actually dead. They fondly imagined

---

Did James favor the Catholic religion?
Upon what pretence did the duke of Monmouth claim the crown of England?
Was Monmouth successful?
Did Monmouth receive pardon?
Did the witnesses of Monmouth's execution doubt that he was living?

that some other person had, from friendship, suffered in his stead, and that they should see him emerge from some concealment.

The punishment of those who had taken part in Monmouth's rebellion was very severe; and the cruelties perpetrated in the king's name by judge Jeffreys and colonel Kirk, in the west of England, have left a stain on their memories, and on that of James II., that can never be wiped away. In the same year, 1685, the duke of Argyle was executed in Scotland for heading a rebellion in that country.

James, having now, as he supposed, suppressed the discontents of the people, thought that he had sufficiently cleared the way for the restoration of popery. Being led on by the vehemence of the queen, and the rash counsels of his confessor, father Peters, he introduced Papists into the army and navy, suspended the bishop of London, and issued a declaration of indulgence to the Roman Catholics and to the other dissenters. He also committed many acts oppressive to the Protestants, and favorable to the Papists.

The measures now taken in favor of the Catholics induced the primate and six of the bishops to present a remonstrance. For this presumption they were committed to the Tower; but on being brought to trial they were acquitted, to the great satisfaction of the people at large, though to the bitter mortification of the king.

One great check on the king's ardent zeal for the restoration of popery, was the knowledge that should his eldest daughter, the wife of the prince of Orange, succeed him on the throne, the whole work would be undone, both the princess and her husband being Protestants, and the prince being universally looked up to as the great support of the reformed religion in Europe. James, therefore, ardently desired a son: and when, on June, 1688, a son was born to him, he thought every thing would prosper to his wishes.

Were Monmouth's adherents punished?
Did James attempt the restoration of popery?
Did the English clergy take alarm at these proceedings?
For what did James desire a son?

That event, however, in fact hastened James's expulsion from the throne. For the people, who had been cheered by the hope of a Protestant sovereign after James's death, now seeing themselves cut off, according to the ordinary course of events, from any further indulgence of that hope became anxious for the king's dethronement; and many persons of rank and consideration entered into secret negotiations with the prince of Orange.

Meanwhile James's conduct seemed nothing but a course of blind infatuation. He looked but at one object, the restoration of popery, and saw neither the rising discontents of the people, nor the increased intercourse which was held with the prince of Orange. At last his minister at the Hague sent to warn him that he might soon expect an invasion from Holland.

On receiving this information James was completely stunned; the letter fell from his hands, and it was sometime before he recovered the power of thinking and acting. When at last he roused himself from this state of consternation and surprise, the only means that occurred to him of averting the coming storm, was to retract some of his late obnoxious measures. But these concessions gained him no credit, and were attributed rather to fear than repentance.

A. D. 1688. At this time a declaration from the prince of Orange, assuring the people of England that he was coming over to redress their grievances, was gladly received throughout the kingdom. On October 31, he sailed from Helvoetsluys with a numerous army and fleet, and landed in Torbay November 5th.

The disastrous issue of Monmouth's invasion was still so fresh in the memories of the inhabitants of the west of England, that at first they dared not join the prince of Orange. In a few days, however, the gentry of Devonshire and Somersetshire flocked to his standard. All England was presently in commotion, and the people combined

---

What was the effect of the birth of a prince of Wales?
Was James blind to the consequences of his own actions?
Was James alarmed at the determination of the prince of Orange?
When did the prince of Orange sail for England?
Were the English rejoiced at the coming of the prince of Orange?

almost universally against their misjudging and ill-advised monarch.

James's dismay and perplexity were at this time very great. The Jesuits who were about him were unable to give him any assistance, and only advised him to abandon the country. The same advice was also strongly urged by the queen: and thus, overruled by the fears and clamor of those around him, he forbore to make even a single effort to preserve his throne.

He sent the queen and her infant son secretly away and on December 12th, he himself left London in the middle of the night, attended only by sir Edward Hales. His intention was to get on board a ship at Sheerness, and to escape to France.

When it was known that the king was gone, and had left no one in charge of the administration, the mob of London rose, and seemed to consider themselves as masters, and set about executing summary justice in the usual manner of mobs. They destroyed all the mass-houses; and finding judge Jeffreys, disguised, and intending to fly the country, they vented their rage on him so unmercifully that he died in consequence.

To add to the general confusion, lord Feversham, commander of the king's forces, disbanded them, and without disarming or giving the pay due to them, turned the men loose on the country. In this extremity, those peers and bishops who happened to be in London assembled, and sent an invitation to the prince of Orange, who now assumed almost all the functions of royalty.

Meanwhile the fugitive king had been discovered at Feversham. He was brought back to London much to the dissatisfaction of the prince of Orange, who had promised his wife that no personal violence should be offered to her father. William, therefore, not only winked at, but even secretly assisted James to make his escape a second time. On the 25th December, this unfortunate monarch landed at

---

How did James meet the prince, &c. ?
How did the king and his family escape ?
What was the first effect of the abdication ?
What happened in London upon the king's abdication ?
Did the prince of Orange easily assume the function of royalty ?
Did William treat James II. generously ?

Ambleteus in Picardy, from whence he proceeded to St. Germains, near Paris, where Louis XIV. received him with great generosity and commiseration. He had reigned about three years.

By his first wife, Anne Hyde, James II. had two daughters; Mary, married William of Nassau, prince of Orange; Anne, married George, son of Frederick III., king of Denmark. By his second wife, Maria Beatrice of Este, he had James Francis Edward, afterwards called the pretender; Mary Louisa, who was to have been a nun, but died before she took the veil.

One of the most virtuous men, and profound philosophers of the time of James II. was the celebrated Robert Boyle, an extraordinary able and good man, who withdrew himself from all the tumults of the unhappy times he lived in, and devoted his life to science and religion. Charles II., after his restoration, pressed Mr. Boyle to become a clergyman, and to accept of some church preferment; but he declined, saying that what he could do for the service of religion he thought would have more effect as coming from a layman.

Sir Christopher Wren was an architect. He was employed to furnish designs for rebuilding the churches that were destroyed by the fire of London. Fifty-eight churches were built by him. Of these St. Paul's is his greatest work. Indeed it is considered to be the finest church in Europe, with the exception only of St. Peter's at Rome.

St. Peter's was above a hundred years in building. The first stone of St. Paul's was laid in 1675, and the whole building was completed in thirty-five years, though some of the decorations were not finished till 1723. It seemed as if the life of the venerable architect was lengthened, that he might enjoy the pleasure of seeing the completion of his great work. He died the year it was finished, aged ninety-one.

Who was Mr. Boyle?
Who was sir Christopher Wren?
Which is the greatest work, St. Peter's or St Paul's churches, and where are both?

CHAPTER XXXIV.

WILLIAM III.

[Years after Christ, 1689—1702.]

William of Nassau was son of William prince of Orange, and Mary, the eldest daughter of Charles I. He was in the thirty-ninth year of his age, when the general voice of the people of England called upon him to ascend the throne. Some years before he had been chosen stadtholder of Holland, and had long been accustomed to an active life, and had shown much firmness and military skill in the wars between Louis XIV. and the Dutch.

William married the princess Mary, daughter of James II. This princess had a fine person, with an engaging countenance, accompanied by an air of great dignity. She was a truly good woman, and little ambitious of governing.

After a long debate in both houses of parliament, it was settled that the prince and princess of Orange should be made king and queen of England, and that the administration of government should be placed in the hands of the prince only. The two houses at the same time made a declaration, called the Bill of Rights, by which the prerogatives of the crown were limited and defined, and the liberty of the subject placed in greater security.

At first all was harmony and satisfaction: but William had not long been king of England before he and his new subjects became mutually discontented with each other. William, a thorough soldier, found the management of a free people extremely troublesome.

The English on their side, were little pleased with a monarch who, instead of living amongst his people in that sort of social way to which their former kings had accustomed them, spent most of his time either alone in his closet, or at a camp which he had formed at Hounslow. And

---

Who was William of Nassau?
Whom did William III. marry?
What was the bill of rights?
Did William and his English subjects suit each other?
Did the English like a military monarch?

when he did show himself in his court, which was very seldom, he did not appear gracious and amiable.

After a time, finding that this secluded way of life made him very unpopular, William tried to rouse himself, and, on various public occasions, exerted himself so far as to conduct himself with affability to those about him, but still the whole bent of his mind was fixed on humbling the power of France, and this more for the sake of revenging the quarrels of his native country, than from any motive in which England was concerned.

Soon after the settlement of the crown of England, the Scots declared the crown of Scotland vacant, and offered it to William and Mary. Thus the title of the new sovereign became established in both kingdoms. Lord Dundee alone collected a body of Highlanders. With a few hundred men he defeated a large body of William's troops at the pass of Killicrankie. Dundee himself was, however, mortally wounded in the action, and died on the day following. His death so broke down the spirit of the Highland clans, that they, after a short time, accepted the pardon offered them by William, and acknowledged his authority.

A. D. 1689. A few months before the battle of Killicrankie, James himself, being assisted by Louis XIV. with arms and money, landed at Kinsale in Ireland. That island, in which the greater part of the people were Papists, still adhered to him. In March, he made a public entry into Dublin, where he was joyfully received. He afterwards laid siege to Londonderry; but the besieged, though reduced by famine to the last extremity, made a most vigorous and obstinate defence, and were at last relieved.

In the month of August in the same year, the duke of Schomberg, William's favorite general, landed in Ireland with ten thousand men, and immediately commenced operations against the *Jacobites*, the name which was given to James's party. The duke, however, met with unex-

---

Did William accommodate his deportment to the English character?
Did the Scots cordially receive William for their king?
Did James II. attempt to recover the crown of England?
Did William himself take up arms against his father-in-law?

pected difficulties; and after James had been above a year in Ireland, William resolved to undertake the war against him in person.

A. D. 1690. June 14, William landed at Carrickfergus with a large body of troops, who, when joined to those already in Ireland under the command of the duke of Schomberg, composed an army of thirty-six thousand well-appointed and disciplined men. James was able to bring nearly as many men into the field; and the two armies came in sight of each other on the opposite sides of the river Boyne, not far from Slane Bridge.

The battle that ensued was decisive, and William remained master of the field. During the heat of the action, the duke of Schomberg was killed by some mistake of his own regiment, who being foreigners, and not knowing the English from the Irish, had levelled their pieces against their own party. The duke was in the 82d year of his age, and had passed the greatest part of his life in campaigning.

When James, from the neighboring hill of Dunmore saw his troops give way, it seems he relinquished the enterprize of recovering his kingdom. He immediately proceeded to Dublin, where he called the magistrates together, and signified to them his intention of leaving the kingdom. In a few days he sailed for France and there lived the rest of his days under the protection of the French king. In the latter part of his life he practised all the austerities of a monk, and died in 1701.

Some few places, after James had quitted Ireland, still held out against William: William, however, soon returned to England, and committed the management of the Irish war, first to the earl, afterwards duke, of Marlborough, and then to the earl of Athlone, who, before the conclusion of the year 1691, reduced the towns that had held out for James, and completely subdued his party.

Those who chose still to follow his fortunes had permis

What was the English force at the battle of the Boyne?
What was the result of the battle of the Boyne?
Whither did James retreat and when did he die?
Who completed the war in Ireland?

sion given them to leave the is.and, and consequently 12,000 of the Irish Catholics retired to France, where they were hospitably received by Louis XIV., and formed into a corps which was long afterwards kept up under the title of he Irish brigade.

Thus was Ireland rendered completely tranquil. In Scotland, after the battle of Killicrankie no resistance had been opposed to the establishment of William's authority, but the Highlanders could not thoroughly reconcile themselves to the loss of their ancient race of kings ; and the Presbyterians, though they were no friends to the Stuarts, yet thought themselves highly aggrieved by William.

William had attempted to introduce episcopacy into Scotland, and this was a cause of dislike to them. A few slight tumults, which these discontents excited, had been soon quelled, and a general pardon was promised to all who on or before a particular day should take the oath of allegiance to William.

It happened that a certain Highland chief, Macdonald of Glencoe, had mistaken the day of taking the oath, and his enemy, the earl of Breadalbane, represented to the king, that Macdonald's misapprehension was a defiance of the royal authority. William accordingly granted a warrant of military execution both against Macdonald himself and his whole clan. A party of the Campbells was sent to Glencoe, and there fell like butchers on the unarmed and unsuspecting Macdonalds.

Nearly forty persons were massacred at Glencoe. The rest made their escape, but many who escaped for the present perished afterwards from the inclemency of the season, or by famine, or died of grief. This horrible outrage caused a general detestation of William's government, and was the beginning of a long series of troubles and sorrows in Scotland. The king tried to exculpate himself by saying that he had signed the fatal warrant in

---

Did any Irish quit their country ?
Were the Scots well affected to the government of William III. ?
What occasion for pardon of the Scots occurred ?
Who misunderstood the condition of pardon, and who misrepresented his motive ?
Who executed the massacre of Glencoe ?

tno hurry of business, without being aware of its full purport.

A. D. 1691. William, who had gone to the continent soon after his return from Ireland, now actively engaged in a war with France. Many of the Protestant states of Germany had joined Holland in a war against France. William took on himself the command of the allied army; and, only making occasional visits to England, spent nearly the whole of the next three years on the continent. Flanders was the chief seat of the war; and in the conduct of it prince Eugene of Savoy, the earl of Marlborough, and the duke of Schomberg (son of the veteran who was killed in Ireland,) greatly distinguished themselves.

A. D. 1692. Louis XIV. made another attempt to effect the restoration of James II. He prepared a numerous fleet for the invasion of England; but it was completely defeated off La Hogue by the combined fleets of the English and Dutch.

Queen Mary, who during her husband's absences from England had the chief conduct of the government, endeared herself much to the nation, acting on many occasions with great firmness and judgment, and at the same time with great mildness. She died of the small-pox, Dec. 28, 1694, and was very sincerely lamented.

William was in England at the time of the queen's death, an event which greatly grieved him. He soon after went again to the continent, and passed there another year in fighting the battles of the allies. The Jacobites at home were still constantly on the watch for any opportunity to disturb the government, and many plots were laid for assassinating him; but the mass of the people were steady to their allegiance.

A. D. 1697. A general peace was made, called the peace of Ryswick, by which the continent of Europe was for a short time restored to tranquillity,

---

Did William justify himself for the massacre of Glencoe?
Who carried on a continental war in 1691, and for some years following?
When did queen Mary die?
Did William wholly possess the love of his subjects?

but towards the conclusion of William's reign an alliance was agreed upon between the emperor, the king of England, and the Dutch, which led soon afterwards to a renewal of the war. William was engaged in making active preparations, when an accident put a sudden end to his life.

On the 21st of February, 1702, as the king was riding to Hampton Court, from Kensington, his horse fell with him, and he was thrown with so much violence that he broke his collar-bone. From the consequences of this accident he never recovered, but on March the 8th, he expired, in the 52d year of his age, and the fourteenth of his reign. After his death, a ring containing some of the late queen's hair was found fastened by a black ribbon round his arm. He married Mary, eldest daughter of James II., and left no children.

King James II. died at St. Germains a few months before William; and his son James Francis was proclaimed king of England by Louis. At William's accession the English parliament had set the claims of James totally aside, and had settled the succession, after William and Mary, and in the event of their leaving no children, on the princess Anne and her children.

William and Mary having no children, and the duke of Gloucester, the only surviving child of the princess Anne having died in the latter part of William's reign, a new act was passed in 1701, settling the crown, on failure of the direct line, on the electress Sophia and her Protestant descendants.

Sophia was daughter of the queen of Bohemia, electress palatine and was grand-daughter of James I. She married the duke, afterwards elector of Hanover, a Protestant prince of the house of Brunswick. The duchess of Savoy who was daughter of Henrietta, youngest daughter of Charles I., protested, as being in a nearer line of succes-

---

Did the peace of Ryswick effectually preserve peace in Europe?
By what accident did William lose his life?
Whom did the parliament pronounce successor to William III.?
In failure of the direct line, who was to succeed the princess Anne?
Who protested against the succession of the house of Brunswick to the throne of England?

sion, against this settlement; but her claims were unattended to, both she and her children being Catholics.

William appropriated the park and palace at Greenwich as a hospital for disabled seamen. The bank of England was established in this reign. The expenses of the king's foreign wars had occasioned a continual drain for money, and he first burdened the country with a *national debt*, the foundation of what is called the *public funds*.

The national debt is an exceeding large sum of money, amounting at the present time in England, to many hundred millions of pounds sterling—a debt which has been incurred at different times by government, which has borrowed money from private persons to pay the army and defray other expenses, and that money, still unpaid, is due to the lenders or their heirs. These receive in return perpetual annuities; or else payment is due to persons who have acquired a portion of those annuities from those who actually lent the money; for these annuities have been divided and subdivided, sometimes into very small portions and have been sold and resold over and over again.

The most famous military man of William's time was John, duke of Marlborough. His family name was Churchill; and his father had some inferior place in the court of Charles II. Young Churchill entered the army at twelve years old, and was engaged in active service nearly the whole of his life, which proved a long one.

Churchill was made earl of Marlborough by William, who had a high value for him, and appreciated his great abilities. Indeed, he was a man of such an extraordinary military genius, that it is said so skilful a commander had not been seen in England since the days of the Black Prince.

Who founded Greenwich hospital?
When was the Bank of England established?
What is the national debt of a country?
Who was the great warrior of William and Anne's reign?
Was Marlborough's genius compared with that of any other warrior?

CHAPTER XXXV

ANNE.

[Years after Christ, 1702—1714.]

The house in which sir Isaac Newton was born.

On the death of William, Anne succeeded peaceably to the crown. She was then in the thirty-ninth year of her age: she had married, in 1683, George, son of Frederick III., king of Denmark, and had many children, who all died in their infancy, except one son, prince George. This young prince lived to be eleven years old. His death caused the most bitter grief of his parents, especially to his mother, who after that event never regained her former vivacity. Anne had a good natural capacity, but it had been very little cultivated. Her temper was mild and obliging.

The undivided administration of government was vested in the queen, prince George having no greater dignities in the state than those of generalissimo of the queen's forces and of lord high admiral. He was a man, indeed, who

---

What were Queen Anne's domestic circumstances, and her personal character?
Had prince George of Denmark any royal function in England?

had no wish to interfere in the management of public affairs. The political animosities between the Whigs and the Tories ran very high during the whole of this reign.

The leading difference in the views of the two parties was on the subject of the succession to the crown, in case Anne should die without children. The Tories were in favor of the pretender and of the house of Stuart, while the Whigs were friends of the house of Hanover and the Protestant succession, as established by the act of parliament in the latter end of William's reign.

Louis XIV. was now become more than ever formidable to all the other states of Europe. The curbing of this exorbitant power, and the placing the archduke Charles, son of the emperor of Austria, on the throne of Spain, were the great objects of the alliance which had been made, towards the close of William's reign, between the Dutch, the king of England, and the emperor.

Anne, on her accession, declared herself resolved to pursue the same line of policy in which her predecessor had engaged so warmly: and she sent Marlborough to conduct the war on the continent, at the same time appointing him ambassador to the Dutch; whose confidence he acquired so thoroughly, that they also invested him with the chief command of their own army.

A. D. 1703. Marlborough, on account of his military talents and his achievements on the continent of Europe was created a duke, and the nation bestowed upon him the manor of Woodstock, and a splendid palace called Blenheim House in commemoration of one of his victories on the banks of the Danube near the village of Blenheim.

After the archduke Charles had applied for the assistance of England in asserting his claim to the crown of Spain; a fleet was sent under Sir George Rooke, to convey the archduke to Lisbon, where he landed. From thence he marched into Spain, with a considerable body of troops, but was unable to make any progress.

Sir George Rooke proceeded into the Mediterranean.

What was the matter of contention between the Whigs and Tories of queen Anne's reign ?
What appointments did the Queen bestow upon Marlborough ?
Who united to restrain the power of Louis XIV. ?
What national honors were bestowed on the duke of Marlborough ?
Who conveyed the Archduke to Lisbon ?

and, after an unsuccessful attempt on Barcelona, attacked and took the fortress of Gibraltar, which has since proved one of the most valuable possessions to England, and has resisted every endeavor to retake it.

A. D. 1705. A fleet was sent, under sir Cloudesly Shovel, having on board five thousand soldiers, commanded by the earl of Peterborough, to the assistance of the archduke. The fleet, taking the archduke on board at Lisbon, sailed for the coast of Catalonia, where he was supposed to have many friends.

Barcelona, though defended by a large garrison, was now forced to surrender, chiefly through the extraordinary vigor and ability with which Peterborough pressed the siege. The English under command of earl Galway were afterwards defeated in Spain, and the cause of the archduke was abandoned, and the Bourbons retained the throne.

At the head of very inconsiderable forces, Peterborough, at one time nearly gained Spain for the archduke, whom he caused to be proclaimed as Charles III., and he almost drove Philip V. out of Spain. But in the midst of his victorious career he was recalled to England, and the command of the army in Spain was given to the earl of Galway.

In 1707, sir Cloudesly Shovel's ship, with three others were wrecked on the rocks of Scilly. Sir Cloudesly perished: and out of the four ships' crews only one captain and twenty-four seamen were saved. In the following year prince George of Denmark died.

The duke Marlborough meanwhile increased his renown abroad, and gained many splendid victories; of which the most celebrated are those of Ramillies, which was fought on the 23d of May, 1706; of Oudenarde, fought July 11th, 1708; and of Malplaquet, Sept. 11th, 1709.

The war was carried on till 1712, and is marked by the adventurous career of Lord Peterborough in Spain as well

---

Who took Gibraltar?
Who conveyed the Archduke to Catalonia?
Was the Archduke established on the throne of Spain?
What were the achievements of Lord Peterborough?
What became of sir Cloudesly Shovel?
What were Marlborough's great victories?
How long did the continental war in which Marlborough engaged last?

as the achievements of the duke of Marlborough but notwithstanding the genius of both, neither of these distinguished men seem to have fulfilled very desirable objects.

Marlborough, from some defect of generosity, could not engage the affections of his countrymen. He was dismissed from all his employments, 1711, and chose rather to live on the continent than in England. Lord Peterborough's enterprises were more splendid than useful. The talent of great warriors in the present age, commands less admiration than it once did. *Great men* are now discovered to be good men, and to love peace better than war.

In January, 1712, a treaty for a general peace was opened at Utrecht; but it was so difficult to adjust the claims of the many different states who had taken part in the war, that the negotiations could not be brought to an end till April, 1713, when the treaty of Utrecht was signed

The chief articles of this treaty which concerned England were, that Louis should resign Newfoundland, Hudson's Bay, and the island of St. Christopher's to the English, that he should abandon the cause of the Pretender, and acknowledge Anne and the Protestant succession.

The Pretender, who had now assumed the name of the Chevalier St. George, protested ineffectually against this article of the treaty. Louis, however, still afforded him protection. He had married a daughter of John Sobieski, king of Poland; a princess of very exalted character, and far superior to her husband both in capacity and merit.

The Pretender had two sons, Charles Edward, and Henry. The eldest was afterwards known as the *young* Pretender, to distinguish him from his father, who is often termed the *old* Pretender. Henry took orders in the Romish church, and was afterwards cardinal of York.

A. D. 1713. The electress Sophia died, in her 84th year; and her son, George, became the head of the Protestant succession. A few months after

---

Were the enterprises of Marlborough and Peterborough very important to the English nation?
When was the peace of Utrecht made?
What were the chief articles of the treaty of Utrecht?
How did the Pretender regard the treaty of Utrecht?
Who were the Pretender's sons?
Who was appointed successor of Queen Anne?

the death of Sophia, the queen fell into a bad state of health; occasioned, it is said, by the intolerable dissensions amongst her ministers.

The Whig party proved in the end the stronger; and at length the queen's death visibly approaching, a letter was sent to the elector of Hanover, desiring him to come immediately to Holland, where a squadron should be in waiting to bring him to England. Heralds were kept in readiness to proclaim king George, the instant the queen should expire. Care was also taken to secure the seaports, and many other precautions were adopted to prevent the Tories and Jacobites from attempting the restoration of the Stuarts.

The queen died August 1, 1714, in the 51st year of her age, and in the 13th of her reign. She married George son of Frederick III., king of Denmark, and had nine children; only one of whom, George, Duke of Gloucester lived beyond the age of infancy. He died July 23, 1700. aged eleven years.

Though Anne was a woman of no very brilliant qualities, yet many lasting benefits were in her reign conferred on the country. Among these was the union with Scotland, a measure which James I. had vainly attempted to accomplish, and which succeeding kings had thought impracticable, and which at last was not effected without much opposition from those whose private interests or prejudices made them adverse to it.

By the terms of the Union the two kingdoms were in future to be considered as one country. The Scots were to retain their own Presbyterian form of church government, their established laws for the administration of justice, and in all matters of property; but it was settled that instead of retaining their parliament, they should send forty-five commoners and sixteen peers to represent them in the English parliament.

Which proved the stronger party, the Whigs or Tories?
When did the queen die, and what was her family?
What was the most important event of queen Anne's reign?
What were the articles of the *Union*?

TABLE.

James I.
Charles I.
Charles II. } sons of Charles I
James II.
{ William III.
{ Mary, daughter of James II.
Anne, daughter of James II.
George I. son of the electress Sophia of Hanover, who was daughter of James I.'s daughter, the electress palatine.
The *old* Pretender, James Francis, was the son of king James II.
The *young* Pretender, Charles Edward, and Henry, cardinal of York, were sons of the Pretender James Francis.

The reign of Anne is certainly a brilliant period of English history, and very few other periods can be named in which so many men of genius flourished together. Of the military and naval achievements of the reign a brief sketch has been given. This period is also regarded as an epoch in the history of taste and literature.

Dryden had died in 1701, one year before the accession of Anne. Locke died only two years after. Pope, Steele, and Addison flourished during her reign, and perhaps did more towards the improvement of the general style of thinking and writing than was done by any other writer.

The Tatler and Spectator, which were chiefly written by Steele and Addison, were the first periodical works that appeared in England, and were read with the greatest avidity by all classes of persons. Dr. Swift, who wrote many political and satirical works, was also one of the greatest geniuses of this age.

Sir Isaac Newton, whose genius towered above that of all his contemporaries, lived all through the reign of Anne, and did not die till 1727. His great work on the system of the universe was published in the time of William III

Newton was not only one of the profoundest philosophers, but also one of the most sincere and humble Chris

---

Was the reign of Anne remarkable for the manifestation of mind?
Who were the more eminent writers of Anne's reign?
What were the remarkable literary productions of this reign?
Who was the most eminent philosopher of this reign?

cians that ever lived. His father was a gentleman of small estate at Woolstrop, in Lincolnshire, and died when he was very young. His mother married again, and sir Isaac was employed by his father-in-law as a shepherd boy.

One day, while Isaac was keeping the sheep, a gentleman passing by observed that he was deeply occupied in some book, and had the curiosity to ask him what it was. To his surprise he found it was a book of practical geometry. This circumstance was mentioned to some of his mother's relations, who rescued him from his humble employment, and placed him at a school at Grantham.

Newton's progress there was quite astonishing, and he was " noted for his strange inventions and extraordinary inclination for mechanics. He had a little shop of tools, as little saws, hatchets, and hammers, with which he amused himself in making models in wood of various things."

Newton's extreme modesty and gentleness of temper were more extraordinary than even his talents and acquirements. He retained the full use of his powers of mind to the last day of a long life, and was never guilty of any one excess, unless it might be that of an excess of study.

Marlborough was a man of extreme calmness and tranquility. Nothing flurried, nothing disconcerted him. His judgment and presence of mind were ready for all occasions. Commanding an army composed of officers and men of different states and nations, whose interests were perpetually clashing, he listened to no cabals or jealousies, but acted in a straight forward manner for the public cause. Of his command of temper one very striking instance is recorded. It has been mentioned that the duke of Marlborough was not beloved by the English, but he possessed some qualities worthy of respect and imitation.

Prince Eugene had proposed, at a council of war, that

Was Newton distinguished when a child?
Did Newton ever exhibit a taste for mechanics?
Were the moral qualities of Newton admirable?
Was the example of Marlborough worthy of imitation?
Did Marlborough decline a challenge?

no attack should be made the next day on the enemy Though nothing evidently could be more judicious than this proposal, the duke positively refused to consent to it. The prince called him a coward, and challenged him; but Marlborough kept his temper, and declined the challenge On this the prince, being violently enraged, left the council

Early the following morning prince Eugene was awoke by Marlborough, who, coming to his bedside, desired him to rise, as he was preparing to make the attack, and added, "I could not tell you my determination last night, because there was a person present who I knew was in the enemy's interest, and would betray us. I have no doubt we shall conquer, and *when the battle is over*, I will be ready to accept your challenge."

Prince Eugene was overpowered by Marlborough's greatness of mind, and asked his pardon for his own intemperate conduct. The duke accepted his apologies, saying, "I thought, my dear prince, you would in time be satisfied."

CHAPTER XXXVI.

GEORGE I.

[Years after Christ, 1714—1727.]

Anne died, as has been said, August 1, 1714, and the elector of Hanover was immediately proclaimed. He arrived in England Sept. 16, and was met at Greenwich, where he landed, by many persons of high office and rank Amongst these was the duke of Marlborough, who had lately returned to England, and whom, both at this time, and ever after, the king treated with great distinction. George, at his accession, was in the fifty-fifth year of his age.

George was a man of plain steady understanding, grave in his manner, and simple in his habits, and had the repu-

---

What reasons did Marlborough offer for his conduct?
Was prince Eugene reconciled to the duke of Marlborough?
Under what circumstances did George I. arrive in England?

tation of being a sagacious politician. He spoke English very imperfectly, and was too much of a German in all his notions and habits to be very popular in England.

George I. had one son and a daughter. The son had married Caroline, daughter of the margravine of Anspach, and at the time of his father's coming to the throne had three young daughters. He was created prince of Wales, and came with his family to England; as did also one of the king's brothers, the bishop of Osnaburg, who was created duke of York.

A. D. 1715. The spirit of party still ran very high in England. The king showed a decided preference for the Whigs. At this the Tories were much exasperated, and they soon began to show a spirit of disaffection to the house of Hanover. Lord Oxford, the great Tory leader, was sent to the Tower, where he remained two years; but the two houses of parliament disagreed so violently as to the proceedings to be taken in regard to him, that he was at last acquitted without a trial. The duke of Ormond and lord Bolingbroke were impeached, but escaped to France. They were then attainted, and their names were erased from the list of English peers.

These severities towards the leaders of the Tories excited great murmurs; and the Jacobites, who had been very active ever since the queen's death, made a strong party in Scotland. The earl of Mar proclaimed prince James Stuart, Sept. 6, 1715, and set up his standard. James, however, was not then in a condition to come and take the crown that was proffered him.

Louis XIV., who had given the Pretender a small supply of arms and ammunition, with the promise of more, died on the first of September this year, and the duke of Orleans, who was regent of France during the minority of Louis XV., (the infant great-grandson of the late king,) was not a friend to the Pretender's cause.

The earl of Mar, nevertheless, continued in arms, and at

Who were the king's family?
What was the state of parties in England in the first years of George's reign?
Who proclaimed James Stuart king of England?
How did Louis XIV. and his successor regard James Stuart's enterprise?
What Scottish nobles befriended and opposed the Pretender?

length assembled a body of ten thousand men, which was further increased by some English Jacobites. On the other hand, the duke of Argyle, who was appointed commander of the king's forces in Scotland, advanced against the rebels at the head of his own clans, assisted by some troops from Ireland.

In the meantime the Pretender's party in the north of England organized themselves in battle array: but they were encountered by the militia and other troops sent against them, and were punished for their attempt. Some were hanged at Tyburn; twenty-two persons were executed in Lancashire, and about one thousand were sent to the North American colonies.

On December 22, the Pretender, after having been long expected, at last arrived in Scotland. He came attended only by six gentlemen. The earl of Mar soon joined him, and he was proclaimed king; and in the expectation that all Scotland would rise in his cause as one man, he fixed Jan. 16, 1716, for his coronation at Scone. But before that day arrived, he was so closely pursued by the duke of Argyle, that he was glad to abandon his rash enterprise, and to get back again to France.

A. D. 1720. The attention of the nation was chiefly occupied by a scheme called the South Sea Scheme. It was principally contrived by sir John Blunt, a busy, speculating man; and the object of it was to enable a company of merchants, called the South Sea Company, to buy up all the national debts and concentrate them into one fund.

Many persons, in the expectation of receiving a high interest, advanced large sums of money towards this purchase; but in a few months the whole was discovered to be a fraudulent scheme. The principal actors in it were punished by parliament, and measures were adopted to give some redress to the injured parties; but a very large number of the imprudent speculators suffered severely.

A. D. 1727. The king, who was much attached to Hanover, and had visited it several times

---

How did the English government treat the Pretender's adherents?
When did the Pretender land in Scotland?
What speculation engaged the English nation, A. D. 1720?
When and where did George I. die?

set out with the intention of going there once more. He had got as far as Delden, a small town near the frontiers of Germany, when he was taken extremely ill. He had set his mind on reaching his brother's palace at Osnaburg, and ordered his people to hasten forwards. But he did not live to get there. It was found, when the carriage stopped at the gate of the palace, that he had already breathed his last. He died June 11, 1727, in the sixty-eighth year of his age, and the thirteenth of his reign.

George Augustus, prince of Wales, succeeded his father.

CHAPTER XXXVII

GEORGE II.

[Years after Christ, 1727—1760.]

An officer and sergeant in the reign of George the First.

The news of the sudden death of George I. reached London June 14, and George II. was proclaimed the next day. He was in the forty-fifth year of his age. His abilities were inferior to those of his father, and his temper hasty He was simple in all his tastes and habits, and singularly

---

What was the character, and who composed the family of George II.

methodical. His strongest feeling, and that which more than any other governed his conduct, was his preference of Hanover to England.

Queen Caroline united brilliant beauty to a strong understanding, and great goodness of heart. When George II. came to the throne, he had two sons: Frederick, the eldest, was twenty years old; William, afterwards duke of Cumberland, was only six years old. He had also four daughters.

A. D. 1736. The prince of Wales married the princess of Saxe-Gotha. In 1737 the queen died, and the king's grief for her loss was sincere and excessive. In the same year a war broke out between England and Spain; and admiral Vernon took Portobello a Spanish settlement on the isthmus of Darien.

A. D. 1743. About this time the peace of the continent was disturbed by a contest for the imperial throne. The emperor Charles VI. died, leaving an only daughter, Maria Theresa, married to prince Francis of Lorraine. The claim of Maria Theresa was disputed by the elector of Bavaria; and nearly all Europe entered into the quarrel. The king of France took the part of elector of Bavaria.

The king of England engaged on the side of Maria Theresa, and sent to the continent an army of 16,000 men, under lord Stair, which was afterwards increased by an equal number of Hanoverians. In the cause of Maria Theresa, the king and his son, the duke of Cumberland, displayed considerable military talent; but England, in the meantime, was suffering by the projects of the Pretender.

In the beginning of 1744, an invasion of England had been attempted by a French force of 15,000 men, under the convoy of twenty ships of the line. James himself, not having sufficient activity to engage personally in this expedition, deputed prince Charles Edward, his eldest son, to join in it. But though this expedition was rendered abor-

---

What took place in 1736 and 1737.
The *imperial throne*, that is, the empire of Germany, was contested for by whom?
What part was taken by England in this war?
Did the Stuarts, aided by France, renew their attempts to reinstate themselves in England?

tive, prince Charles ventured in the following year to try his fortune in the northern part of the island.

Having procured a sum of money, and a small supply of arms, on his own credit, prince Charles sent to inform his friends in Scotland that he hoped soon to be with them. In June, 1745, he embarked with a few Scotch and Irish gentlemen in a small frigate; but the vessel which carried a supply of arms for the expedition, was disabled in the passage. Meanwhile the frigate pursued her destined course. On the 16th of July Charles landed at Borodale, in Lochaber, and was soon joined by a considerable number of Highlanders.

A moment more favorable for this enterprise could not have been chosen. The king of England was in Hanover; the duke of Cumberland, with the most serviceable part of the army, was in Flanders; and the ministers and parliament were divided by political disputes: but Charles could not make the most of these advantages; his want of arms, and the loss of the officers who were to have come, but were prevented, disabling him from making any attack on the strong English garrisons, which were in the heart of the country, at Fort William and Fort Augustus.

The news of the Pretender's arrival in Scotland, threw all England into commotion. The lords regent, to whom the conduct of affairs had been left during the king's absence, sent to hasten his return; and in the meantime issued a proclamation, offering a reward of 30,000*l*. to any one who would seize Charles Stuart. Charles, in retaliation, set the same price on the head of the elector of Hanover.

The prince, advancing to Perth, proclaimed his father king. His army still kept gathering numbers; and, Sept. 16, he took possession of the town of Edinburgh. The castle, however, still held out. General Guest, an experienced officer, commanded there; and, having a strong garrison, was determined to stand a siege.

Sir John Cope, meanwhile, who commanded the king's

When did prince Charles Edward land in Scotland?
What circumstances favored or retarded Edward's project?
What effect was produced by the appearance of the Pretender in England?
Did the Pretender take Edinburgh?
What was the result of the battle of Preston-pans?

forces in Scotland, approached Edinburgh with all the troops he could muster; and, Sept. 20th, he encamped about nine miles from the town, at Preston pans. The next morning Charles marched to meet him; and the half-armed Highlanders attacked the king's troops with so much fury, that the cavalry fled with precipitation. The total defeat of the infantry soon followed. They fled, leaving on the field all their baggage, and, what the prince wanted most of all, their arms, ammunition, and a train of field artillery.

By this victory the rebels acquired possession of a considerable part of Scotland. The castle of Edinburgh still held out, and was blockaded by the rebels. Charles, however, at the earnest entreaty of the inhabitants whom general Guest had alarmed by the threat of destroying the town, and indeed by actually beginning to fire on it, *raised the blockade;* that is, he ceased the attempt to take the castle—he withdrew his troops.

The popularity at this time of the Pretender's cause was greatly increased by the good conduct of the prince himself, who showed himself both vigorous in action and prudent in council, and bore his success with moderation. The king of France, seeing that his affairs were prosperous, sent him a supply of small arms, cannon and officers, and promised him that a large body of French should be landed in the south of England.

On this assurance Charles passed the borders of Scotland. He entered Carlisle Nov. 6th. Leaving a garrison there, he marched onwards; and on November 29th fixed his head-quarters at Manchester. He was there joined by about two hundred English jacobites, and then proceeded to Derby.

The rebel army was now within four days' march of London. Indescribable alarm and consternation prevailed in that city. Those who were in London fled into the country, while those in the country flew to London, every person thinking the place he was in the place of danger. The king, who had returned from Germany on the first

---

Did prince Charles take Edinburgh castle?
Did the French nation afford further aid to the Pretender's cause?
How far did prince Charles advance into England?
How were the people of London affected, and how did George II. meet this emergency?

summons, was all activity, and intended to have taken the field in person.

Prince Charles's army was sometimes successful; but a final battle between his adherents and the English army took place at Culloden, in Scotland, April, 1746.

The fatal action of Culloden over, Charles, seeing that all was lost, rode off the field with a few followers These he soon dismissed, and led a wandering life for nearly five months, concealing himself in different parts of the Highlands, and owing his preservation to the fidelity of the poor inhabitants, who could not be tempted to betray him by the great reward which was offered for his apprehension, and who concealed him in their huts and caves, at the risk of their own lives.

At last Charles, with a few faithful friends, found means to get on board a French privateer. Under the shelter of a thick fog he passed through the midst of a British squadron; and at last, after many difficulties and dangers, landed safely at Morlaix, in Bretagne; but so worn out by the fatigues and hardships he had undergone, that he was scarcely to be known as the same handsome sprightly youth who had left France full of animation and hope the year before.

Frightful scenes followed in Scotland after the decisive victory at Culloden. It is deeply afflicting that the reputation of a brave man should be sullied by such dreadful cruelties as must ever stain the memory of the duke of Cumberland, who commanded the king's forces. It is said that, in a district of nearly fifty miles round Lochiel, there was, in the course of a few days, neither house nor cottage, neither men nor cattle to be seen; so complete was the ruin, silence, and desolation.

The jails in England were filled with rebels, whose trials now followed. Many were executed—many were transported to the plantations in America, and some few were

---

What action finished the enterprise of prince Charles?
Whither did Charles go, after the battle of Culloden, and what admirable integrity and fidelity was shown by some of his adherents?
How did Charles appear when he returned to France?
Did the English government treat the rebels with generosity and humanity?
What punishments were inflicted upon the leaders of the rebellion?

pardoned. Lords Balmerino, Kilmarnock, and Lovat, and Mr. Ratcliffe, who were among the principal persons concerned in the rebellion, were conveyed to London and executed.

The rebellion being subdued, the duke of Cumberland returned to the allied army in Flanders, where the war continued a short time longer. At length a general peace was signed at Aix-la-Chapelle, October 7th, 1748.

A series of encroachments made by France on the British colonies in North America, gave rise, a few years afterwards, to a new war with that country, which broke out in the year 1755. This war involved eventually the whole of Europe, and is often entitled the seven years war. In its commencement it proved unfavorable to England.

The English colonies, those which are now entitled the United States of America, were on their western side greatly exposed to the French, who possessed both Louisiana and Canada, and were attempting to connect them by a chain of forts, stretching in the rear of the English settlements. The French had instigated also many of the native tribes of the Americans to join in attacks on the English provinces.

In the commencement of these disputes in America, general Washington, who afterwards gained so much distinction in the war which ended in releasing the United States from their dependency on England, first signalized himself though then a very young officer, by his conduct of an expedition sent from Virginia to watch the motions of the French on the river Ohio.

In 1756 several expeditions were undertaken by the English commanders in America, but the more considerable of them failed of success. The operations of the year 1757 were also unfavorable in that quarter to the British arms: but in the year following the fortunes of the war appeared to take a decisive turn; and in 1759 and 1760 the whole province of Canada was subdued, and the

---

When was the treaty of Aix-la-Chapelle signed?
What war broke out in 1755?
Were the English colonists in America disturbed by the French?
When did Washington first distinguish himself?
Was the French power in America limited by the English?

French power was annihilated in that part of the American continent.

This great object, however, was not achieved without the loss of one of the most popular and distinguished commanders whom the English army has ever had to boast of; namely, general Wolfe, who was killed in the moment of victory at the siege of Quebec, in 1759.

In the meantime the war was carried on in Europe with great animosity. France attacked and took possession of Hanover. The northern European powers, except Prussia, and its king, Frederick the Great, were combined against the king of England. But Frederick's sagacity and military skill finally extricated him from the hazardous situation in which he was placed by the combination of so many enemies.

Frederick was assisted both with money and troops from England, where the energy of a very able minister, Mr. Pitt, afterwards earl of Chatham, infused great spirit into the conduct of affairs. In the battle of Minden, which was fought in 1759, the English forces had a considerable share. Lord Clive was very successful in the East Indies; and at sea the English flag was triumphant over the French.

The king was now become an old man; but he enjoyed a degree of health and bodily vigor very unusual at his advanced age, and which seemed to give the promise of a much longer life. But, October 25, 1760, George II. died suddenly

Political parties ran very high in this reign. Sir Robert Walpole, sir William Pulteney, Mr. Pelham, the duke of Newcastle, and Mr. Pitt, afterwards earl of Chatham, were successively leaders of the administration

---

The names of Anson, Hawke, and Boscawen, are the most distinguished in the naval history of this reign.

The sequel of the history of the misguided and unfortu-

Where was general Wolfe killed?
Was the continental warfare of Europe still in operation?
What were the successes in England in 1759?
When did George II. die?
Who were the principal ministers of George II.?
Who were the principal naval commanders of the reign of George II

nate prince Charles, may properly be added in this place. Soon after his return to France, Louis, in consequence of one of the conditions of peace in the treaty of Aix-la-Chapelle in 1748, withdrew his protection from him. He then retired into the territories of the pope. He for a long time kept up a secret correspondence with the English Jacobites; and once, if not oftener, he came privately to London.

After a time, prince Charles disgusted his friends by his misconduct, and they totally abandoned his cause. This prince, who excited so much sympathy in his youth, and seemed then to possess many hopeful qualities, degenerated afterwards into a vicious character. He assumed the name of count D'Albany, and died in 1784, unpitied and unlamented.

Prince Charles had an only brother, the cardinal of York, who, after his brother's death, sometimes assumed the name of Henry IX. He lived to be an old man, and died at Rome in 1807. In him the unfortunate family of Stuart became extinct.

CHAPTER XXXVIII.

GEORGE III.

[Years after Christ, 1760—1789.]

George III. had completed his twenty-second year, when the death of his grandfather placed him on the throne. He had resided with his mother, the princess dowager of Wales, between whom and George II. there existed no cordiality; and having thus been in a manner excluded from court, and not interfering in any of the political parties of the day, he had led what might be called a retired life, associating only with the small but select circle which was collected round the princess.

What became of prince Charles Edward?
What was the termination of Charles's life?
Who was the last of the Stuarts?
Under what circumstances did George III. succeed to the throne of Britain?

This was in some respects a disadvantage to him, as it gave him an awkward manner, which an earlier introduction to general society might have remedied. His usual way of speaking was hurried and confused; but when he was called on to speak in public, his delivery was graceful and impressive.

The ruling principle of his mind was religion. George III. found his greatest happiness in the tranquility of domestic life, and it has been said of him that a better father, husband, son, and brother, never existed. His heart was open not only to kindly affections towards his own family, but also to a general good will towards mankind. His charities were extensive and judicious, and there is not one cruel or unfeeling action recorded of him during the course of his long life.

George III. married August 7, 1761, Charlotte, princess of Mechlenburgh Strelitz. The last public service which the veteran admiral lord Anson performed was that of bringing the new queen to England.

The war was for sometime continued with vigor, though the nation was become weary at the great expense at which it was carried on, particularly of the expenses which were lavished in Germany. Proposals were made for a general peace; but these were overruled, and Spain taking part with France against England, engaged that nation against the Spaniards. Some British forces were sent to the defence of Portugal, and the Spaniards, who made an invasion of that country were repulsed.

Amongst the events of this busy time, it is difficult to select the most important. It must suffice now to say that the British arms were every where successful. Several valuable islands in the West Indies were taken from France. The rich town of the Havana, in Cuba, Manilla, in the East Indies, and the rest of the Philippine islands, were taken from Spain; and many considerable prizes were made at sea.

Was George III. a good man?
Who was the queen of George III.?
Was the continental war popular in England, and how was it extended to Spain?
Were the British successful in the war?

France and Spain became at last anxious to put an end to a war which had proved so disastrous to them, particularly to the latter, and a general peace was concluded at Paris on the 10th of February, 1763.

By this peace, the island of Minorca, several islands in the West Indies, and Goree, in Africa, were restored to France. The river Senegal was given up to England. In the East Indies all the forts and factories taken from the French were restored. The Havana was restored to Spain, and the Spaniards in return ceded Florida to the English, and agreed also to make peace with Portugal.

The history of political parties in Britain cannot be intelligible to young readers; and the history of the war of England with the American colonies belongs to American history—to that we refer the student.

The country now called the United States of America, was originally peopled by English and other Europeans, and was governed by the laws of England. The first emigration began in 1607, and in 1764, the country had become populous and wealthy. The English government levied taxes on the Americans, which the latter deemed oppressive and refused to pay.

From this dispute arose a war of seven years duration. Hostilities commenced in 1775, and continued till the 17th of October, 1781, when lord Cornwallis, the British commander, surrendered to general Lincoln, an officer commanding under Washington, the American commander-in-chief. France took part with the colonies during the war.

The success of the Americans in this contest was due to the justice of their cause; to an indomitable spirit of civil liberty which grew primarily from the sense of their own moral dignity, and inherent power; and also,

---

When was a general peace concluded?
How were colonial possessions apportioned by the peace of 1703?
Is the history of political parties intelligible to the young?
What was the cause of hostility between Britain and the American colonies?
What was the duration of the war of independence, and what part in it was taken by the French nation?

in great measure, to the extraordinary character of General Washington, a true patriot, who thought nothing of his own aggrandisement, and every thing of acheiving and establishing American Independence. After the conclusion of the war, he was twice elected President of the United States. In this station his constant policy was to maintain peace, with foreign nations and to promote the best interests of his own country. He died December 13th, 1799.

The war with America, although very popular in England at its commencement, had not been undertaken or carried on without opposition from many able men in parliament. One of the most distinguished of its opponents was the famous William Pitt, earl of Chatham. He strongly resisted the taxing of America in the first instance, and afterwards expressed satisfaction that the Americans refused submission to the tax.

Lord Chatham with a wise foresight always predicted that the colonies would succeed in their resistance to the oppressive measures of the parent country. He assumed the principle that the moral energy of a whole nation is stronger than the physical power of an invading army and that, of course, the attempt to compel the Americans to abandon their fixed determination would ultimately fail, as the event proved.

Lord Chatham was seventy years old, when he appeared for the last time in the House of Lords, April 1778, and spoke with great eloquence and solemnity upon the question of the American war; but while the words of remonstrance rose to his lips, he fell back in convulsions and was immediately surrounded by the awe-struck and astonished members. He was soon conveyed to his own house, but never recovered from this fatal attack. He died a few weeks after. The people of England took a less enlightened view of the American war; generally they were in favor of it, and the result was neither expected by them, nor agreeable to their wishes.

To what causes may the success of the Americans be attributed?
Did the wisest men in England approve of the war?
What was lord Chatham's opinion of this war.
How did lord Chatham die, and how did the English nation regard the conclusion of the war?

France, during the American war, had contrived to enlist both Spain and Holland as her allies in the war. Russia, also, Sweden and Denmark, though they did not actually take part in the war, yet were manifestly indirect enemies of England, and united to form what was called an *armed neutrality.*

England, nevertheless, amid all these disadvantages, maintained the contest with the European powers, upon at least equal terms. At sea, not to make mention of other indecisive or less important engagements, her fleets, under the command of lord Rodney, gained great victories, one over the Spaniards on the 16th January, 1780; another over the French fleet in the West Indies. Some islands were taken in the West Indies; but on the other hand some were lost. In the East Indies the British arms were successful.

A. D. 1783. In the beginning of this year peace was concluded between the belligerent powers. England acknowledged the Independence of the United States; gave up to France the islands of St. Lucia and Tobago, in the West Indies; the river Senegal and a few forts in Africa; and made some cessions also to the same power in the East Indies. Minorca and Florida were surrendered to Spain.

The United States, after the ratification of the treaty, sent Mr. Adams, one of the most eminent statesmen, and afterwards president of the United States, in the capacity of envoy to the English court. The king, who had previously declared to some of his attendants that he looked forward to his first interview with this new minister as to the most critical moment of his life, received him very graciously, and said to him, "I was the last man in the kingdom, sir, to consent to the Independence of America: but, now it is granted, I shall be the last man in the kingdom to sanction a violation of it."

In the beginning of this reign there was a continual change of ministers. Lord Chatham, the duke of New-

---

How did England maintain her power against her enemies?
What were the important transactions of 1783?
What was the reception of Mr. Adams at the court of Great Britain?

castle, lord Bute, Mr. G. Grenville, the marquis of Rockingham, the duke of Grafton, lord North, Mr. Fox, and lord Shelburne, held successively the chief offices in the administration. In 1783, Mr. Pitt, second son of lord Chatham, was made prime minister, and with only one short interval retained that nigh office twenty-two years.

In the study of history, the young reader will often inquire, Why do governments make war? Why is the history of nations the history of wars? A true history would rather describe the religion and manners of a people—the arts which increase their comforts, and the sciences which improve their minds, than limit itself to the quarrels and violences of nations.

The *great* men of an age are they who think most profoundly, and act most worthily, and leave behind them something to instruct those who may live after them. Bacon is the great man of James's reign; Milton is more glorious than his contemporary Cromwell; and Newton ten thousand times superior to the duke of Marlborough.

In the progress of this history we have come to the period of the French revolution, a change in the French government into which the English nation largely entered, and it would bring into view the character and actions of Napoleon Bonaparte. The events of the revolution and the genius of the French Emperor, are themes too ample for a few pages—they belong to the history of France and of modern Europe, and to those histories the student will be referred.

It remains to say a few words upon modern warfare. In ancient times, *the desire of property*, of taking from others, instead of toiling for the fruits of the earth—and, *the lust of dominion*, that is, the desire of the restless and ambitious, like Alexander and Cæsar, to be called master and monarch by millions of men, instigated military leaders to

---

What does true history describe?
Who are great men?
To what does the history of the French revolution belong?
What were the occasions of ancient warfare?

invade distant and extensive territories, and to make subjects and slaves of the proper owners of those territories.

In modern times the love of wealth still urges plans of dominion, as is shown in the British conquest of India; but often, modern wars have been made to preserve what has been gained before; to establish certain principles; to repel encroachments of other powers, and to preserve the *balance of power*.

The revolutionary war of America was mutually carried on by the British and Americans, that the latter might become an independent state and govern themselves; and that the former might preserve the power already possessed, and increase their wealth from the growing resources of their American subjects. Providence overruled the contest by favoring the just cause, and frustrating the selfish policy of the adverse power.

Of wars to *establish principles*, the part taken by the English government in the French revolutionary war is an example. A *principle* is a rule intended to regulate actions, or it is a truth that belongs to something. The *principle* assumed by the English government was, hereditary princes shall reign, and their subjects shall not depose them. Princes must be protected by other princes, or all monarchs will be in danger.

The balance of power is a sort of equality of princes and nations, so that the government of each nation acts by its own will, having power to do so, without fear of another great power, or danger from any such power. If the monarchs of all continental Europe should declare against England, should seize the English colonies, and could by their combined fleets drive English ships from every sea, the *balance of power* in Europe would be destroyed, and England would be insignificant. When the English have seen governments uniting against them, they have declared war and humbled the powers that would humble them, and thus prevented for any long time, the existence of an overwhelming dominion in Europe.

What are the occasions of modern wars?
What were the respective motives of the English and Americans in the revolutionary war?
Why did the British take part in the French revolution?
What is intended by the phrase *balance of power*?

France is one of the most populous and highly civilized countries of all Europe, but the state of the nation towards the close of the last century was truly unhappy. The *wealth of the country*, that is, the soil and the money, chiefly belonged to two classes of persons—the nobility and the ecclesiastics. The nobles owned very extensive estates, and the convents, that is, communities of monks and nuns, possessed also great tracts of land and large revenues.

There were indeed merchants, mechanics, and laborers, but all these were enormously taxed to maintain an extravagant court, to make roads and fortifications, and to pay other public expenses; while the nobles and the clergy were, as much as possible, exempted from all burdens, and lived for the most part in idleness and luxury; the poor people, moreover, were left in extreme ignorance.

The sufferings of the poor, and the want of money to carry on the government, made it necessary to change the laws, in order to relieve, if practicable, the distresses of the nation. A convention of deputies was called from the different provinces of the kingdom for this purpose. This convention, and that party in the country who preferred the established order of things, could not agree in the means of redress, and a frightful state of anarchy and bloodshed followed.

The party opposed to the *ancient regime*, or established rule, became so exasperated against the king, Louis XVI., his family, and all their adherents, that, after a trial before the convention, they pronounced sentence of death upon Louis. Afterwards the queen, and great numbers of persons of high rank and great worth, were beheaded for what was called *political offences*, which signified that they were attached to old institutions, or wished to restrain the violences of the revolutionists. This period of the revolution has been aptly termed *the reign of terror*.

The English government assumed the principle, that it

What was the condition of the French people towards the close of the 18th century?

What were the relative advantages of the higher and lower classes of France?

Who inflamed the passions of the French people?

What is signified by the phrase—Reign of Terror?

What part was taken by the English towards the French?

was the cause of humanity, and of all just government, not to acknowledge the authority of the French Republic, and to take up arms to reinstate the monarchy, and punish the usurpation. There were many persons in England who thought their government had no proper concern in French affairs. Mr. Pitt, the son of lord Chatham, and prime minister in England promoted the war with France, and Mr. Fox a very able and distinguished statesman was among the chief leaders of the opposite party.

A. D. 1792. Some of the continental powers also took part in the French contest. Prussia and Austria united to restore the authority of Louis while that unfortunate monarch was a prisoner. Louis was executed Jan. 1st, 1793.

Such was the commencement of a most unparalled contest, which, with little intermission, distracted Europe for above twenty years, and was attended with a series of more signal events than any other, perhaps, in the history of the world.

Holland was among the countries that opposed the French revolution, but the French took Amsterdam on the 16th of January, 1795. The rest of Holland, and the other provinces, then submitted, and taking the title of the Batavian republic, entered into an alliance with France.

Before that time the duke of York, the king of England's second son, was sent from England to the assistance of the Dutch, with a considerable army under his command. In this campaign he had some partial success; but in 1794 he was compelled to retire.

From the commencement of the revolution the French arms were eminently successful. From the year 1796 to 1815 the history of France is connected with the great talent, and extraordinary fortunes of Napoleon Bonaparte, whose history is itself a study, and cannot be detailed here Bonaparte's vigilance was actively engaged against the enlargement of English power.

What part was taken by the continental powers, &c. ?
What happened in Holland 1794—95 ?
What eminent individual distinguished himself in Europe from 1796 till 1815 ?

A. D. 1797. During this year, however, two great naval victories were gained: one over the Spaniards, who had been prevailed on to declare war against England; the other over the Batavian republic The first of these actions was fought off Cape St. Vincent on the 14th of February. The Spanish fleet, amounting to twenty-seven sail of the line, was attempting to join a French armament, but was attacked and completely defeated by sir John Jervis, afterwards created earl St. Vincent. The battle with the Dutch was fought on the 11th of October. Admiral Duncan, who commanded the English fleet on this occasion, was also raised to the peerage.

On October 17th a definitive treaty of peace between France and Austria was signed at Campo Formio, in Italy: and thus England was left alone in the great contest which she was carrying on against her powerful enemy.

A. D. 1798. On the meeting of parliament in January, the king intimated that he had received intelligence of a design entertained by the French government to attempt the invasion of England. Whether this danger was real or only imaginary, it had the effect of uniting men of all parties in England in one common bond for the public safety.

In the summer of the same year a serious rebellion broke out in Ireland, which raged chiefly in the counties of Wicklow and Wexford. This rebellion was, however, soon suppressed; chiefly by the prudence of marquis Cornwallis, who on this occasion was appointed lord lieutenant; and a body of about one thousand French troops, who disembarked at Killala on the 12th August, surrendered on the 8th of September.

A. D. 1798. Bonaparte sailed from Toulon with an armament, consisting of thirteen ships of the line, six frigates, and transports, containing, an army of 30,000 men. He took Malta, and thence proceeded to Egypt, with the view of forming a settlement there, which

---

What memorable naval battles took place 1797?
When was England left alone in the war with France?
What alarmed the English nation in 1798?
When did rebellion break out in Ireland?
What motive induced Bonaparte to go to Egypt?

might afford means for making some future attack, by way either of the Red Sea or of the Persian Gulf, on the British dominions in India. He was pursued to Egypt by admiral Nelson; who, on his arrival, found the French fleet at anchor in Aboukir Bay.

An engagement followed, in which the English obtained a signal victory. The battle lasted through the night. L'Orient, the French admiral's ship, a vessel of 120 guns, was blown up at midnight with a terrible explosion; and when the morning arrived, only two ships of the line and two frigates remained of the whole French fleet. All the rest were either taken or destroyed. On the occasion of this achievement, Admiral Nelson was created a peer, by the title of Baron Nelson of the Nile.

The war on the continent was renewed in 1799, and in the autumn of that year an English army, under the command of sir Ralph Abercrombie, was disembarked at the Helder Point in Holland. The duke of York afterwards took the command; but the enterprise finally miscarried, and the troops re-embarked and returned to England.

The French government, at the close of this campaign, underwent a new and remarkable change, the more remarkable from its direct connection with the extraordinary fortunes of Bonaparte. That general, though the fleet which conveyed him to Egypt was entirely destroyed by lord Nelson, had conquered Egypt, and had invaded Syria; but found his career stopped at Acre by Ghezar, the Turkish pasha, assisted by some English troops, under sir Sidney Smith, who distinguished himself greatly in the defence o that town.

Bonaparte, repulsed from Acre, returned to Egypt, and then ventured on a step, the singular success of which must always be ranked among the most extraordinary parts of his history. Having received intelligence of great discontents in France, he resolved even to forsake the army he commanded, in order to try his fortune at home in this troubled state of public affairs.

Who was defeated at the battle of the Nile?
Were the English troops successful in 1799?
Was Bonaparte successful in Egypt, and who repulsed him in Turkey?
Why did Bonaparte leave the army in Egypt?

Bonaparte escaped from Egypt in August, 1799; and immediately on his arrival in Paris, was able to effect a dissolution of the government. The directory was abolished, and the executive administration was committed to three consuls, of whom he procured himself to be made the chief.

A. D. 1800. In this year was accomplished a legislative union between Great Britain and Ireland; nearly on the same principles on which in the reign of queen Anne, the union had been framed between England and Scotland. Twenty-eight peers, and one hundred commoners, were admitted from Ireland into the English parliament; or rather into the parliament of the united kingdom of Great Britain and Ireland; the title which was now formally adopted as the proper designation of the British isles.

A. D. 1801. In this year Denmark, Sweden, and Russia, were suspected by the English government of a combination to restrain the maritime power of Britain. To counteract this confederacy, an armament under admiral sir Hyde Parker, but of which lord Nelson was the efficient commander, was despatched against Copenhagen in the month of March, 1801. Lord Nelson, on arriving before that capital, instantly made the attack After an exceedingly severe engagement, several Danish ships were destroyed or captured, and the town itself was thought in the utmost danger.

At this moment lord Nelson offered terms of an armistice, which were accepted by the prince of Denmark The English fleet then proceeded to Carlscroon; but its farther operations in the Baltic were interrupted by the death of the emperor (Paul) of Russia. His son and successor, Alexander, immediately disclaimed all hostile intentions, and entered into an amicable convention with England.

The French still kept possession of Egypt. A British force, which was sent to drive them out of that country

---

When did Bonaparte become first consul?
When was the union with Ireland accomplished?
Upon what pretext did the English attack Copenhagen?
What checked the English operations in the Baltic?
When were the French expelled from Egypt?

about this time effected its purpose, though not without the loss of its brave commander, sir Ralph Abercrombie, who was mortally wounded in the first engagement.

While these events were taking place, the public attention was excited in England by the sudden and unexpected resignation of Mr. Pitt, who had been prime minister twenty-one years. He was succeeded by the duke of Portland and Mr. Addington, afterwards created viscount Sidmouth. These ministers opened a negotiation with France, which was at length concluded by a definitive treaty, signed at Amiens, March 27, 1802. Hostilities were renewed in 1803.

A. D. 1804. Bonaparte was proclaimed emperor of France. He had now acquired an unlimited sway, not only in that country, but also over a great part of Europe. Holland, Italy, Spain, and Portugal, crouched before him. England alone stood independent

On the 21st of October, 1804, lord Nelson, with a fleet of 27 ships of the line, encountered the combined fleets of France and Spain, amounting to 33 sail, off Cape Trafalgar. Nelson received, during the action, a mortal wound by a ball fired from the mizen-top of a French ship. When he found himself wounded, he covered his face with his handkerchief, and concealed the stars and orders that decorated the breast of his coat. He took this precaution that he might not be known, fearing lest his crew should be disheartened by knowing that their admiral had fallen. He was carried down to the surgeon's room, where he lived three hours; long enough to know that his fleet was victorious.

Twenty of the enemy's ships had struck, or surrendered during the engagement. But most of the prizes were wrecked in a gale that sprung up in the night. Four only were saved and brought to England. By this victory the navy of France was destroyed, and Britain established more completely than ever her decisive superiority at sea.

What change was made in the English ministry in 1801, and when was the peace of Amiens signed?
What was the position of Bonaparte in 1804?
Who fell at the battle of Trafalgar?
What was the consequence of the battle of Trafalgar?

Mr. Pitt, who had come again into administration in the year 1804, died on the 23d of January, 1806, and was succeeded as prime minister by his great political rival, Mr Fox. But the new administration did not last long. Mr Fox died on the 13th of September; and on the 25th of March, in the year following, another ministry was formed, of which Mr. Percival was usually considered the head.

A. D. 1807. Expeditions were sent to the Dardanelles, to Egypt, and against the Spanish settlements on the river Plate, in South America; but none of them were attended with any advantage. Another expedition was despatched against Copenhagen, which succeeded, after bombarding the town, in gaining possession of the whole Danish fleet, which was safely brought to England

A. D. 1808. Nearly the whole continent of Europe was under the control of Bonaparte. Russia was alienated from England. The emperor of Germany had been compelled to surrender a large portion of his territories. Many of the German princes retained their dominions only as tributaries of the French emperor. The king of Prussia had felt his power, and had seen him make a triumphant entry into Berlin.

Bonaparte reigned over all the north of Italy. He drove the king of Naples from his throne, on which he placed Murat, one of his own generals. He made the king of Spain a prisoner in France, and placed his brother, Joseph Bonaparte, on the throne of Madrid. Portugal was also reduced under the dominion of this great conqueror, and the royal family of that country had emigrated to their South American territories. Holland was erected into a monarchy, and bestowed on Louis Bonaparte.

The papal power was also overthrown, and the pope became an unwilling resident in France. Louis XVIII. the brother of the late king of France, who (on the death of the dauphin in a prison in Paris) had become the representative of the Bourbon family, had at this time but little prospect of being ever restored to his rank. He was liv-

---

When did Mr. Pitt and Mr. Fox die?
What expeditions were undertaken by the English in 1807?
What was the state of northern Europe in 1808?
What was the state of Italy, &c.?
Where were the Pope and Louis XVIII. in 1808?

ing in great retirement in England, and called himself the count de Lille.

In the spring of this year, the Spanish nation, exasperated by the cruelties committed by the French in Madrid, roused themselves to exertion, declared war against France, and sent deputies to England to implore assistance. An expedition of about ten thousand men was sent to their assistance, under the command of sir Arthur Wellesley, and arrived at Corunna on the 20th of July.

On communication with the Spanish leaders in that district, it was thought best to proceed in the first instance to Portugal, for the purpose of expelling general Junot, who had the command of a French army in that country, and was in possession of Lisbon.

The English landed at Mondego Bay, and defeated the French in a battle at Vimeira, which was fought on the 21st of August; after which the French army retired to the strong position which covered Lisbon; and a convention was in consequence entered into by sir Hew Dalrymple, who had subsequently taken the command of the army for the evacuation of Portugal by the French troops.

In the month of November, sir John Moore, who had arrived with a reinforcement of 12,000 men, led the British army into Spain. General Moore was, however, compelled to retreat; and, after a most severe and calamitous march, through a difficult country, and in most inclement weather, he arrived at Corunna, Jan. 16, 1809.

Soult, the French general, overtook and attacked Moore when on the point of embarking. The British, though suffering under extreme fatigue and anxiety, beat off the French, though with great loss. Sir John Moore was amongst those who fell. His friends were able to spare a few moments, amidst the confusion of the night succeeding the battle, through the whole of which the troops were embarking, to inter the body of their lamented commander on the ramparts of Corunna.

Why was the peninsular war commenced?
Why was the English army sent to Lisbon?
How did the English proceed in Portugal?
Who led the English army into Spain?
Under what circumstances was sir John Moore killed?

A. D. 1809. In the month of April, sir Arthur Wellesley, having been again appointed to the command of the British army in the Peninsula, landed with reinforcements in Portugal. He obliged the French to abandon Oporto, and soon afterwards entered Spain: but he was compelled eventually to withdraw into Portugal.

A. D. 1812. In this year the United States of America declared war against England. The chief events of this war properly belong to American history. It was occasioned by disputes concerning the commercial and maritime privileges of the Americans, and ended honorably to our country

The tide of success on the continent of Europe was now beginning to turn. Bonaparte on arriving at the pinnacle of greatness, alienated all his allies, and at length undertook to invade Russia. There nothing but disaster and defeat overtook his hitherto invincible armies. It has been calculated that of the 400,000 men who had composed the invading army, not more than 50,000 re-crossed the Russian boundary on its return. On the 4th of December, Bonaparte himself left the army, and set out on a rapid journey to Paris.

These reverses of the French army in Russia roused the other nations of Europe from their state of subjection to the power of Bonaparte. Prussia was the first to shake off the yoke, and to join the advancing armies of Russia. Bernadotte, the crown prince of Sweden, allied himself to the same cause. Austria also declared war against France: and in the month of November, in the same year, the prince of Orange was recalled by the Dutch from his long exile, and entered the Hague amidst the acclamations of the people

Denmark joined the allies in the following January. Several great battles were fought in this campaign. That of Leipzig, on the 18th of October, was completely decisive against the French, who were rapidly driven back to their own country, pursued by the immense armies of the allies.

What did sir Arthur Wellesley accomplish in 1809?
Under what circumstances did the war with America terminate?
What was the end of Bonaparte's invasion of Russia?
How did the sovereigns of Europe regard Bonaparte in 1813?
What victory was gained by the allies in 1814?

who had now no fear for the success of the war, and were eagerly contemplating he invasion of France. Early in the winter the allies crossed the Rhine. On the 30th of March, 1814, they gained a victory before Paris, and the next day entered that city in triumph.

The contest in Spain in the meantime was not concluded In the years 1811 and 1812 there had been much hard fighting in that country, and the English gained many victories. But the French army was so superior in number, that lord Wellington, after having advanced to Madrid, was obliged, in November, 1812, to retreat to the Portuguese frontier. In the following year, however, 1813, his success was complete.

Lord Wellington drove the French entirely out of the Peninsula, and on the 7th of October entered France. The concluding achievements of this army, in the spring of 1814, were to enter Bordeaux, which had declared its attachment to the Bourbon cause, while the great contest in the neighbourhood of Paris was still undecided, and where the British troops were welcomed as deliverers; and finally the defeat of marshal Soult, in a severe battle at Toulouse, on the 11th of April.

On the 2d of April, the French senate declared that Bonaparte had forfeited his throne: on the 4th, he signed an act of abdication: on the 28th he embarked at Frejus, on board an English frigate, and was conveyed to Elba, a little island on the coast of Italy, which was assigned to him by the allied powers. The empress, Maria Louisa, and her infant son, to whom Bonaparte had given the title of king of Rome, had previously gone to Vienna.

On the 6th of April, a decree of the senate had been passed for the recall of the Bourbon princes; and Louis XVIII. made on the 3d of May a solemn entry into Paris. All these extraordinary events passed so rapidly, that they seemed more like the winding up of a romance than like realities.

What was done by Lord Wellington in 1812 and 1813?
What was done by the English army on the continent in 1814?
When did Bonaparte go to Elba?
When did Louis XVIII. enter Paris?

May 30th, peace was concluded between the allied powers and France. The limits of France were reduced by this treaty nearly to those which she had possessed in 1792 Her colonies, with a few exceptions, were restored. England retained Malta, and the Cape of Good Hope, and the small island of Heligoland. The adjustment of many complicated questions, which remained to be settled between the continental powers, was reserved for a congress appointed to meet at Vienna.

In the beginning of June, the emperor of Russia, and the king of Pussia, paid a visit to England. They were accompanied by Blucher, a veteran Prussian general, and by Platoff, hetman of the Cossacks, men who had borne a distinguished part in the late achievements of the allied army. The visit of these distinguished strangers was celebrated in London, and other parts of the kingdom, with extraordinary rejoicing and festivity. Peace with America was soon afterwards restored.

Early in 1815, a general alarm was spread throughout Europe by the escape of Bonaparte from Elba. He landed March 1st in the south of France. He was everywhere received with joy by the soldiery. Louis XVIII. fled from Paris early in the morning of the 20th of the same month, and Bonaparte entered that capital in the evening of the same day, and resumed the government without opposition

His first attempt was to conciliate the allies, to whom he proposed to maintain the peace, on the terms which had been lately settled with Louis. But the allies unanimously rejected the proposition, and began immediately to put their armies in motion, with the resolution of once more displacing this unprincipled disturber of the world.

The English and Prussians were first in motion. To prevent their entrance into France, Bonaparte, at the head of 150,000 men, marched to the Netherlands. June 15th, the French and Prussians had the first rencontre at Charleroi. The engagement was renewed on the 16th, and on

---

What limits were assigned to France by the allied powers?
What distinguished persons visited London in 1815?
When did Bonaparte re-enter Paris?
Did the allies refuse all terms with Bonaparte?
Where did Bonaparte encounter the allied armies?

the same day another division of the French army had a severe conflict with the English at Quatre Bras. On the 17th, the British army retreated to an advantageous post near the village of Waterloo.

About ten o'clock, June 18th, began one of the hardest fought battles recorded in history. It raged furiously during the whole day, and terminated in the defeat of the French army. Bonaparte, when he saw his guards give way, exclaimed, "It is all over; we must save ourselves." And, so saying, he quitted the field of battle, attended by five or six officers, and arrived at Paris on the night of the 20th of June. Seeing no prospect of being able to retrieve his ruined fortunes, he proceeded a few days afterwards, to Rochefort, with the intention of making his escape to America.

Bonaparte actually embarked with that intention; but the Bellerophon, an English man of war, being in sight, from which it would have been impossible to escape, he resolved to surrender himself to the English captain. The Bellerophon, as soon as he arrived on board, sailed for Torbay, where he continued on board that vessel, till it could be concerted between the English government and the allies what would be the best and securest place of confinement for so very important a prisoner. The island of St. Helena was at last determined upon. In this island he continued a prisoner till his death, which took place May 5th, 1821.

The English and Prussian armies advanced rapidly after the battle of Waterloo, and invested Paris on the 29th and 30th June. A few days afterwards the city capitulated. The Austrians and Russians had now crossed the Rhine. On the 8th Louis XVIII. re-entered his capital; but the English and Prussians retained military possession of it till the final restoration of peace. The terms of the peace were settled in October.

Thus finally terminated that long contest in which Europe was involved by the French revolution, a contest

---

What was the catastrophe of Waterloo?
Whither did Bonaparte escape from Waterloo?
What happened to Bonaparte subsequently to his escape?
Whither did the allied armies proceed after the victory of Waterloo?
Did the peace of 1815 conclude the war in Europe?

which had raged with unexampled fury, and with few and brief intermissions, for a period of more than twenty years

The prince of Wales (since George IV.) had married in 1795, his cousin, the princess Caroline of Brunswick They had an only daughter, the princess Charlotte, born January 7, 1796; who, on May 2, 1816, married prince Leopold of Saxe-Coburg. To the unspeakable grief of the whole nation, this young princess, who possessed many popular qualities, died, November 7, 1817.

A. D. 1818. The queen died after a lingering illness The duke of Kent, the king's fourth son, died January 23, 1820. He had married the sister of prince Leopold, and left an only child, the princess Victoria, then not a year old, the present queen of England.

George III. having at intervals of his life been subject to insanity, sunk at length into complete derangement of intellect. He died January 29, 1820, in the 82d year of his age, and the 60th of his reign; during the last nine years of which he had been in a melancholy state of blindness, deafness, and mental incapacity. He married, Sept. 8, 1761, Sophia Charlotte, princess of Mechlenburg-Strelitz, and had nine sons and six daughters.

The expenditure of life and money by the English nation in the war with France, has been of doubtful benefit to the country · but the destruction, by lord Exmouth, of the Algerine tyranny over the sea was of great importance to the interests of humanity and of commerce. The Algerines, and the other Barbary states, had for many centuries been accustomed to treat as slaves all the unhappy persons whom they took as prisoners. After the conclusion of peace in 1814 when the hostilities which had so long raged in Europe no longer disturbed the navigation of the Mediterranean, their depredations on the trading vessels of some of

---

Who was the princess Charlotte, and when did she die?
When did the queen and the duke of Kent die?
When did George III. die?
What naval achievement in the reign of George III. was favorable to human happiness?

the Italian states increased, and became seriously alarming They captured the vessels, and made slaves of the crews

In the spring of 1816, lord Exmouth was sent from England to remonstrate with the dey of Algiers on these depredations : and the dey in consequence released some Christian slaves, and made fair promises for the future. Soon after this, and, as it is said, without the permission or even knowledge of the dey, a body of Algerines attacked some Italians who were engaged in fishing for pearls at Bona. When this news reached England, the people were much exasperated at the apparent want of faith of the dey, and lord Exmouth was again sent out, with orders to compel the Algerines to keep their promises.

On the 27th of May, 1816, lord Exmouth came in sight of Algiers, with a large armament and sent to demand of the dey to set all his Christain slaves at liberty. Receiving no answer, after having waited some hours, he began to fire upon the town. The dey's magazines, arsenals, and shipping, were destroyed before his eyes, and great damage done to the town. The next morning the dey sent to inform lord Exmouth that he would agree to the terms demanded; and before noon most of the Christian slaves were released, and the English fleet in a few days sailed from Algiers.

The victory of lord Exmouth was not the only service rendered to humanity in this reign. During the short period of Mr. Fox's administration, an act was passed for the abolition of the negro slave trade between Africa and the West Indies.

CHAPTER XXXIX

CONCLUSION.

GEORGE IV.

[Years after Christ, 1820—1830.]

George III. not only reigned the longest, but also lived to a greater age than any other English king. He was

---

Who was sent from England to remonstrate with the dey of Algiers ?
When did lord Exmouth compel the dey of Algiers to submit to his demands ?
When was the slave trade abolished ?

more distinguished by the domestic virtues, and for sincere piety, than for political wisdom; but, during his long reign, English mind was advancing, and English power and prosperity, were increasing.

George III., for many years of his life a maniac, from October, 1788, to April, 1789, was prevented from exercising the duties of a sovereign; and from October, 1810, to January, 1820, he lived under entire deprivation of reason. These ten years were the period of the regency. The prince of Wales, afterwards George IV., was appointed to the royal function and dignity; and, till his father's death, was styled the Prince Regent.

George IV. was crowned king, July 19th, 1821. He died at the age of sixty-eight, June 26th, 1830. George IV. received an excellent classical, and a neglected moral and religious education. He might have been instructed in the duties of a man and a sovereign prince; but he was *never made to feel* that his example might sanction vice, or recommend virtue, and that his natural abilities made him eminently capable to do good to the great kingdom over which he was set.

The dissipated and frivolous life of George IV. while a young man, made him unpopular in England; but the first time that he ever spoke in the House of Lords, he declared: "I exist by the love, the friendship, and the benevolence of the people; and their cause I will never forsake as long as I live." This expression of just sentiment awakened in the public mind all the feelings of love and trust due to a patriot prince.

A. D. 1795. George IV was married to his cousin Caroline of Brunswick, whom he never loved, and from whom he was afterwards separated. They had but one child, the princess Charlotte, who died in 1817 Queen Caroline was accused of many crimes, and was brought to a trial on account of them. Whether or not she was guilty, the public opinion is not determined. She died, 1821, and was relieved from the misery and disgrace of doubtful innocence.

Was George III. a good man?
Why was the Prince of Wales made regent?
What was the character of George IV.?
How did the prince of Wales commend himself to the English people

George IV. visited different parts of his dominions, and was greeted with enthusiasm in Ireland, Scotland, and Hanover. The latter years of George IV. were passed in retirement. A secluded cottage in Windsor Park, was his favorite residence : he caused royal palaces to be repaired and built, but of the latter he never took possession.

George IV. seldom met his parliament in person—very rarely held courts, that is, he rarely received the great nobility, foreign ministers, and distinguished strangers, and he seldom appeared in any public place. He died of dropsy in the summer of 1830, and was committed to the earth with splendid ceremonies, but without the regrets of the grateful and the good.

Much might be said of the progress of arts, literature, and science, in these latter reigns of the English kings ; but the history of arts and artists, of literature and scholars, of science and philosophers, is too ample to find room in these pages. A list of the names of men of genius would afford no just notion what they were, and what they have done.

There also remains much to be told concerning the various discoveries and improvements that have been made during the last sixty years in almost every branch of art and science : balloons, steamboats, telegraphs, machines for spinning and weaving, &c. There never was any former period in which human talent and ingenuity were exercised so much or so well.

Maritime discovery in this age has done wonders, and English travelers have made important discoveries. The expeditions of Cook and Burney, Franklin, Parry, and Ross, have greatly increased human knowledge ; and the

---

What were the circumstances of George's domestic life ?
Did George IV. visit his dominions ?
What were the habits of George IV., and when did he die ?
Can a proper history be given here of English literature ?
What was the state of arts, &c. during the reign of George IV ?
What are the great enterprises of the reigns of George III. and his son ?

great enterprises of humanity, the abolition of the slave trade, the Bible Society, and missionary adventure to every neglected portion of the earth, may be traced to British origin. The reign of George IV. is marked by *Catholic Emancipation*. It was mentioned in another part of this history, that no office of government could be exercised by a Roman Catholic ; and on this account the Stuarts were expelled from the throne of Britain. An act of parliament, 1829, removed many disabilities from the Catholics, and admitted them to privileges not previously allowed them: this is Catholic Emancipation.

WILLIAM IV.

[Years after Christ, 1830—1837.]

William Henry, duke of Clarence, succeeded to the throne on the decease of his brother George IV. On the accession of William IV., the English nation manifested a general consciousness of suffering from injustice and misgovernment, and they insisted moreover their own right to redress their grievances.

The kingdom was indeed wealthy and prosperous. The face of the country was covered with roads, canals, bridges, and public and private buildings of unsurpassed magnificence. The soil was under skilful cultivation. England was at the head of the maritime powers of Europe. Its manufactures, commerce, and foreign colonies, were immense sources of industry and wealth.

The other side of the picture was frightful: the national debt was augmented beyond the means of the country to pay; the poor rates were *quadrupled;* one-sixth of the population were paupers. The taxation, since the accession of George III., was more than quadrupled; and the state was burthened by the extravagant salaries of government functionaries, and the payment of numerous pensions.

Who possesses the great wealth of England? The no-

What is Catholic Emancipation ?
Is England highly prosperous ?
What were the causes of popular discontent in England ?
Who possess wealth, and who are very poor in England?

bility, the aristocratic commoners, the merchants, bankers, and great manufacturers, have a superabundance; but the laboring classes,—they who cultivate the soil, and who work for the rich in sundry ways, and multitudes who can obtain no work, who people the almshouses and hospitals, are the hungry poor,—and their ignorance and want demand redress.

All these evils the people believe a wise government might remedy. The people demand this remedy. They have insisted that a better representation in parliament should be granted, and a reformed parliament was obtained, (1832.)

William IV. conceded every thing that he could. It may be hoped that a system of reform then commenced will be progressive, and misery may be mitigated, and national virtue be strengthened in that dominion of earth, of which it may be said, " that the world never before saw so vast an amount of wealth and power under one head, as that under the control of the British government."

It would be doing injustice to English history, to afford no information of the British empire in India. The trade of Europe with India, has been more or less extensive from time immemorial. From the discovery of the Cape of Good Hope, (1496,) this trade became easy by means of navigation.

An English East India Company, that is, an English company to carry on traffic with India, was formed in 1600. This company quarrelled with the French, Dutch, and Portuguese, who also traded to India. The English built a factory at Calcutta, 1736. They required troops to defend them there, and a proper force was employed.

The native princes of the country quarrelled: the English aided some, and invaded others, and gradually subdued them, till the revenues derived from the India trade, and British possessions in India, amounted (1728) to 22,851,424l. The history of British India is very inter-

---

What may be supposed to be a remedy for these national grievances?
What may be the result of better government in Britain?
When was the India trade commenced?
When were the English first established in India?
What is the present extent of British power in India?

esting, and is very extensive in its details—too much so to be further related in this place.

William IV. reigned seven years, and died June, 1837. He was succeeded by the princess Victoria, daughter of his brother, Edward duke of Kent. This young lady, born 1819, had been carefully educated, and the English people, not averse to female rule, looked for a prosperous and happy reign. In the present age of the world the influence of a British sovereign is much less than in former times:—public opinion, general morals, the diffusion of knowledge, and a just representation of the nation in Parliament set limits to the uses and abuses of prerogative; still, an enlightened mind, a firm spirit, and a virtuous example shed lustre upon the throne, and wisdom and goodness so exalted give a tone to public counsels, and political measures, that exert a salutary and ennobling power upon a free people.

CHAPTER XL.

REIGN OF QUEEN VICTORIA.—PART I.

[Years after Christ, 1837–1856.]

The young princess was at her accession almost exactly eighteen years old. Even at this early age she was seen to enter with remarkable dignity and propriety on the high station which had fallen to her lot. She retained the late king's ministers in office, and went in person, July 17th, to dissolve the Parliament, and read her speech on this occasion from the throne. She also opened in person, in the November following, the first session of the new Parliament. The elections of the members of the House of Commons were found to support the choice of ministers which she had made. In the following year her coronation was celebrated, June 28th, and was accompanied by numerous indications of her great and general

---

How long did William IV. reign, and when did he die?
In what manner did Queen Victoria enter upon her duties?

popularity. A rebellion had broken out in Canada in the preceding November, but peace was restored after a short struggle; and in 1838 the Earl of Durham was sent out as Governor-General of the British possessions in North America. The two provinces of Upper and Lower Canada were consolidated, and the seat of government transferred from Toronto and Quebec to Montreal. Various changes were also introduced into the political constitution of this colony.

At the close of the year 1839 a political association of men who entitled themselves Chartists broke out into open riot at Newport, in Monmouthshire. A body of these confederates, aided by the secrecy with which the use of the Welsh language enabled them to clothe their proceedings, collected in the neighboring hills, and marched down at night, and by surprise got possession of the town. This disturbance was immediately quelled, by the courage of a small body of soldiers, headed by a spirited magistrate, and three of its leaders were apprehended, and tried, and condemned to death, but their sentence was commuted to transportation for life. The Chartist principles, however, have become too prevalent among working miners and manufacturers, and also among large bodies of laborers, not to render it desirable to state them particularly. The Charter, as it was called, in which these principles were embodied, proposed five *points*. The first of these was the grant of universal suffrage in the election of members of Parliament; the second was that of voting by ballot, a system of secret voting by which a man may avoid the declaring openly for whom he votes; the third point is to have annual parliaments; the fourth, that the members be paid for their services; and the fifth, the abolition of that qualification in respect of property which all members of Parliament are now required by law to possess, namely, £600 a year if member for a county, and £300 if member for a city or borough. Hardly any person of knowledge or observation can imagine that the extreme changes thus proposed could be pro-

---

What rebellion broke ont?
Who were the Chartists?
What were their demands of reform?

ductive of real benefit to any rank or order of men. But still this Charter has been espoused, as has been said, very extensively among the working classes, and, as will be seen hereafter, has been brought the more before the public eye by the example of the revolution in France of 1848. It has much resemblance also to the constitution which has been adopted, though in a very different state of society from our own, in the United States of America.

On the 10th of February, 1840, the Queen married her first-cousin, Prince Albert of Saxe-Coburg, a nephew of the Duchess of Kent, and of Leopold, king of the Belgians. The prince-consort, while he kept himself wisely aloof from all political parties in the state, was studious to promote by every means in his power our most useful charities and national institutions. Both his own habits, and those of the Queen, were of a highly English character. They often retired from the fatigues of their public life to the comparative quiet of a villa at Osborne, in the Isle of Wight, in sight of the great arsenal of Portsmouth and the roadstead of Spithead, and they had an occasional residence also at Balmoral in Scotland. It was among their relaxations to make sea excursions in the royal yacht, in which they visited both Ireland and Scotland more than once. In September, 1843, they crossed the Channel, and paid a short visit to the King of the French at the Château d'Eu, near Treport, in Normandy; the first visit of any English sovereign to France since Henry VIII. In the October of the following year Louis Philippe returned this visit to the Queen at Windsor; and in August and September, 1845, the Queen and Prince Albert made a tour in Germany, and on their return passed another day or two at the Château d'Eu. They then doubtless little thought that before three more years should expire, the King of the French would once again need that hospitality in England which he had sought amid the misfortunes of his early life, and which was renewed after the loss of his crown in 1848.

Among what classes do Chartist opinions prevail?
When, and to whom, was the Queen married?
What are the domestic habits of the Prince and Queen?

In April, 1840, war was declared by England against China. Canton was blockaded, and the island of Chusan taken possession of, in the same year; and an invading army, under the command of Lord Gough, afterward (in August, 1842) penetrated to the very walls of Nankin, and dictated a peace. By this peace, the island of Hong Kong was ceded to England, and a large sum of money paid by way of an indemnity for the expenses of the war; and, besides Canton, the only port to which foreign traders had previously been admitted, four other Chinese ports were opened to commerce with the rest of the world. The terms of this treaty have, on the whole, been faithfully observed. Keying, the Chinese commissioner who was employed to adjust the treaty with the *barbarians*, as the English and other Europeans are called in China, expresses himself as follows in the report which he presented to his own government on this occasion: "I, your servant, have examined and found what are the unwarrantable demands of the said barbarians, and they are deserving of the utmost hatred." He then, however, proceeds to argue that, as they have taken and kept possession of various places, which are not given up, and have not retired, it will be a difficult matter to get them back. "It is a difficult matter," he adds, "to contend with them on the waters. Should it not therefore be allowed them to return to us our territory, and allow them to trade, since they are willing respectfully to pay the duties? Just now they are sensible, and repent of their errors, and are as obedient as if driven by the wind; and when again in mutual friendship, benevolence, and truth, all things will go on well."

While this war was thus carrying on in China, another was also entered into with the Pacha, or viceroy, of Egypt, Mehemet Ali. This war arose out of a long contest between the Pasha and his titular sovereign, the Sultan of Constantinople, in which all the greater powers of Europe at length interfered in the Sultan's behalf. In 1840 an English squadron, under the command of Commodore

---

Against what country did England declare war? and when?
What was the object of this war?
What was Keying's opinion of the barbarians and their demands?
With whom was another war commenced?

Napier, joined the Turkish fleet, and took Beyrout, and afterward destroyed Acre, both which places, together with the whole coast of Syria, had been for some time in the possession of Mehemet. From Acre the Commodore proceeded to Alexandria, and prepared for an attack on that city. But a treaty was then agreed on, by which Syria was restored to the Turks, and the government of Egypt secured to the Pacha, and made hereditary in his family. The intercourse and commerce of Egypt with Europe, and especially with England, has, since this period, greatly increased. The Upper Nile, and the relics of high antiquity to be found on its banks, have been explored with success; and Cairo, where the climate is always serene and delicious during the winter months, has become a place of frequent residence for invalids. Mehemet himself fell at length into a state of imbecility. His son, Ibrahim, was nominated viceroy in his place, September 1, 1848, but died November 10th in the same year, and was succeeded by his nephew, Abbas, the eldest grandson of Mehemet. Mehemet himself died August 2, 1849. Ibrahim had visited both France and England in the autumn of 1845 and the spring and summer of 1846.

The events which have taken place, during the present reign, in the British dominions in India, are far too intricate to be here detailed, and yet some brief notice of them must not be omitted. The vast surface of that great peninsula has been in general tranquil. But, on the western frontier, the British forces which had invaded Afghanistan, a large territory to the west of the Indus, were compelled by a rising of the people to retreat from Cabool in January, 1842, under the most distressing circumstances, and were cut off in the passes of the mountains while on their retreat; one person only escaping at the time to tell the tale. In the following year another war broke out in Scinde, a district at the mouth of the same great river, the free navigation and command of which is of the first importance, both to the commerce and the security of the upper provinces. General Sir Charles Napier gained here

---

What is said of Cairo?
What events took place in India?
In what country did another war occur?

a great victory at Meance, February 17, 1843, and afterward took Hyderabad; and, on March 24th, gained another victory at Dubba. The tranquillity of Scinde has been, since that time, undisturbed. Another war, however, broke out subsequently in the district entitled the Punjab, an Indian name derived from five rivers by which it is watered. These rivers take their rise on the western side of the Himalaya mountains, the highest in the world, which bound Hindostan on the north, and, after flowing through the Punjab, run into the Indus. This fine country was inhabited by the Sikhs, a hardy and warlike race, who, on the 12th December, 1845, and the following days, crossed the Sutlej, the river by which they were bounded on the south, thus invading the British territory, and on the 18th made an attack on a British army at Moodkee. In this attack they were repulsed, and they were subsequently compelled to retreat, and were afterward defeated at Ferozeshah on the 21st and 22d of the same month; and again, at Aliwal, January 28th, and at Sobraon, February 10, 1846, when they were driven back across the Sutlej with immense slaughter. In 1848 the war was renewed. A bloody but indecisive action was fought at Chillianwallah, January 13, 1849, in which the British army was commanded by Lord Gough. This indecisive battle, though called a victory, was, in England, at first regarded as almost a defeat; and Sir Charles Napier, whose great success, a few years before, in the war in Scinde, had acquired for him an exceedingly high reputation, was appointed to succeed Lord Gough as commander-in-chief. The disappointment, however, which arose from the battle of Chillianwallah* was soon relieved by the intelligence of the capture of Mooltan, and of a decisive victory obtained by Lord Gough at Goojerat, February 21st. The result of this victory was an unconditional surrender of the Sikhs, and the annexation of the Punjab to the British dominions.

* Nearly the spot, as is supposed, where Alexander the Great gained his victory over Porus.

Did a war break out in the Punjab?
Who commanded the British troops?

During the course of these events in distant lands, the domestic peace of England had happily not been interrupted by any hostility with either the powers of the Continent of Europe, or with the United States of America. The strong feeling of the desirableness of universal peace, and especially of peace with this great country, which took its origin from our own shores, appears to acquire, every day, a more and more powerful influence in subduing those occasional asperities and jealousies which, in the intercourse of nations, are apt to arise.

The changes, however, in the commercial and manufacturing policy of our country have not been less, or less important, during these peaceful years, than the changes might have been from war to peace, or from peace to war. The Parliament which had been elected on the Queen's accession was dissolved in June, 1841, and the new elections appeared to show that the administration of Lord Melbourne had lost much of its hold on public opinion. Consequently Lord Melbourne resigned, and Sir Robert Peel came into office at the head of a new ministry, September 1st, in that year. The study to remove, as far as possible, all legislative fetters on both commerce and manufactures was among the first principles of the new government. Almost all the import duties on foreign goods were greatly diminished—a measure which has been followed by a great increase in the export of the British manufactures, which are sent abroad in exchange for those goods, and by which, in fact, they are purchased. The most important bearing of this policy was on the heavy duties which, for the sake of protecting the British agriculturist, had been now levied, ever since the peace of 1815, on the importation of foreign corn. An act for modifying these laws was passed in the session of 1842; and in order to compensate the loss of revenue, necessarily consequent on these changes, a new property or income tax of sevenpence in the pound was imposed on all incomes above £150 a year. A subsequent act for the

---

Was the peace of England disturbed?
Were changes made in the policy of the country?
Who came into office?
What is said of import duties?

nearly absolute repeal of the corn-laws was carried through Parliament in 1846, and received the royal assent June 26th in that year. The contest which arose on that occasion was unusually bitter and vehement. Most of the county members in particular, who had previously been among the minister's chief supporters, now took part against him, and accused him of deserting the conservative principles on which he had come forward in public life. Hence another change of ministry. Sir Robert Peel resigned, and a new administration was formed under Lord John Russell, July 4th.

Amid the agitations arising from these causes in England, the failure of the crop of the potato in 1845 and 1846, plunged the Irish, who have long been greatly dependent on this plant for food, into the deepest distress. This distress was also aggravated by a deficiency of the corn crop of 1846, not in Ireland only, but also throughout England and almost the whole of Europe. It was partially relieved in 1847, by an abundant harvest, by a grant of ten millions from Parliament, by a vast private subscription, and by emigrations to America and other countries. It has also been attempted, by the enactment of a Poor-law for Ireland, and by measures intended to promote the agriculture and encourage the industry of this fertile island, to render its great natural resources available to the support of its inhabitants. But the benefit to be derived from these attempts has as yet been very imperfect, and has been, moreover, seriously impeded by various tumults and even insurrections. These have been headed by vehement orators, who clamored for a repeal of the union with England, and thought, or pretended to think, that they might look to political changes for remedies only to be found in soocial tranquillity, and in promoting the sympathies of all ranks with one another. Mr. Smith O'Brien, a man of one of the families of highest rank in Ireland, took the lead in a riot in Tipperary, in which two or three lives were lost, in June, 1848; but this riot was

---

Who next became prime minister?
What crop failed in Ireland? did other crops fail?
Did tumults arise in Ireland?
Who was Smith O'Brien?

instantly suppressed; and he and some of his followers were subsequently arrested and tried for high treason, and found guilty, but their lives were spared, and they were transported for life.

In the following year, 1849, Queen Victoria visited Ireland, and was received with the greatest demonstrations of respect and regard. It appears to be probable that the royal visits to Ireland will be frequently repeated in future; and the more probable, inasmuch as the Lord Lieutenancy of that island is likely to be abolished—an office which, though never better filled than of late, by Lord Clarendon, is thought both to be of needless expense, and also to introduce a complexity in the relations with the government in London, which it is wise to remove. The reasons which operated for the retention of the office at the period of the union have long ceased to exist: and the rapidity and certainty of those methods of communication which recent years have introduced, bring now the remotest parts not of England and Scotland only, but of Ireland also, into almost immediate contact with each other. There is not any thing for which we have to be more thankful than that neither those most painful calamities which have taken place in Ireland, nor yet a great distress which has prevailed in the Highlands of Scotland, nor any agitation of parties, or opposing interests, in any other parts of the empire, have appeared to blind any considerable number of the inhabitants of our own island to that wisdom which seeks its good in tranquillity; or, it may be hoped, to that spirit of religion which submits in hope and faith to the Supreme Disposer of events.

Far happier in this respect has been the fortune of England than that of France, Italy, Austria, Prussia, Portugal, or Spain. In France, where an under-current of vehement democracy had subsisted all through the seventeen years of the reign of Louis Philippe, a new and sudden revolution broke out February 22, 1848. On the 24th the prisons were thrown open, the palace of the Tuileries

---

How was the Queen received in Ireland?
For what should England be thankful?
Compare the fortune of England and that of other countries.
What new revolution broke out in France?

was taken possession of and plundered by the mob, and the King and Queen forced to fly to England, where they found an asylum at Claremont—a place still the property of their son-in-law, Leopold, king of the Belgians, whose first wife had been the short-lived Princess Charlotte of Wales.

In this new revolution in France, which was followed immediately by the proclamation of a Republic, many of the watchwords and theories of the Revolution of 1789 were brought forward over again by the actors in it. *Liberty, equality,* and *fraternity* were proclaimed in every street and by all its orators, as their maxims or principles; and many declarations put forth that an organization, as it was called, of labor might be formed which should abolish poverty, and that it was the business of the State to find work for all who could labor, as well as to support the old and infirm.

These doctrines and this example could not be without some effect in England and Ireland. March 13th, a numerous meeting of the *Chàrtists* was held on Kennington Common. A convention of Chartist delegates met in London, April 4th; and on the 10th a great body of their delegates and partisans, wearing rosettes of white, green, and red, assembled in John Street, Fitzroy-square, and adjourned in procession to another meeting on Kennington Common. The crowd thus assembled was supposed to amount altogether to the number of 23,000 or 25,000, and the leaders had intended to proceed to the House of Commons to present their petition. Much apprehension was entertained that some serious disturbance, similar to those which at Paris, Vienna, Berlin, and other capitals, had produced such bloody and disastrous events, might on this occasion take place. Intimation was consequently given that the procession, if attempted, would be stopped by force. The shops were shut in all the great thoroughfares. Bodies of horse and foot police were posted at the approaches of the several bridges over the Thames. A large force of regular troops were stationed, by the sagacious provision of the Duke of Wellington, out of sight in

---

What the effect in England?
What measures were taken by the Duke of Wellington?

various places. The great commander watched in person on this day over the safety of London, and ordered the measures taken for its security. Also a very large body of special constables volunteered their services in all parts of the town. Under these circumstances the meeting on the common passed off quietly; the crowds which had assembled and paraded through the streets in other parts of London dispersed without tumult; and the general feeling that the principle of order and respect for property is far too strong in England to be assailed with success, or with any possible advantage to any rank or class of society, is thought to have received a very strong and useful confirmation from these events. The riot in Ireland, which was headed by Mr. Smith O'Brien in the month of June in this year, has been mentioned already. A meeting, in which the same Mr. O'Brien had taken part, and in which very inflammatory speeches were made, and an address voted to the French Republic, had previously been held in Dublin, March 20th. This address was presented in Paris, April 3d.

The example of France, or rather the great explosion which had taken place in that country, had at this time communicated itself, or was in progress of a rapid communication to almost all the other countries of Europe, in most of which the seeds of revolution, or, at least, of discontent with their governments, were already sown. In Tuscany, the Grand Duke had, on February 11th in this year, granted a representative constitution to that great and flourishing duchy. On the 18th of the same month the inhabitants of Milan expelled the Austrian viceroy, and on the following day the flag of Italian independence was hoisted in all the towns of Northern Italy. The King of Sardinia, in the vain expectation of uniting Lombardy to Piedmont, afterward joined in the same cause, and a long series of fierce hostilities followed. The Austrian power, however, at length resumed its ascendency. Milan capitulated to the imperial general, August 4th, and Venice, after a most

---

Were the seeds of revolution in any of the countries of Europe?
What occurred in Italy?
Did reforms result from these disturbances?

determined resistance, August 22, 1849. Vehement and bloody contests took place also both at Naples and in Sicily. In Rome Pius IX., who had been elected Pope on the death of Gregory XVI. in June, 1846, granted to his States, March 14, 1848, a Legislature, consisting of a Senate and a Chamber of Deputies. These reforms, however, were either inadequate to the occasion, or gave an impulse to demand further concessions. The Pope, unable or irresolute to face the opposition thus excited, fled in disguise on December 24th of this same eventful year, and escaped to Gaeta, in the kingdom of Naples. France subsequently embraced his cause, and by sending an overwhelming force, took Rome, after a most brave resistance, July 3, 1849. A comparative tranquillity was then restored, and the Pope has since (April 12, 1850) returned to his capital.

Germany, in the mean time, was not less disturbed than Italy. An insurrection took place at Vienna, March 13, 1848. The Emperor of Austria fled to Innspruck, May 18th, but returned to Vienna August 15. In the latter end of May a Congress assembled at Frankfort, in which it was proposed to consolidate all the German states under some new constitution; and in the following March the Archduke John, brother of the Emperor of Austria, was elected Lieutenant-General of Germany, and accepted the office. But these proceedings failed to effect any permanent good. In the end of October new conflicts took place in Vienna, and the popular party, consisting of the lowest dregs of society, became ascendant for a time. At length the Emperor's authority was again established, and an army of Hungarians was defeated, which had come to aid his opponents. A war in Hungary followed, in which the Austrians, though met by the bravest and most determined resistance, were at length victorious. In this war with Hungary Russia lent her powerful aid to the Austrians.

To conclude as briefly as possible what remains to be said of the convulsions of Europe during the year 1848.

Was Germany agitated by insurrections?
Any war in Hungary?

Fierce and bloody tumults took place in Berlin in March of this year, and were renewed in June. The Danish provinces of Schleswig and Holstein, desirous to annex themselves to Germany, revolted against Denmark, and the King of Prussia espoused their cause. Switzerland also, and both Spain and Portugal, were full of conflict and animosity.

The Dowager Queen Adelaide died, after a long decline, at the age of fifty-seven, December 2, 1849. No person in any rank of life ever died either more loved for her quiet virtues or more conspicuous for her kindly and liberal charities. No one ever felt more sincerely that worldly greatness is as nothing in the sight of God; and she had desired, a short time before her death, that the ceremony of embalming, and much of that state which is ordinary at royal funerals, should be set aside at her own.

Under the head of the preceding reign, a brief account has already been given of the commencement of that great system of Railways which has since produced most important changes throughout our whole land. The greediness of gain and the extravagant expenditure into which adventurers, who thought that they were about to obtain enormous profits, imprudently plunged, brought on at length in some cases ruinous losses, and in others an alarming panic, which appeared to reach their crisis in 1847, and by which many of these undertakings have been overwhelmed, others suspended, and all depressed. But still these railway communications, throughout almost our whole island, subsist, and indeed, on the whole, increase, and daily ripen into some new benefit or commercial advantage. And yet even the metamorphosis of the railway, although it has changed almost the whole aspect of England to the traveller's eye, is a less marvel than that of the Electric Telegraphs, which are constructed on almost all the more considerable railway lines, and by which messages may be sent and answers received, and informa-

---

The character of Queen Adelaide ?
What great public improvements were undertaken ?
The railways ?

tion of every kind transmitted, from one end of England to another, with the speed of thought.

The whole system of the Post-Office has also been subjected during the present reign to great alterations, and received essential improvements, introduced chiefly at the suggestion of Mr. Rowland Hill. The charges for the postage of letters had long been felt to be much too high, and were known to check in an injurious and unkindly degree the communications both of the middling and the poorer classes with one another. The postage of a letter from London to Oxford was eightpence, and to Edinburgh a shilling, and so in proportion for other distances. Instead of this expensive scale we have now had, ever since January 10, 1840, the daily gratification of receiving our letters, and from any part either of Great Britain or Ireland, at the cost of one penny if not of more than half an ounce weight. Many other alterations also have been made of the former system. Franking has been abolished; the mails are now dispatched from London by the railways, and not by mail-coaches, and twice instead of once a day, and to some places oftener. Besides these changes, a cheap money-order office has also been established, by which all but the mere village postmasters may transmit to each other orders for the payment of any sums not exceeding five pounds. The effect of a transition from a very dear system of the same sort to this cheap system is highly remarkable. In the quarter ending January 5, 1840, which was before the alteration, 40,763 money-orders were issued in England and Wales, for sums amounting altogether to £67,411. The number issued in the quarter ending January 5, 1849, was 4,203,727, and for an amount of £8,151,295. The number of letters which passed through the post-office in the week ending December 22, 1839, was 1,585,973, and in the week ending February 2, 1849, 6,849,196.

It was observed, in the account of the last reign, that the Houses of Parliament were destroyed by fire in the

---

What improvements in the post-office?
Who was the author of the law or change?
What are cheap money-orders?
Were the numbers of letters increased?

year 1834, and that designs were subsequently made by Mr. Barry, and approved of, for rebuilding them. The more important portions of the new buildings are at length nearly completed, and the House of Peers was opened in 1847. The Custom-House, also the Royal Exchange, which were destroyed by fire, the one in 1837 and the other in 1838, have been rebuilt: and the new Exchange was opened by the Queen in state in October, 1843. The Tunnel under the Thames, begun in the preceding reign, was completed in March of the same year. The British Museum, which has been constantly increasing its treasures of antiquity, art, and science, and attracting a larger number both of readers and visitors, has been almost rebuilt at great expense, and on a most extensive scale. The Xanthian marbles, brought from Lycia by Sir Charles Fellows, were opened to public view, February 6, 1843. The still more remarkable sculptures discovered at Nimroud, the supposed site of ancient Nineveh, by Mr. Layard, were placed in the Museum June 21, 1847. Many more, and not less successful researches, have since been made in the same region by this intelligent and enterprising traveller, which will supply eventually additional illustrations of the oldest histories in existence, and of the sacred history in particular.

Neither yet have the improvements in this vast metropolis been confined to the restoration and enlargement of public buildings, or to the accumulation of new stores in the Museum. Almost a new city has sprung up to the north of Hyde Park; and a new park on the northeast of London, to which the name of Victoria Park has been assigned in honor of the Queen, affords a breathing-place to the inhabitants of that part of the town, of which they had long been in want. Many more improvements both in London and in many provincial towns might be pointed out, but must be here passed by. It ought not, however, to be omitted that a commencement has been made of extensive efforts to remedy the want of suitable dwellings

---

What buildings were erected?
What ancient sculptures were brought to England?
The tunnel under the Thames?
Where is the Victoria Park?

for the poorer classes, and to supply them with better means of comfort and cleanliness than are attainable in the narrow courts and unhealthy neighborhoods in which they are commonly crowded. To this end many model lodging-houses, and baths and wash-houses, some of them on a very large scale, have been constructed in London and other places. A bill also was introduced, in April, 1850, into Parliament, by which the burial of all persons who die in London must be transferred to cemeteries at some distance from town.

The reasonableness of these provisions, or rather the urgent necessity by which they are dictated, has been brought the more forcibly before the public mind by the reappearance, in the autumn of 1848, of that alarming disease the Asiatic cholera, of which the previous ravages in 1831 and 1832 are not forgotten. This disease, which lasted nearly a year, has been even more fatal on this recent visitation than on the former. It is aggravated by nothing more than by want of cleanliness; and the great majority of its victims has always been found among the ill-drained and ill-ventilated habitations of the poor.

The pacific and commercial intercourse of England with her colonies, and with foreign nations, during the period here spoken of, has steadily increased, and the resources of emigration and colonization have every year appeared to become the more necessary to furnish the means of employment and support for the increased multitudes of our countrymen. Upper Canada, notwithstanding the distractions of which that colony has been the scene, has attracted a perpetually augmenting number of settlers. The United States, and especially its immense western territory, has absorbed many more. Australia, though with some reverses, has yet on the whole rapidly increased both in population and wealth; and the islands of New Zealand have not taken the less hold of English enterprise and industry because placed at the very opposite extremity of the globe.

At the same time our means of communication with

What has been the intercourse of England with her colonies?
To what countries have emigrants gone?

18

both America and our Indian empire have been almost as much facilitated by the increase and improvement of steam navigation, as our intercourse with the different parts of our own island by the introduction of railways. Steam navigation, though brought very generally into use between the several ports of the United Kingdom, and many of those of the continent of Europe, in the reign of George IV., was opened to America in 1838; the "Great Western," steamship to New York, reaching that port June 17th in that year, after a passage of fifteen days. The communication with India, which used to occupy, in the long voyage round the Cape of Good Hope, a period of from four to five months, and often more, is now effected, and almost with certainty, in five or six weeks. Or, to speak more particularly, what is called the overland passage to India is now commonly made by steam navigation to Malta and Alexandria, and then again by Cairo and across the desert to Suez, and thence by the Red Sea. By this route the transit from England to Bombay is ordinarily accomplished in from thirty to thirty-five days, and that to Calcutta in ten days more.

To these events thus more peculiarly appertaining to our own history it remains to be added, that in the course of the last few years discoveries of gold have been made in California, which carry back the mind to the early history of the settlement of the Spaniards in Mexico, and which have excited scarcely less cupidity. It may also be added, that it appears to be likely that the system of railroads will be extended across the vast continent of America, and that a ship-canal, which had long seemed to be among the day-dreams of geographers, is at length about to be constructed across the Isthmus of Panama, by which the Atlantic and Pacific Oceans will be joined.

To these great results both of skill and of enterprise in almost all the accessible portions of the globe, it was, for a time, hoped and wished—but we must now at length fear vainly wished—that the arctic regions of the western hemisphere might furnish gratifying addition. These re-

---

What has been the effect of steam navigation?
Of the discovery of gold in California?

gions, although bound up in a chain of ice, which has as yet proved impassable, have provoked, even by the difficulties which they present to the navigator, and by past failures, the desire to penetrate them, and to accomplish the problem of the northwest passage from Hudson's Bay to Behring's Straits.

Among the attempts to attain this object, that of Sir John Ross, who sailed from England in 1829, is one of the most memorable. But he was unable to proceed farther than to Repulse Bay, where he was blocked up by the ice, and long remained unheard of; and was almost despaired of, when, after not less than four years' absence, he returned, to the great joy of his friends and the public. Sir John Franklin, who had previously explored these icy regions in 1819–'22, and reached in 1825–'27 the coast of the northern sea by a land journey from Canada, undeterred by the failures of the many previous attempts to effect the passage by sea, sailed on another trial in May, 1845. But no tidings have been yet received of him, although many efforts have been already made to send him assistance, or to ascertain his fate.

CHAPTER XLI.

REIGN OF QUEEN VICTORIA.—PART II.

[Years after Christ, 1851—1853.]

The year 1851 will be long remembered as the year of the Great Exhibition of the Industry of all Nations. The design of this Exhibition, if not suggested, was at least supported from the first, and energetically and successfully carried through, by Prince Albert. The building in which it was held was remarkable as well for the novelty of its design as for its great extent. It was erected in Hyde Park, and covered nineteen acres of ground. This vast

The northwest passage?
The great exhibition?

building was constructed of glass and iron, and was found admirably suited for the display of the immense variety of objects of every description of interest which were there brought together from all parts of the world. The contents of this fragile edifice were valued at more than two millions sterling, and this open display of so great wealth was a proof of the security which England enjoyed. The undertaking was completely successful. The Exhibition was kept open for twenty-three weeks, and the number of persons admitted to it during that time was more than six millions. Thousands of visitors were conveyed from all parts of the country by cheap excursion trains on the various railroads; and altogether it may be safely said that never before was an equal amount of gratification and instruction so widely diffused.

This splendid work has since been copied in other buildings of great extent raised for purposes of exhibition at Paris, New York, Dublin, and Manchester, and the original materials have been bought by a company, and removed and reërected at Sydenham, with some alterations of design, as a permanent structure, which still retains the fanciful title, popularly bestowed on its predecessor, of the Crystal Palace.

In the year 1851 a discovery was made of extensive gold fields in Australia, and this has led to a great increase of emigration to that colony.

The close of the following year, 1852, was marked by the death (September 14) and public funeral of the Duke of Wellington. The funeral took place in St. Paul's Cathedral (November 18) with every demonstration of national sorrow and respect. Not many days later (December 1) the reëstablishment of the French Empire under Prince Louis Napoleon, the nephew of the first Napoleon, the Duke's old antagonist, was proclaimed by the Legislative Assembly of France. The new Emperor was immediately acknowledged and congratulated on his accession

How long kept open?
To what country was there a great emigration?
Whose death is mentioned?
What empire was re-established?
Who was the emperor?

by the English ambassador at Paris. He has ever since steadily maintained the closest alliance with England. Friendly visits have been exchanged between the monarchs of these two great countries; and we may trust that the two nations are fully awake to the benefits of mutual peace, and that all unchristian feelings of national jealousy and dislike have passed away.

The increase of commerce and the improvement in communications have scarcely ever flagged during the whole period of which we are now speaking. New lines of railway have been opened, not in our own islands only, but also in our principal dependencies, Canada, India, and even Australia. But the most remarkable application of science to the uses of life in modern times has been in the Electric Telegraph. This discovery enables intelligible signs to be transmitted instantaneously by electricity from one end of a wire to the other, however distant. This principle has rapidly been reduced to a system. Lines of wires have been extended in a few years over a great part of the civilized world, and means have been found for carrying these wires under the sea, imbedded in a cable ingeniously contrived, which protects them from injury.

The first Submarine Telegraph, crossing the Straits of Dover, was successfully laid September 27, 1851. In less than seven years from that date, after great difficulties and several failures, the signal triumph was accomplished (August 5, 1858) of laying a cable across the Atlantic from Valentia on the Irish coast to the shores of Newfoundland. We cannot deny ourselves the pleasure of recording the words and adopting the prayer, first carried from the New World to the Old by this, the greatest work of modern days: "Glory to God in the highest, and on earth peace, good-will toward men." *

We must now recur to the mention made in a former page of the point which had been reached by Arctic dis-

---

* Another cable was successfully laid between the same places in the summer of 1866.

What means of communication have increased ?
Where was laid the first submarine telegraph ?

covery in the year 1850. Since that time the long-sought Northwest passage has been at length found to exist, though for the purposes of commerce it can never be of any real service. The Investigator, commanded by Captain McClure, entered the Arctic seas by Behring's Straits in the summer of 1850. After taking up his winter quarters on the shore of Baring Island, he proceeded to explore the neighboring regions by parties travelling over the frozen sea. On the 26th of October he discovered a passage leading into Barrow's Strait, and thus communicating through Davis's Strait with the Atlantic Ocean.

During the whole of the next season (that of 1851) the ice never broke up sufficiently to enable the voyagers to extricate themselves from their position; but eventually, though compelled to abandon their vessel, and to seek a different route for their return, and after encountering difficulties too long to be here detailed, they returned to England.

Meanwhile no trace of Sir John Franklin and his brave companions was discovered. Every year, however, added to the conviction that it was impossible that they could still survive, and in 1854 evidence was obtained which sets the melancholy fate beyond all doubt. An enterprising traveller, Dr. Rae, while engaged in making a survey of the shores of Boothia, fell in with some Esquimaux who told him of the death by famine in the year 1850 of a company of white men about forty in number. Dr. Rae was unable to attempt to reach the spot at which this event occurred; but he obtained from the Esquimaux, in confirmation of their story, many articles known to have belonged to the lost voyagers, which had been found on the scene of the sad tragedy, near the mouth of the river Back.

Extensive discoveries, in a very different region, and it is hoped of much more practical utility, have been recently made in the interior of Africa. Dr. David Livingstone, an adventurous missionary traveller, returned to England in the winter of 1856, after a period of more than sixteen years spent in the heart of that great continent. In that

---

What is said of Captain McClure and Sir John Franklin?
By whom were discoveries made in Africa?

time he traversed about 11,000 miles, the greater portion of that long distance through a country never before visited by any European. In the vast tracts of Africa south of the equator, Dr. Livingstone found flourishing kingdoms and an intelligent population, inhabiting a fertile country situated in a not unfavorable climate. This territory is traversed by a fine navigable river, the Zambesi, flowing into the Mozambique channel.

In the year 1853 a war broke out between Russia and Turkey, in which England and France were speedily called upon, as allies of Turkey, to take a principal share. This memorable and important war arose out of an attempt on the part of the Russian Emperor Nicholas I. to take advantage of the weakness of Turkey for the purpose of extending his own influence and dominions in the direction of Constantinople. His whole design extended to a complete dismemberment of the Turkish empire. He even ventured to propose to Sir Hamilton Seymour, the British ambassador at St. Petersburg, that our own country should connive at his project, seizing Egypt, or some other important possession, as our share of the spoil.

In pursuance of these ambitious projects, the Emperor Nicholas ordered Prince Menzikoff, his ambassador at Constantinople, to make various demands which the Sultan could not possibly grant, and, in short, to pick a quarrel with him. On the refusal of these demands the ambassador left Constantinople, May 22d. On the 2d of July the Russian army crossed the Pruth, the boundary between Russia and Turkey, and took possession of Wallachia and Moldavia, these being the whole of the Turkish territories north of the Danube. This was the real beginning of the war, which was formally declared against Russia by the Porte in September, 1853, and by France and England in the March following.

The first heavy blow was struck by Russia. A powerful fleet from Sebastopol surprised a small and undefended Turkish squadron in the harbor of Sinope, and

---

What war broke out in 1853?
What was the cause?
What were the designs of Russia?

totally destroyed it. This disaster occurred November 30th.

The early spring of the following year was occupied by a campaign on the Danube, in which the Turks under Omar Pacha displayed unexpected steadiness: with very inferior numbers they repulsed the Russians in many engagements, and concluded a successful campaign by the brilliant defence of Silistria, from which the Turks, aided by two British officers, drove back the enemy with great loss. Shortly afterward the Principalities in which the war had broken out were occupied, at the request of the Turkish government, and with the acquiescence of Russia, by Austrian troops; and these provinces thus became for the time neutral, and the war was removed to another scene.

For many years the Russians had been engaged in fortifying the harbor of Sebastopol in the Crimea, in building extensive docks and arsenals, and in collecting a large fleet and warlike stores of every kind. The whole of the Crimean peninsula was a comparatively recent acquisition of this great power, having been taken from Turkey in 1783, and this military establishment on its shores was now manifestly designed for aggression upon the Turkish dominions. Accordingly, the English and French generals, who had arrived at Varna, resolved to attempt its destruction, and an allied army of 56,000 men was transported across the Black Sea, and safely landed on the 14th of September, 1854, on the shore of the Crimea, a few miles south of the small town of Eupatoria. The British were commanded by Lord Raglan, a division being under the orders of the Duke of Cambridge, and the French by Marshal St. Arnaud. The united army immediately began its march toward Sebastopol. On September the 20th they came in presence of the Russians under Prince Menzikoff, who had taken up a strong position on a range of heights on the southern bank of the river Alma. After a short but bloody contest the English and French stormed

---

What occurred on the Danube?
What place was strongly fortified?
What was the number of the allied army?
Who commanded the English? who the French?

the heights, and the enemy retreated in confusion to Sebastopol. The victors continued their march, and by a détour to the left arrived on the 25th at the village of Balaklava, of which they took possession, together with the small but safe harbor of the same name. A few days later commenced the siege of Sebastopol, a siege memorable for its length, for the endurance and pertinacity shown both in the attack and in the defence, for many acts of heroism on both sides, for the great scale on which the operations were conducted, and it must be added, for the unparalleled sufferings of nearly all who took part in it. The first grand attack took place on the 17th of October, with a general bombardment both by sea and land. This attack produced little impression, but the fire of the Russian forts and of the newly-raised intrenchments inflicted considerable loss on the allies, especially on the English ships and the French batteries.

Among the incidents of this great siege were the disastrous action of Balaklava (October 25th), in which the British light cavalry brigade made a charge, from which not one-third of the whole body returned; and the desperate fight of Inkerman (November 5th), in which the British were assailed under every disadvantage by an overwhelming force. On that day the Coldstream Guards crossed bayonets with fresh bands of the enemy eleven times; and the British infantry having exhausted their cartridges were defending themselves with stones, and the butt-ends of their muskets, when a French division under General Bosquet came to their support, and the Russians were driven back with heavy loss. Throughout the whole winter the privations endured by the British troops were most severe. The inclemency of the weather, the severity of the labor entailed by the great extent of the trenches, and the insufficient supplies of food and clothing—all these causes produced an excessive mortality among our troops, especially among the new recruits and fresh regiments. All this time the Russians also were suffering very great

---

What place did they besiege?
When and how was made the first attack?
What desperate fight occurred?
What were the privations of the British troops?

losses and privations, chiefly in the long and arduous land march, by which alone reënforcements could be sent to the besieged.

During the whole of this trying time intense anxiety was of course felt at home. The management of the war became the subject of great agitation throughout the country, and a violent attack was made in parliament on Lord Aberdeen's government. The result of this movement was the fall of that minister, and the establishment of a new administration under Lord Palmerston.

With the beginning of spring, the efforts, private and public, made for the comfort and relief of our troops, began to tell; the condition of the army rapidly improved, and the besiegers gained ground. Among the efforts here referred to, several were complete novelties in the annals of war. A railway was constructed from Balaklava to the camp for the conveyance of stores and artillery. A submarine telegraph was laid under the Black Sea, bringing the allied camp into immediate communication with Paris and London. Least of all should it be forgotten that during the progress of this siege a number of English ladies went out as nurses in the military hospitals, at Scutari and elsewhere, under the superintendence of Miss Florence Nightingale. The ministrations of this devoted band were completely successful. The influence and example of Miss Nightingale and her companions introduced many salutary reforms into the treatment of the sick and wounded soldiers, while their personal attention to the sufferers touched their feelings and cheered their spirits in the very highest degree. At this period the alliance was strengthened by the accession of Sardinia, and a small but well-appointed army from that kingdom shortly afterward joined the besieging force.

As the spring advanced the siege was pushed with great vigor. Repeated bombardments inflicted terrible loss upon the garrison. Still the defence was conducted with the utmost obstinacy. An assault made simultaneously by the English and French on the 18th of June was repulsed with

---

What is said of Lord Aberdeen and Lord Palmerston?
What efforts were made for the relief of the soldiers?
Who among the English ladies was foremost in the good work?
What is said of Sardinia?

loss, and it was not till the 8th of September that a decisive success was gained. On that day the Malakhoff tower was taken by assault by Marshal Pelissier, who had now succeeded to the command of the French troops. At the same time a part of the defences called the Redan was assaulted by the British, entered, and held for nearly two hours. At length our brave troops, too few to advance further, and exposed to a destructive fire from the interior defences, were compelled to retreat to their own lines with heavy loss. However, the success of the French was decisive. The whole town was commanded by the Malakhoff, and was now no longer tenable. The Russians retreated in the course of the night across the harbor to the fortified heights on the northern side. At the same time they destroyed the remnant of their own fleet, of which the greater part had been sunk across the mouth of the harbor, as a bar to the entrance of the allied ships, at the very commencement of the siege. On the next day the allies took possession of Sebastopol. No further change of importance took place in the position of the contending forces in the Crimea until the peace. The interval was employed by the French and English engineers in blowing up the docks and fortifications, and removing the cannon and other military and naval stores.

The throne of Russia was now occupied by the young Emperor Alexander II. His father, Nicholas, the originator of the war had died on the 2d of March in this eventful year (1855), of a broken heart. Both the English and French generals who had led the allied forces in the first invasion of Russian territory were also dead; Marshal St. Arnaud having survived the victory of the Alma only a very few days, and Lord Raglan having died just ten days after the bloody repulse of the 18th of June.

The taking of Sebastopol was the turning-point of the war. In other parts operations were less decisive, because there were no means of bringing the enemy to action. In

---

What place did the British capture?
What did the Russians do?
What stronghold was now taken?
Who of the generals died?
What was the turning-point of the war?

the North, in the two years 1854 and 1855, our fleets, throughout all the months during which the Baltic is unfrozen, swept that sea unresisted, the Russian fleet sheltering itself behind the fortifications of Cronstadt. The only events of importance in that quarter were the taking of the strong fortress of Bomarsund in the Aland Isles in 1854, and the bombardment of Sweaborg in 1855. On the latter occasion steam gunboats were employed with great success.

Vessels of the same class were also found highly effective in a series of operations in the Sea of Azoff and at the mouth of the Dnieper. In these quarters the English and French inflicted great loss on the enemy by the destruction of stores and magazines, upon which their armies depended for support.

The only considerable success obtained by the Russians, to set off against so many reverses, was on the side of Armenia, where the important town of Kars was surrendered to them (November 26, 1855). Even there the Turkish troops, though wretchedly appointed and provided, made a most gallant defence, and were reduced at last only by famine. The honor of the defence is principally due to an English officer who conducted it, General, now Sir William Fenwick Williams of Kars.

In the beginning of the year 1856 a negotiation for peace was set on foot at Vienna, and a suspension of hostilities agreed on. This negotiation happily proceeded to a successful conclusion, and a treaty was signed at Paris (March 30th). The great object of the war, the security of Turkey, is effectually provided for by several articles of this treaty, especially by one in which the navigation of the Black Sea is forbidden to the ships-of-war of all nations. But perhaps the most important effect of all the events of the two years of the war has been the correction of the very exaggerated estimate of the military power of Russia, which had prevailed ever since the disastrous retreat of Napoleon from Moscow in 1812. The total loss to

---

What was done by the British fleet in the Baltic?
Who defended the town of Kars?
When and where was peace concluded?

the British army during the war was stated at about 4,000 who were killed or died of their wounds, 15,000 who died of disease, and 3,000 disabled.

In the year 1852 a war took place with the Caffre tribes in South Africa, and another with the Burmese Empire. In 1856 hostilities broke out with Persia in consequence of the seizure by that power, influenced as was supposed by Russian intrigues, of the city of Herat. These were brought to a speedy and favorable conclusion by the capture (December 9th) of Bushire on the Persian Gulf by a force which had been dispatched from Bombay under General Outram.

In the same year a dispute arose with China on the subject of an alleged breach of treaty by the seizure of a small vessel, called a lorcha, trading under the English flag in the Canton river. This trifling question grew into a serious contest in consequence of the refusal of Yeh, the Chinese viceroy of Canton, to enter into any communication with the British Admiral. Several attacks were consequently made on Canton and the neighboring forts, but these operations afterward slackened, in consequence of the sudden and urgent demand for troops occasioned by the breaking out of the great mutiny in India, presently to be related. Hostilities were, however, resumed in the spring of the present year (1858). Canton was stormed, and Yeh taken prisoner. Later in the season an expedition was sent up the river Peiho, by which the capital itself of the Chinese empire was seriously threatened. These proceedings have been entirely successful, and a treaty of peace has been concluded at Tien-sin, which provides for the toleration of Christianity, and for a large increase of intercourse between Europe and that vast territory.

In 1857 a most formidable insurrection broke out in the Indian army. For many years the East India Company had maintained a large force of native troops under British

---

What was the total loss of the British army?
Where did other wars break out?
Why the dispute with China?
What place was captured, and who taken prisoner?
Was Christianity tolerated by treaty?
Did an insurrection break out in India?

officers, and armed and disciplined in the European manner. These Sepoys, as they were called, were a fine body of men, and had done excellent service in many wars; and notwithstanding several instances of insubordination, very great confidence was placed in them generally.

The cause of the outbreak is even now scarcely certain. Some strange, unfounded suspicion of an attempt about to be made by the British authorities for their forcible conversion to Christianity seems to have found its way into the minds of the Sepoys, both Mohammedan and Hindoo. This alarm was founded, or pretended to be founded, on the issue of new cartridges, adapted to the improved firearms now used by all our infantry, and which it was supposed were greased with the fat either of the cow, which is a sacred animal with the Brahmins, the highest caste of Hindoos, or of swine, which are an abomination to the Mohammedans, as to the Jews.

The first very serious outbreak of this mutiny took place early in May, at Meerut, a military station about thirty miles to the north of Delhi. The insurgents murdered their officers and their families, and marched to Delhi, where they were joined by the garrison, consisting entirely of native regiments, and the atrocities committed at Meerut were here repeated. They also took the nominal king of Delhi, the lineal descendant of the Mogul sovereigns, a feeble old man, who was then living in that magnificent capital a pensioner of the East India Company, and proclaimed him Emperor of India.

Throughout the vast plain of the Ganges the native regiments mutinied one after another, till the great Bengal army absolutely ceased to exist. In some stations the British officers were sufficiently forewarned to enable them to escape: in others they were ruthlessly murdered, with their wives and children, by the troops they had lately commanded. Those who escaped either took refuge in a few hastily fortified places, or joined the only force still able to keep the field for the British government. This force, though far outnumbered by the trained soldiers

What were the causes of the war?
Where was the first outbreak? among what troops?

composing the rebel garrison of Delhi, was yet boldly posted in the attitude of a besieging army in front of that great capital, and held its ground till joined by reënforcements of both British troops and Sikh auxiliaries, whom Sir John Lawrence, governor of the Punjab, had dispatched to its succor. This little army, thus strengthened, assaulted and took Delhi, capturing the king and his family, on the 20th of September, before a single soldier from England had arrived on the scene of action.

In the mean time, at Cawnpore on the Ganges, and at Lucknow, the capital of Oude—a turbulent district, which had been annexed only the year before to the East India Company's dominions—parties of English were surrounded by the insurgents. At both places a large number of women and children had taken refuge. At Cawnpore the means of defence were soon exhausted, and the garrison was reduced to the greatest distress. A native chief, Nana Sahib, in whom the British thought that they had reason to place confidence, had taken command of the besiegers. To this traitor General Wheeler, the commanding officer in Cawnpore, in an evil hour capitulated, under a solemn pledge of safe conveyance by water to Allahabad. On the faith of this agreement, men, women, and children all gladly went on board the boats provided for them, but were scarcely afloat when they were fired on and massacred (June 27th), with the exception of about one hundred and fifty women and children, who were taken back into Cawnpore as prisoners. But these also were murdered in cold blood a short time afterward (July 16th). The occasion of this savage deed was the victorious approach of General Havelock. This brave man, the very pattern of Christian chivalry, with no more than 2,000 followers, drove the rebels through Cawnpore, defeated them again at Bithoor, and immediately set out on the desperate attempt to raise the siege of the Residency at Lucknow.

About half-way between Cawnpore and Lucknow, this

By whom was Delhi captured ?
Did the mutineers commit great outrages ?
Who was Nana Sahib ?
The surrender of Cawnpore ? the treatment of the prisoners ?
Who was General Havelock ? his character ?

little band of heroes, now sadly reduced, gained its ninth victory over a force of rebels many times exceeding their own in numbers. But they were now too much weakened by their very successes to be able to proceed farther, and found it absolutely necessary to return to Cawnpore, there to await that help which they knew was coming. Happily this arrived before it was too late. General Havelock was joined by Sir James Outram with fresh troops; and these two brave men then immediately advanced, and after desperate fighting, and with terrible loss, led their troops into the Residency of Lucknow (September 25th), where they found its defenders reduced to the last extremity. Even then it was impossible to withdraw the garrison, incumbered as it was with numerous sick and wounded, besides several hundred women and children, in the face of an enemy so many times superior in numbers: they therefore joined their forces to those of the garrison, and after repairing and extending the fortifications of the place, remained on the defensive.

At this time the troops which had been sent from England began to arrive. Sir Colin Campbell, who had been appointed to the command, reached Cawnpore in November, and by a series of most skilful operations and brilliant victories broke through the lines of the besiegers, and finally rescued the brave defenders of the Residency with all the women and children, and brought them off in perfect safety, after a siege of no less than five months' duration. Not many days after this happy deliverance the brave General Havelock died from the exhaustion consequent on his long exertions and anxieties. With his name must be mentioned those of Niel, Nicholson, and many other heroes whose loss their country had to deplore during this disastrous struggle. Sir Colin Campbell's flood of good fortune did not desert him. He rapidly followed up his great success, defeating and dispersing the mutineers on every side, taking their towns, and reducing them to a mere mass of fugitives.

Did he gain many victories?
Who brought fresh troops?
What is said of Lucknow?
What is said of the success of Sir Colin Campbell?

Thus, by the firm attitude assumed by the British in India, surprised and outnumbered as they were, and placed in a position of unexampled peril, by the prompt and powerful support sent out from home, and by the distinguished talent and valor of their commanders, and of many other most able men in every rank and of all conditions, the most formidable military revolt which has ever been known was crushed into mere fragments in less than a year. It is likewise to be observed that throughout the whole of this critical period, neither the mass of the population of India nor the princes of the country have shown any sympathy with the mutineers. The insurrection was, moreover, confined to the Bengal Presidency, the Madras and Bombay troops having, with few exceptions, proved trustworthy.

A most important change in the government of India, of which the necessity had long been foreseen, has been accelerated by the events which have been now related. The great East India Company was abolished, and its vast empire transferred to the direct dominion of the Crown, September 1, 1858.

The state of the English royal family is now as follows: A Princess Royal, Victoria Adelaide Mary Louisa, born November 21, 1840; Albert Edward, Prince of Wales, born November 9, 1841; Alice Maud Mary, born April 25, 1843; Alfred Ernest Albert, born August 6, 1844; Helena Augusta Victoria, born May 25, 1846; Louisa Caroline Alberta, born March 8, 1848; Arthur (named after the Duke of Wellington), born May 1, 1850; Leopold George Duncan Albert, born April 7, 1853; and Beatrice Mary Victoria Feodore, born April 14, 1857.

The Princess Royal is now the Princess Frederick William of Prussia, having married (January 25, 1858) the King of Prussia's eldest nephew, and after his father the heir of that crown.

Prince Albert died December 14, 1861, deeply lamented by the English people.

Did the mass of the population show sympathy with the mutineers?
What change was made in the government of India?
What is said of the royal family?

QUACKENBOS'S STANDARD TEXT-BOOKS.

Elementary History of the United States. Made easy and interesting for beginners. Brought down to the present Administration. Splendidly illustrated. 16mo, pp. 216. 65 cents.

Illustrated School History of the United States, with numerous Maps, Plans of Battle-fields, and Pictorial Illustrations. Brought down to the present Administration. 12mo, pp. 538. $1.30.

First Book in English Grammar. 16mo, pp. 120. 45 cents.

An English Grammar. 12mo, pp. 288. 80 cents.

Illustrated Lessons in Our Language. 12mo, pp. 180. 55 cts.

First Lessons in Composition. 12mo, pp. 182. 80 cents.

Advanced Course of Composition and Rhetoric. A Series of Practical Lessons on the Origin, History, and Peculiarities of the English Language, Punctuation, Taste, the Pleasures of the Imagination, Figures, Style, Criticism, and Prose and Poetical Composition, with Exercises. *New and revised edition.* 12mo, pp. 450. $1.30.

A Natural Philosophy. Embracing the most recent discoveries in Physics, and exhibiting the application of Scientific Principles in every-day life. Accompanied with 335 Illustrations, and adapted to use with or without Apparatus. 12mo, pp. 450. $1.50.

A Primary Arithmetic. Beautifully illustrated. 16mo, pp. 108. 22 cents.

An Elementary Arithmetic. 12mo, pp. 144. 40 cents.

A Practical Arithmetic. 12mo, pp. 336. 80 cents. KEY to the same. 18 cents.

A Mental Arithmetic. 16mo, pp. 168. 35 cents.

A Higher Arithmetic. A comprehensive treatise for advanced pupils. Designed as a thorough preparation for the Counting-house. *Recently published.* 12mo, pp. 420. $1.10. KEY. 65 cents.

D. APPLETON & CO., PUBLISHERS,
549 & 551 *Broadway, New York.*

Illustrated School History of the World,

FROM THE EARLIEST AGES TO THE PRESENT TIME.

By J. D. QUACKENBOS, A. M., M. D.

1 vol., 12mo, 473 pages.

This new School History is written in a style that is a model of clearness, eloquence, and elegant condensation.

It is not a mere record of wars, but portrays as well the social life of the nations, ancient, mediæval, and modern, their progress in science, literature, and the arts, discovery, invention, and civilization.

[*Specimen Engraving.*]

EGYPTIAN OBELISK.

It leaves insignificant details and repulsive statistics out of view, but presents all that is of real consequence, dealing, in fact, with many interesting parts of the world's annals which have been heretofore comparatively overlooked.

It condenses the whole history of the past into a moderate-sized volume that can be readily mastered in the course of the ordinary school year.

It treats ancient countries in the light of the most recent discoveries.

It brings down the history of every country to the present year, with invaluable freshness and accuracy.

It is profusely illustrated with artistic colored maps, ancient and modern, and with magnificent engravings from spirited designs, in which the truth of history is rigidly preserved.

It is full of pleasant stories, which relieve the narrative, while sometimes they give a more vivid view of men and manners than whole pages of description would do.

It is adapted to every school, public or private, in which General History is taught.

Every possible device has been resorted to, in order to make this manual an attractive school-book, to render the learning of history easy, and to imbue the pupil with a taste for historical reading.

D. APPLETON & CO., Publishers, 549 & 551 Broadway, New York.

Book of Oratory.

By EDWARD C. MARSHALL, A.M. 12mo, 500 pages.

An Abridgment of the above. 12mo, 237 pages.

Marshall's "Oratory" presents superior claims to the attention of teachers of elocution, by reason of the choice character and great number of its selections, their novelty, variety, and peculiar adaptation to school purposes. It has been compiled expressly to meet the wants of common schools and academies, containing pieces of every style and length, and widely differing in difficulty of execution, so that the beginner and the proficient in the art may alike suit themselves from its pages. There is a freshness about the extracts that strikingly distinguishes them from the stereotyped selections in the old text-books. They consist of choice specimens of prose and poetry from the most distinguished American and English authors—from such master-minds as Webster, Clay, Calhoun, Everett, Prentiss, Wirt, Randolph, Channing, Longfellow, Bryant, Hood, Brougham, Scott, Byron, and Shakespeare.

In no other work is so perfect a picture of American eloquence presented, the statesmen of all sections of the Union being fully represented. The student who desires to form a just estimate of his country's orators, and to improve himself by the use of the admirable models which they have left, will find all that he can desire in this volume.

From the Evangelist.

"A large and admirable selection of pieces for declamation, copious and varied, and well chosen with reference to speaking. The range of selection is almost universal, at least among modern writers in prose, verse, and drama. The editor is a practical teacher of elocution, and evidently has a wide acquaintance with literature. It is as good a work of the kind as we ever saw."

Introduction to the Study of Art.

By M. A. DWIGHT, Author of "Grecian and Roman Mythology" 12mo, 278 pages.

This work is the result of practical teaching, pursued for many years. It is nothing more than it purports to be—an introduction, intended to give some idea of the requirements of art, and to aid the beginner in its study. The rules presented are deduced from the works of the best masters, and are founded exclusively on nature. The young artist, too generally left to the vague and ill-directed promptings of his own genius, will find in this volume a safe and faithful guide, with whose aid he can avoid the rocks on which others have split, and make the most satisfactory progress in his studies. There is no misunderstanding the teachings of the author. Their clearness and direct practical bearing enhance their value, and will recommend them not only to schools of design, but to all institutions in which Drawing is taught.

CONTENTS.—Imitation, Taste and Style, Form and Proportion, Muscles and Joints, Gravity of the Figures, Drawing of the Figure, Prospective of the Form. Light and Shade, Color and its Laws, Expression, Composition, Classification of Pictures Portrait Painting, Landscape Painting, Ancient Pictorial Art, Symbolic Colors, Symbols Emblems, and Sculpture.

D. APPLETON & CO.'S PUBLICATIONS.

Bryant and Stratton's Commercial Law:

For Business Men, including Merchants, Farmers, Mechanics, etc., and Books of Reference for the Legal Profession. Adapted to all of the States of the Union. To be used as a Text-Book for Law Schools and Commercial Colleges, with a large variety of Practical Forms most commonly required in Business Transactions. By AMOS DEAN, LL. D., Professor of Law in the Law Department of the University of Albany. 1 vol., 8vo, 549 pages.

The design of this work is to present, in a condensed form, those logical principles which are of the most common use in the various transactions of business; thereby supplying an educational want, which is becoming more and more imperative, as the modes and relation of business grow more complex, intricate, and extended.

The forms appended are with a view both to illustrate and to serve the common purposes of business. To secure both these objects, a careful selection has been made of a few deemed the best adapted to answer the purpose of the one, and meet the wants of the other.

Education:

Intellectual, Moral, and Physical. By HERBERT SPENCER, Author of "Social Statics," "The Principles of Psychology," and "Essays: Scientific, Political, and Speculative." 12mo, 283 pages.

From the New York Teacher.

"This work originally appeared in four Essays, in the British Reviews. They are first collected and published in book form in this country. The book marks an era in the discussion of education. We deem it of so much importance as to deserve something like a review in a future number. In the mean time, we commend it to the attention of all who wish to see the subject discussed in a profound and philosophical manner. The work is advertised in the present number. We are happy to learn that the author's more elaborate works are about to be issued by subscription, in a serial form. The publishers of the present book will receive subscriptions in this country, and have already the names of our leading scholars and authors."

www.ingramcontent.com/pod-product-compliance
Lightning Source LLC
Chambersburg PA
CBHW051736300426
44115CB00007B/583